AF474011

Nihil

Joshua Hagler
IN NEW MEXICO

Introductory text by John Yau

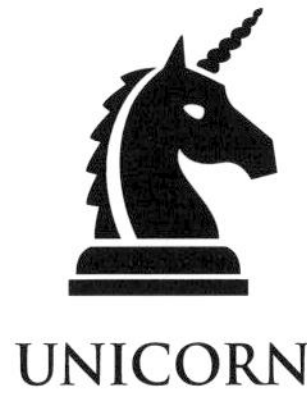

UNICORN

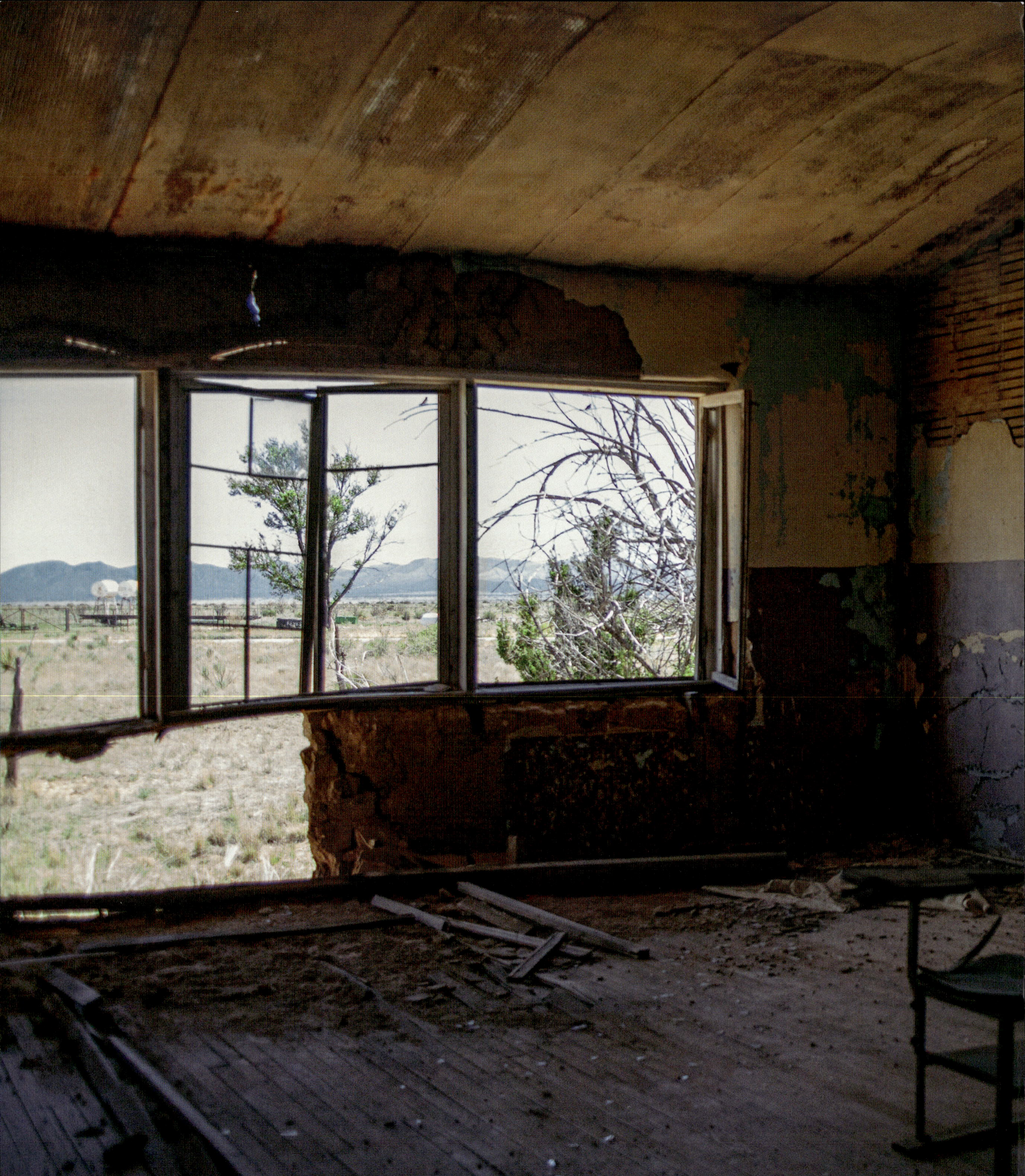

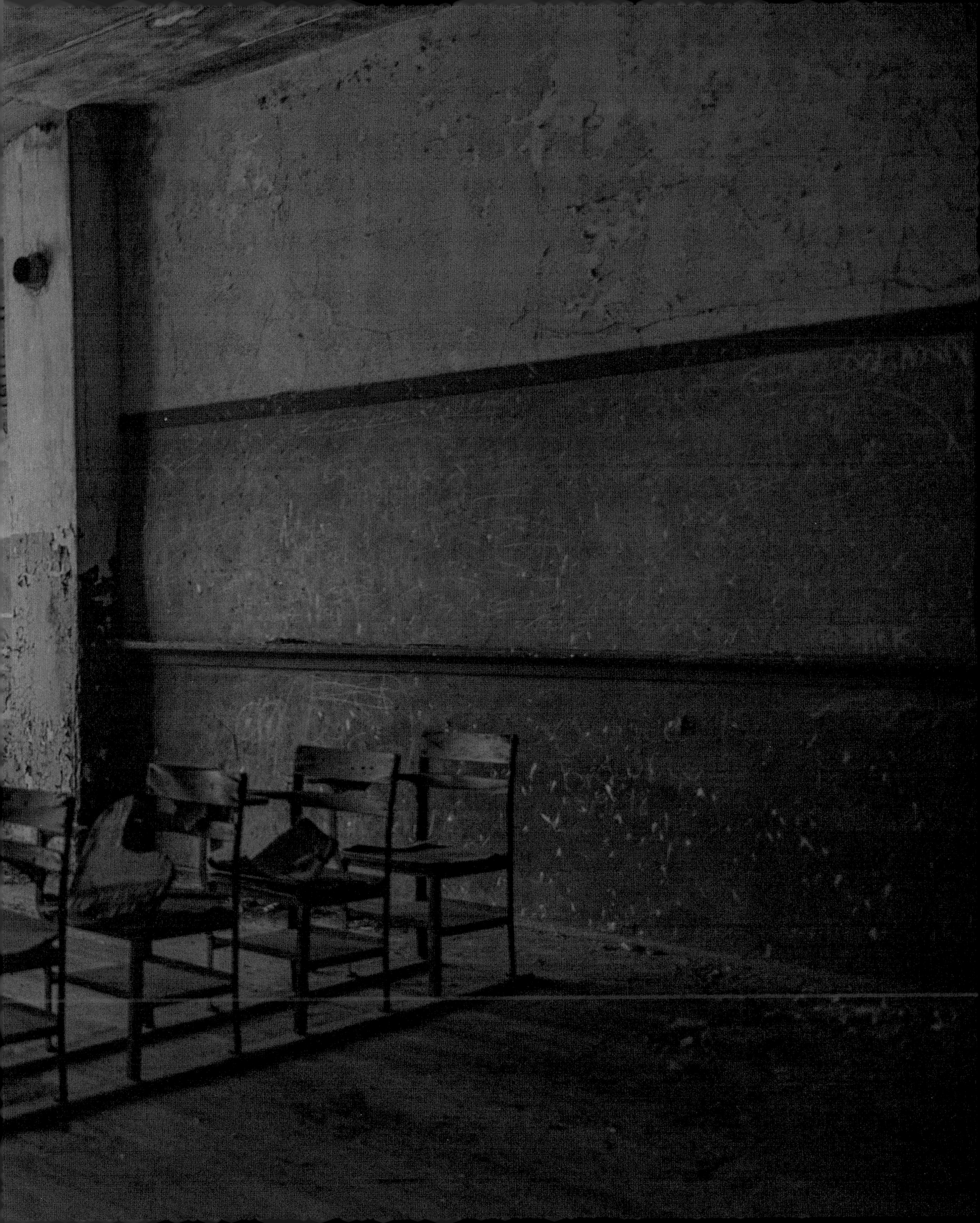

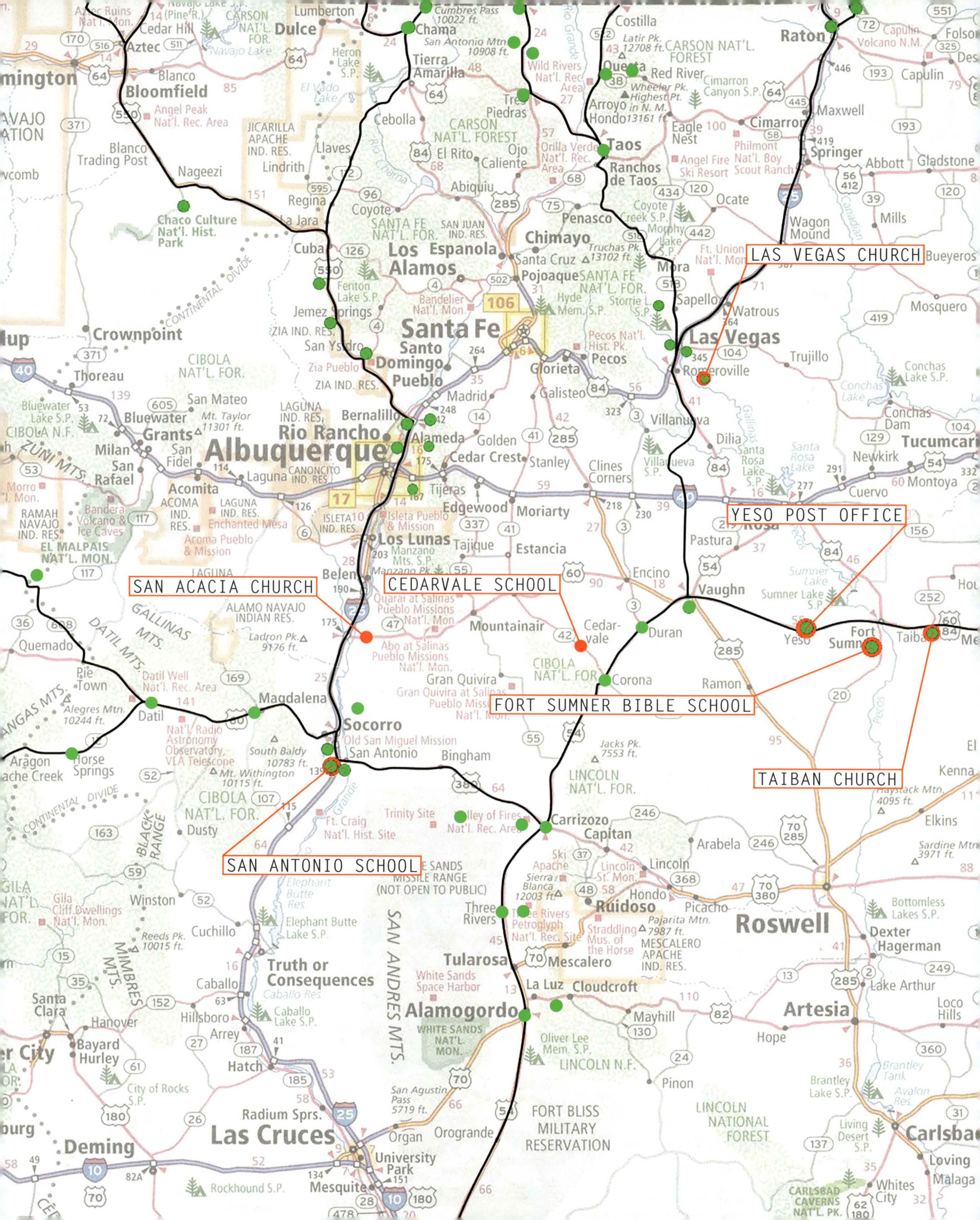
LAS VEGAS CHURCH
YESO POST OFFICE
SAN ACACIA CHURCH
CEDARVALE SCHOOL
FORT SUMNER BIBLE SCHOOL
TAIBAN CHURCH
SAN ANTONIO SCHOOL
Santa Fe
Albuquerque
Rio Rancho
Las Vegas
Los Alamos
Espanola
Taos
Raton
Socorro
Roswell
Alamogordo
Las Cruces
Truth or Consequences
Artesia
Tucumcari
Deming
Los Lunas
Belen
Grants
Farmington
Bloomfield
Aztec
Dulce
Chama
Cimarron
Springer
Vaughn
Duran
Corona
Carrizozo
Ruidoso
Tularosa
Magdalena
Datil
Mountainair
Moriarty
Estancia
Encino
Yeso
Fort Sumner
Taiban
Romeroville
Cedarvale
San Antonio
San Acacia

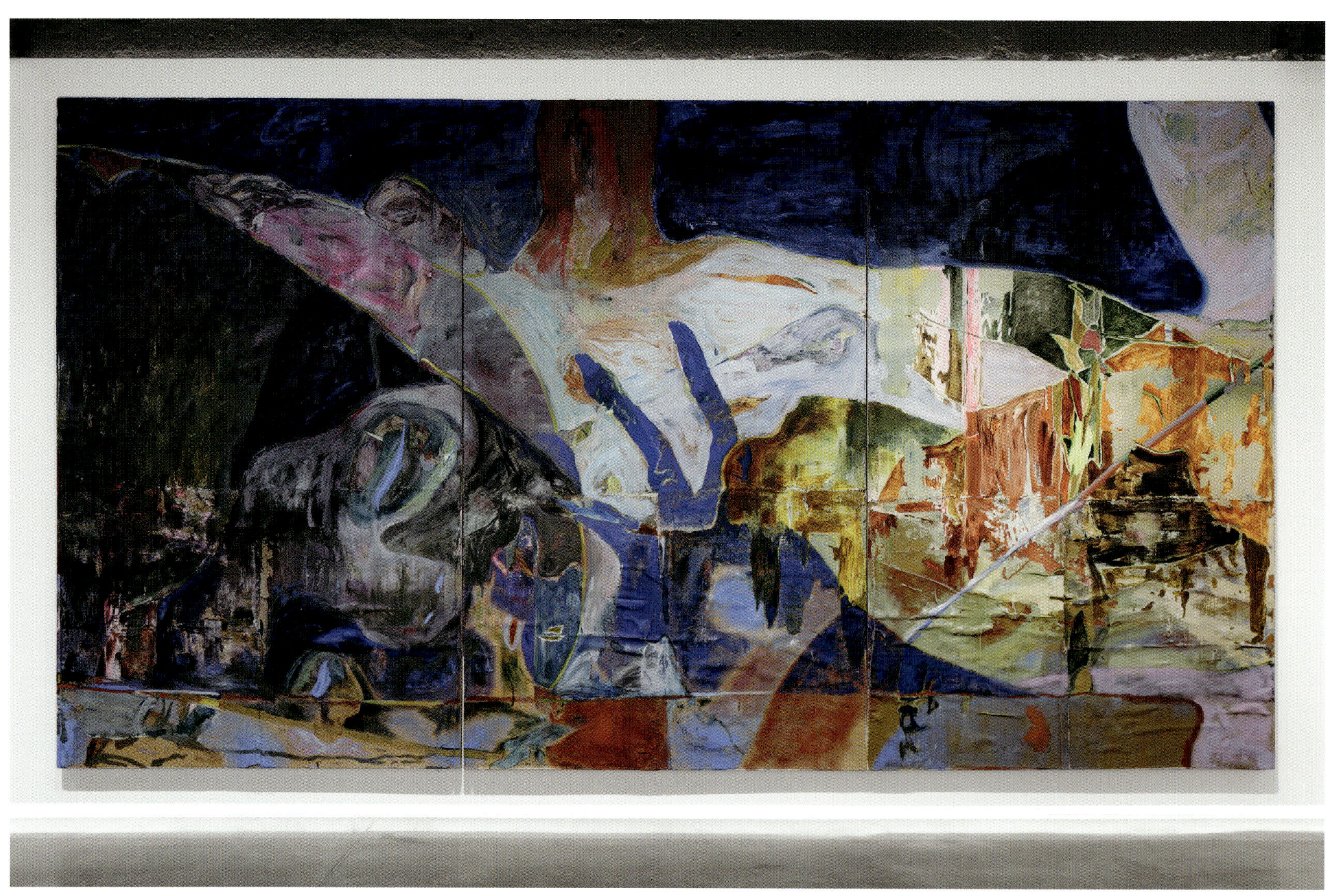

THE HOUR INSTALLED IN SOLO EXHIBITION *THE LIVING CIRCLE US* AT UNIT LONDON, 2021

TIME AND CHANGE
John Yau

I.

Rainer Maria Rilke (1875–1926) ended his poem "Archaic Torso of Apollo" with a command: "You must change your life."[1] From people embarking on a diet to artists pursuing a vision, Rilke's sentiment is expressed by many but heeded by few. The artist Joshua Hagler (b. 1979) is a recent exception. This book documents *Nihil*, a project that Hagler started in May 2020 and worked on for four years until 2024.

The starting date is significant for three reasons. He began developing *Nihil* after a successful exhibition, *Chimera*, at Unit in London (July 19–August 31, 2019), during the height of the Covid-19 pandemic, and two months before the birth of his daughter. It was during this period of heightened isolation that Hagler decided to place one of his paintings in an abandoned school (Cedarvale) just outside Corona, New Mexico. This action, which he would repeat in different ways over the next four years, is the seed from which *Nihil* grew.

Hagler explains: "I simply wanted to know what it would feel like to put work in an empty structure and to find out how much I was capable of doing on my own."[2] This explanation brings to mind the writings of French philosopher Gaston Bachelard (1884–1962). In *The Poetics of Space* (1958), he wrote, "A house that has been experienced is not an inert box. Inhabited space transcends geometrical space."[3]

This is the paradox that Hagler began to reflect upon: the structures in which he installed his art were not inert boxes, the antiseptic white cube of the gallery. They were formerly the sites of daily rituals, private and public moments: uninhabited spaces haunted by the noise of what had been written on their walls and the silence of their authors. Who were they writing to? Would their messages ever reach their destinations? They were places full of visible and invisible history, layers of dust, footprints left behind.

By putting work in abandoned schoolhouses and churches—places of study and worship—Hagler began to think concretely about the relationship between art and time. He was situating his work, which no one would see, in a walled structure marked by time and graffiti. On a literal level, he was physically and symbolically declaring his independence from the art world that was just beginning to recognize him and from the self that made those works. After all, was carefully installing a painting in a cast-off building not the opposite of hanging work in a gallery? In the noisy silence of these disheveled spaces, where he would often sit and meditate, Hagler was able to ask elemental questions about what it means to be an artist: who am I painting for, and why?

When Hagler asked these questions, he began what could be characterized as a shamanic journey in which the landscape and abandoned buildings became portals and mirrors full of signs, offering a way of seeing himself (and the world he had previously lived in) differently. For me, the significance of Hagler's reevaluation goes beyond the changes he would make to his work—it addresses issues that are part of the very fabric of the art world. What is an artist? What is the purpose of art? Is it to enlighten, distract, or comfort the viewer? What would it mean to make art that rejects these commonplace goals?

Hagler may have first installed his work in an abandoned schoolhouse on a whim, but he is not a person who believes the universe is random and arbitrary. This is why he titled the project *Nihil*, which is Latin for "nothing." In an interview, Hagler describes the place (or "nothing") he found himself in, and the realizations that it stirred up in him:

> There comes a point—fifteen years in my case—where it does seem completely stupid and useless to try to "say something" any longer.... To come to a place in which there is simply nothing left to say is terrifying, but it amounts to a powerful shift in perspective, of no longer trying to speak to a momentary audience, which has its momentary tastes and ideological positions. The place I

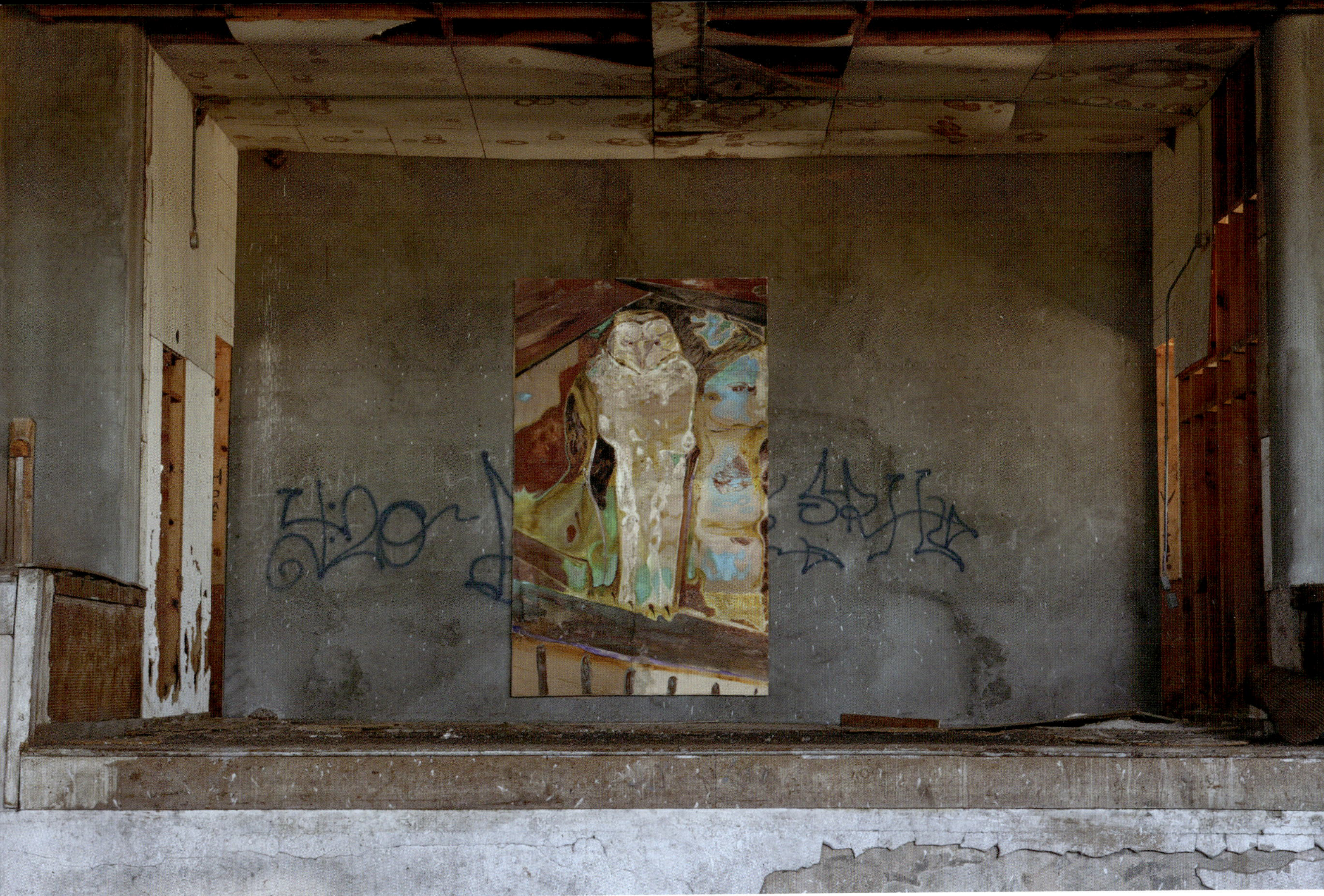

A DOOR IN THE DARKNESS INSTALLED IN THE ABANDONED CEDARVALE SCHOOL

> find myself is groundless, as the Buddhist teacher Pema Chödrön would put it; it exceeds where my attempts at philosophical ideas can take me. It has meant shifting from trying to participate in the social and political moment ... to thinking in terms of a singular intention toward a specific person, either in the present or in another time, or even to a place, a particular landscape, for example. It has meant forgoing the public language of consensus ... for a private language of greater awe and compassion.[4]

Instead of turning away from this feeling of "nothing," Hagler embraced it. In *Nihil*, using the music and thinking of the deeply religious Estonian composer Arvo Pärt (b. 1935) as structuring devices, Hagler established a set of formal constraints that would direct the choices he made, while allowing for improvisation and the unexpected to play a role. It was a way of melding formal restrictions with imagination's unlimited freedom. Aware that this contradiction lay at the heart of his project, and thorough in his thinking and planning, Hagler conceived of *Nihil* as a way to take everything he could think of into account.

By placing *Arbos*, a sketch of a geometric tree made by Pärt to determine his choice of notes for his composition of the same name, over a map of New Mexico, Hagler established what roads he would drive down. In the physical space he created, where choices became limited and opportunities unpredictable, he was able to decide on the non-repeatable palette he would use in each of his layered, process-oriented paintings. The more he restricted his choices, the more his imagination was able to burst free in unpredictable directions. This enabled Hagler to step back from his life, look at it, and see the different kinds of isolation and absences he had experienced, starting with the death of his brother when he was a young boy, and the persistent absence it left in him.

With the rules established in advance, Hagler found a way to let go of his old self—the one "trying to speak to a momentary audience"[5]—and discover what he was and could be when no one was around. Abandoning approved-of subject matter and what had become for him a style, he untethered himself and went on to change his work so that it was consistent with having no message. Instead of trying to assimilate and become part of the art world (an external structure), which he had worked at for many years, Hagler was empowered by *Nihil* to attain the "shift in perspective" he deeply desired.

Both the time and the place Hagler chose to formulate *Nihil* are important to its birth. It was not a coincidence that the idea for *Nihil* came to Hagler after he placed his painting in an abandoned schoolhouse in New Mexico, where the layers and histories of different cultures intersect and overlap amid a land where the physical evidence of deep time is constantly visible under a changing sky, and various myths are to be found everywhere, starting with Roswell, where rumors of a UFO crash began in 1947.

A recent transplant from Los Angeles, Hagler and his wife, the artist Maja Ruznic (b. 1983), were in this vast, constantly changing landscape during a pandemic. During this time Hagler formulated a set of rules that facilitated a way for him to come face to face with himself and—in the process of doing so—to discover and track what selves emerged.

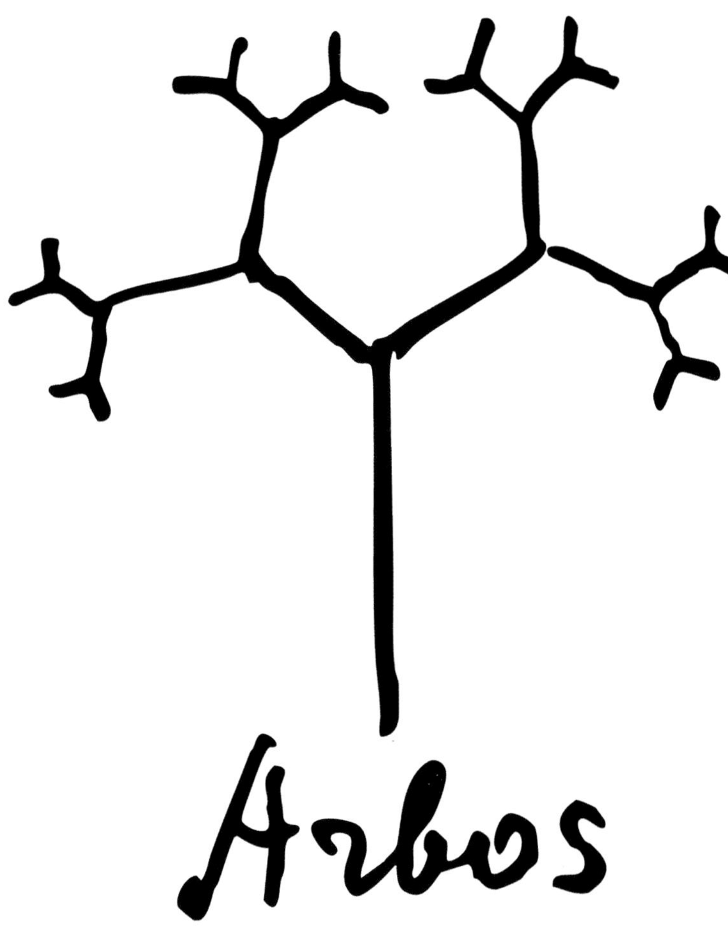

ARVO PÄRT, MUSICAL DIARY, 1994–95, P. 20

II.

The shaman is a capacious, egoless being who becomes attentive to both the visible and the occult, that which is hidden in plain sight. The journey is simultaneously inward and outward, a discovering of one's capacity to leave one's physical body and inhabit another, living or dead, human or animal. It is not about "style," which, the poet Robert Kelly wrote, "is death." The shamanic artist is not in pursuit of what Manny Farber, in his bracing, brilliant essay "White Elephant Art vs. Termite Art" (1962), called "the pursuit of the continuity, harmony, involved in constructing a masterpiece."[6] This was the goal that Hagler rejected.

In his paintings, and their eroded surfaces and blurring of figure-ground distinctions, Hagler achieves two things. The layering and scraping parallel the geological strata and millennia of erosion that are visible in the buttes of New Mexico. They are a record of the journey, in which a process of addition and subtraction continues until the work is completed. The journey shares something with the path Farber believes separates termite art from white elephant art: "A peculiar fact about termite tapeworm-fungus-moss is that it goes always forward eating its own boundaries, and, likely as not, leaves nothing in its path other than the signs of eager, industrious, unkempt activity."[7]

Impressive in scale, with a surface abraded by Hagler's open-ended process, *The Hunger Artist* (2024) is a largely tan, orange, and purple painting depicting a tiger standing on its hind legs, scratching the wall of its enclosure. Hagler installed it on the distressed walls of the abandoned Cedarvale School. He hung a painting on a wall of peeling paint for a public that did not exist, and left it exposed to the world until he returned.

Hagler describes the inspiration for *The Hunger Artist* on his website:

> I had several visualizations, dreams, and in one holotropic breathwork session, a powerful physical sensation of encountering and merging with a mountain lion. In the snowy Sandia Mountains [New Mexico], I had tracked one a short distance before sanely turning back. When I wanted to draw one, I didn't try to find it in the wild or turn away from the idea altogether; I went to the Albuquerque Zoo where I drew imprisoned cats of all kinds, including lions and tigers.[8]

Connecting this experience to Franz Kafka's (1883–1924) short story with a very similar title is telling. "A Hunger Artist" (1922) tells the story of a nameless performer who travels with his manager across Europe, seeking a location to lock himself in a cage and fast for public spectacle. Unsurprisingly, things devolve when he refuses to comply with his "impresario" and end his fast after 40 days; eventually, he ends up in a circus where he starves to

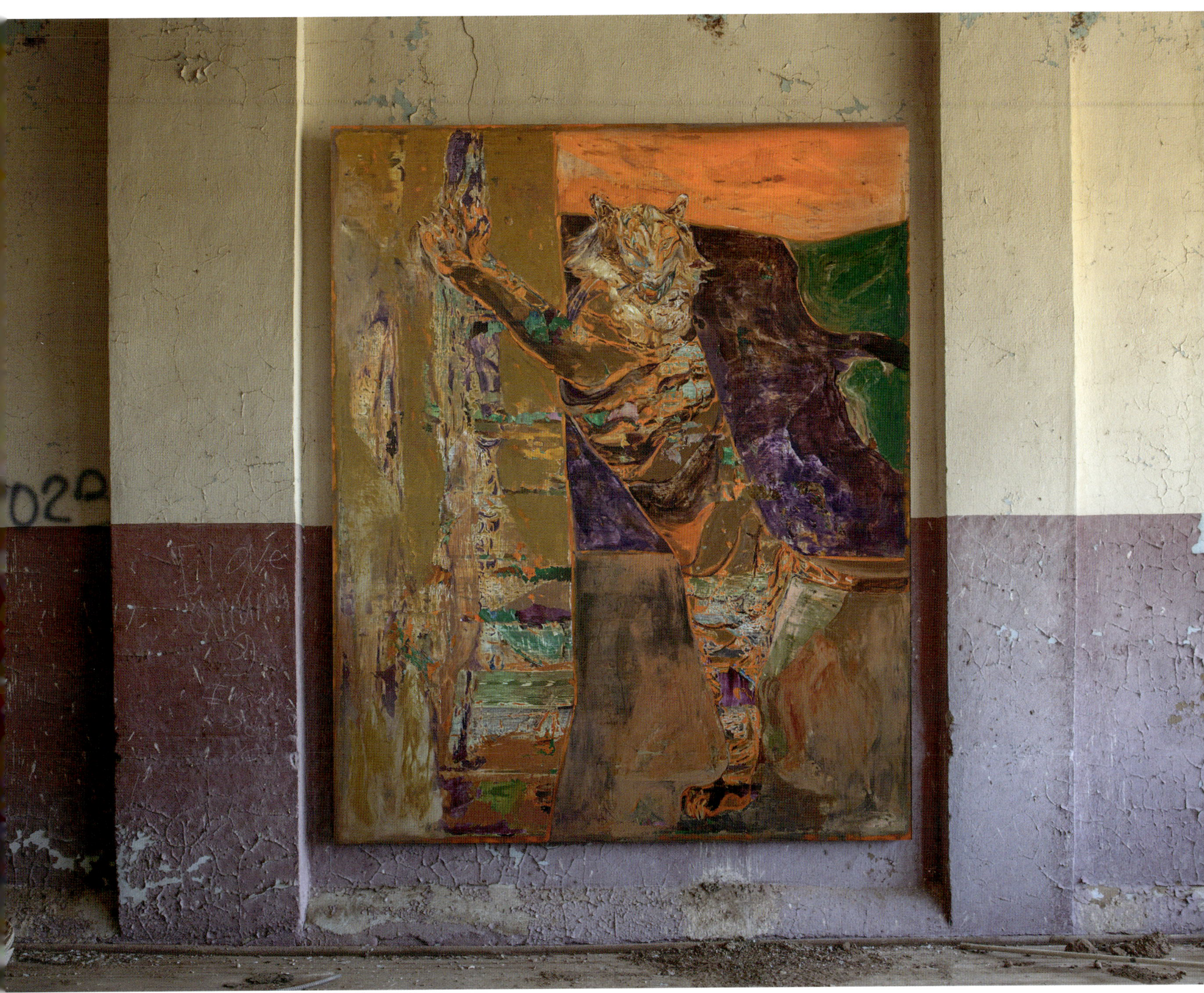

THE HUNGER ARTIST, INSTALLED IN AN ABANDONED SCHOOL AT CEDARVALE, NEW MEXICO

death, shunned by those around him, including audiences. After he dies, the circus reclaims the cage for a panther, which draws huge crowds. In this story, Hagler saw parallels with the dilemma he was facing: who do I make my art for? Am I a performer who is supposed to make a spectacle of myself?

III.

Hagler incorporates a wide range of materials in the paintings, drawings, and sculpture that comprise *Nihil*. The discarded books, pages, and posters he paints in oil, wax, charcoal, graphite, and oil pastel look, in some cases, as if they are abandoned. The colored wax both covers the surface and preserves it. Sometimes the surface is semi-transparent, and we can almost read what is beneath the wax. The stained pages remind us that what once might have been news is now an artifact from a lost time. The ghostliness of the images, their tormented surface, evokes a world that is remote and immediate, sensual and violent.

The paintings in *Chimera* used well-known works by Max Beckmann (1884–1950) and Emil Nolde (1867–1956) as springboards. Hagler neither appropriated nor parodied his sources. They provided the structure upon which he built up his own painting. He was not interested in social irony. In *Nihil,* Hagler responded to the inner and outer world of his daily life, the intense feeling of solitude he felt, the untold and unheard stories the abandoned buildings whispered to him, and the world he encountered.

When he titled a painting *Costco Portrait (The Mental Body)* (2023), he was referring to the source: he had made quick drawings of the women working at Costco along one of the routes he had marked out that went through Albuquerque. In contrast to the paintings in *Chimera,* Hagler did not rely on a safety net. When he no longer sought refuge in a signature style (or brand), used a well-known work as a source, or resorted to resemblance, how could he tell if the painting—it was a portrait, after all—was good or bad? Did those terms of judging mean anything anymore?

In *Tractatus Logico-Philosophicus* (1921), the only book-length philosophical work that Ludwig Wittgenstein (1889–1951) published in his lifetime, he famously wrote: "The limits of my language mean the limits of my world," and also: "What can be shown cannot be said."[9] As Wittgenstein understood it, language was only able to paint a picture of hard facts and data. Other than saying that *Costco Portrait (The Mental Body)* is a painting, I cannot say what it is. I can only point to it with my words.

IV.

There are five sculptural forms in *Nihil*, all made in 2023 out of rawhide. Ranging in color from a dirty off-white to an earthy brown, three of the sculptures are titled *Autumn Pilgrimage*. Two of them are standing. When the light passes through them, they have a buttery glow. The hide becomes a hooded cloak and skin without a body. If they are penitents, it is unclear what order they belong to.

The works are uncanny, calling up forgotten lives, as well as a ritual intrinsic to El Santuario de Chimayó, an adobe church just north of Santa Fe. In the week before Easter, thousands of people make a pilgrimage to the small church, with many taking dirt from the ground because they believe it has the power to heal. And yet, on making this association, we must resist being literal. The pilgrimage that Hagler's figures have undertaken is not known. We see the figures as surrogates for the artist and the viewer. What destinations do we want to reach as we journey toward our own mortality?

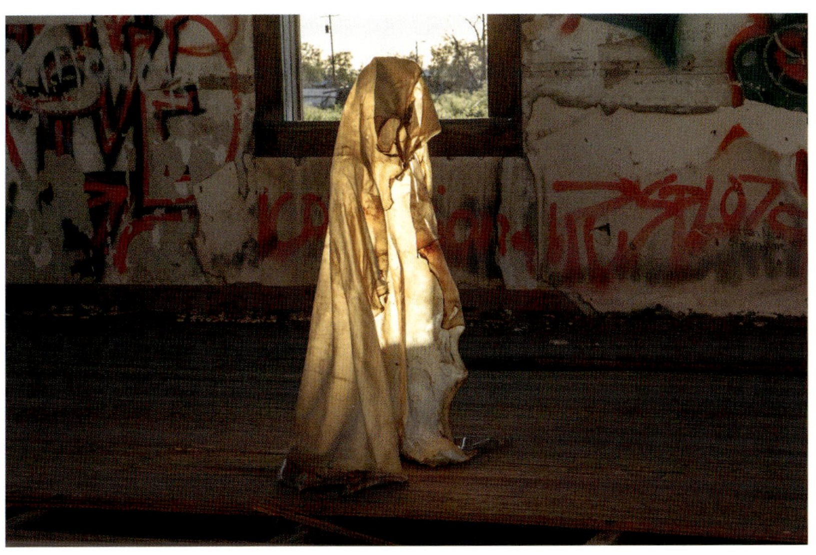

AUTUMN PILGRIMAGE, INSTALLED IN AN ABANDONED CHURCH AT TAIBAN, NEW MEXICO

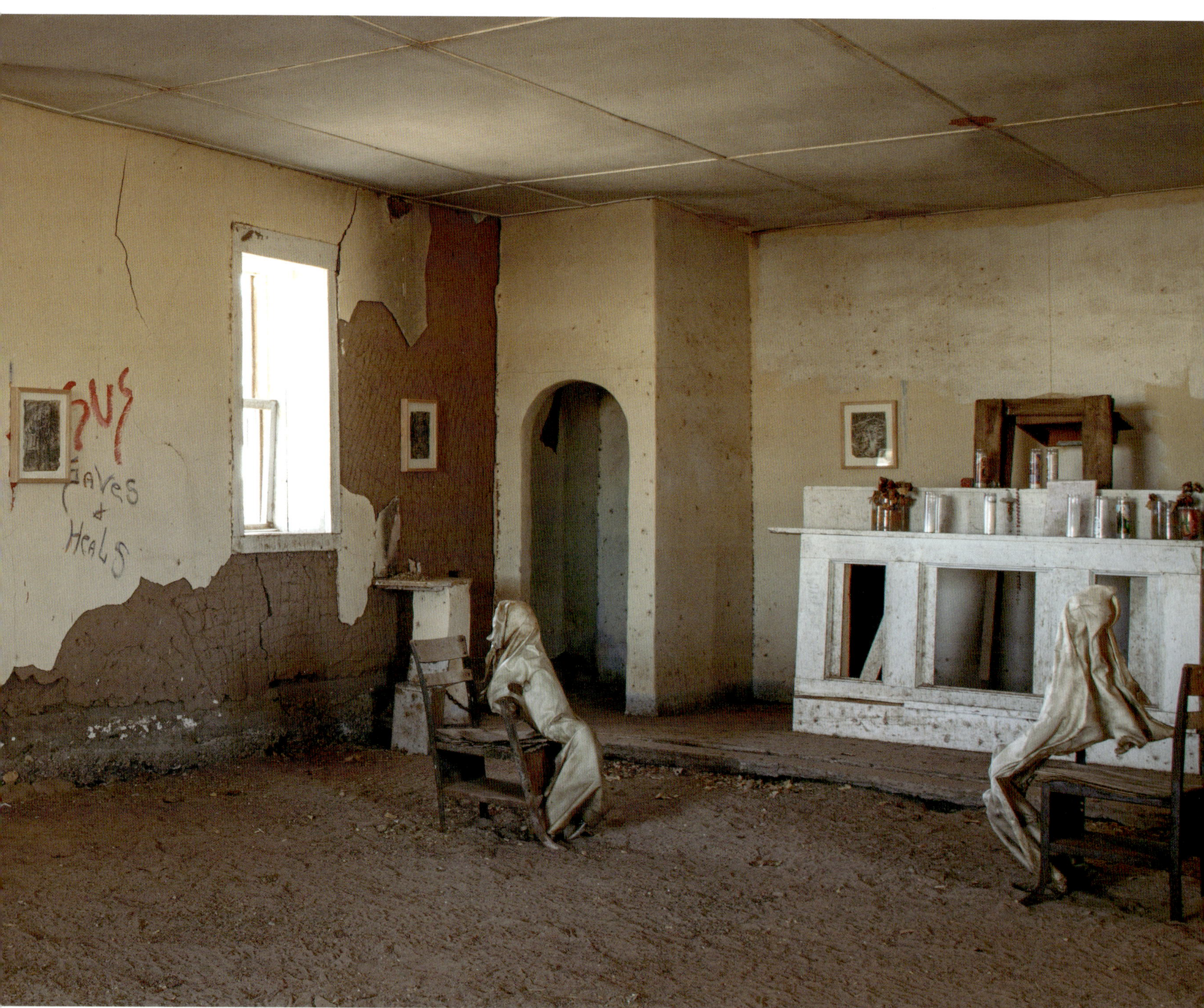

MOON IN WATER, INSTALLED IN AN ABANDONED CHURCH AT SAN ACACIA, NEW MEXICO

Titled *Moon in Water*, the other two sculptures are seated uncomfortably in found wood-and-steel chairs. Are they novitiates? Why have they stopped and what are they thinking? The sculptures' resistance to being read literally is very compelling. They are neither reassuring nor comforting, and why should they be?

V.

The Book of Hours (Yeso, New Mexico, 1957) is titled after Yeso, New Mexico, a ghost town of a half-dozen houses that was founded in 1906, when the railroad was extended to this spot. The only business was a post office, which prompts us to wonder whether Hagler made a connection between the work and the town. The painting is a blackish-brown grid of rectangular sheets that have been affixed to a larger, muddy-colored surface. The grid suggests a book, whose pages have been carefully torn out and covered with layers of paint.

Books of Hours are collections of prayers, readings, and psalms that are recited at eight set times during the day to the Virgin Mary, the Mother of God, in the hope that she will plead to God on behalf of the individual. Hagler titled his painting after Rilke's *Book of Hours: Love Poems to God* (1905), which the poet wrote in his twenties after a trip to Russia. Moved by Leo Tolstoy and Boris Pasternak, who were deeply religious men and writers, he returned to Germany and began writing down poems that he believed were co-authored by a divine presence:

> We must not portray you in king's robes,
> you drifting mist that brought forth the morning.
>
> Once again from the old paintboxes
> we take the same gold for scepter and crown
> that has disguised you through the ages.

> Piously we produce our images of you
> till they stand around you like a thousand walls.
> And when our hearts would simply open,
> our fervent hands hide you.[10]

This is what Hagler said about his painting: "For this reason, I dated the work 1957–2021, as, more and more, I think of time itself as a collaborator." [11]

Rilke's poems are written by a man who has journeyed inward: "I love the dark hours of my being. My mind deepens into them."[12] Full of longing and the feeling of being broken, the poems contain neither messages nor answers:

> I yearn to belong to something, to be contained
> in an all-embracing mind that sees me
> as a single thing.[13]

What are we to make of Hagler's *The Book of Hours (Yeso, New Mexico, 1957)*? Do we need to know that he found a 1957 catalog selling hydraulic pumps for wells, which he incorporated into the painting? While we can see there are seven rows and seven columns of seven pages, do we also need to know there seven layers of paint? Will we connect Hagler's use of seven to its recurring significance in the Bible: from the Book of Genesis, in which God created the world in six days and rested on the seventh, to the Book of Revelation, with its seven churches, seven seals, seven trumpets, and seven bowls? Or that he installed the painting in the abandoned office in Yeso, New Mexico, essentially returning it to the site where it was born?

VI.

There are three drawings in graphite, charcoal, oil pastel, and wax on the pages of a found Baptist notebook that are dated 1981 to 2024. These served as studies for the monumental triptych *The Hermit* (2024). The work

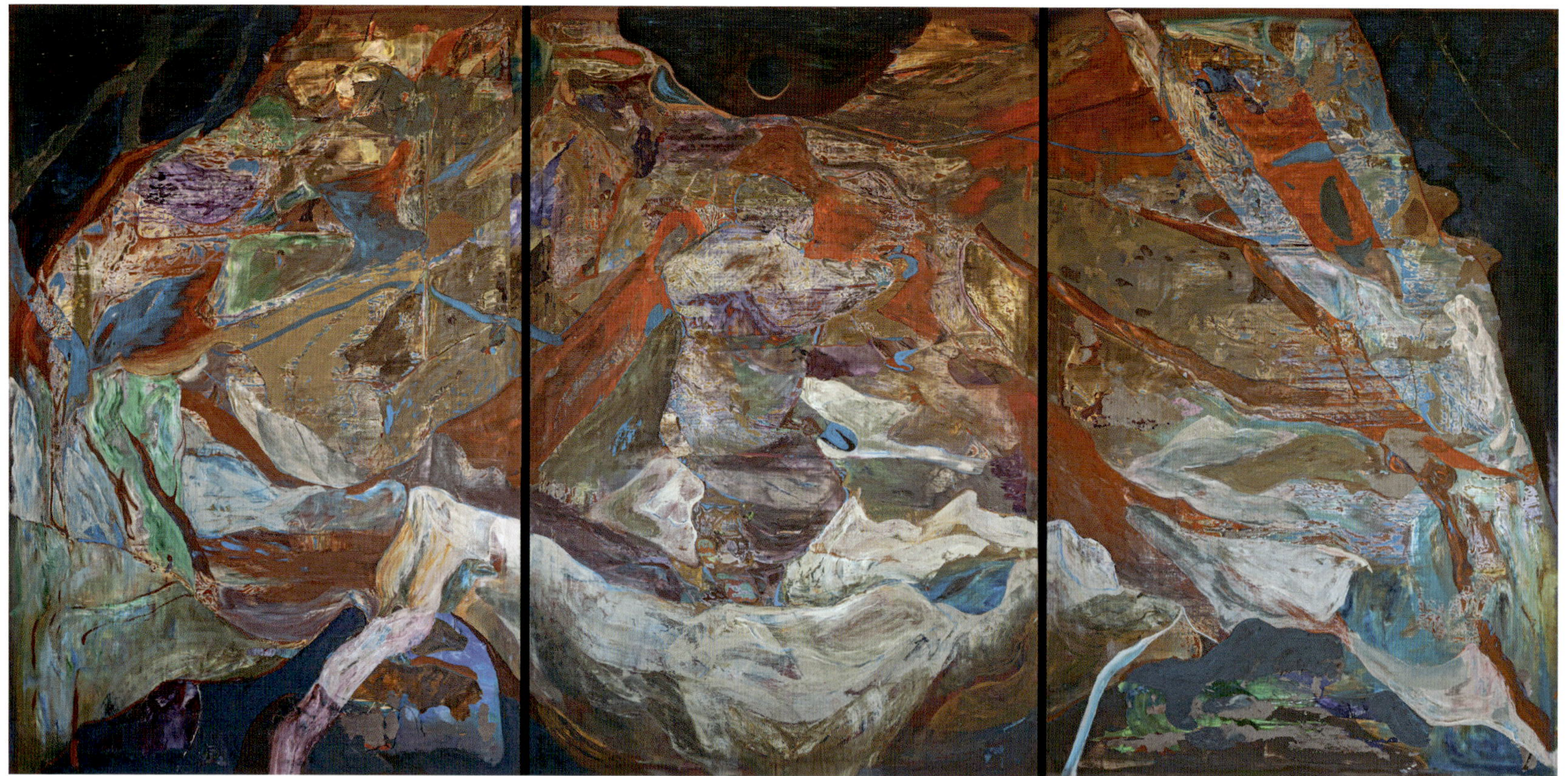

THE HERMIT

depicts what looks like a nude man, either leaning against a rock or standing, pointing at the night sky, which is framed by twin buttes. In the middle of the sky floats a lunar eclipse. With their worked surfaces, the different-colored, interlocking planes and shapes become a visual puzzle.

In the foreground, a ghostly white shape with tints of blue, green, and violet stretches across the triptych, hovering between figural form and geological accretion. The blurring of the figure-ground relationship evokes various associations that transcend formal issues. Taking the painting's title as a cue, the viewer is invited to reflect upon Hagler's considerations of the relationship between the physical body and spiritual presence, matter and transcendence. It is through this lens that we consider his figure-ground relationships, his layers of accretion and eroded surfaces. Done in time, they embody time passing. His paintings, drawings, and sculptures feel open and vulnerable.

Hagler belongs to the group of visionary artists who look inward in their search for higher consciousness. They can be world builders, like the poet and printmaker William Blake (1757–1827). They can see a world that others never notice. When Antonin Artaud (1896–1948) entered the land of the Indigenous Tarahumara people in Mexico, he saw a mountainous landscape marked by what he understood as the indecipherable imprints of higher spirits. John of Patmos is believed to be the author of the Book of Revelation, the only apocalyptic book in the New Testament. In it the author describes visions that include a seven-headed dragon and a woman clothed with the sun and a crown of twelve stars. Banished by Roman authorities, John lived a reclusive life on the island of Patmos in the Aegean Sea. A hermit, he came to symbolize an individual living an ascetic life of introspection, away from the world, its dogmas, positions, and vying for power.

This is the path that Hagler formulated in his project *Nihil* after leaving Los Angeles and relocating to New Mexico. Hagler has identified this path through his choice of subjects such as the hermit and tiger. It is a path where logic and consensus are shed in favor of visions and dreams.

1 poets.org/poem/archaic-torso-apollo (accessed January 2025).
2 joshuahagler.com/nihil (accessed January 2025).
3 Gaston Bachelard, *The Poetics of Space*, translated by Maria Jolas, 1964, p. 47.
4 hopperprize.org/joshua-hagler-interview/ (accessed January 2025).
5 Ibid.
6 Manny Farber, "White Elephant Art vs. Termite Art", 1962, p. 242: moca.org/storage/app/media/cropped-images/02_White%20Elephant%20Art%20vs.%20Termite%20Art.pdf (accessed January 2025).
7 Ibid., p. 242.
8 joshuahagler.com/word/already-paradise (accessed January 2025).
9 medium.com/@lcsterling/the-limits-of-my-language-mean-the-limits-of-my-world-68b94fc1d119 (accessed January 2025).
10 onbeing.org/poetry/gods-true-cloak/ (accessed January 2025).
11 joshuahagler.com/word/nihil-1 (accessed January 2025).
12 tumblr.com/peelsofpoetry/172781193319/i-love-the-dark-hours-of-my-being-by-rainer-maria (accessed January 2025).
13 uuwestport.org/i-am-prayer-again/ (accessed January 2025).

TENETS OF NIHIL

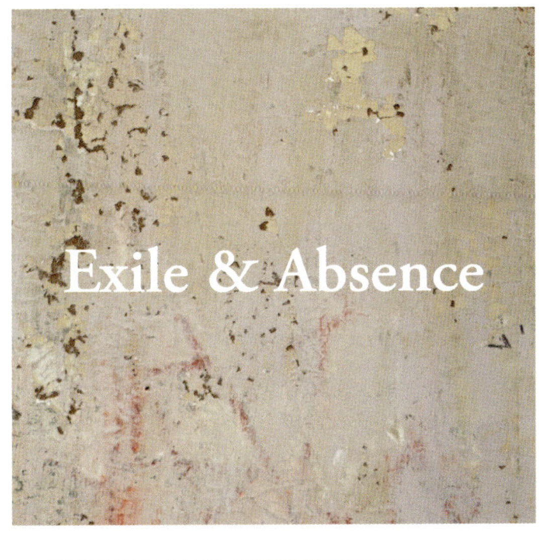
Exile & Absence

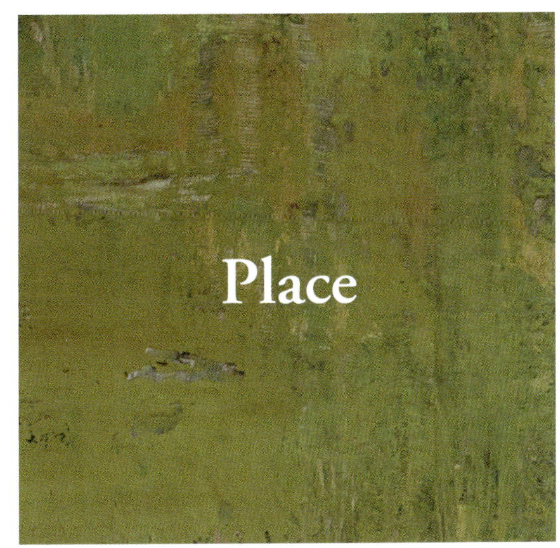
Place

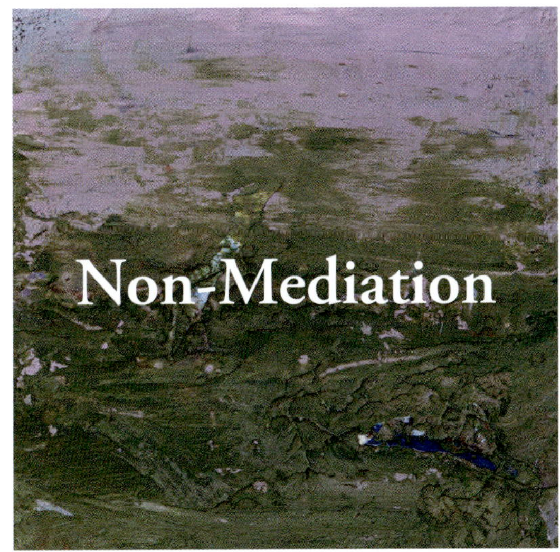
Non-Mediation

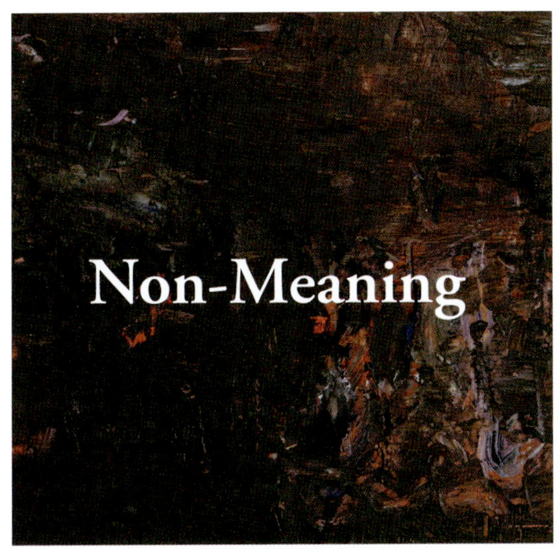
Non-Meaning

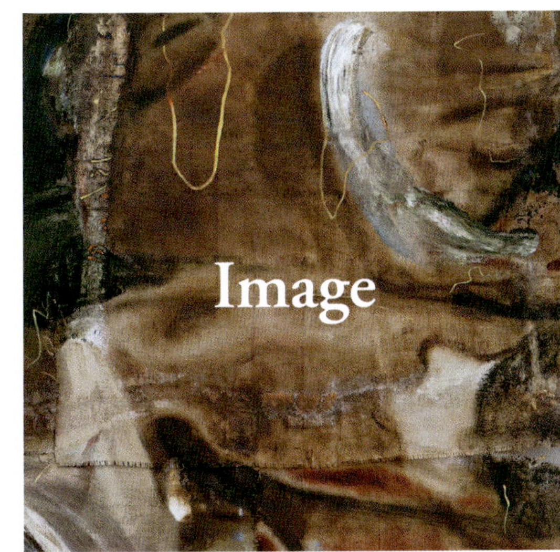
Image

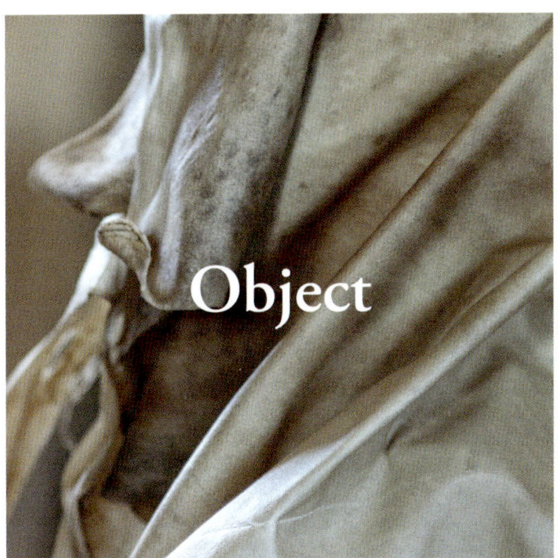
Object

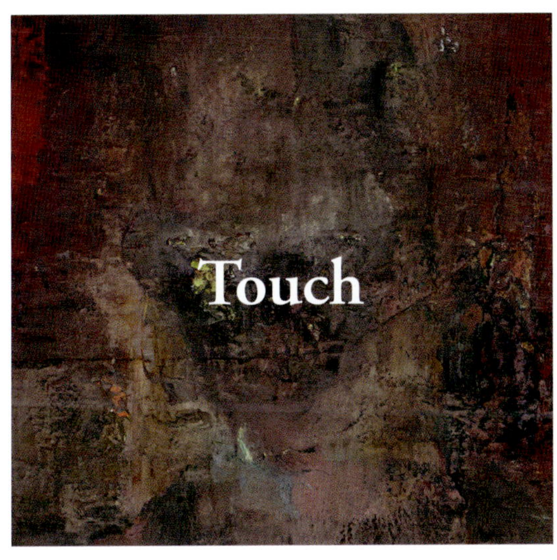
Touch

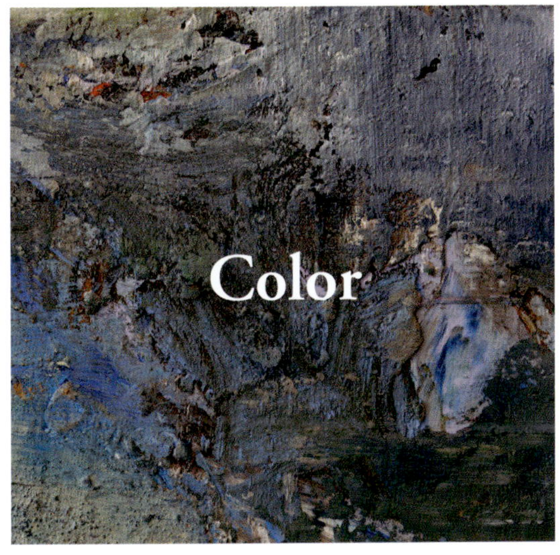
Color

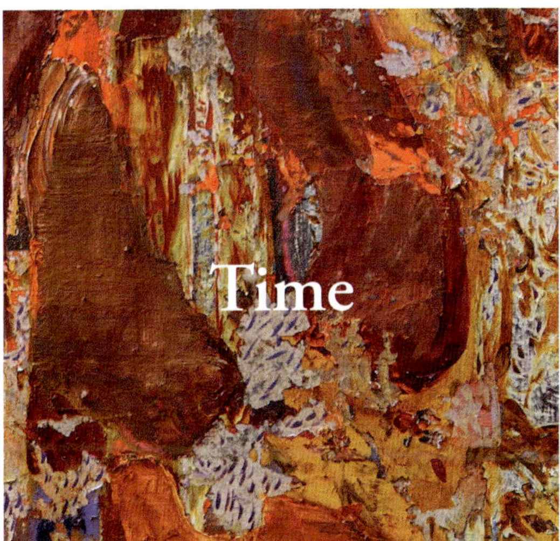
Time

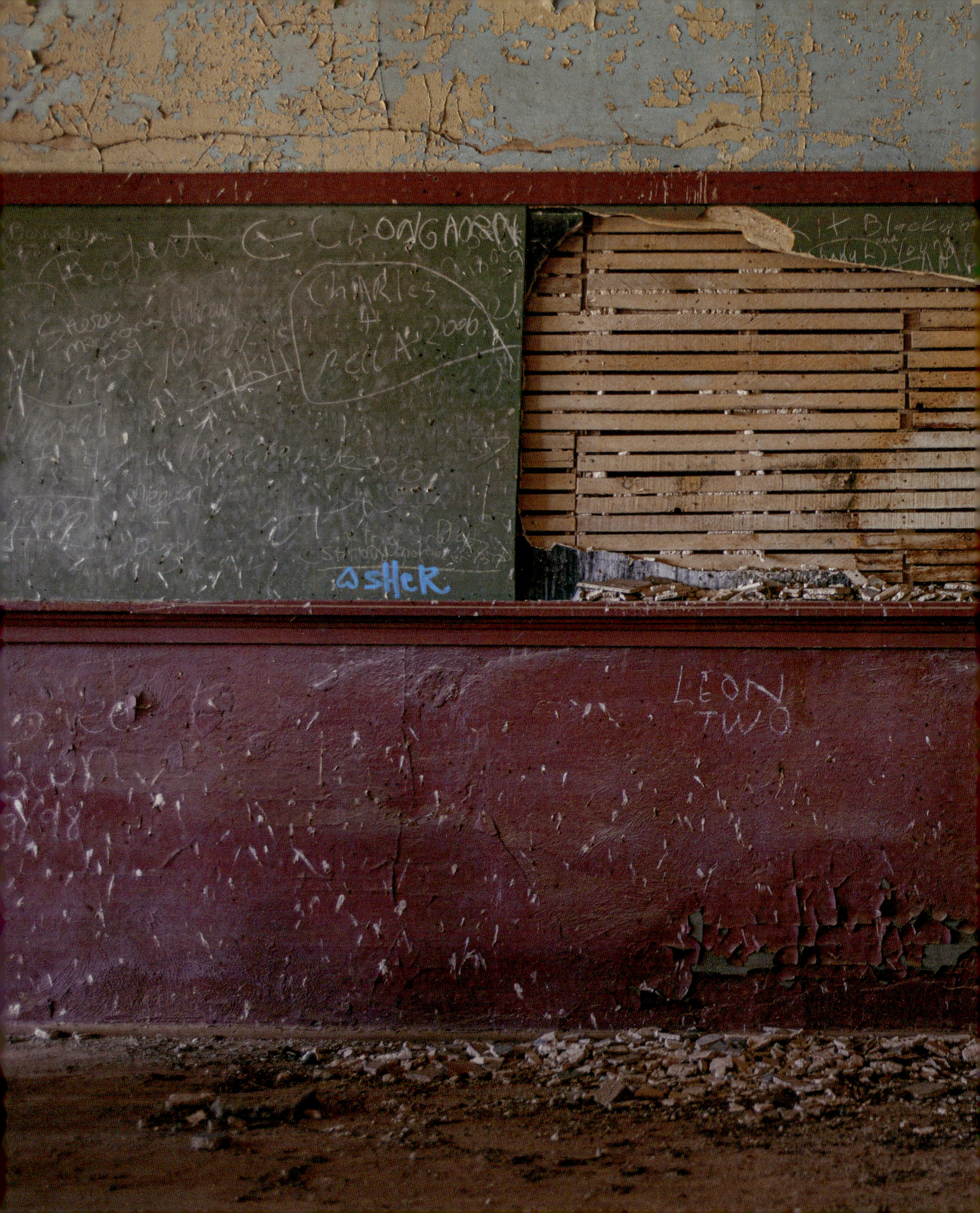
asHER
LEON
TWO

CEDARVALE SCHOOL

When there is nothing left to say, the work can begin

On little more than a whim, in May 2020, two months before my daughter was born, and at the height of Covid-19, I installed work at the abandoned Cedarvale School just outside Corona, New Mexico. It was the first of several deserted structures in which I would do so. I simply wanted to know what it would feel like to put work in an empty structure and to find out how much I was capable of doing on my own.

From that day through the summer of 2024, the abandoned New Mexico schools, churches, and post offices where I installed paintings and sculptures became, for me, like a single architecture. There was the sense that this architecture on this land, with its many rooms and hidden treasures, contained the unconscious self. In roaming the unpopulated regions of New Mexico, it was as if many times and places hovered before and behind one another within a single moment or space. In little time, I began making work specifically for certain walls, alcoves, and rooms. Each time, it was as though a certain quality of consciousness had returned to its source. My phrase for this process, in these spaces and within myself, is Repatriation of Soul.

This book is not a monograph of all the work I made in four years but a chronicle of this four-year experience.

...

From the moment I arrived in New Mexico in late 2017, after 15 years in San Francisco and Los Angeles, my work changed. My interests changed, my very feeling for what was important or even real changed. I began collecting scraps of anything and everything to paint on, mostly because I was too broke to afford store-bought canvas and linen. I seemed immediately to identify with the forgotten and ignored, which suggests a long-term psychological consequence of my work being overlooked and excluded from things in those 15 years in California. Whatever I had imagined my life was supposed to be about, it wasn't.

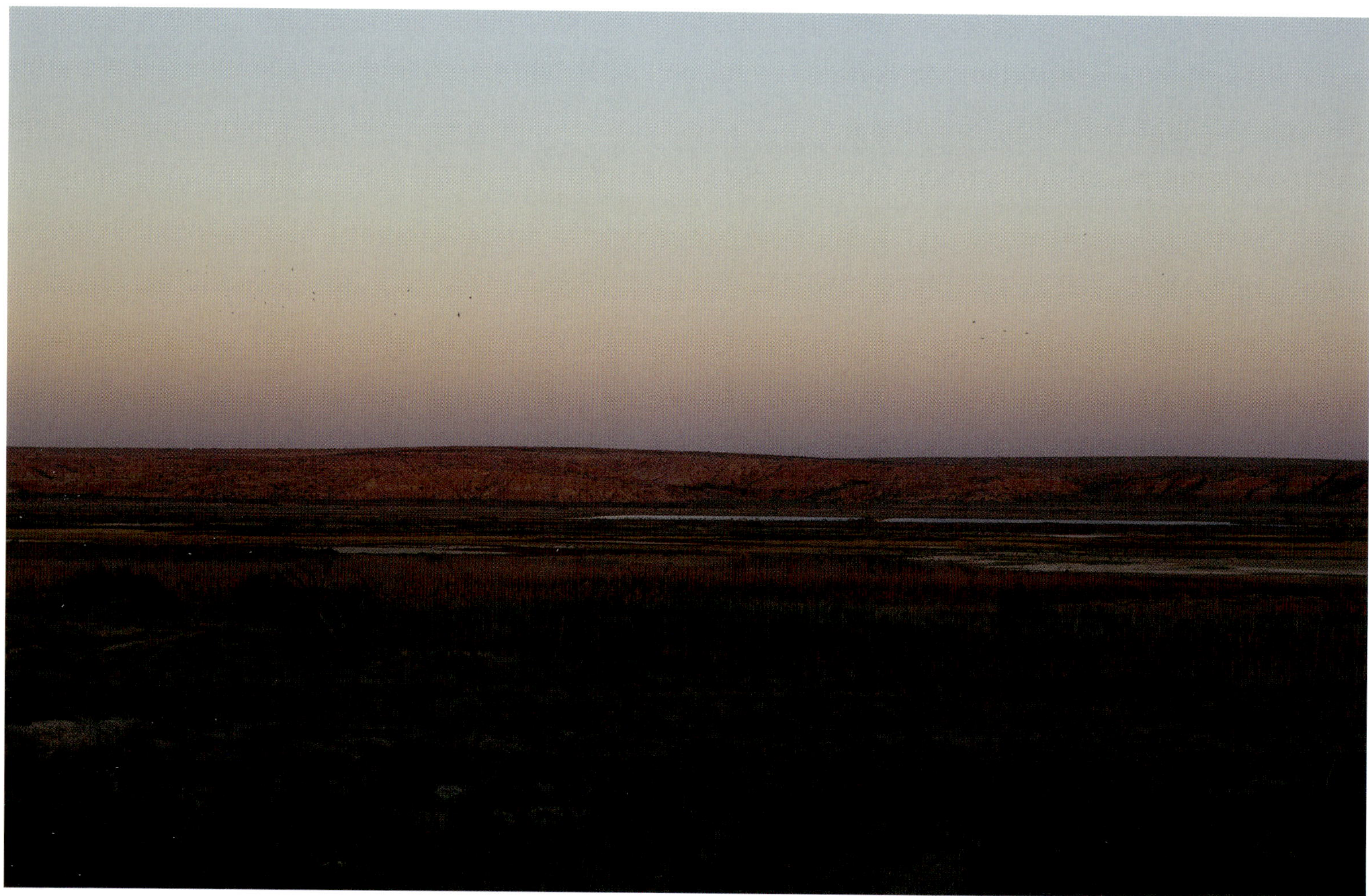

BITTER LAKE WILDLIFE REFUGE, ROSWELL, NEW MEXICO

The images in my paintings were now dissolving further and further into abstract fields, and some of those images came out of dreams, something I had never before allowed in my work. Of all factors, I believe it was sound, in the most general sense, that seemed at the heart of the work's visual changes, perhaps because things had become much quieter than in LA and I could hear again—I could hear myself hearing, listening with what Nietzsche called "ears behind ears."[1] And very soon, my musical interests changed as well.

I remember a specific morning while still living in Roswell. I was jogging through the local park and saw a boy of about eight flying a kite. Arvo Pärt's 1976 "Für Alina" (then a recent discovery) played at a low volume on my headphones, through which I could still hear people and birds. As I listened to this spare and haunting song and watched the boy's kite, I began weeping. I stopped there, kneeling and watching. Reflecting on that moment, I feel I understand it now: within the short length of the song and the visual frame of the overcast day with the boy and his kite, a compression of loss and innocence intermingled so that an expansive space for some kind of personal surrender was made possible. Symbolically, the boy was both my younger self and my late brother, who died when I was not quite this boy's age. I had long conflated my failure as an artist (still defining success in social and economic terms) with a failure to redeem his loss, a loss that was, itself, a tragic consequence of long unspoken transgenerational trauma within my family.

Sound had a new presence all around me. During meditation, whether in my own back yard or out in the nearby desert hills, I began to notice sounds like very small bells, but sleeker, like the sound effect of a sharp object quietly unsheathed in the distance. This subtle sound would come in and out, over or under sudden gusts of wind, chirping birds, the quiet croaking of crows, the stomping or snorting of a wild horse, a distant train, military aircraft overhead, even the faraway sound of cartoons from inside the house where my daughter played. There is a way in which, when one is patient, everything around oneself begins to take on structure: the held breath (this is the picture), the inhale (step into the picture), and the exhale (let go of the picture). The mind seems either to discover or to invent an interjecting order around which the aural world weaves.

Arvo Pärt's famous musical innovation, the "tintinnabuli" structuring of his work (literally meaning "little bells"), is to do with fleeting, individual "broken" voices moving in and out of one holistic voice within which all operate. Though I assume nothing of Pärt's own thinking, I tend to understand the relationship between the broken and the whole not as hierarchical, but as co-poiesis, with one evoking the other in mutual need and consequence.

...

I do not remember exactly when the word "nihil" first flashed into my mind, but it simply did: the five letters, not as a brainy question or concept, but as a "pure, clear word" as poet Stanley Kunitz was well known for putting it, unconnected to anything I was doing, reading, or thinking about at the time. Yet, day after day, as my obsession with Pärt's music grew, I would see this word in my mind's eye. I understood early what it meant: *I have nothing left to say, and even if I did, what would be the point of saying it?* And the very next thought was (this seems to me a miracle now): *well, if there's nothing left to say, then I'm free from making work about anything at all*. It would probably seem ironic to Pärt himself to learn that, freed from the need for messaging in art, I began leaning on tintinnabuli to structure a work in lieu of conceptualism. What about his way of composing music could be translated into color, layers, shape, form, touch?

The more questions I asked, the more the structure for *Nihil* developed. I had wanted one-to-one translation from sound to vision. Ultimately, it was not really possible, but from this growing feeling for structure, *Nihil*'s nine tenets developed (see p. 23), which governed something of both the work's process and its ethical values.

The route I contrived for the excursions made through New Mexico came from Pärt's tree drawing, which he had once used as an organizing principle for his piece "Arbos."

This is how it was that *Nihil* took shape. Having nothing left to say, I listened—to Pärt, to the landscape, to its emptiness—and, in listening, everything was given. My only task was to catch it when it came.

1 *The Portable Nietzsche*, edited and translated by Walter Kaufmann, Penguin Books, 1976, p. 516.

Exile & Absence (*The Archaic Brother*)

In *Nihil*, exile is the necessary precondition for beginning the work. Exile is the consequence of being outside the social order of things. This failure to belong comes from a refusal to confer deferentially to the implicit or explicit expectations and requirements of the social group. The language might well develop and deepen over time, but it does not mean the social order perceives a need for it. The language of consensus is the language of obviousness. In *Nihil*, it is understood that nothing obvious is worth saying, but only obviousness can be widely discussed. In the social order, it is the discussion—and the game of discussion—that matters more than the work. In *Nihil*, however, and in the exile that ensues, it is precisely the opposite.

Exile begins at the point at which I give up hope of belonging or communicating. What for a while, on the far side of hope, is an experience of alienation eventually makes real freedom possible. Freedom begins with the embrace of emptiness, which is also vastness. This is possible, in *Nihil*, by developing a relationship with place—in my case New Mexico—and shifting communication from a primarily social or public concern in the present to an intimate individual concern over a course of time extending beyond my own life. Concepts such as relevance no longer seem relevant to me. Once the impossibility of joining is finally accepted, I discover I was in exile all along. Most of us resist becoming aware of the falseness of belonging for as long as the situation allows, but the unavoidable stage of angst and heartbreak we attempt to avoid is only momentary in the scheme of things. Exile is the beginning of freedom that follows this loss of hope. To do the work of *Nihil*, the work must not seek to matter. It must become free.

In practice, exile means a few things. First, I must leave the densely populated metropolis for the sparsely populated landscape. This landscape must begin as a stranger because all discoveries ought to be made with no greater sophistication than when a child discovers the world beyond the home of her parents for the first time. I must not know where I am, nor be allowed to return to where I was. In time, place reveals itself as myself, both alien and familiar. All my life, I have awaited my arrival here without knowing. Exile transubstantiates into repatriation. The soul remembers the soul, arriving at last at *axis mundi*.

In exile, the eye is trained to notice absence as the most potent presence in the visual field. Absence is home to the Archaic Brother and the source of it. After all, the first stage of exile began when I was a young boy, when my brother suddenly vanished. His trace was to be found everywhere and nowhere. This vanishing happened not once, but rather is always happening, to the memory, the body, the painting. As he vanishes to the outside world, little by little, year after year, he appears in the forgotten places of New Mexico. This is where the Archaic Brother is to be found: in the negative space between junipers, in the floors and ceilings of abandoned churches and schools, in the middle distance from where I sit to where the fires in the mountains rage. The Archaic Brother is the very archetype of absence. All matters of absence pertain to the Archaic Brother, and only out of absence can he be present. The presence felt in painting, for example, is to do with absence, with the epistolary substance between my exile and his.

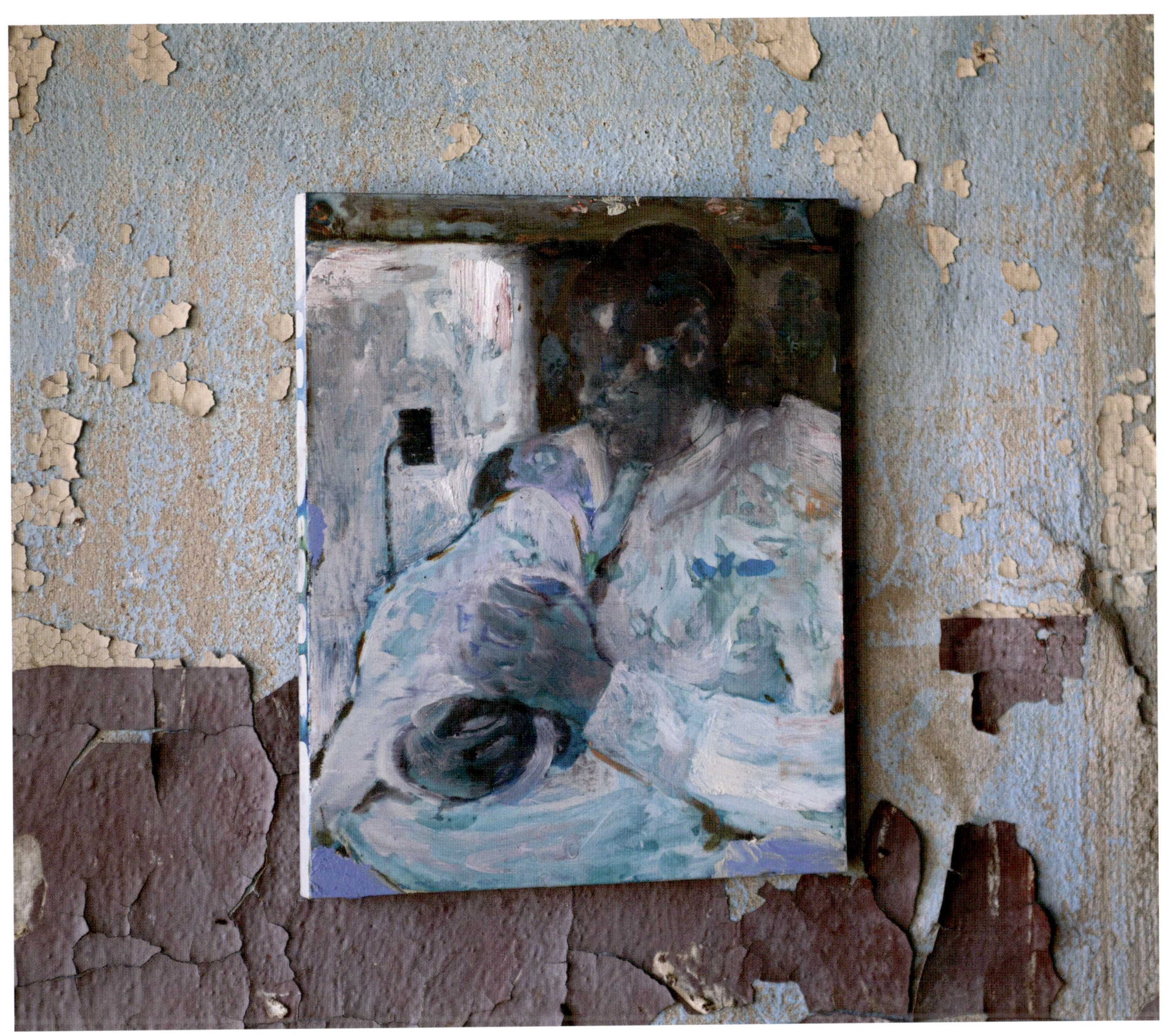

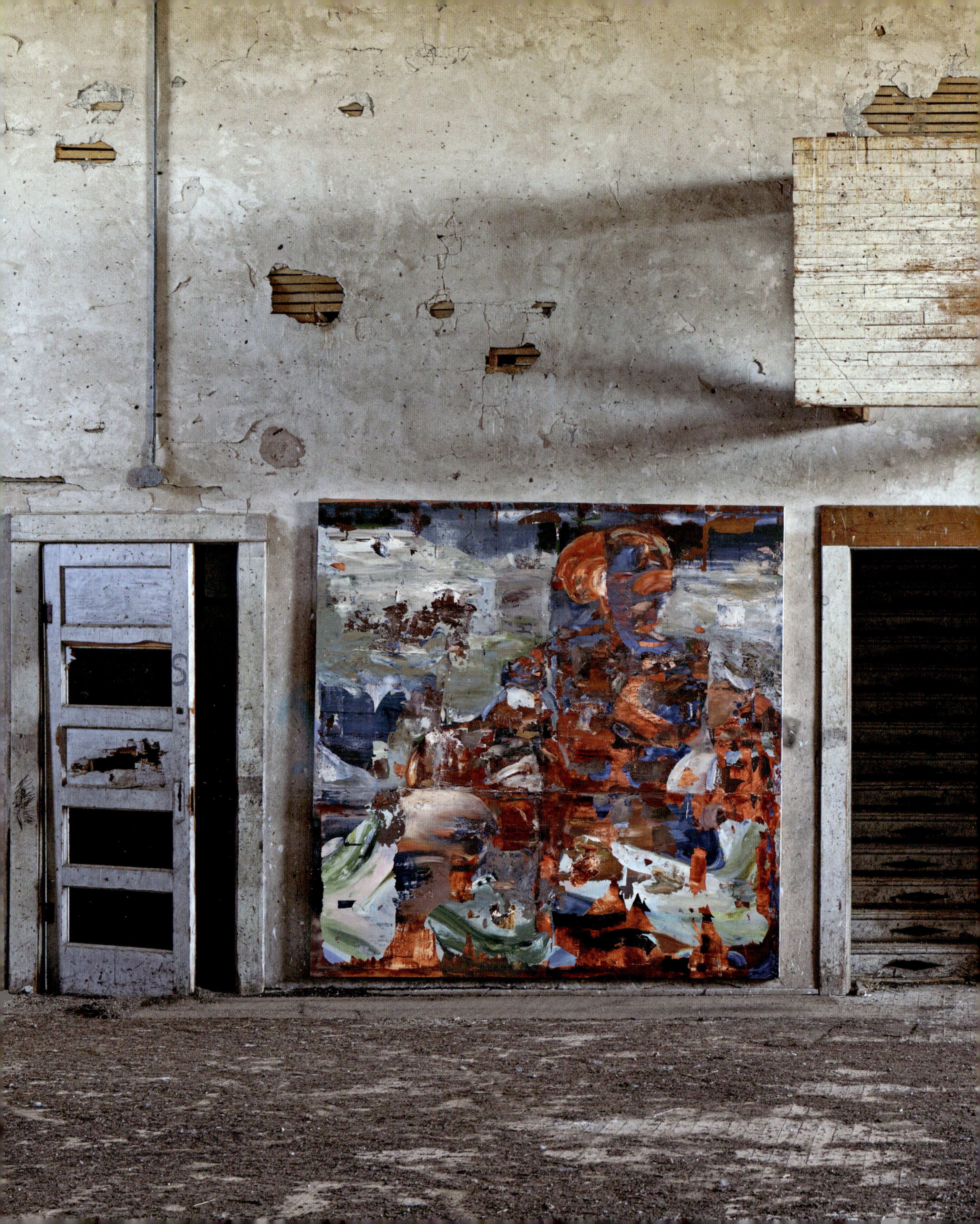

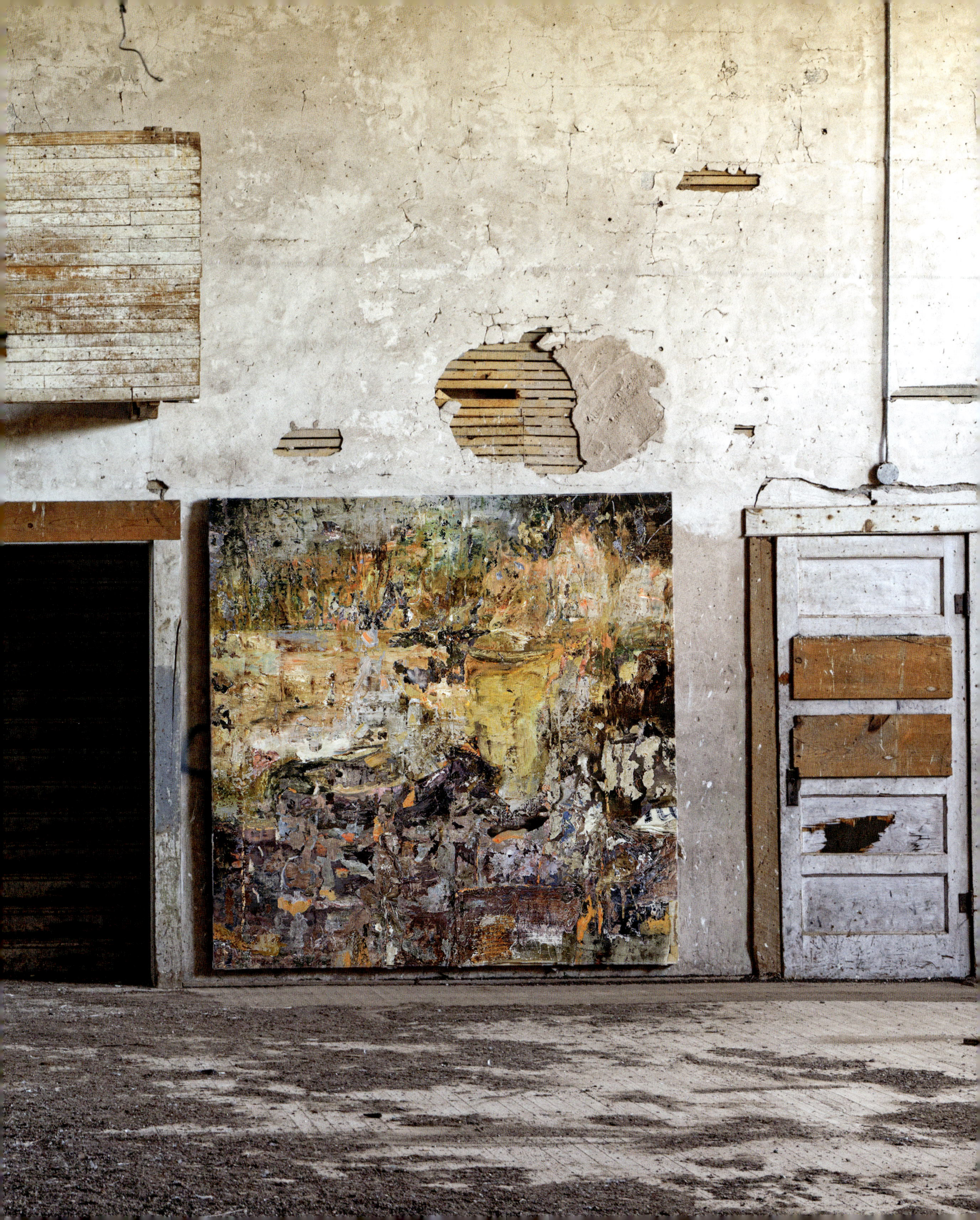

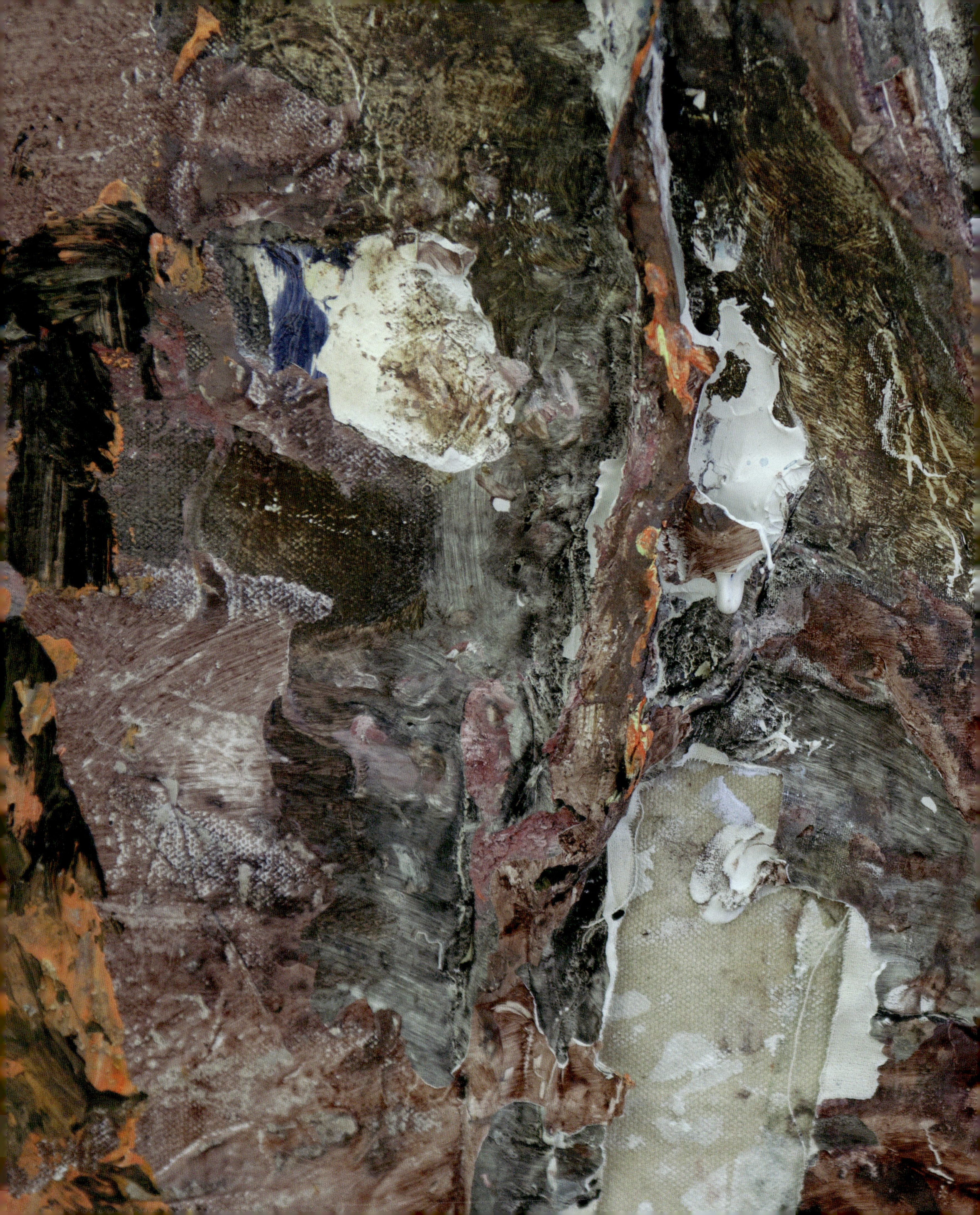

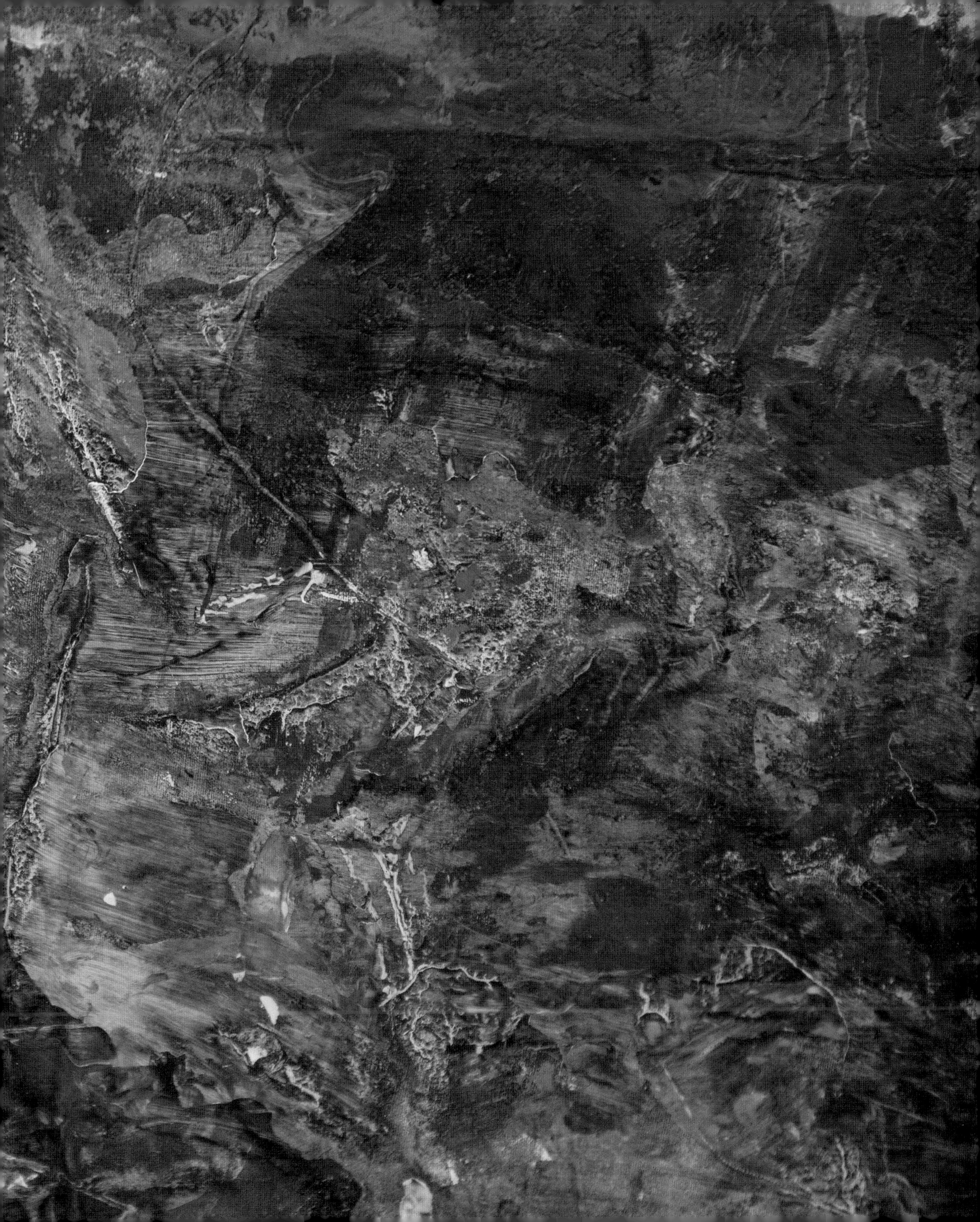

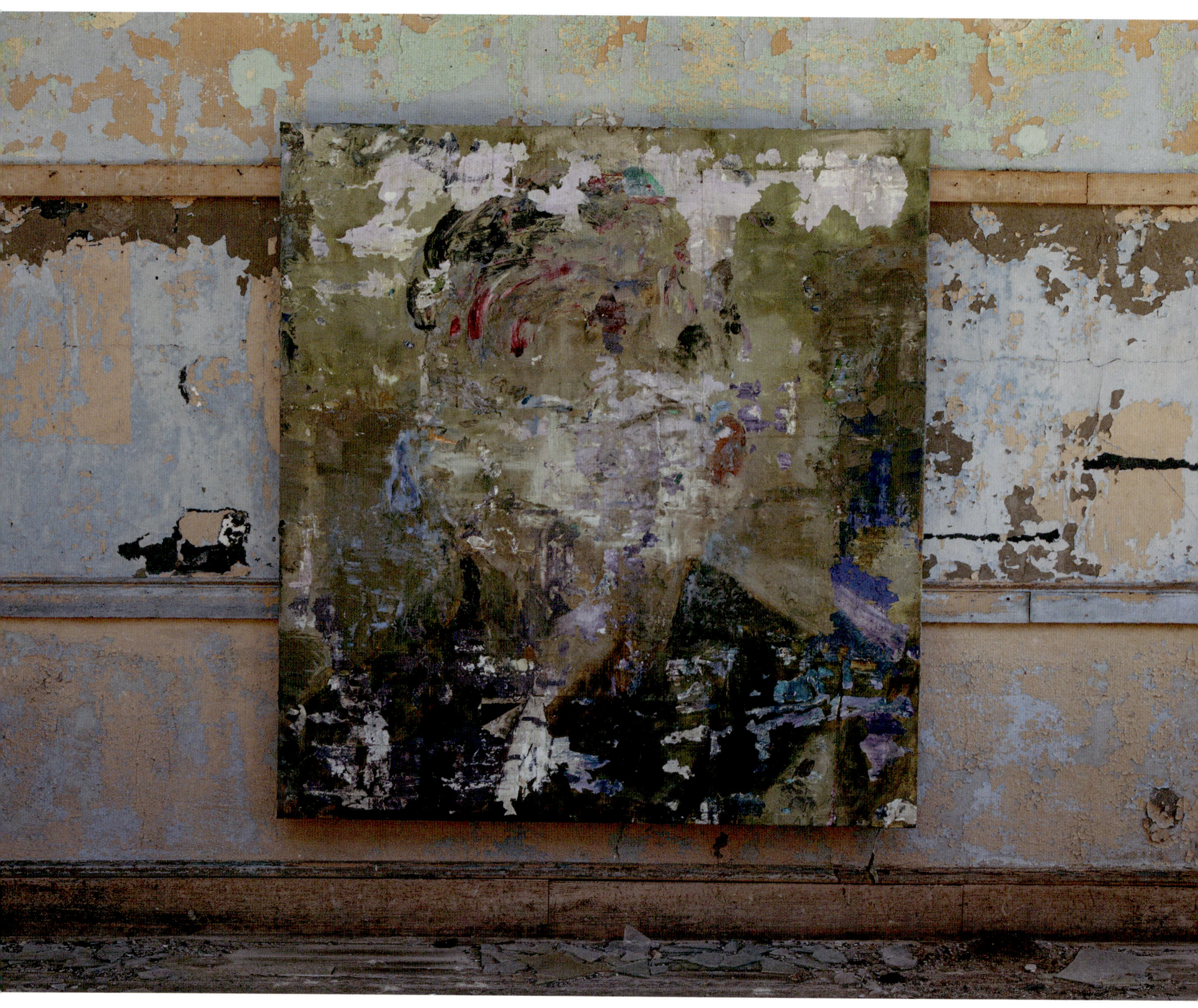

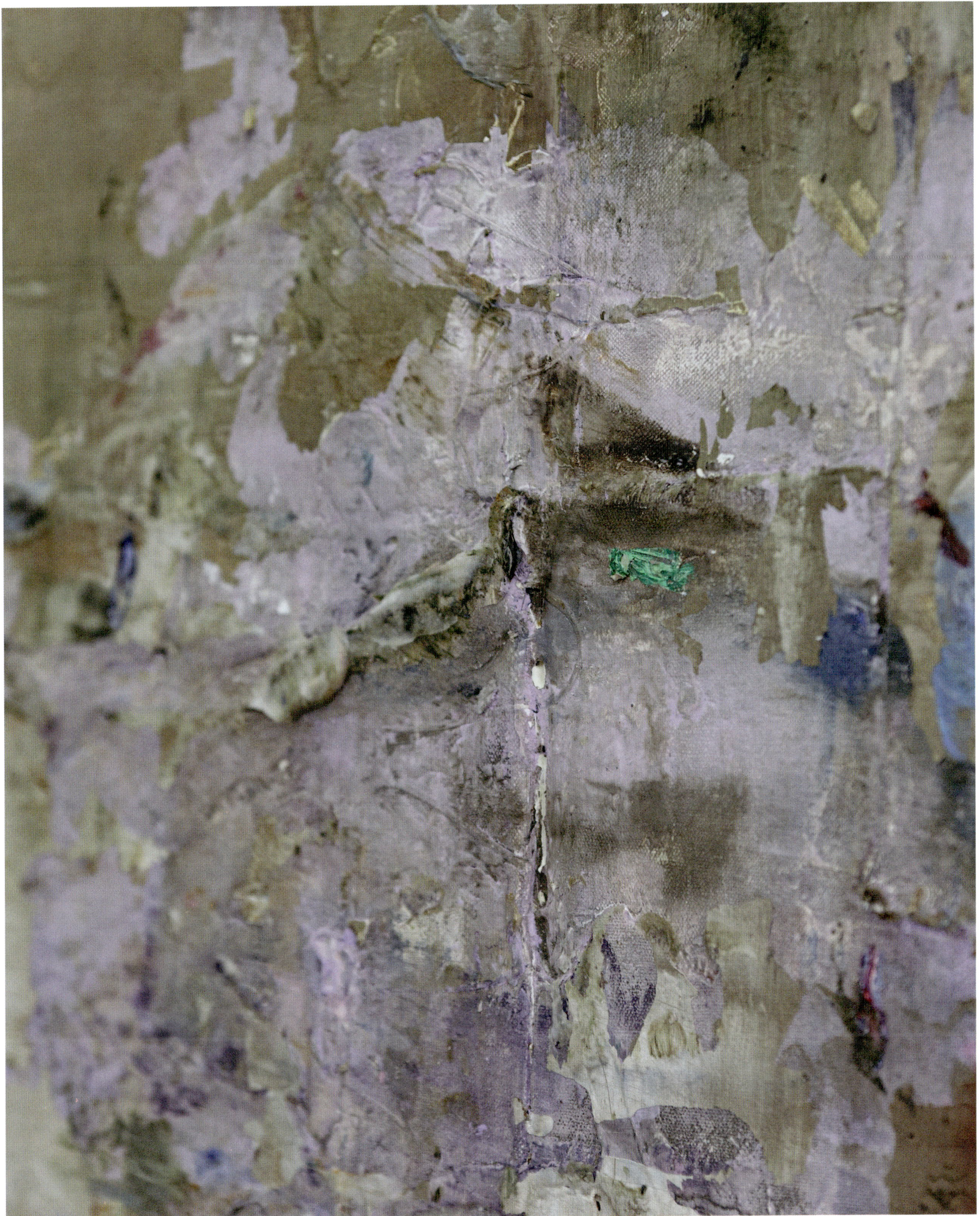

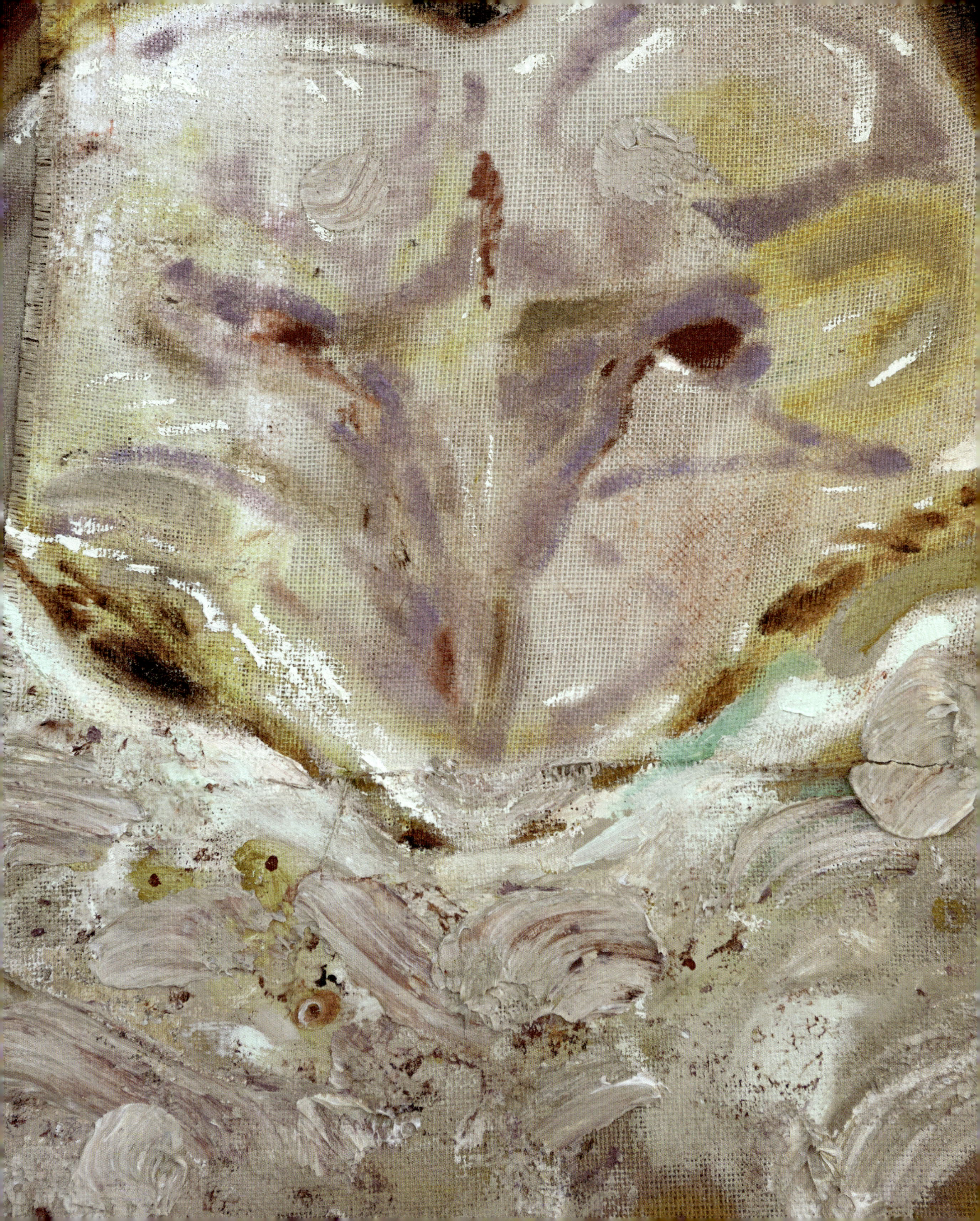

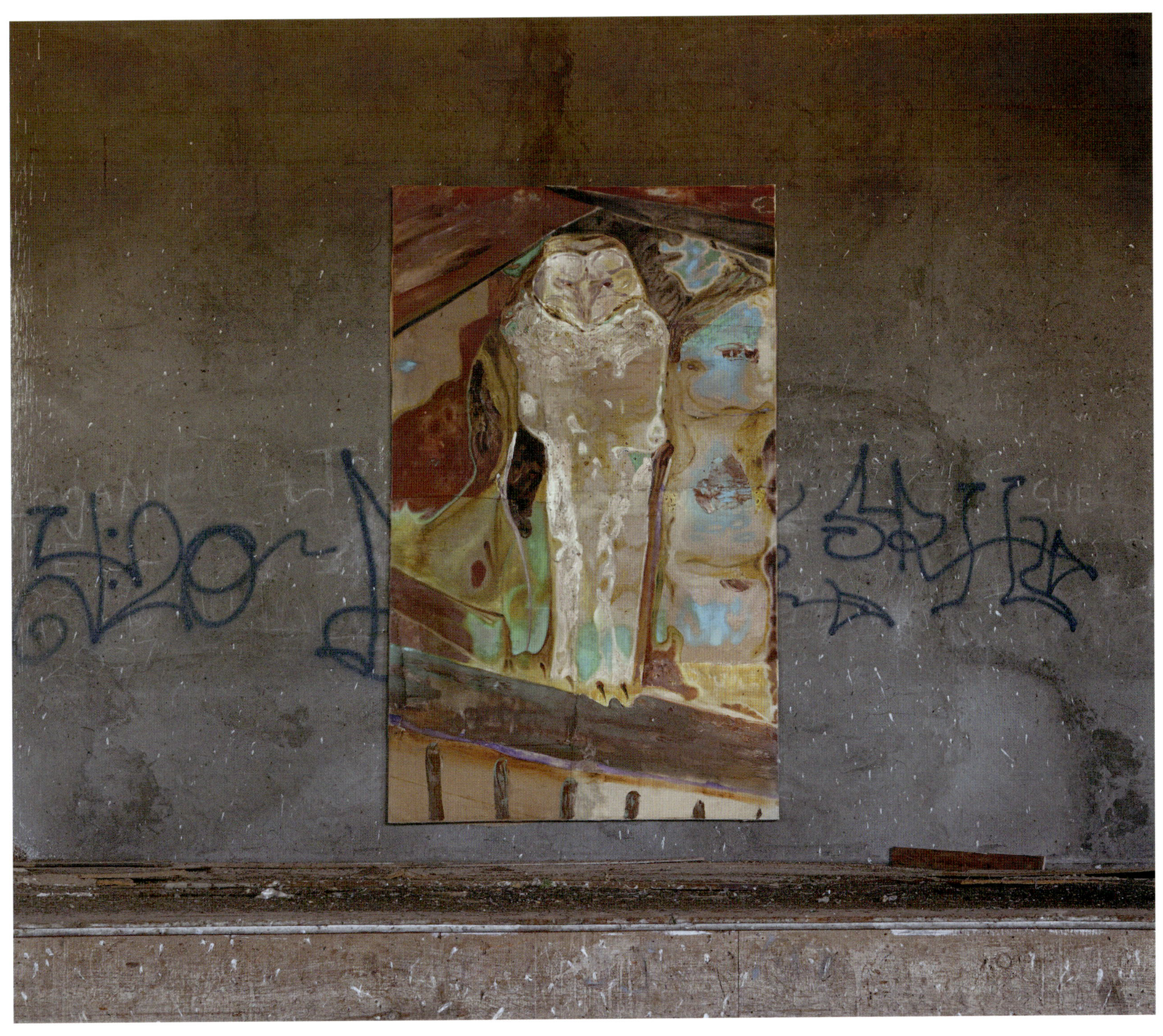

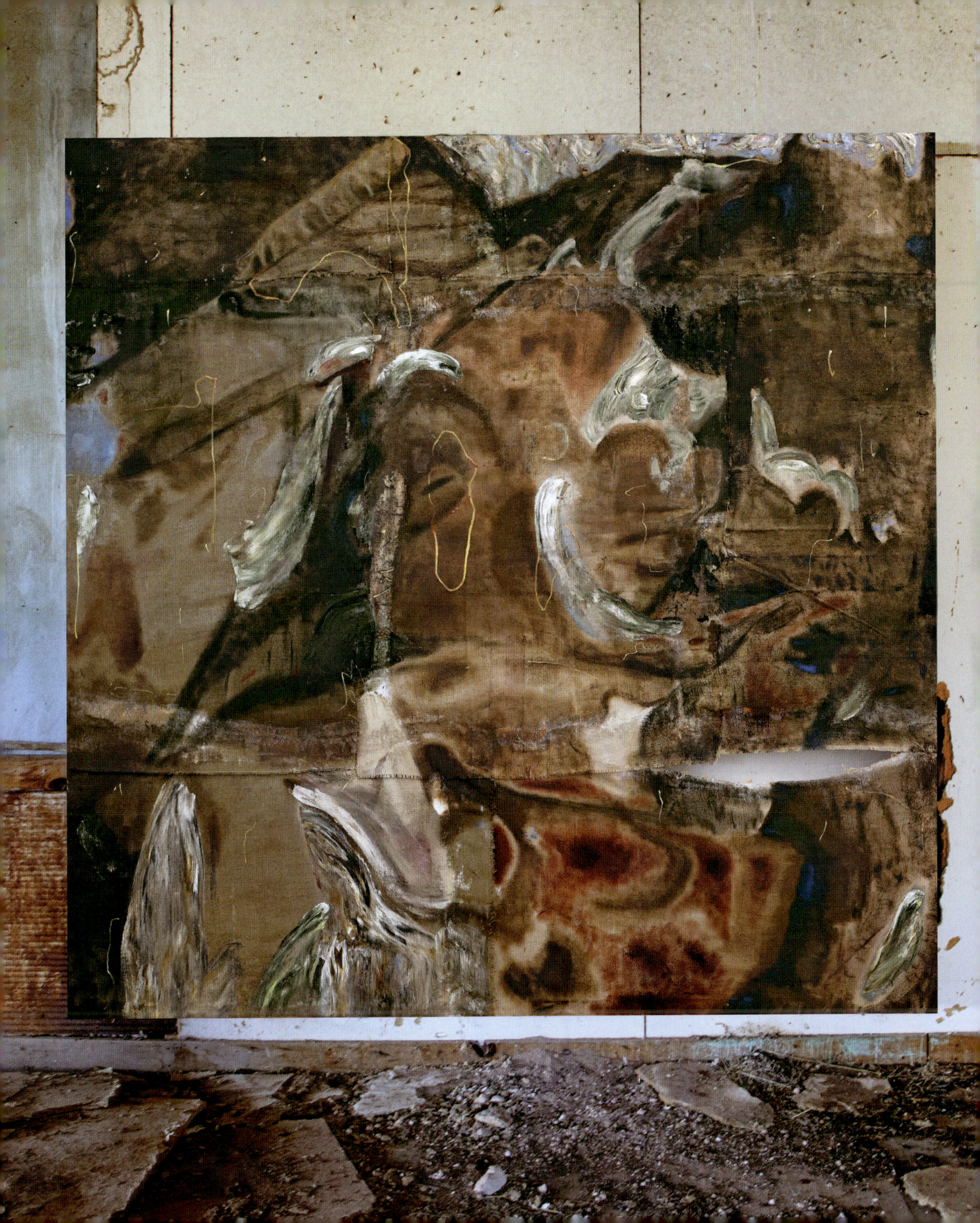

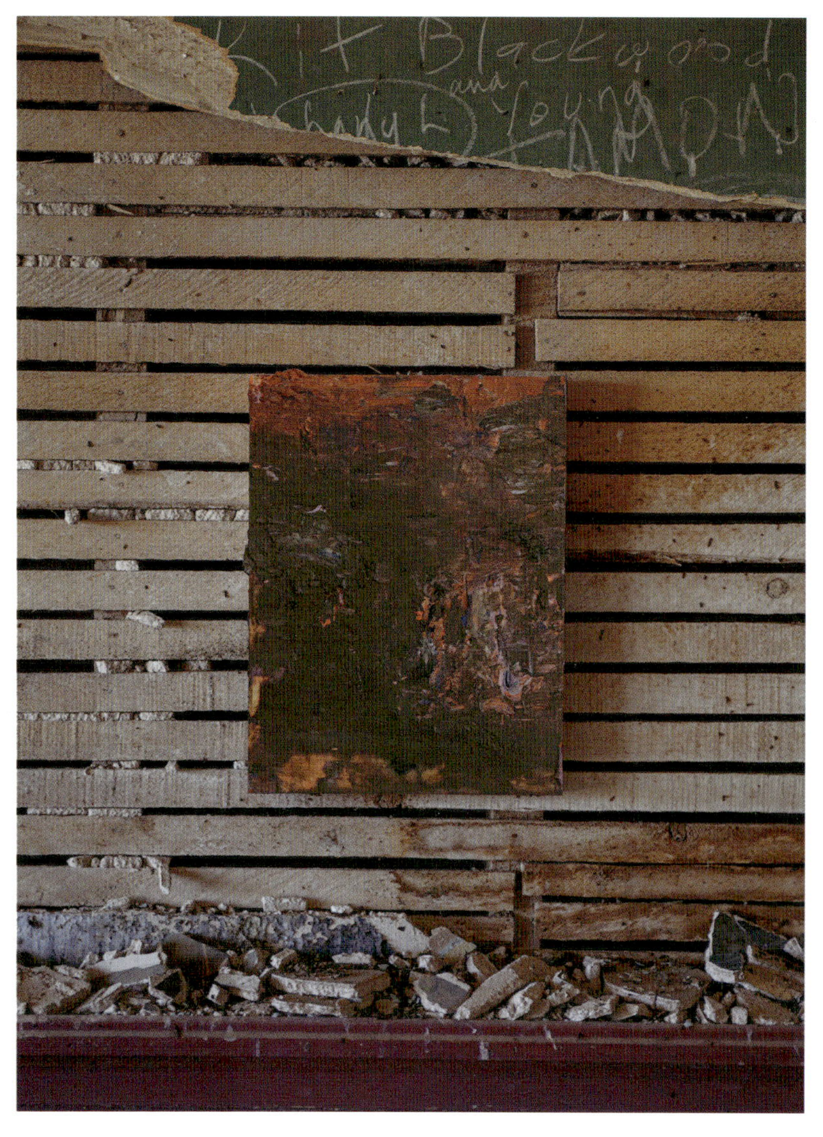
Blackwood

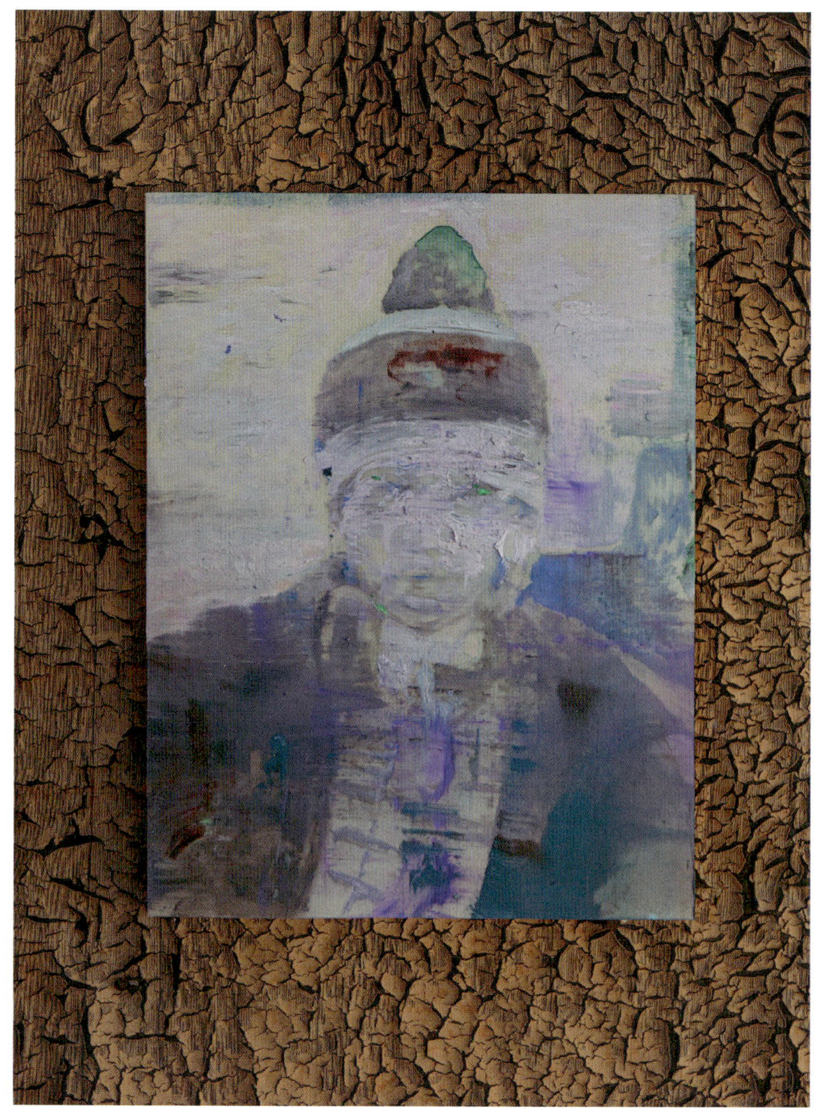

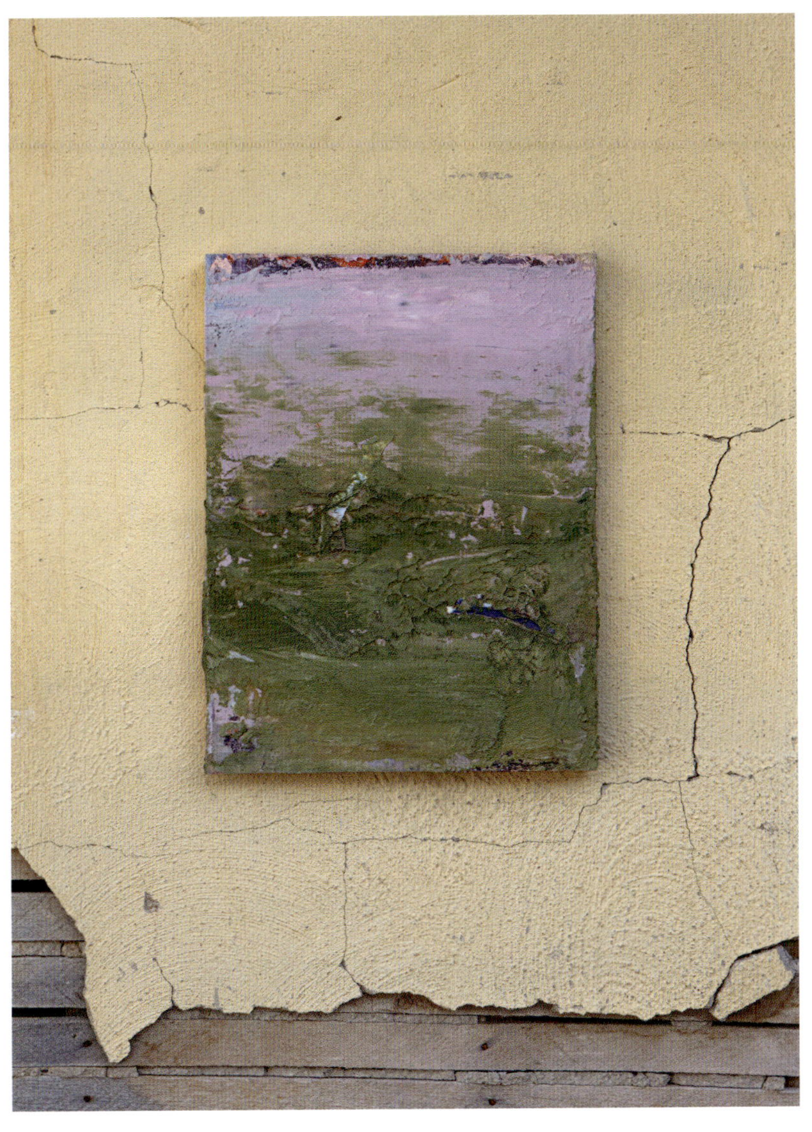

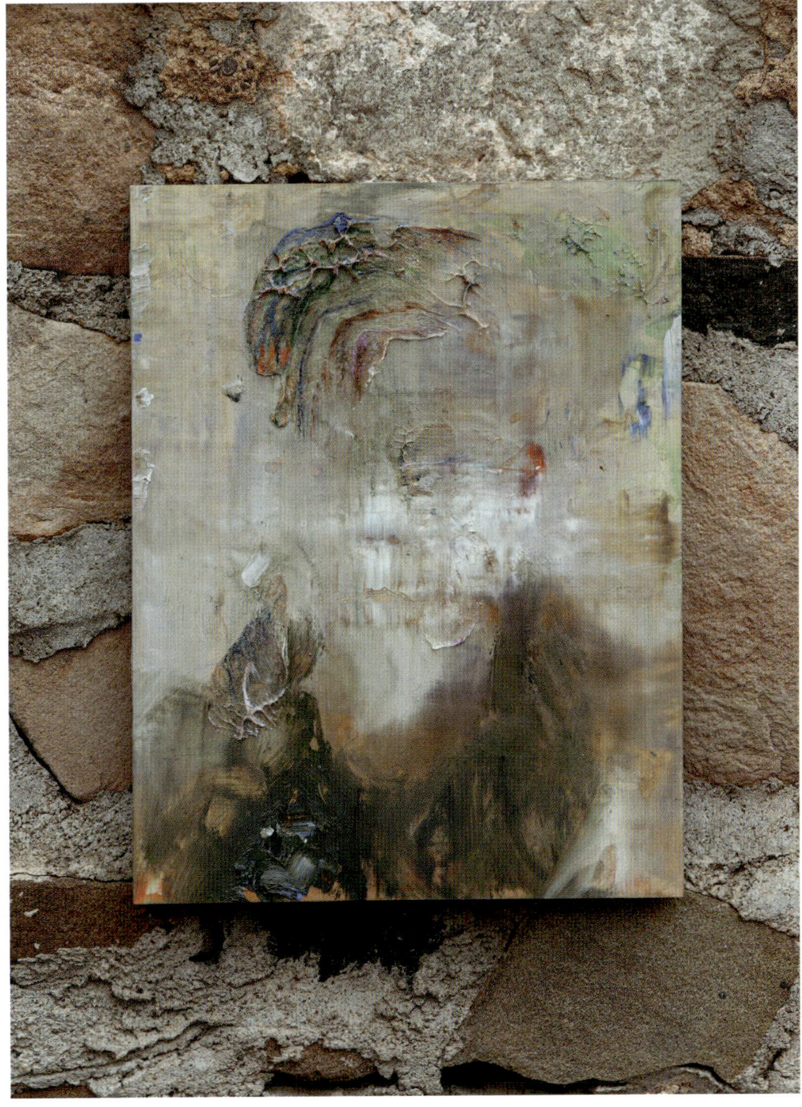

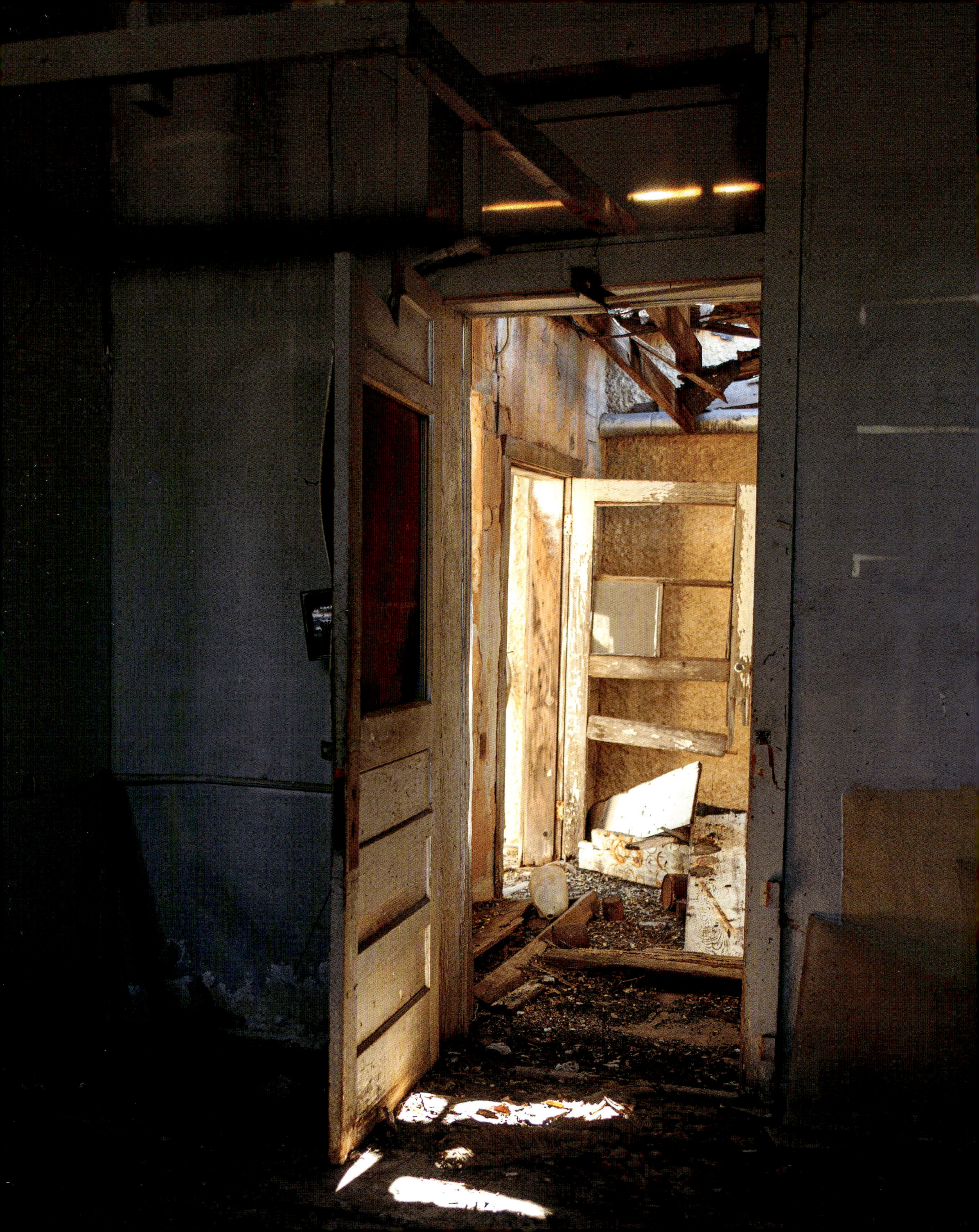

YESO
POST
OFFICE

A Book of Hours

Dear darkening ground,
you've endured so patiently the walls we've
built,
perhaps you'll give the cities one more hour

and grant the churches and cloisters two.
And those that labor—will you let their work
grip them another five hours, or seven,

before you become forest again, and water,
and widening wilderness
in that hour of inconceivable terror
when you take back your name
from all things.

Just give me a little more time!
I want to love the things
as no one has thought to love them,
until they're worthy of you and real.

I want only seven days, seven
on which no one has ever written himself—
seven pages of solitude.

from *The Book of Monastic Life* by Rainer Maria Rilke, 1905[1]

Titled after a Rilke poetry collection, *Book of Hours (Yeso, New Mexico, 1957)* is constructed from pages ripped out of a 1957 catalogue for Aermotor Company, a manufacturer of wind-powered water pumps. I found the catalogue buried among the detritus of an abandoned post office in the ghost town of Yeso, New Mexico. It had evidently been left there from that time. For this reason, I dated the work 1957 to 2021, as, more and more, I think of time itself as both medium and process.

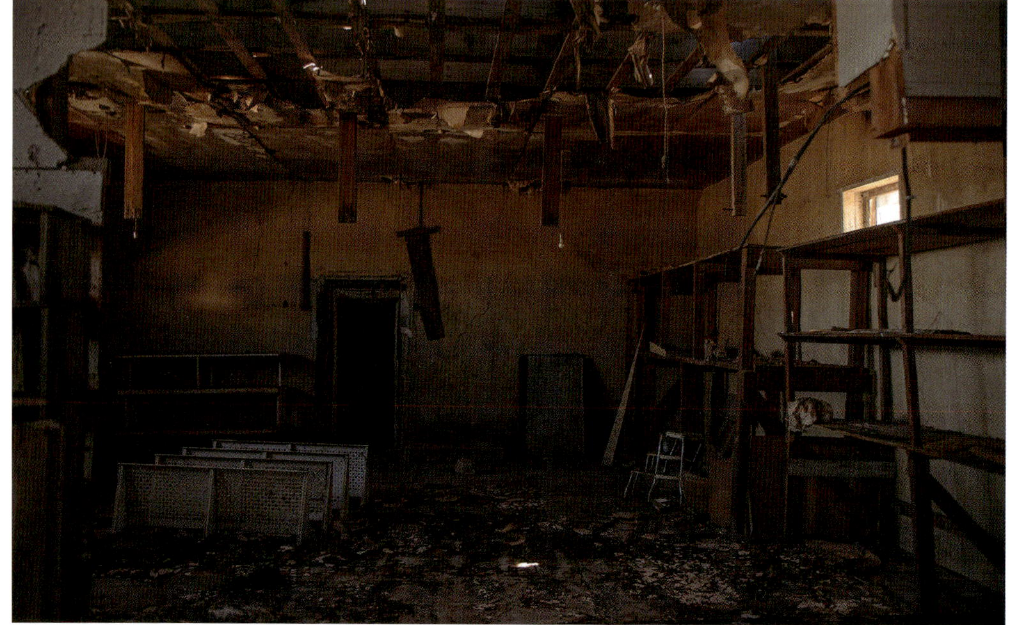

ABANDONED POST OFFICE IN YESO, NEW MEXICO

There are many layers of color in the work, namely turquoise, yellow, and pink; and the inherent colors of the pages themselves. Each color in oil was added semi-opaquely on top of the other. When all three colors had been layered, I began the process again, eventually covering the work in the dregs of all previously mixed colors on my palette from various other paintings, so that it had the appearance of mud. There are seven layers of paint, along with seven rows and seven columns of seven pages affixed to canvas.

It was because of this painting that I began collecting from these spaces the very raw material that I would return to them, however changed. The instinct made some kind of strange and immediate sense to me, and it was soon codified into the "Object" tenet of Nihil (see p. 23). Like the other eight principles, it gave me a way to think about and work with whatever I might find. I called these kinds of works the "Out of Existence" series: very small paintings or *things* (depending on how one sees it) made from objects left behind. Objects included such things as flattened pails with bullet holes, wood shingles, car wreckage, aluminum trays, pieces of toilet seats, and, my favorite, objects I could not identify. Each object implied a past, if no longer an identifiable function. One soon gets the strange feeling, working with lost things, that each hides a secret; a quiet *something* seems dug up with it, and from it. It is as if the simple choice to exhume one thing from its surroundings is to sacralize it, to designate it as an object of devotion, of single-pointed attention in a quiet space.

Each individual piece requires months of patience. It will sit unattended for long periods before being brought out and looked at again. The objects are scattered around the studio appearing like so much junk, on tables, chairs, the floor, a windowsill. I never know what to do with each object, how to make it into something. Often it is already perfect. The more perfect the object, the more likely it is to fail as an "Out of Existence" work, because, on some level, the very point is that it should feel found and not made. Yet to do that requires a particular kind of touch, a touch both knowing and unknowing—unlike the touch

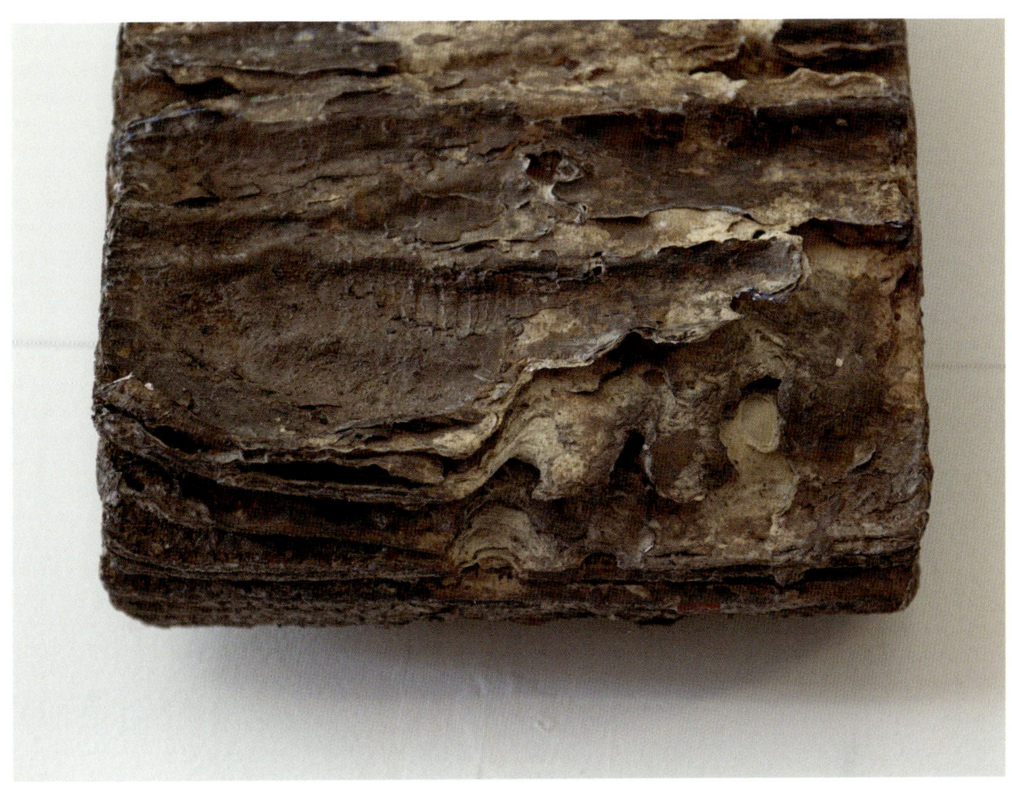

OUT OF EXISTENCE XVII (DETAIL), OIL, WAX, AND MATTE MEDIUM ON PETRIFIED LEDGER, ABOUT 1957–2021

of image making, which is to do with plans and styles. Sometimes, there is very little to do to or with the object, but invariably it requires months of it sitting for me to finally accept that doing anything more is pointless. Always, there is the anxious question: "Is this or isn't this?"

How am I to have the audacity to call a half-decayed scrap of something an *artwork*? But also, why does it matter what I call it? I catch a stray thought: I do not like art, and I do not want it. Somehow these works cause me to see that I mostly hate art. When, in contemporary life, is art not swallowed whole by the twin contexts of money and politics, of market and propaganda? When is it not created in service to that world and because of that world?

When I close my eyes to imagine a clear pure *thing*, nothing comes. No good idea is in me; it escapes and survives me only in the object. The object gives itself to the eye and hand, even as my conscious mind has nothing to offer. There is a mode of being, a human peculiarity, made possible by how the right object, fitting in the hands, narrows the eyes and then relaxes them. How a whole body is electrified even though the mind cannot grasp the cause, and is brought into a rested state of attentiveness.

In some sense, this kind of work is an admission of having nothing left to say. This sounds, from a certain distance, like loss or failure, but in practice, saying nothing is the work's liberation, its best hope for authenticity. *Nihil*, as a project, was a trick I played on myself to get out of the way of the work. Its paradoxes and ironies grew layered. Sometimes I wonder whether *Nihil* was the accidental means by which it became possible for the unconscious to unveil itself, approximating something like dream space, on which absence and memory come to call.

1 abbeyofthearts.com/blog/2007/11/19/dear-darkening-ground/ (accessed March 2025)

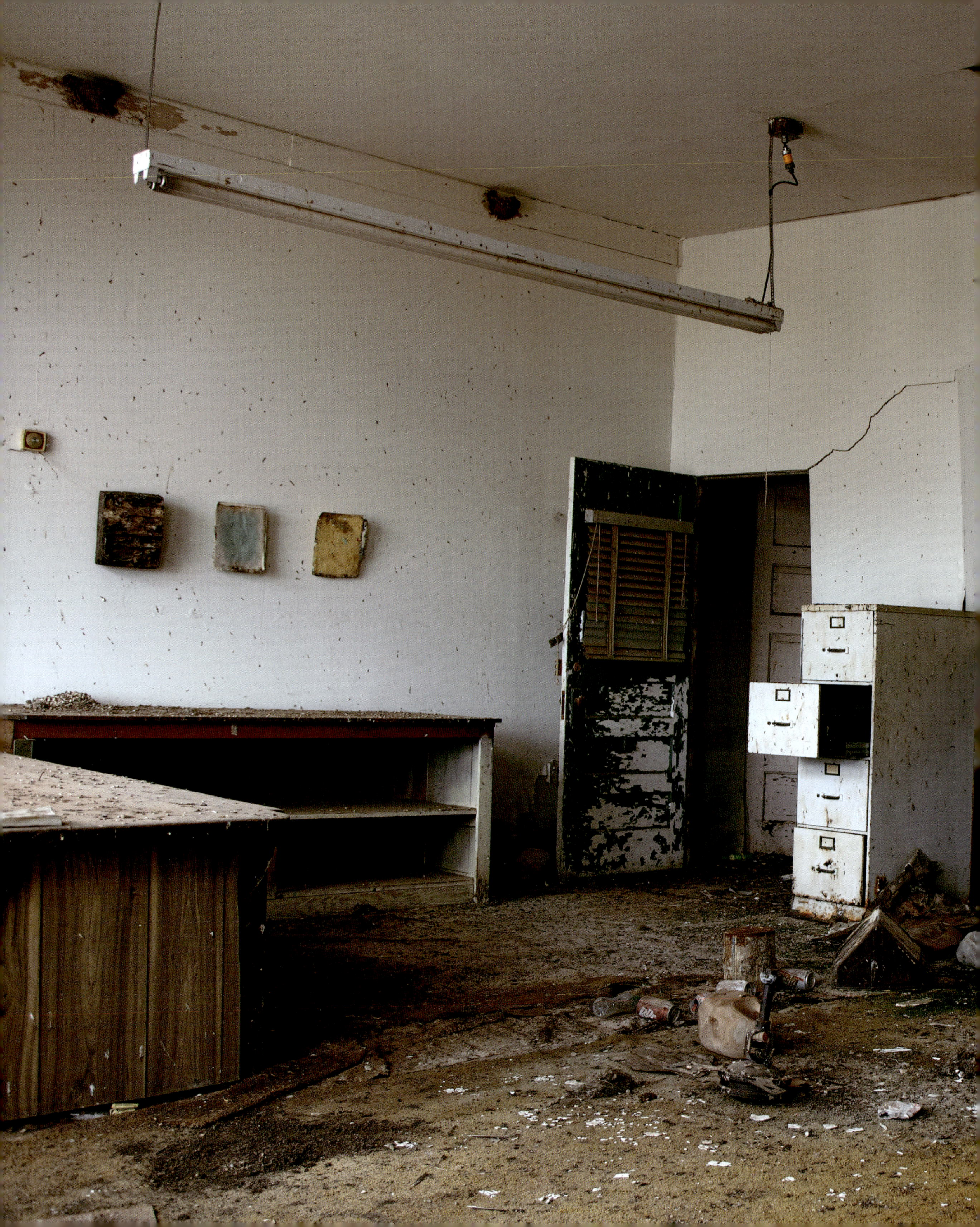

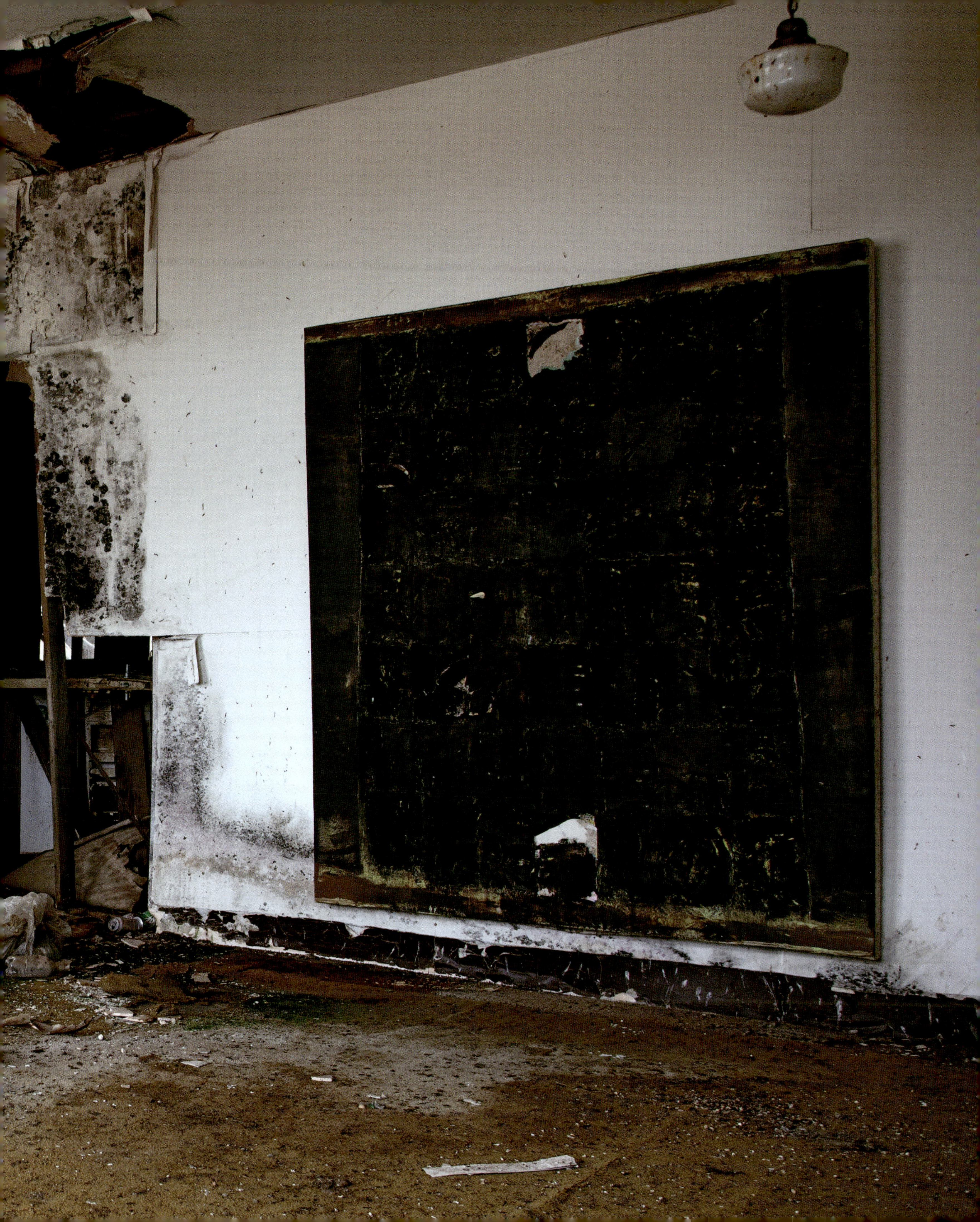

Place (*Where I Am Is What I Am*)

The source of all work in *Nihil* begins with the specificity of place and my relation to it. A route must be fashioned as a means of limiting the overwhelming choices, in terms of where one might travel, within a given set of boundaries. The primary information from which all work is derived is the immediate world within my reach and in my line of sight.

Because the *Nihil* structure emerges as a response to composer Arvo Pärt's tintinnabulation system for making music, I lean on him again to figure out a route that will shape how I navigate through New Mexico. Pärt often uses small drawings or glyphs as a starting point for structuring a work, and so I overlay his sketch of a tree on the map of the state, because only this drawing (of all his drawings) can come close to following the roads that run through the state.

All along the way, I make drawings of what I see. I collect objects left behind in forgotten and abandoned spaces, especially objects I do not understand. I take photos once in a while to aid memory. In deserted structures, I take the dimensions of windows, doors, and walls with a measuring tape. I take liberally, with the idea of returning what I find, though changed through the process of working with it. Some places become sites for the installation of future work.

I sit for meditation when possible. The ideal is to be with reality and not in abstraction. Yet always there is a sense of thinness, as in a veil that has a front and back. Scale and enumeration seem suspicious. I do not know what I believe here. Is what I see empty or full? Is it many or a continuum? Is it happening now or has it happened already? Is it just one possibility of the world or the only one? The approach in *Nihil* is that if I thought I knew, it would be a lie. It is better not to know. Yet a place has a certain identity that cannot be ignored. It asserts itself subtly.

I begin with the idea that I only want to draw what is there. In little time, I become too aware of how I see, of how certain things, shapes, patterns of light, and so on, repeat themselves.

To become aware of how I see where I am is to become aware of when I see what I am.

I want to see without prejudice, but seeing itself is a prejudice. The visual cues, traces, and echoes that arrest me do so because they retain a familiarity I cannot begin to explain. Even though I am in a canyon, ruin, forest, or desert that I have never before encountered, I see because I remember. Poet Louise Glück wrote:

"We look at the world once in childhood, the rest is memory."[1]

The ghost in the landscape is shaped out of my own life, translocated from time to space. Or my consciousness was never my own, but a small piece of something dislocated from within itself. Or there is no one here at all. I am always at the River Lethe,[2] waiting.

1 "Nostos" in the collection *Meadowlands*, HarperCollins, 1996, p. 53.

2 We gave our daughter the middle name of Aletheia, an archaic Greek word for the unconcealment of hidden memory. Flowing through the Greek underworld, it was believed, was the River Lethe. It was said that to drink from its waters was to expunge one's memory of the previous life, but that if one did not drink "more than his measure," something of that life might be remembered, a foothold to begin the inner work of coming back to oneself. Before classical philosophy, it was thought that the poets held the keys to Truth, in the form of sung speech, and that in the reclaiming of what was forgotten, a part of oneself was restored by song. To sing the right words was to begin the process of restoration of the self. In modern language, we might use terms like "wholeness," "individuation," or "self-acceptance" to get close to the idea of Aletheia. I might make the claim that in contemporary life, the steady stream of images surrounding us at all times is like the River Lethe. It is not the *something* set apart from the *nothing*, but the constant rush of nothing that causes us to forget who we are. We must be pulled out, must not drink "more than our measure," and can only begin to see with any depth once we confront, in ourselves and in the world, what we, in our fearful shallowness, had thought to be empty. There we find not emptiness as we usually think of it, but a depth of feeling we did not know we possessed. A kind of gnosis (mystical knowledge) is restored, soul returning to soul.

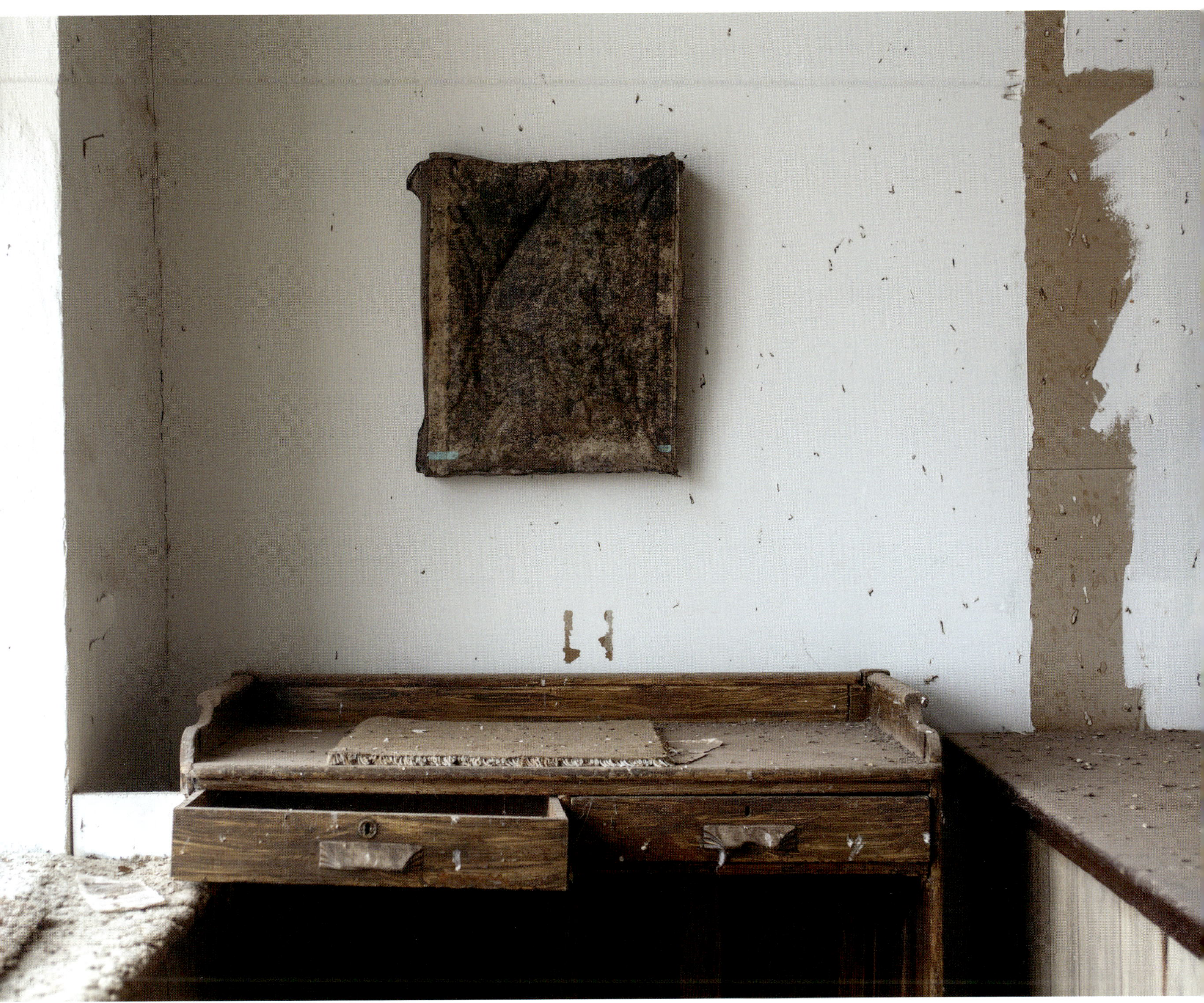

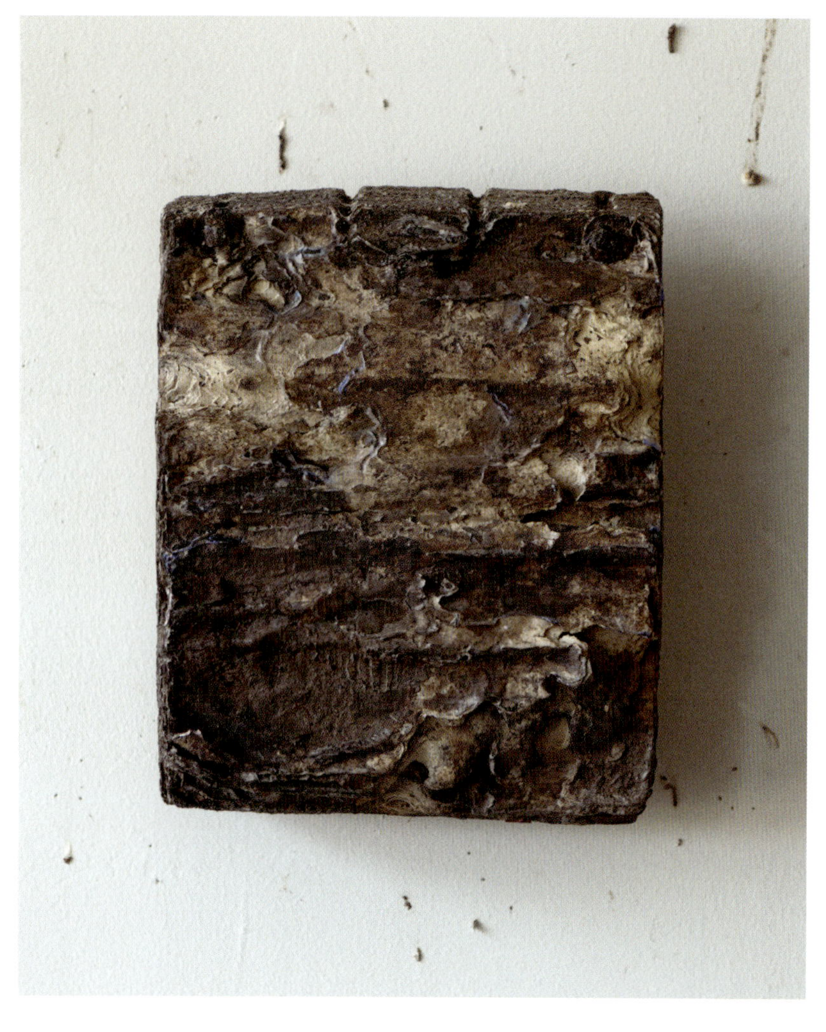

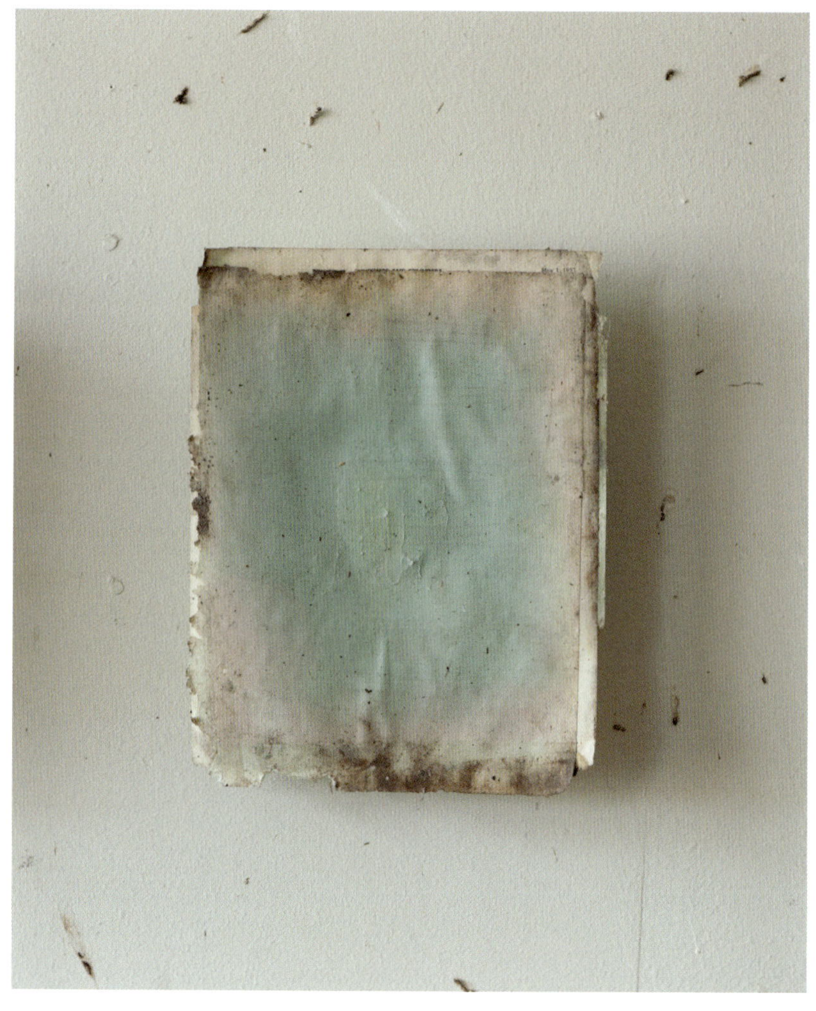

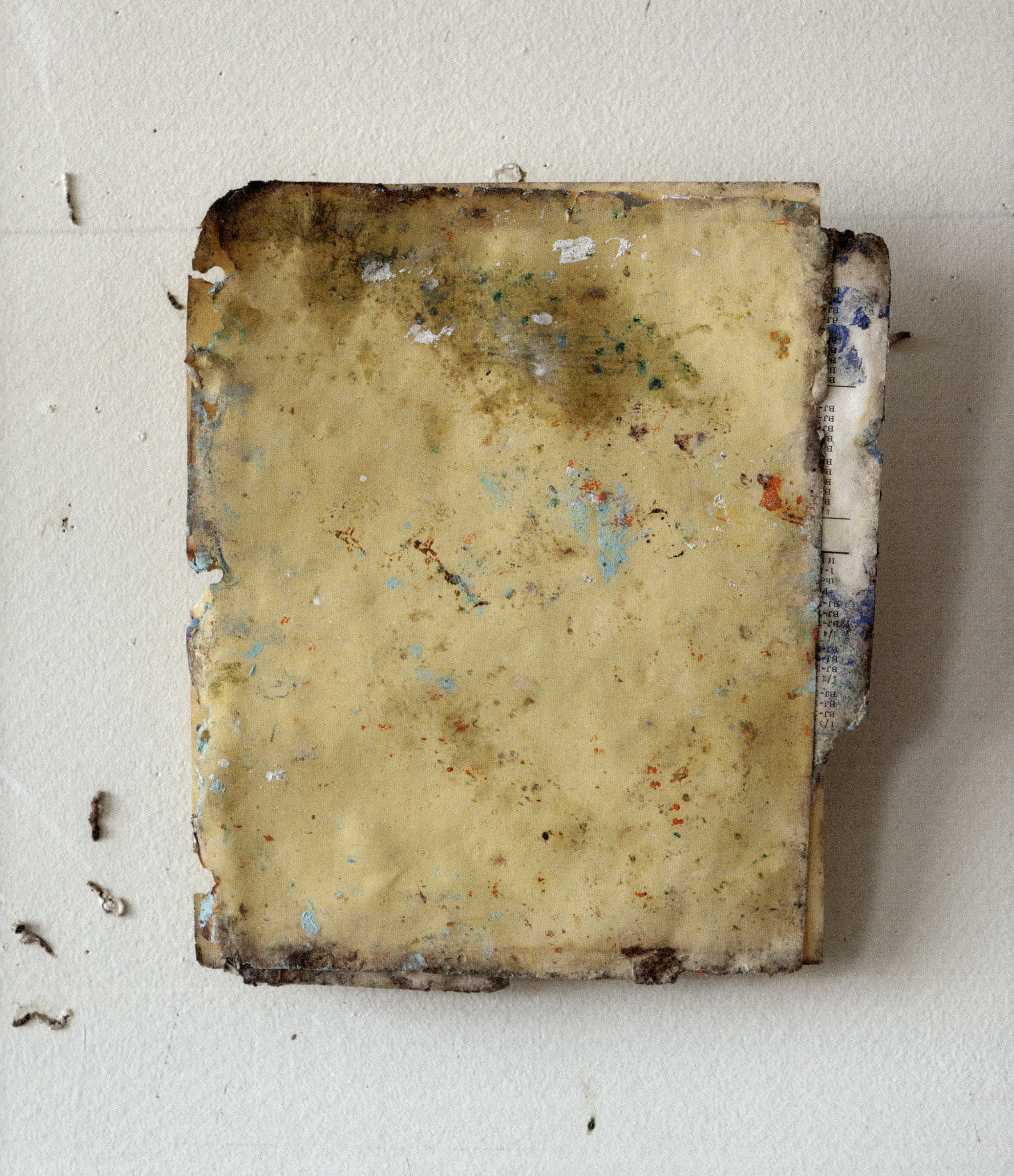

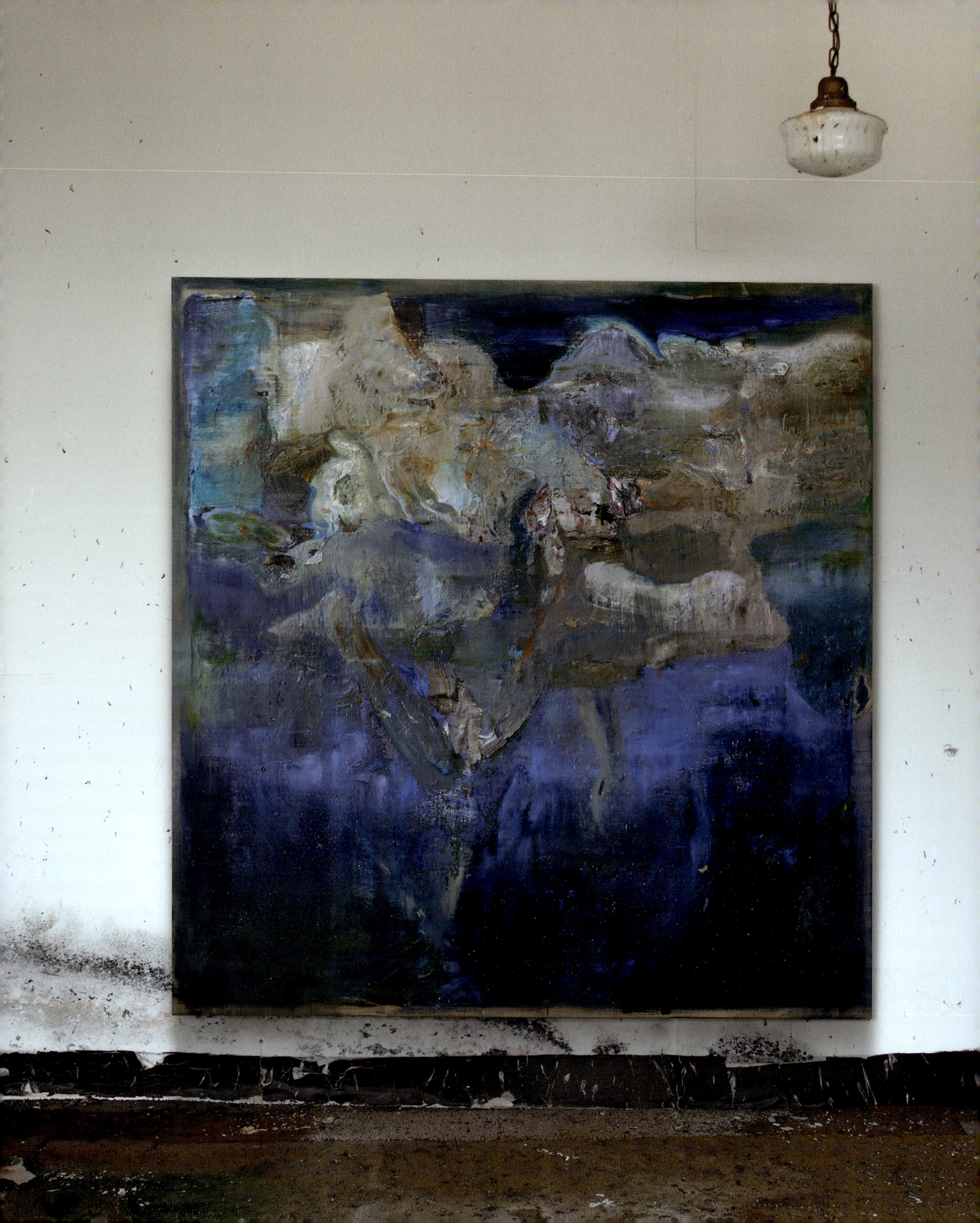

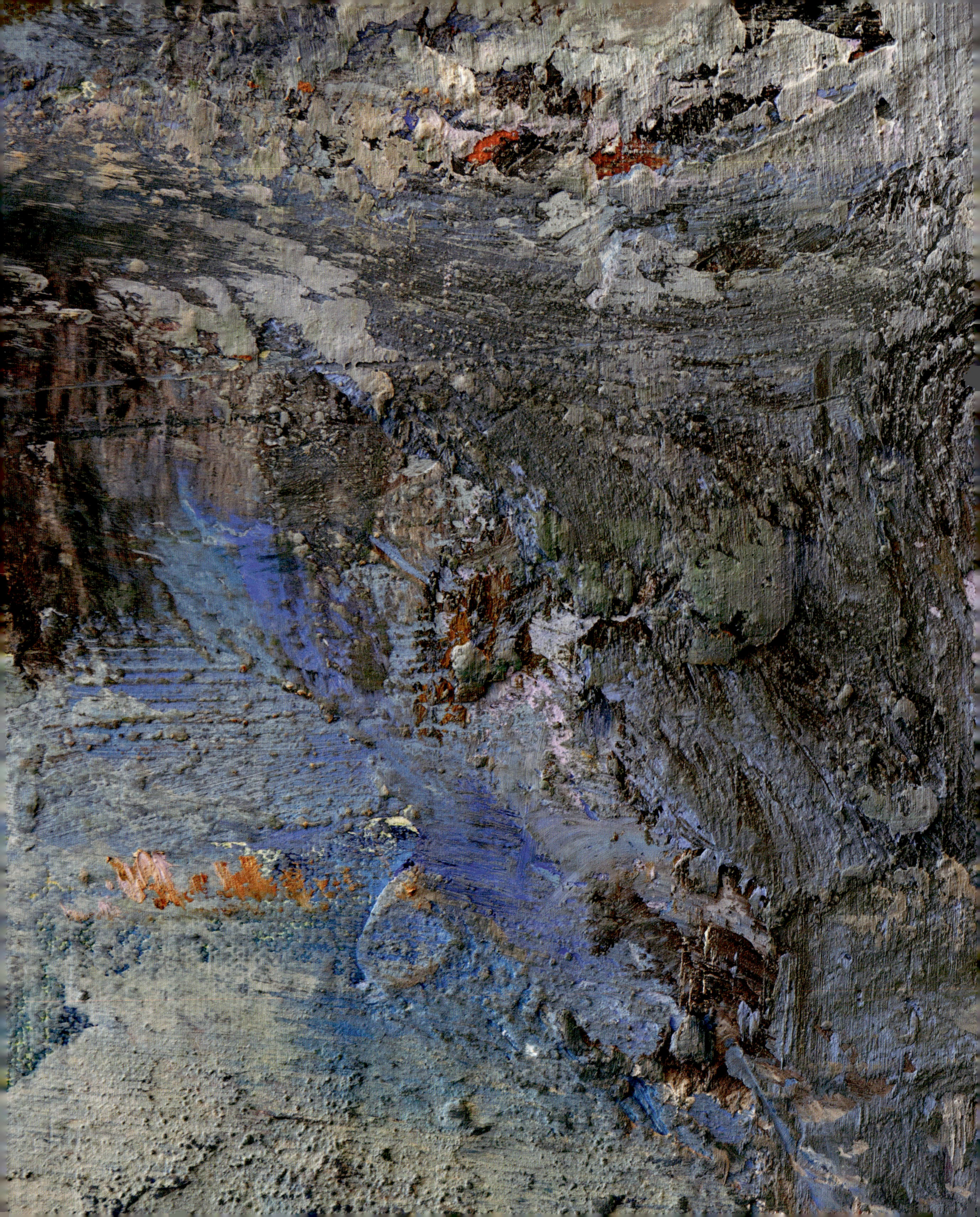

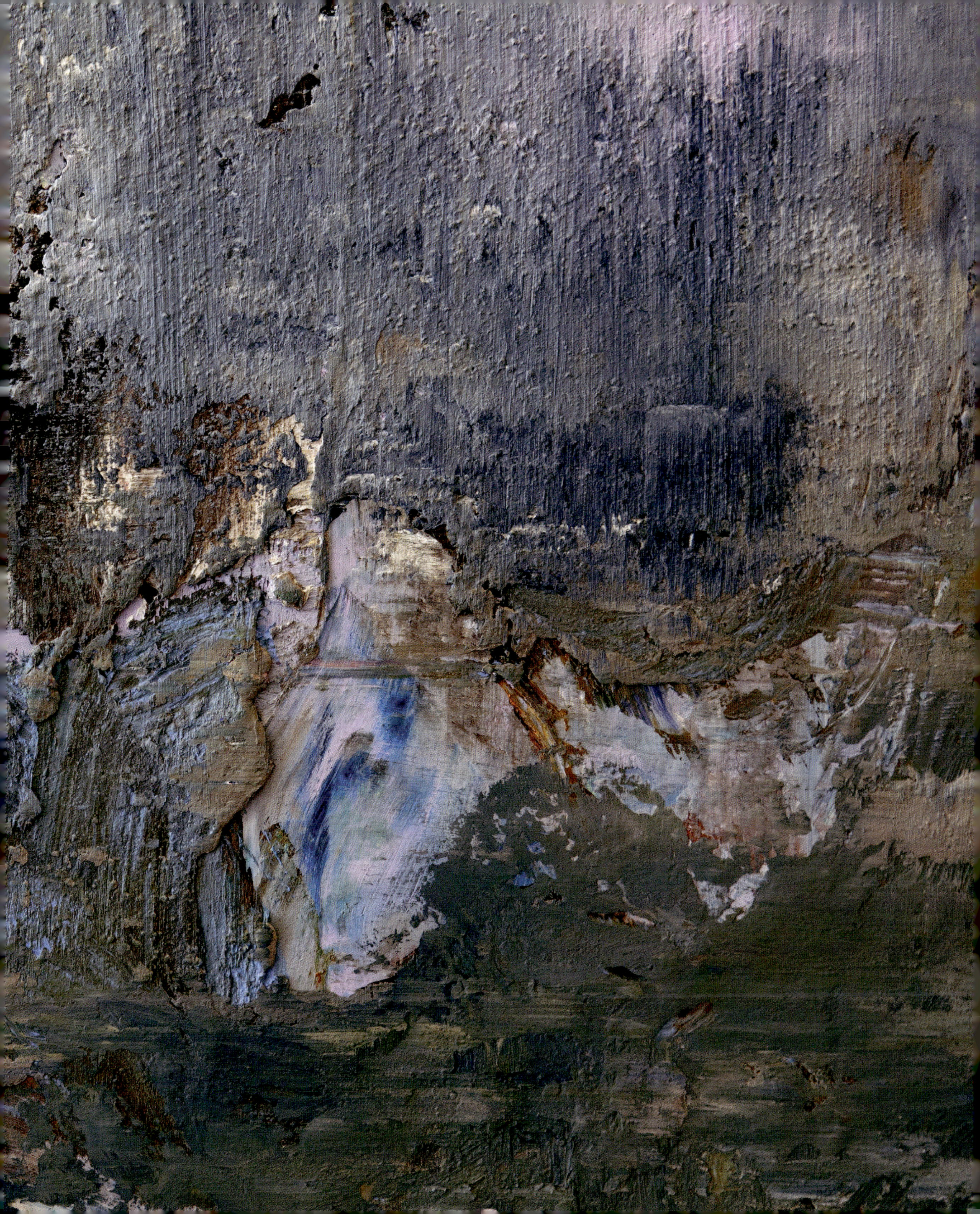

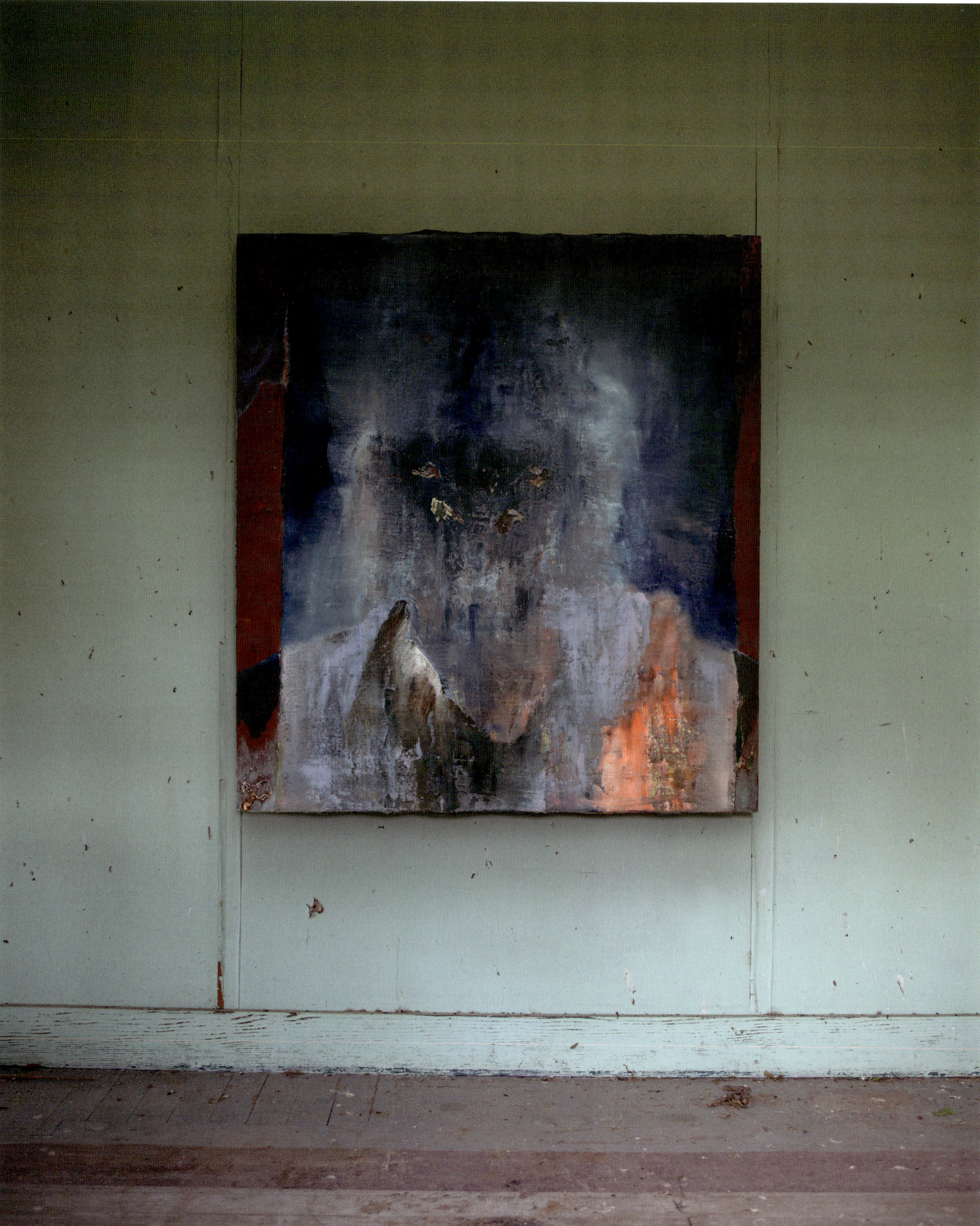

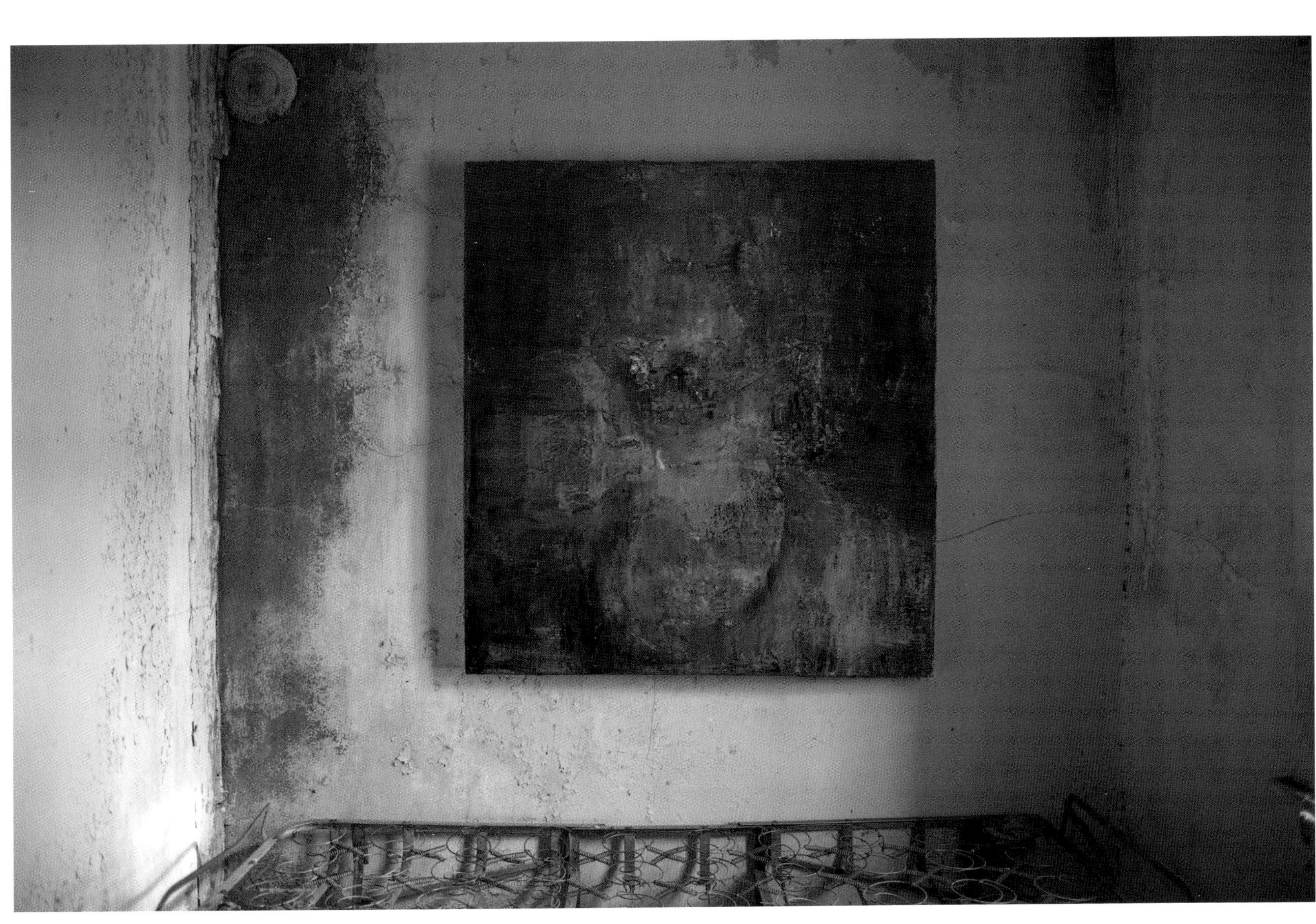

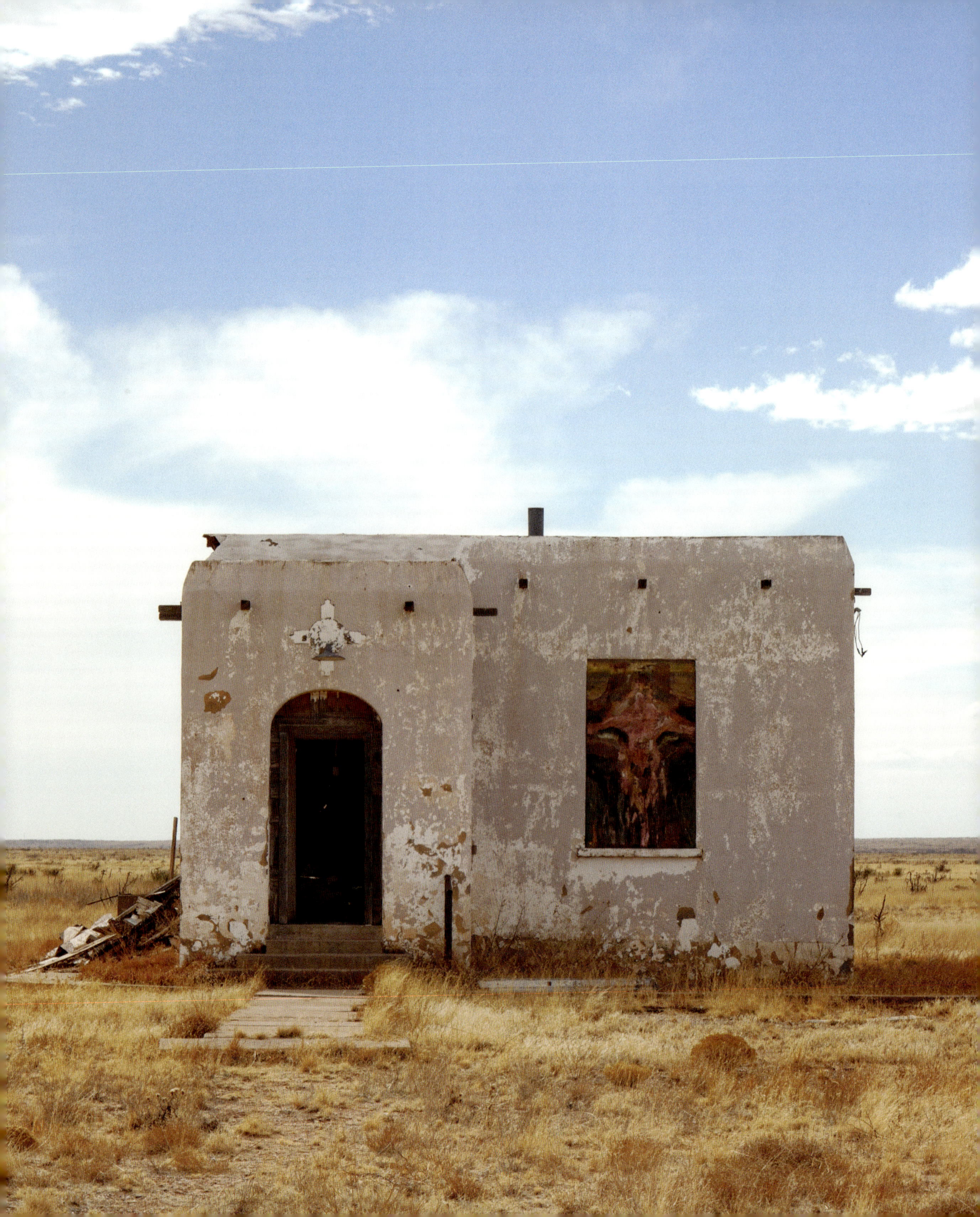

FORT SUMNER BIBLE SCHOOL

Out of Existence

Unlike any other site I visited over the four years, the abandoned bible school near Fort Sumner seemed devoid of visitors. Other sites are in constant flux: changed by graffiti and vandalism, clothing and beer bottles left behind, and objects that I had seen before later vanished. Half the roof caved in here some time ago, around 2005 I would guess, the most recent date I can find written on a wall. Perhaps it was built around the time New Mexico became a state, in the 1910s or 1920s; nearby tombstones are engraved with similar dates. The mural I discovered here remains unchanged, unvandalized. Often I wonder about the artist: these blue dashes on the blackboard, the array of red triangles spraypainted over the old bulletin board, all seeming like an encoded language. I imagine the blue marks kept a tally, the red contours and triangles another kind of account. I do not see it as tagging or self-conscious artwork. Different impulse. Different aims.

I know nothing about the artist, yet I am arrested by a strange and ineffable familiarity. There is a universal desire, I think, to reach through a veil of some kind, to seek contact with others, or an other, however despite ourselves, however unconscious. I sense that instinct here, or I project it because it is my instinct. Or I wish it to be as true about the artist as myself, knowing I am about to pull this panel off the wall and bring it to my studio. I want to collaborate with the unknown artist. On some level, I want to know the artist.

...

Nihil began with the hope that I might avoid meaning or narrative, and yet, almost from the start, I have found meaning everywhere I have looked. The remnants of years gone by are always strewn about the studio. A petrified shoe I once found in another abandoned space, for example, sits alternately on or under my painting table, and continues to take on layers of paint; who knows why? For a while, it rested on top of a plastic piece of car fender. The relationship between the shoe and fender brought about a memory of a boy I went to middle school with when my family lived in rural Illinois, a boy named Lucas who was killed in a car accident.

Lucas was a sixth grader in my chorus class. My friend Mike and I were in seventh. My own middle-school years were plagued by bullying. I was harassed and beaten up because it was thought among some of my classmates and teammates that I was gay: such was the sort of town I grew up in. I will often describe those years as being governed by a kind of trickle-down cruelty or prison-yard mentality. I fell in line. If I was ranked in the bottom quarter in terms of social status among the other kids, Lucas was at the bottom. I might have seemed effeminate to my classmates, but Lucas was a boy everyone assumed to be gay. Mike and I, sitting behind him in chorus, took many opportunities to remind him, making each other giggle at our own clever puns and jokes. Lucas never once looked back at us that I can remember and sat in humiliated stillness toward the front of class, waiting for the teacher to enter. This is how I passed my pain on, my frustration, fear, and shame. Though I no longer remember how the semester or year passed, I do remember what soon happened to Lucas.

To this day, I cannot think of him without tears, which encompass all the feelings that one could imagine might come along with crying. Mainly, it is to do with regret, with the knowledge that every day of this boy's life at school was a living hell to which I contributed. That what happened to him was so deeply unfair and grotesque I cannot appeal to any compensatory sentiment to redeem it. How can I ask forgiveness of a boy I never really knew and only barely remember? I cannot shake the feeling that the significance of the story, in terms of my being pulled toward it for so long, is to do somehow with the loss of my own brother, that both boys seem to call out of a profound silence and invisibility cloaking their memories. I think again of the anonymous artist, but I do not know why.

...

It was a spontaneous decision to put the shoe beneath the painting, yet as soon as I did, I was overwhelmed again with this memory. This is the 24th work in the "Out of Existence" series, and its title was always meant to contain two opposite meanings simultaneously negating and affirming a subject, which is also enacted in the process of adding and removing paint, layer after layer. The trace of an anonymous hand. The trace of my hand.

Nihil can be interpreted as a functioning contemplative practice. What has happened

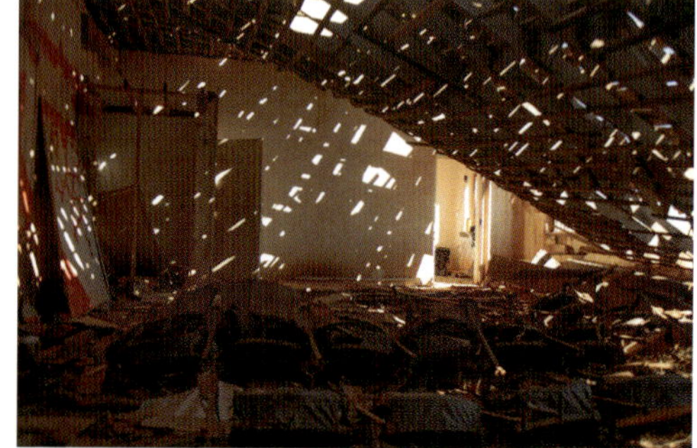

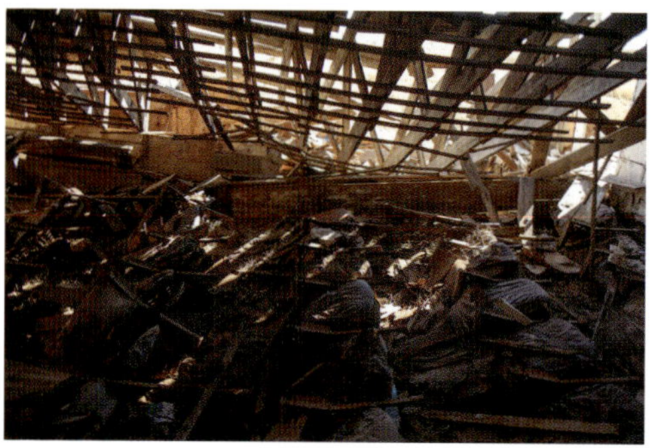

ABANDONED BIBLE SCHOOL NEAR FORT SUMNER, NEW MEXICO

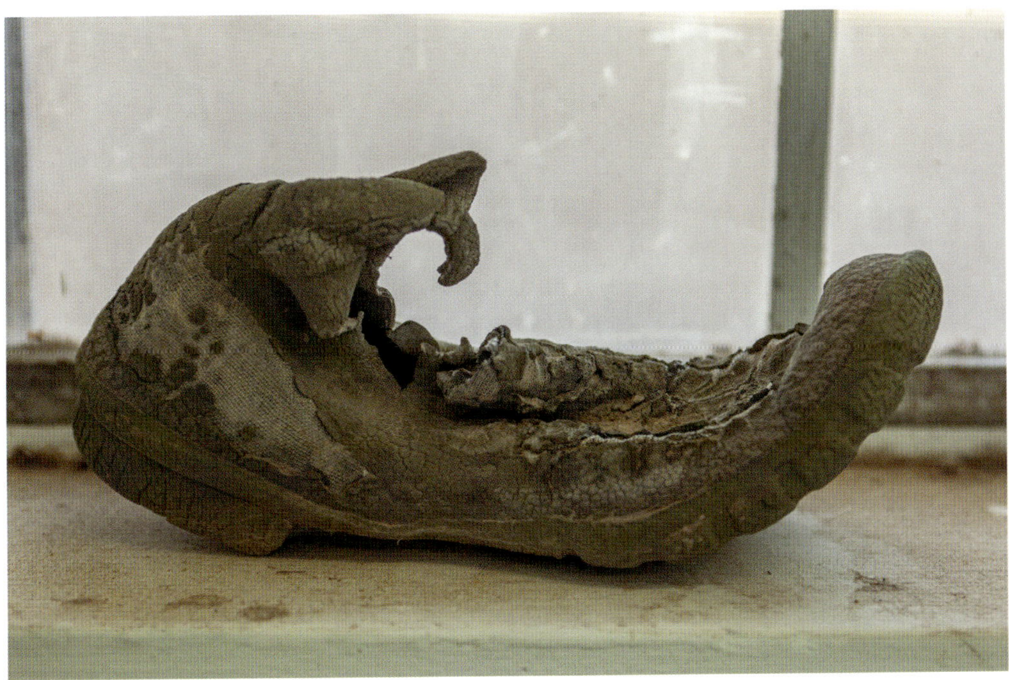

PETRIFIED SHOE AT THE ROSWELL STUDIO

is a kind of knowing acceptance of an emptiness hovering just behind the ocular frame and echoed within it. One grows compassionate toward one's own brokenness, which seems to be the precondition for real openness. I do not know what I know, but I know when *something is happening now*. A feeling for *something* in the vicinity of oneself seems to become trustworthy, as if from across a little distance, on the other side of a screen or veil, and yet all within oneself. All of this seems a byproduct of spending time alone attentively in vast quiet spaces. One does not try to justify the experience, but treats it respectfully, delicately, and wants simply to know what there is within the frame and to let it grow in magnitude in one's inner life. When my heart is stirred by noticing Lucas, my brother Danny, and the anonymous artist all in one breath, I take that seriously, even if I cannot report on its nature or meaning. Somehow their consciousness is to do with my own, and I respond with the assumption that it matters, here and now in the presence of this abandoned bible school and the flat desert landscape that holds it. At the smallest scales, through this veil, between my life and theirs, consciousness is transpersonal. It is not something I *have*, but something within which I feel myself somehow *directed*. From this boundary between us, I feel another quality of consciousness is made possible. The same consciousness, it seems to me, which bound them to the earth while they were here is what, to this day, binds their memories not simply to my own imagination, but to the consciousness in which I swim: theirs, mine, and of all the imaginational vestiges that stir deeply in this place.

...

When the day comes that I return the painted bulletin board to the abandoned school, it seems to disappear. At first, I do not know how to understand that. It seems obvious that the space itself is what is most important here, the light coruscating in specks and shards along the wall, the blackboard with its handwritten confessions obscured by the blue dashes of the anonymous artist, the rows of fold-out seats half-engulfed in the detritus of ceiling fallen to floor. The painting is barely a fact.

I should have expected this from the start. I have become bored of the obvious image, of puppeteering. Have I not been trying to find a way out of painting by finding a way through it? Is the presence of an object not all that remains of my belief in the value of art? Here, it occurs to me, I have been rescued from making yet another painting. In fact, by the look of it, I have hardly made anything at all. Yet the object, for me, becomes the veil, the emptiness behind it and in me, now made tangible, if only slightly more visible. I am able to prioritize what Carl Jung calls the "spirit of the depths" over the "spirit of the times." Joan of Arc said that nothing she had to say in her trial could "touch its process." Here I have offered something that no one will ever see in life in this way, momentarily reclaimed by its place of origin. My photograph of it is not the evidence, as it cannot place anyone in the room. My evidence touches no process, and that might be its only rescue.

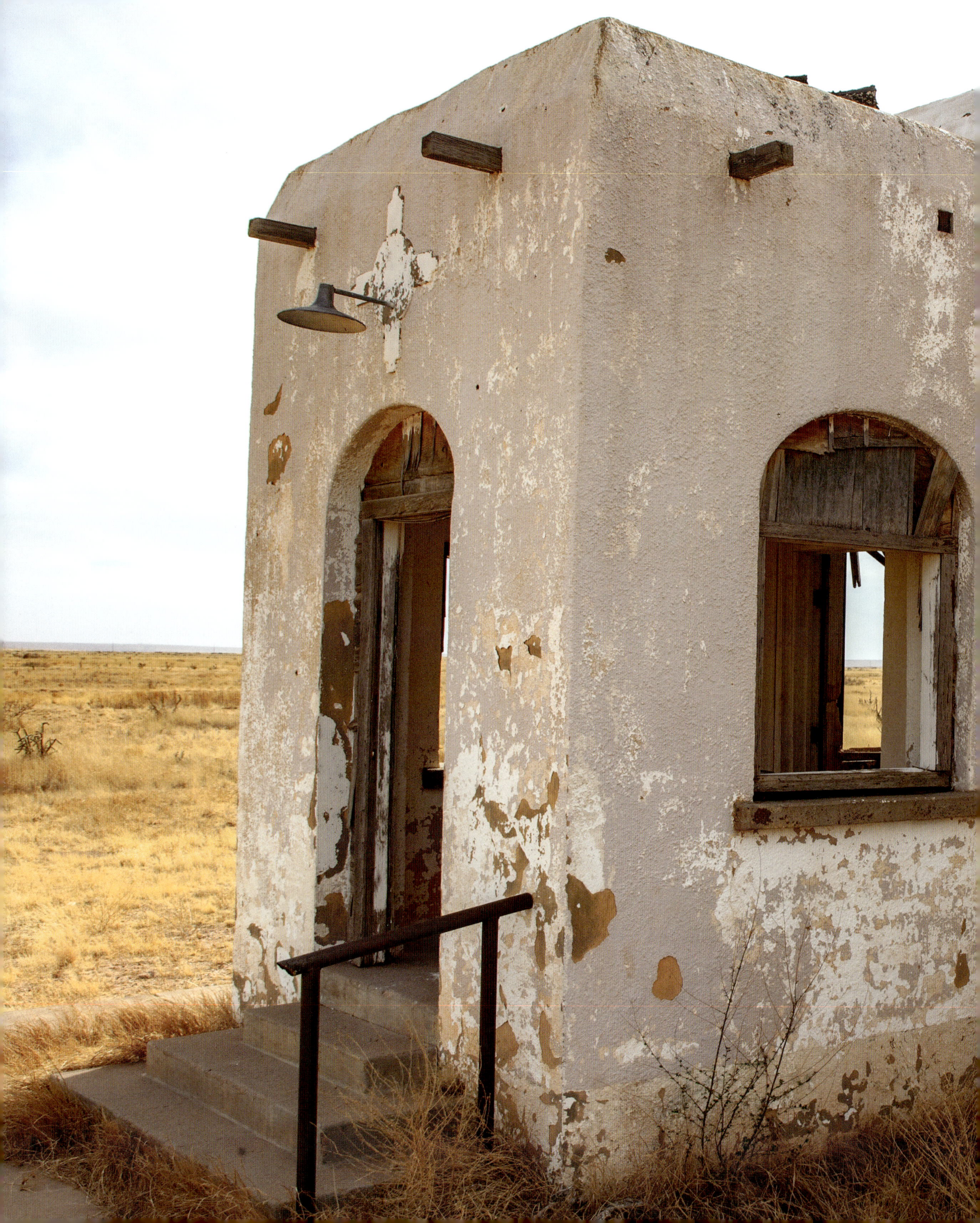

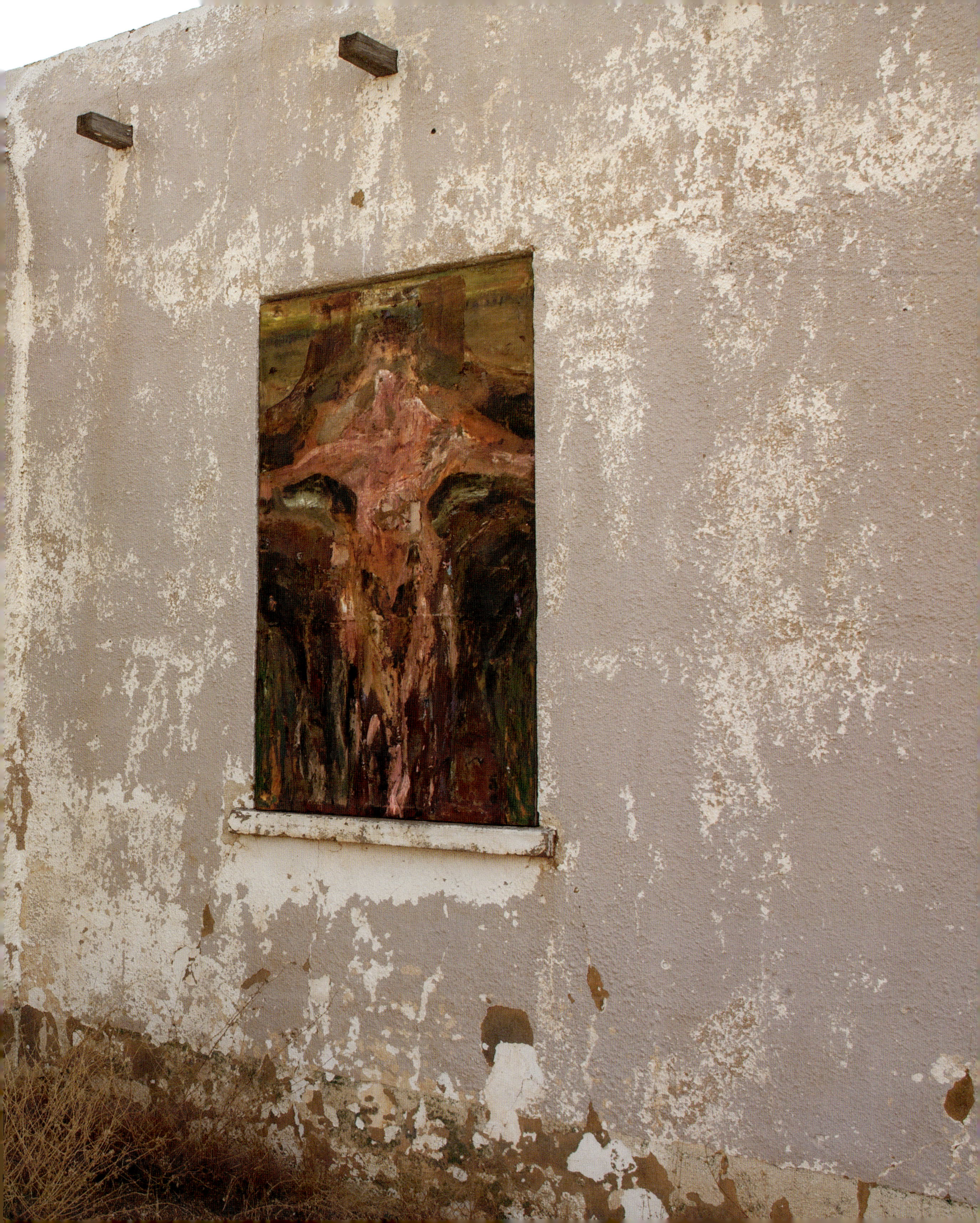

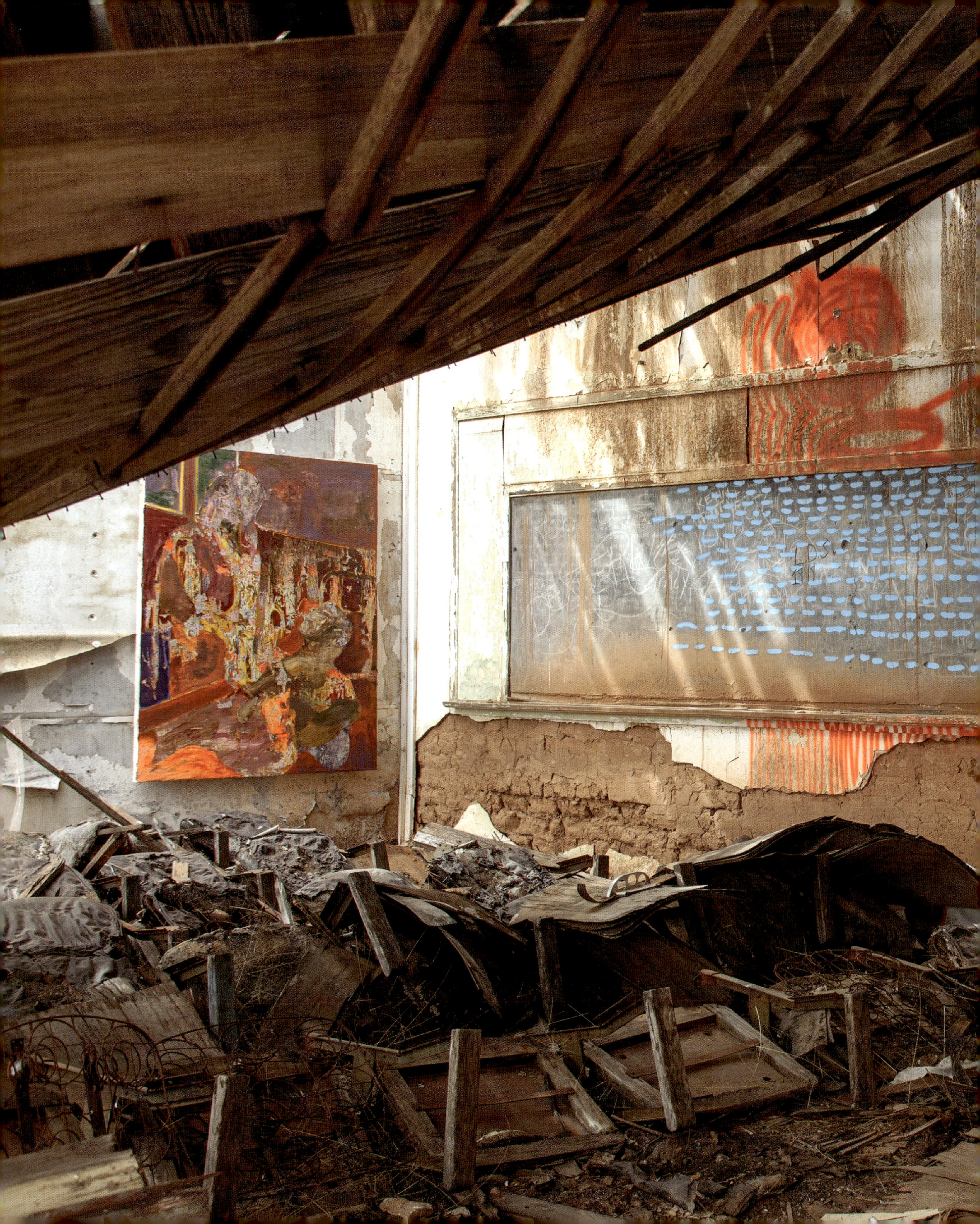

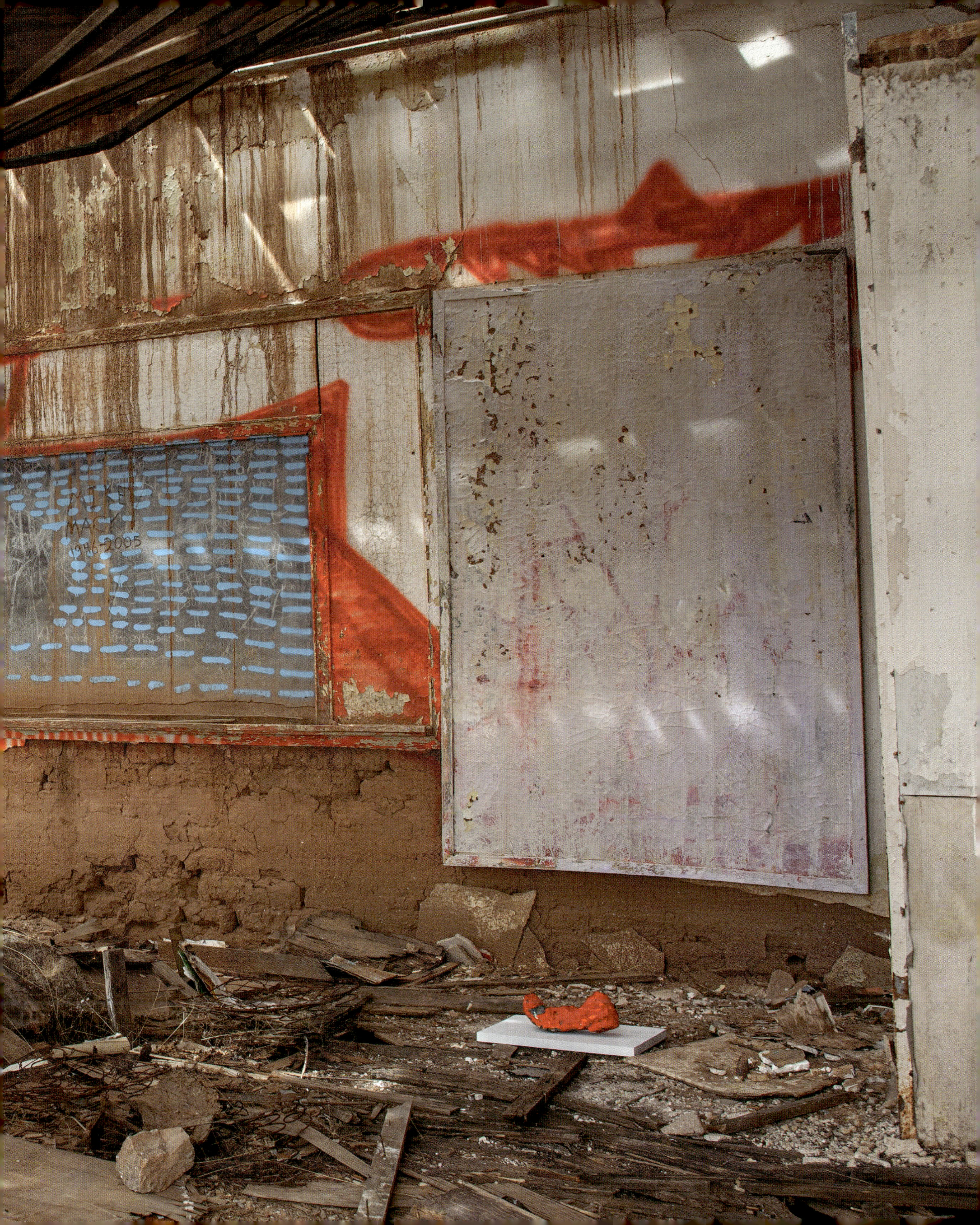
MIKE
MACY

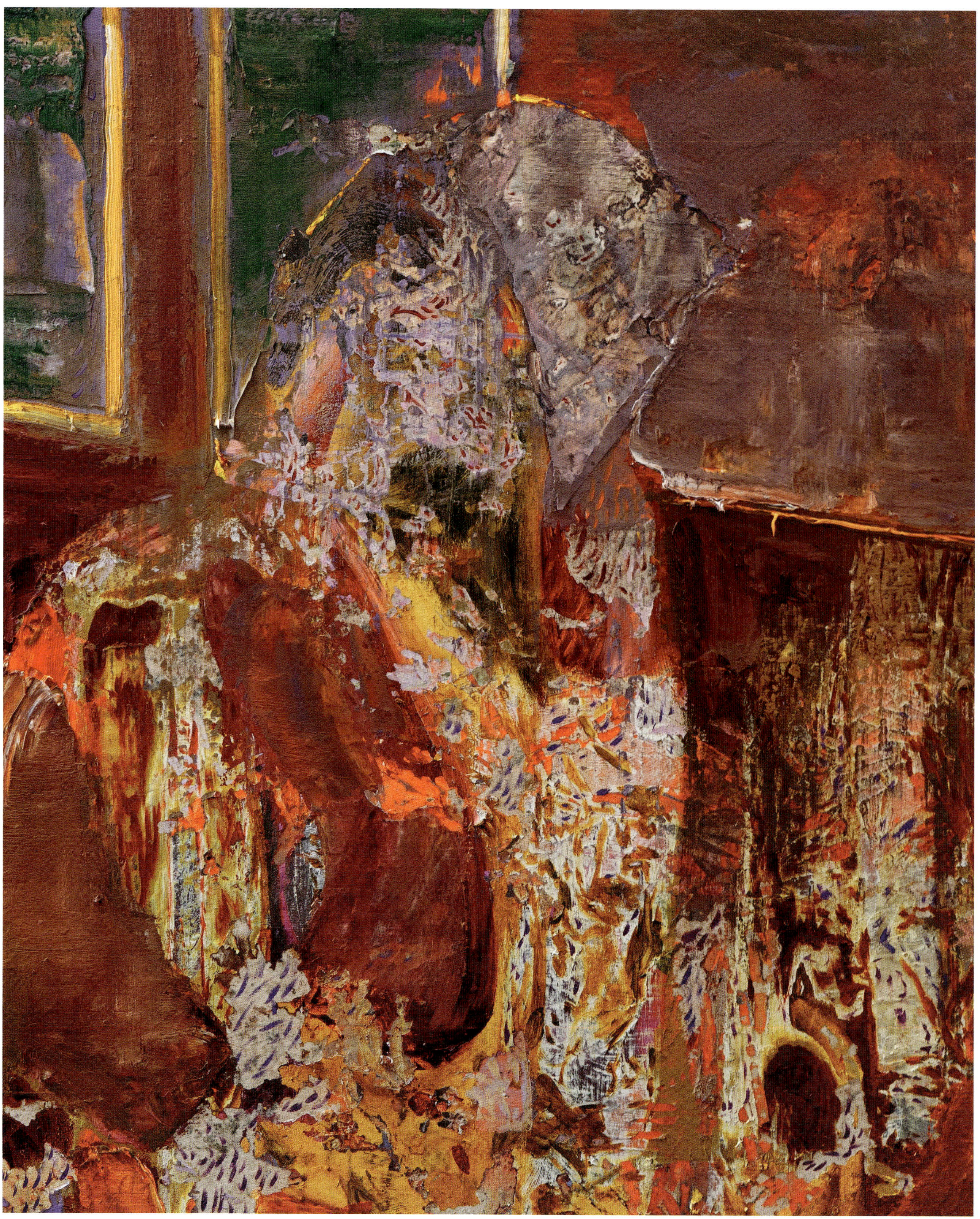

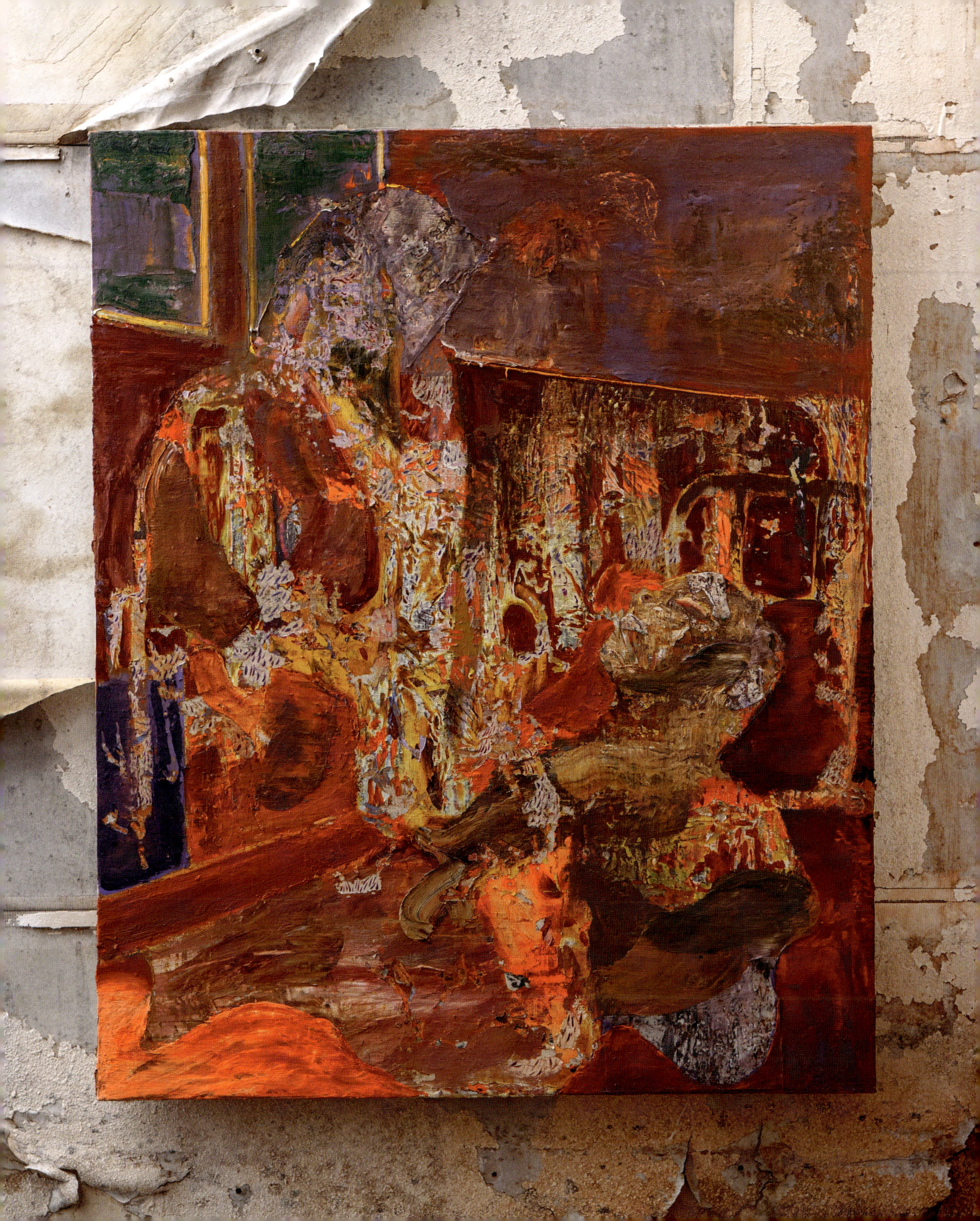

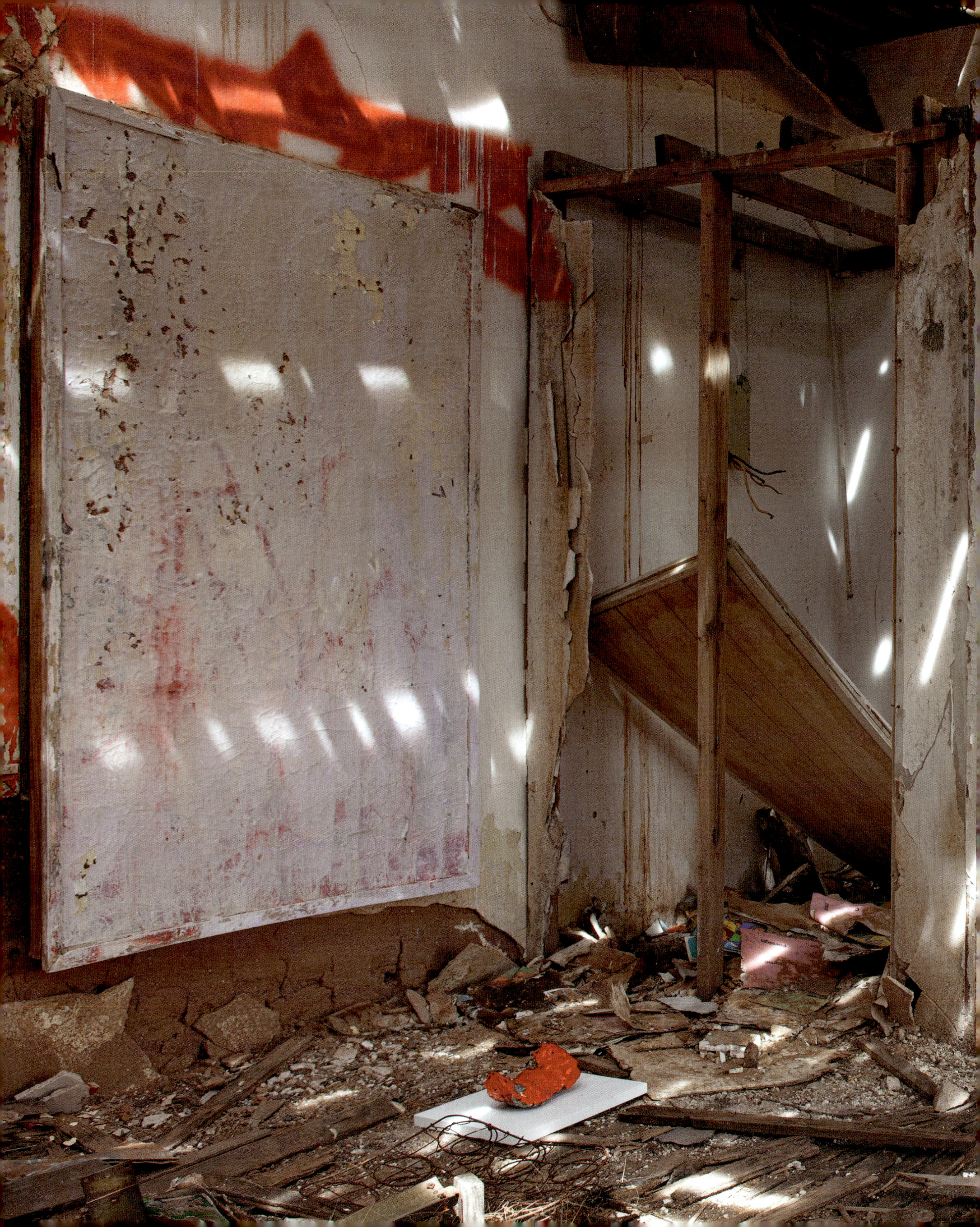

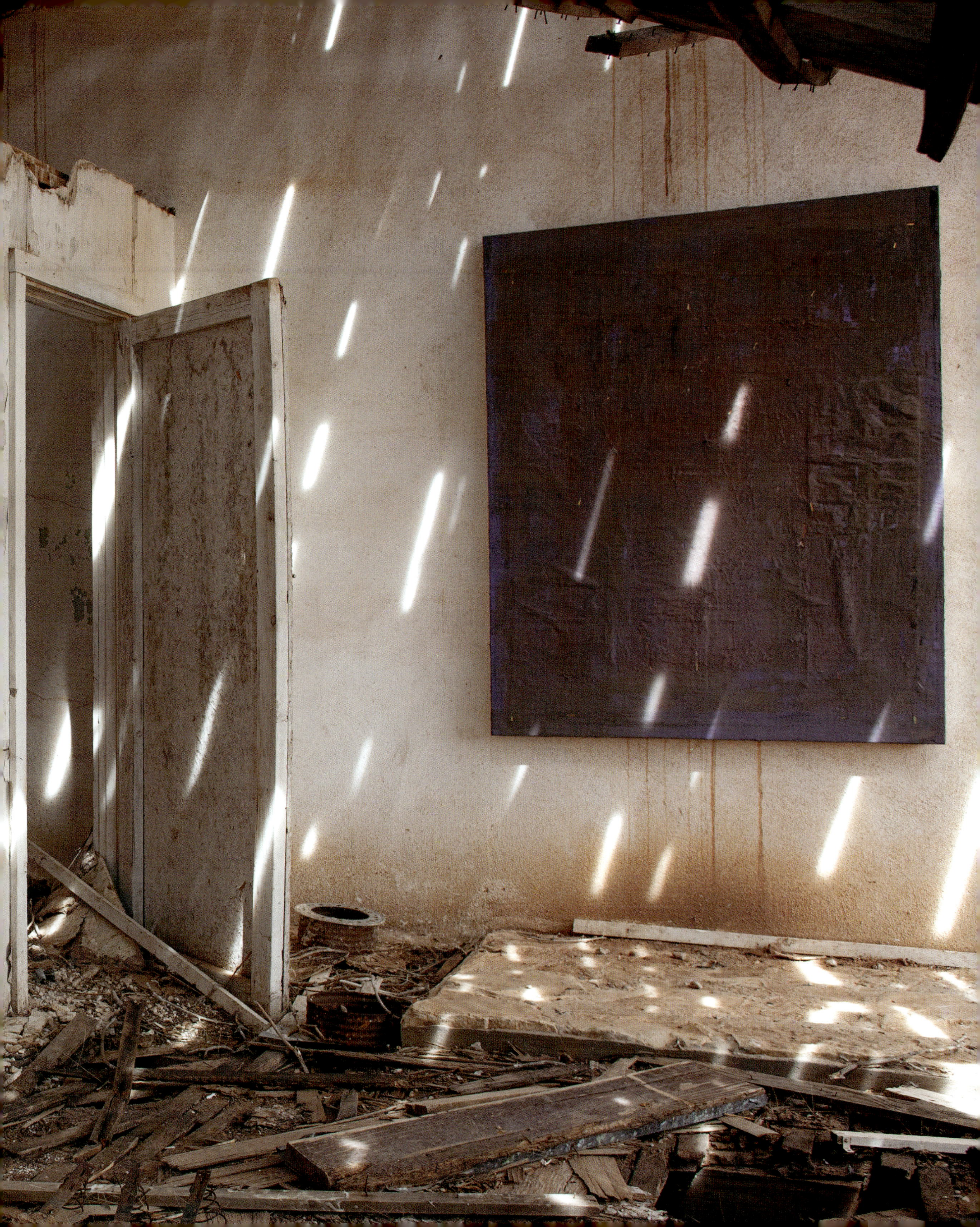

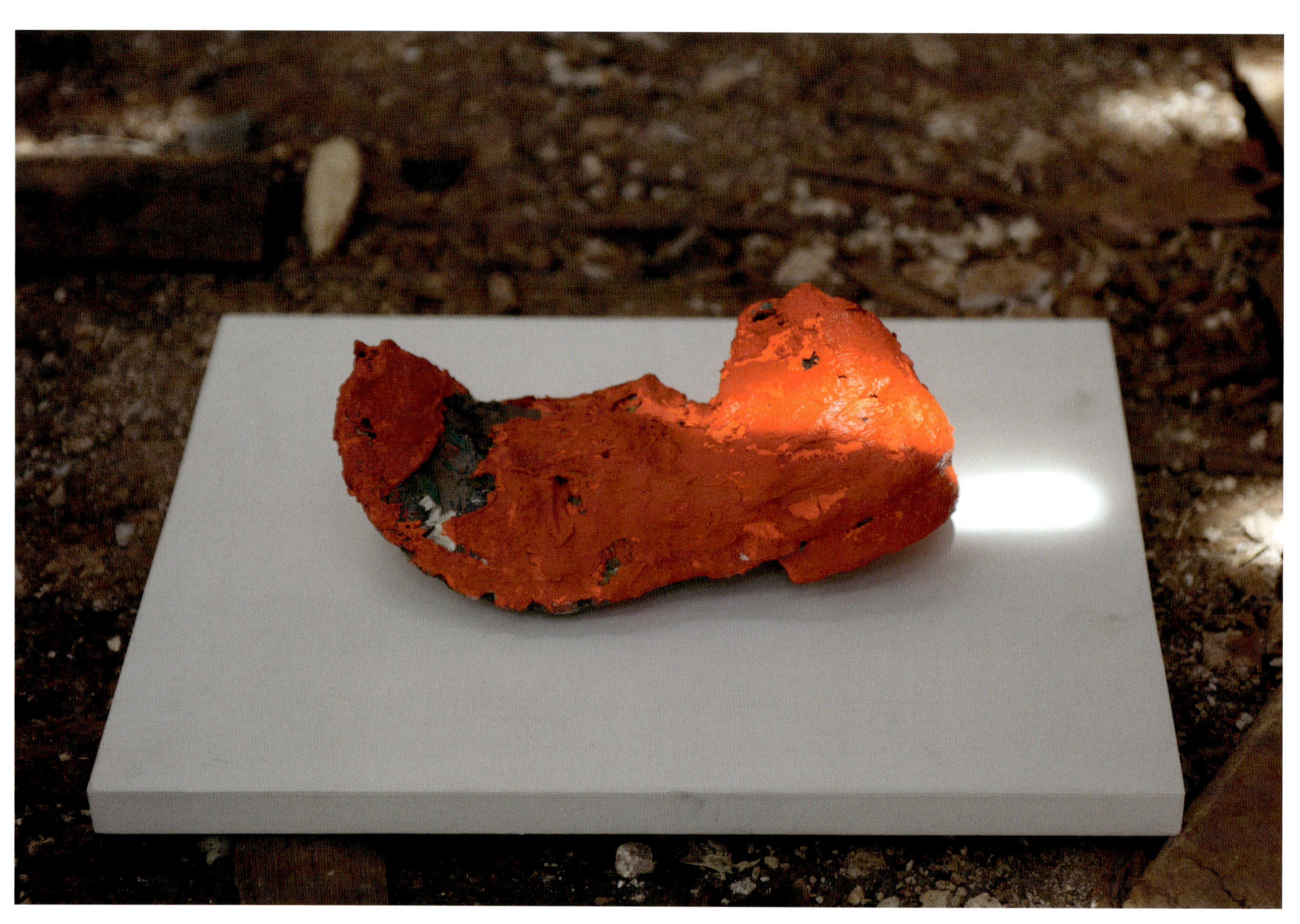

Non-Mediation *(The Impossible Ideal, with Strategies for Cheating)*

An implicit question in *Nihil* is how direct can my experience of the world be? How much mediation between myself and the world can be removed? Does the question make any sense at all? Is it not mediation itself that makes possible my experience of the world?

The Internet, social media, books and print publications, movies and television, memes, fashion, intellectual information, topical issues, history and politics (pragmatically speaking), and any other cultural production within which the arts typically exist are removed from the realm of possible visual information for use in *Nihil*. Inevitably, however, this is not all there is to mediated experience. Mediation is too subtle a problem. It cannot be whittled down to nothing.

I can draw a juniper without thinking "juniper" only if I draw through the landscape continuously, and then what I have drawn most certainly is not a juniper. Whatever idea of tree arises comes from the memory of tree. It is this memory, among other factors, that constitutes mediation. After all, is mediation, ontologically speaking, not to be found in the very accrual of life itself?

The attempt to remove mediation speaks to an ideal of merging, I suppose, between the self and the world beneath the world of ideas. Here, the usefulness of language dead-ends because whatever world I mean to infer would not be that world if it could be described. *Nihil* wants to whittle everything down to nothing, to discover and embrace emptiness fully.

Knowing my ideal to be an impossibility, cheating becomes not only possible, but necessary, because it makes all the subtlest forms of mediation visible to me. What I want, ultimately, is not so much to end up with "nothing" (nothing is nothing), but to isolate and rely only on the forms of mediation closest to my unconscious desires and motivations. In this way, the unconscious might be made conscious: it might actualize itself in the work to its fullest potential.

An example of good cheating in *Nihil* is to make drawings of imagery found on garbage and objects in abandoned spaces. Because it does not violate the dogma to draw what I see along the *Nihil* route, if I see an image printed on torn-out pages of magazines, for example, I have only drawn what I found. Most images I find are out of time, not current to events going on in the world now. They are themselves memory. I am drawing, to the fullest degree possible, unmediated mediations.

Here we find the mystery and paradox at the center of every aspect of *Nihil*. On one hand, I am giving preference to what I discover over what I already think about the world. And yet what I discover seems, again and again, to reflect how I have always seen things. Even as my views and opinions change over time, there is something essential to who I am that has not changed since I was a child. I do not know why I cannot escape my own subjectivity, but what is even more mysterious is why there should be any subjectivity at all to the world. Even from the position of a single life's repeated experiences of synchronicity there seems to be a non-coincidental subjectivity at work in the world itself. The individual life is reflected in the world in equal measure to the world's reflection in the individual life. The images I find, for example, just happen to be the sort of images I have been dealing with for as long as I can remember. The kind of solitude found in sparsely populated places matches the kind of solitude that leaves its trace in my earliest memories. I follow an arbitrary tree-shaped route, but the route only follows my yearning to return my soul to the earth. To give the work's destiny over to arbitrariness is another way of clearing the path for the unconscious to actualize its own unveiling.

In *Nihil*, I encounter my own ghost wherever I am. Somewhere I am already dead. Somewhere I have not yet been born. And everywhere I find my ghost; I find the ghost of the world, already gone, always becoming.

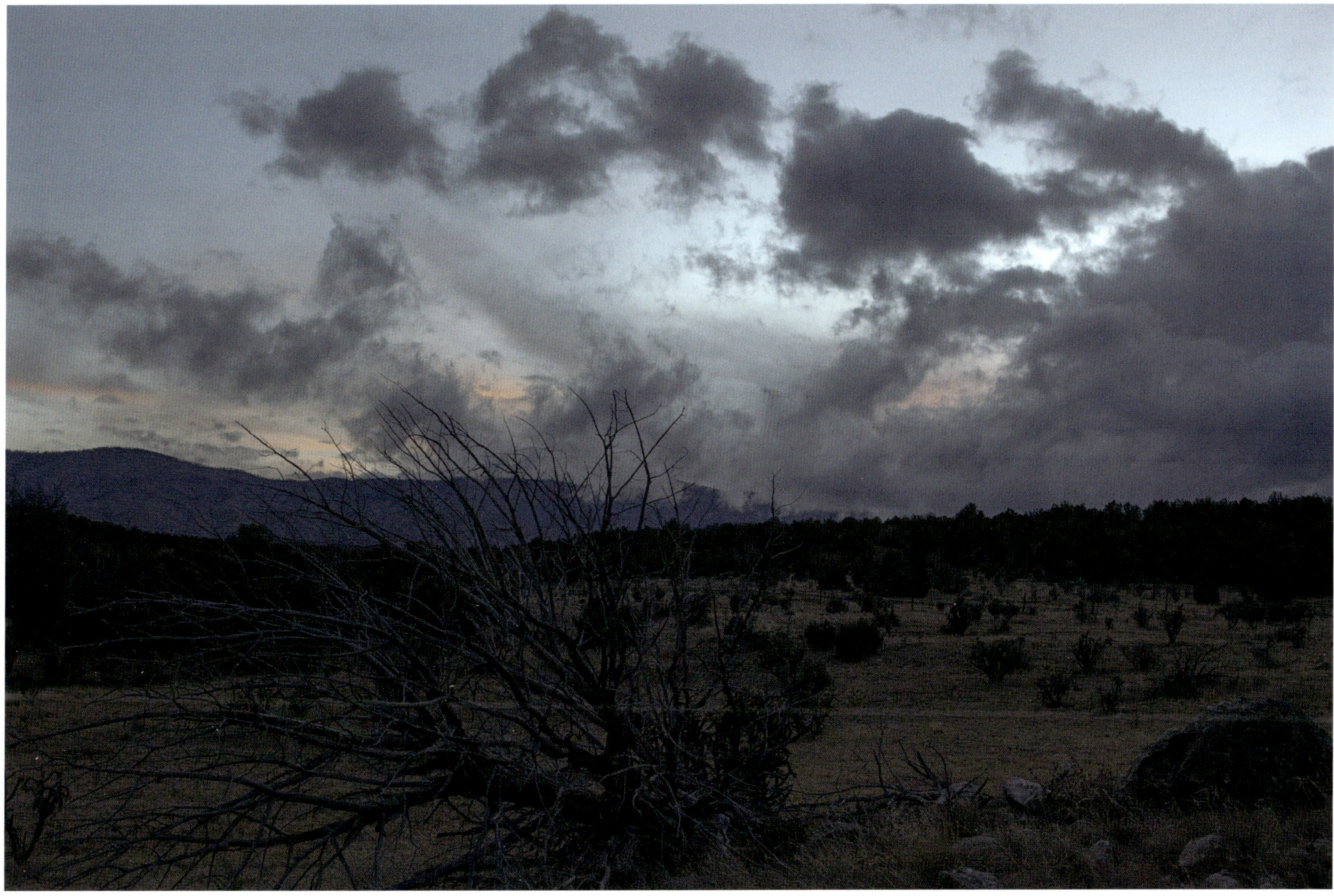

LINCOLN NATIONAL FOREST, NEW MEXICO, 2021

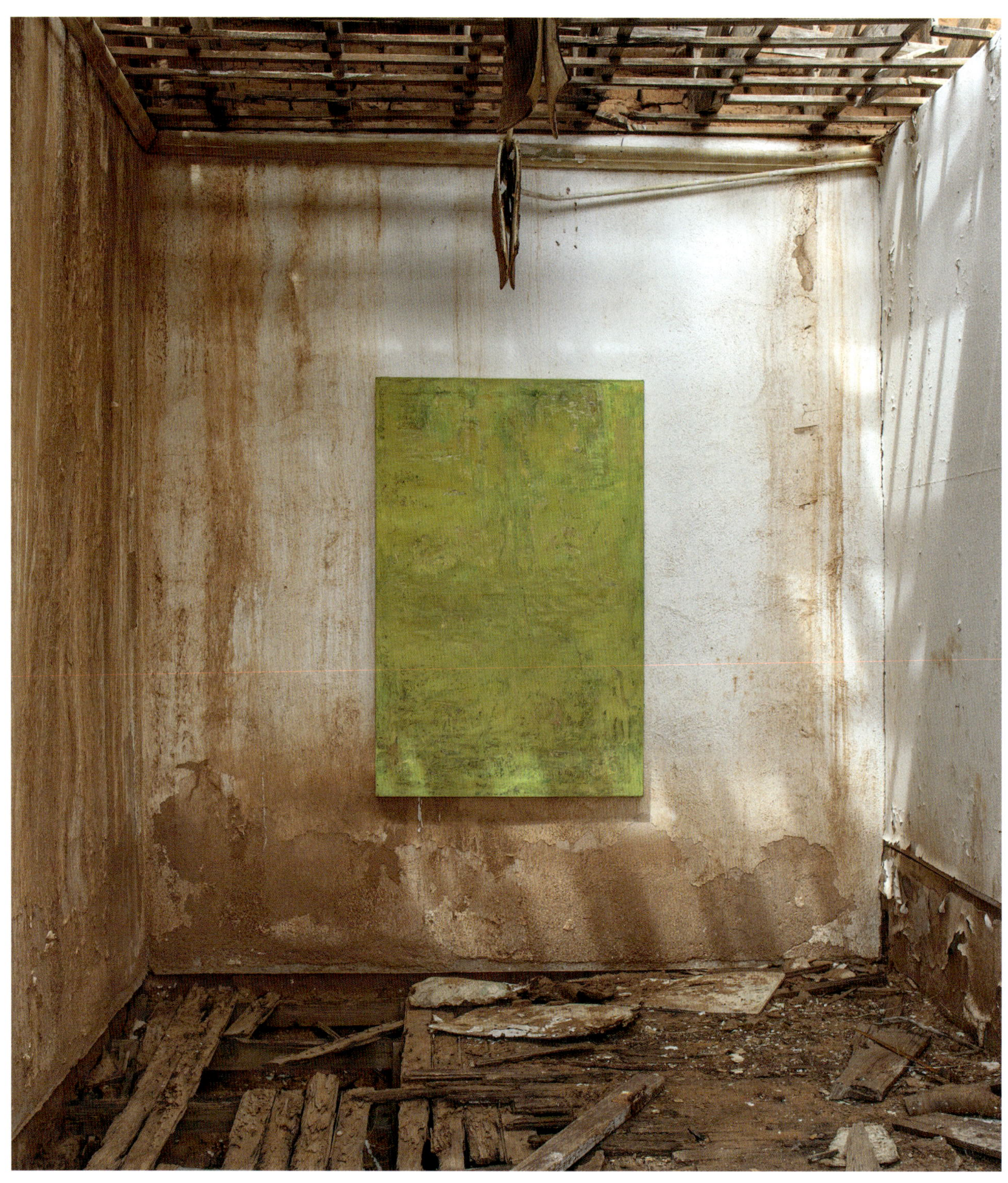

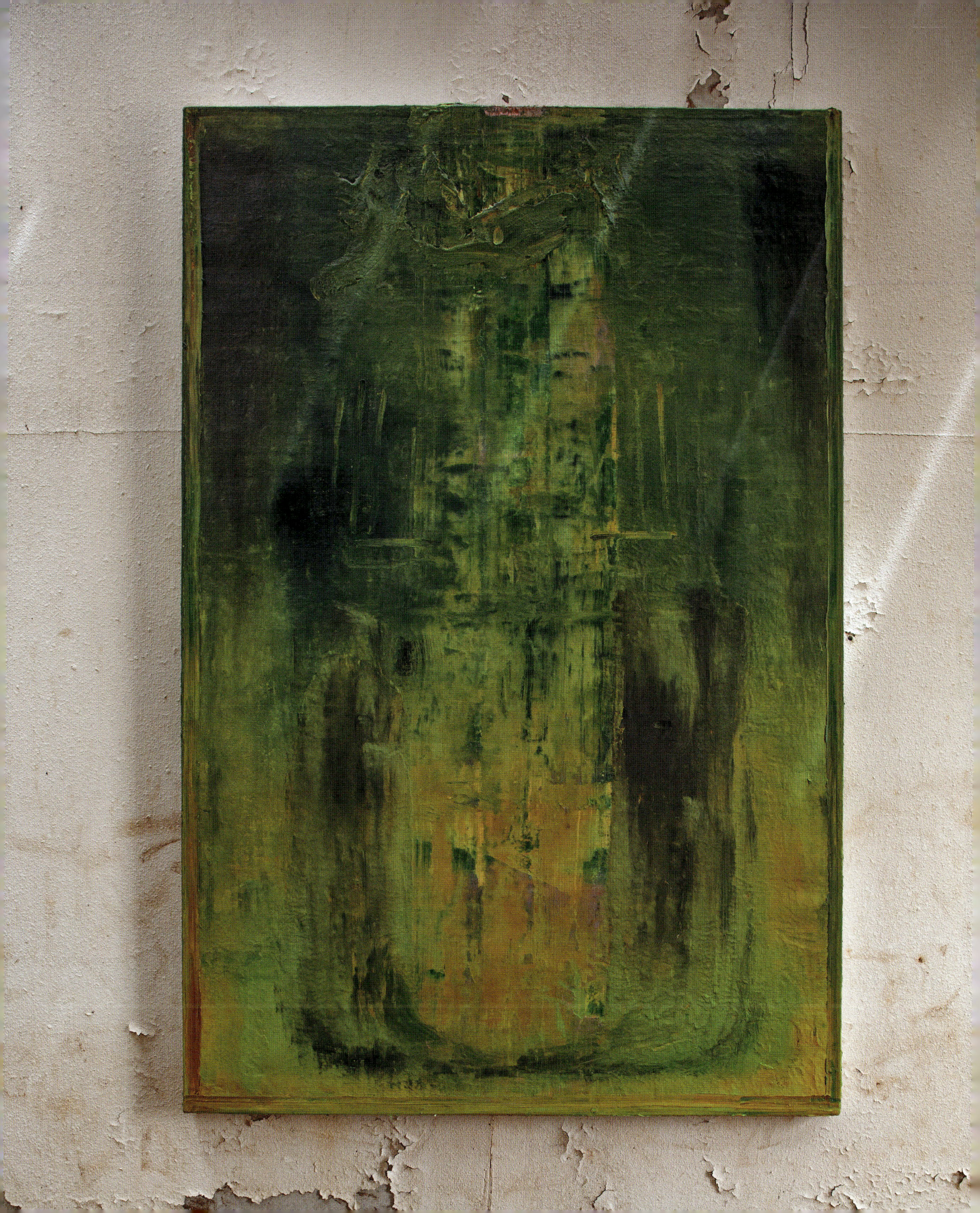

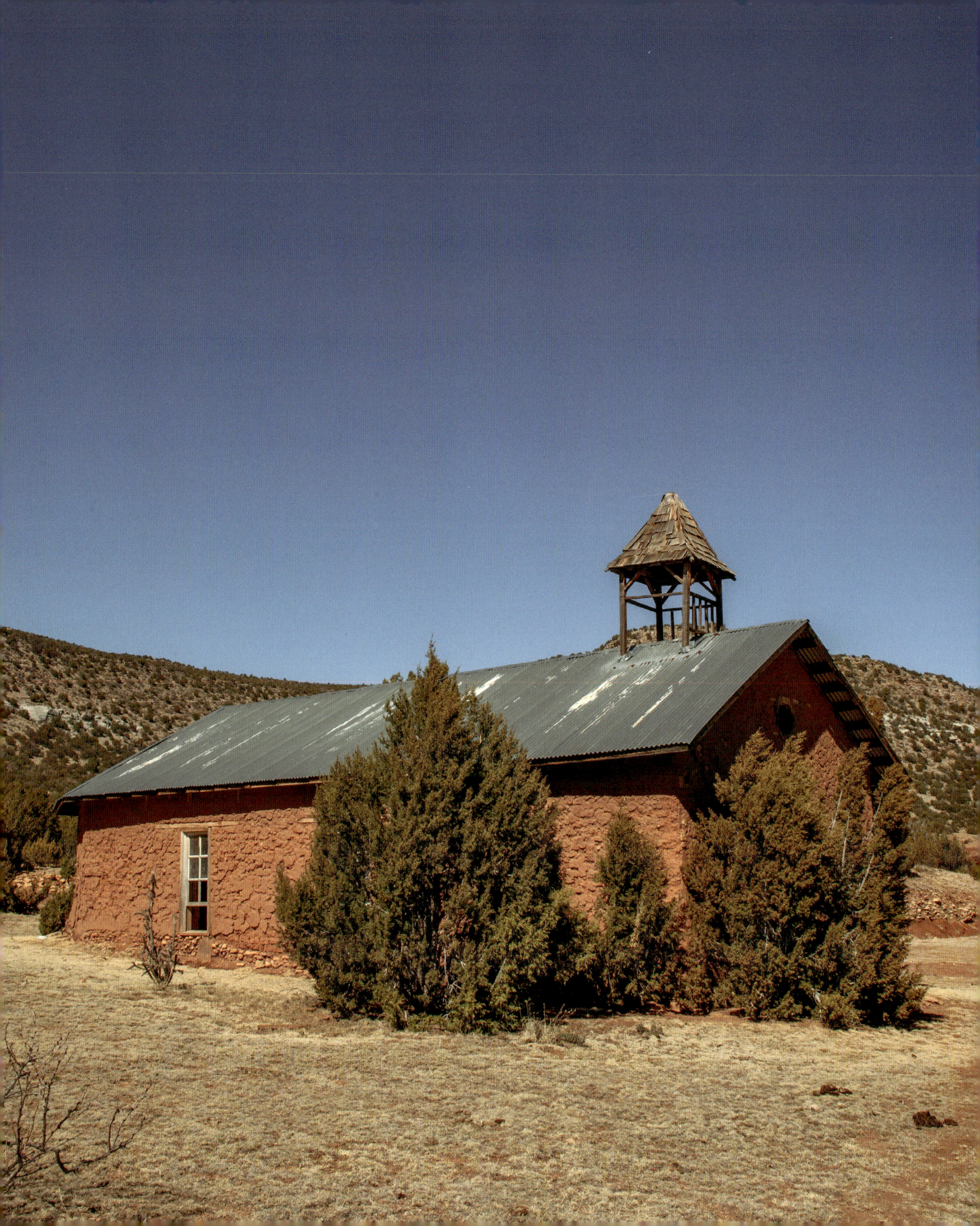

LAS VEGAS (NEW MEXICO) CHURCH

The Summer Triangle

During the hot, windy spring of 2022, much of New Mexico burned. The largest among the many fires raged near the small college town of Las Vegas, which just so happens to sit on the *Nihil* route.

My friend, the remarkable realist painter Cedra Wood, lived nearby and volunteered to guide me through the area as we attempted to approach the fires. Though checkpoints marking evacuation zones sensibly prevented us from getting in the vicinity, smoke was everywhere, and airplanes flew in lines, filling with water in nearby Lake Isobel, only to circle back and drop it on the fire. We drove into encampments where firefighters and volunteers lived for the duration of the disaster. Everywhere we went, I sketched.

One of the sites Cedra showed me was an abandoned church, and five months later I made an installation for *Nihil* there. The most obvious and immediate obstacle was that a single glass-less window presented the only passage in or out.

The trouble was that I wanted to make a triptych for the apse, or, in any case, the area where the altar would likely have once been situated. Yet the only way to get it into the church would be either as something that could come apart in many small pieces, or something on paper or fabric that could be rolled tightly enough to fit through.

The first of the works I began was *A Friend Who Waits before a Bridge Leading into Fire (Vega, I Dreamt I Saw You)*, painted on 35 individual square-foot wood panels that could fit through the window. Somehow trying to paint the fire was not working, and I began looking at the sketches I had made of religious icons at other nearby sites and of Cedra herself. What became important to the piece was that my drawings of her were made while she sat at the foot of a bridge marking the boundary between us and the evacuation zone. What began as a landscape painting of sorts was turning figurative, even as I scraped out layer after layer of legible imagery.

...

I am someone who sees words in my mind's eye, different, for example, from my wife Maja Ruznic, who sees colors and shapes. "Nihil" was a word hovering in the air, day after day, for about a year or so prior to it becoming a project. And then I began to see the word "Vega" each day as I worked on the painting. It seemed to come out of the word "Las Vegas," so I tried to ignore it as nothing more than a meaningless fragment. Each day, I worried about our own nearby mountains catching fire, at least in part an object of projection for a namelessly acute anxiety I felt increasing by the day.

In recent days, Maja had been explaining the vagus nerve, the main nerve in the parasympathetic nervous system, which controls things like digestion, heart rate, and the immune system. Many of the symptoms I had been experiencing, she suggested, seemed to be connected to the vagus nerve, specifically when it is understimulated.

After about three days of seeing the word "Vega," I experienced a sudden paroxysm of uncontrollable weeping. It would turn out to be a panic attack, disabling even my ability to speak or stand upright. I had something akin to an out-of-body experience in which it felt as if I had no interior, as if I were hollow, merely a fugitive skin or exoskeleton, and I could smell something awful that I could only think of as death. It was as if an inner self had been violently ripped from an outer self and gone missing. I was soon to pick up my daughter from daycare, but knew I could not take care of her, and that realization caused me to break down totally and to feel as if I would truly die.

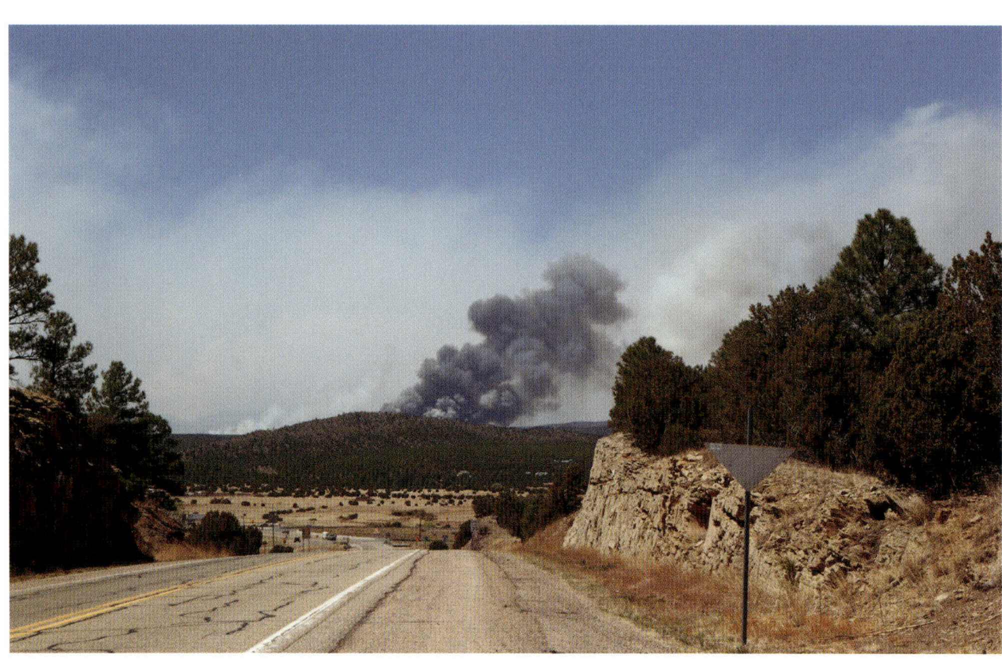

HERMIT'S PEAK FIRE NEAR LAS VEGAS, NEW MEXICO

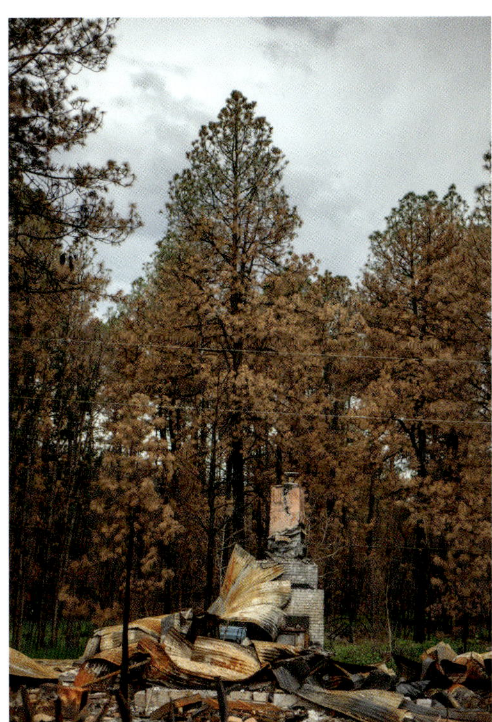

DESTROYED HOMES IN THE 2022 FIRE'S AFTERMATH

For three days afterward, I experienced what I can only describe as euphoria, and I genuinely wondered whether I was bipolar. That thought, however, did not particularly bother me, and the rest of the painting came quickly and easily. Life resumed and I felt like myself, not euphoric, though better somehow, and lighter than before. I began to think of the whole episode as a kind of necessary exorcism somehow responsible for expediting a transformative process, bringing forward a potentiality that had been bottlenecked for too long.

I have experienced nothing like it since.

...

In *A Friend Who Waits before a Bridge Leading into Fire (Vega, I Dreamt I Saw You)*, the central figure, leaving behind any resemblance to my friend Cedra or of the fire itself, appears more or less birdlike, an accidental result of the subtraction process and my improvisational response to the loss and transformation of imagery. It was a great delight, as I began looking into the word "Vega," to learn that the star is represented as an eagle or vulture in East and West Asian and North African mythologies. Because of the stars displayed near the ceiling in the abandoned church, I liked recalling that Vega is an actual star. In Arabic etymology, the word means "to fall," and that seemed significant as well, given that it was what I had done just days ago.

After further research, I discovered that the Vega star is one of three comprising the Summer Triangle, not a constellation but an asterism, formed along with the stars Altair and Deneb. These three bright stars from the Lyra, Aquila, and Cygnus constellations, respectively, are visible from New Mexico in the low eastern sky during summer.

In Chinese mythology, Altair and Vega were long-ago lovers permitted to meet again only once every eon through the mediation of Deneb. Reflecting on my panic attack, I could not escape the sense of "splitting" within myself, a disintegration between something like ego and soul (or whatever words best approximate the dilemma); that one part of myself should always feel suppressed in order that the other might somehow operate. To give names to the many parts of life's hidden mysteries, I think, is a basic human proclivity embedded in all of mythology. Deneb, it seems to me, was a kind of gift, an attack and release, expediting a necessary surrender as preparation for "re-constellating" my own identity, which, had probably been the unconscious drive for creating *Nihil* to begin with.

Vega's title, I like to point out, describes an actual moment by a bridge with a friend on a day in which we were chasing fire: *a friend who waits before a bridge leading into fire*. Yet once the literal thought and imagery vanishes, we are left with a title indicating something more symbolic or universal. *Altair...*, for example, was created by looking at sketches I made on a day out on the *Nihil* route with my studio manager Sam Staffan, as we scoured the countryside and wilderness in the aftermath of the fire. And just as the imagery of the fire and of Cedra disappeared, so too did the images of the aftermath and of Sam. The next painting came easily, was birdlike, and took on a similar symbolic title, *A Friend Who Waits beyond a Bridge Swallowed by the Fire (Altair, I Dreamt I Saw You)*.

The central painting (the last completed) is most legible, I think, because the crucified Christ is indelible in culture. This image was not contained in earlier layers, and I did not know it would sit on top. I mention this because I do not intend it as a message to a public, from the perspective of either a religious believer or a skeptic. It is a simple unsurprising fact, here in New Mexico, that I find so much Catholic imagery everywhere I go. The top layer of the *Deneb* piece comes from studies I made from a very old, very small statue of Christ I found in Corrales, which is missing its arms. I called the finished painting *A Friend Who Waits beneath a Bridge Setting it on Fire (Deneb, I Dreamt I Saw You)*.

The first time I saw the three works together was in the church where these photos were taken. I did not know the sum of what I had made until that point. They seem to me not so much a triptych but an... asterism. They come from their own worlds, but they can be seen together. Not insisting on them as a triptych means that they will likely go their own ways again, and in their own times.

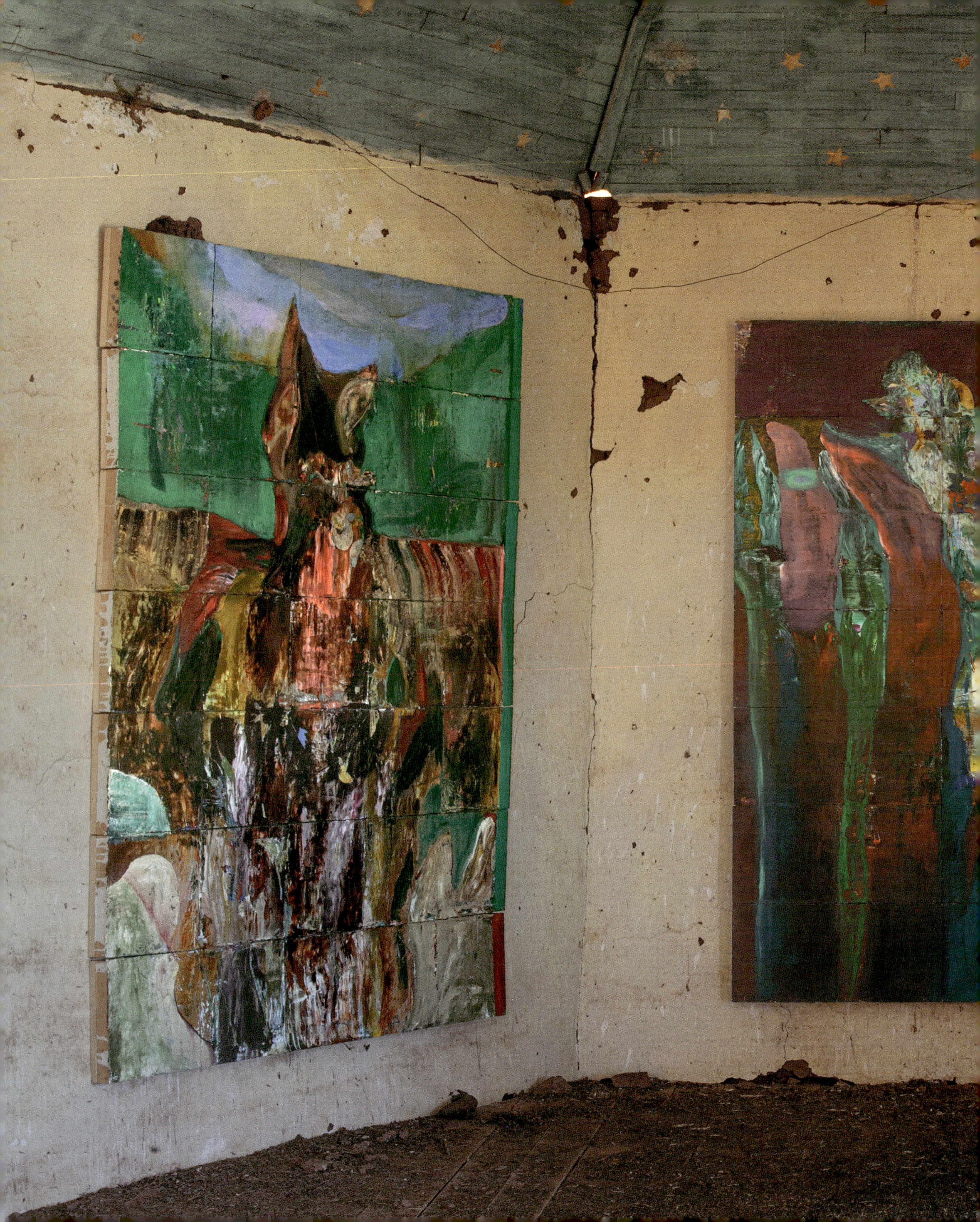

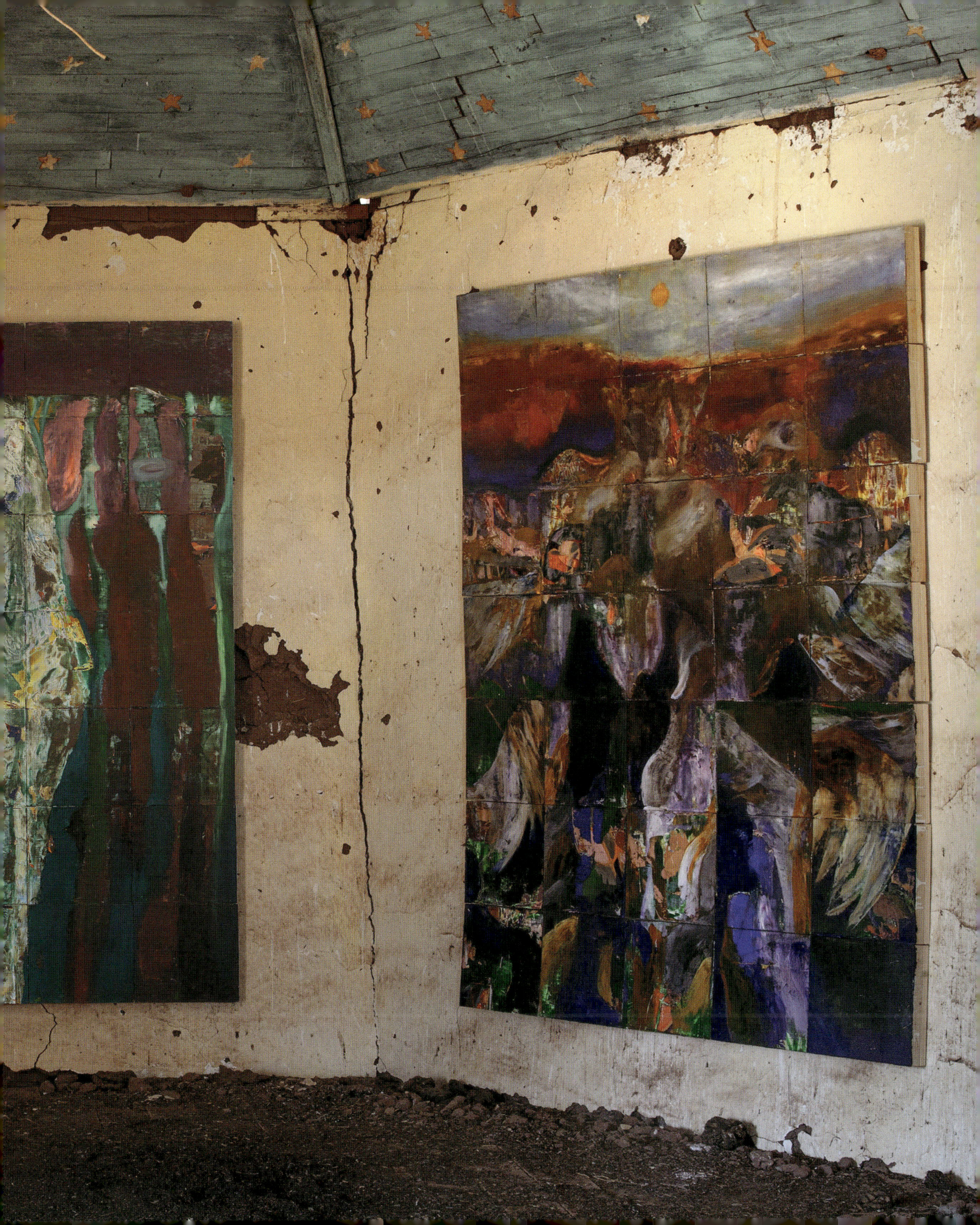

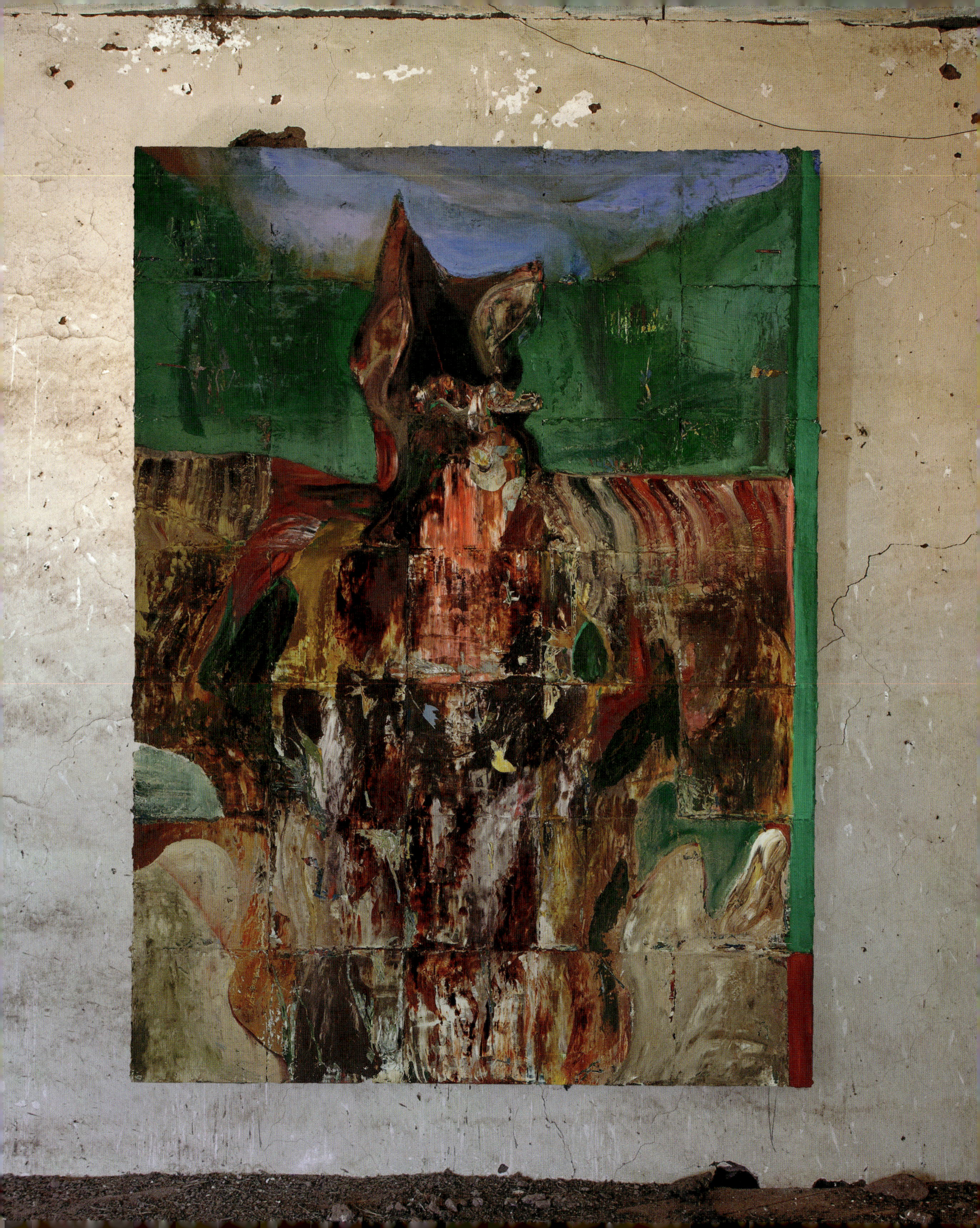

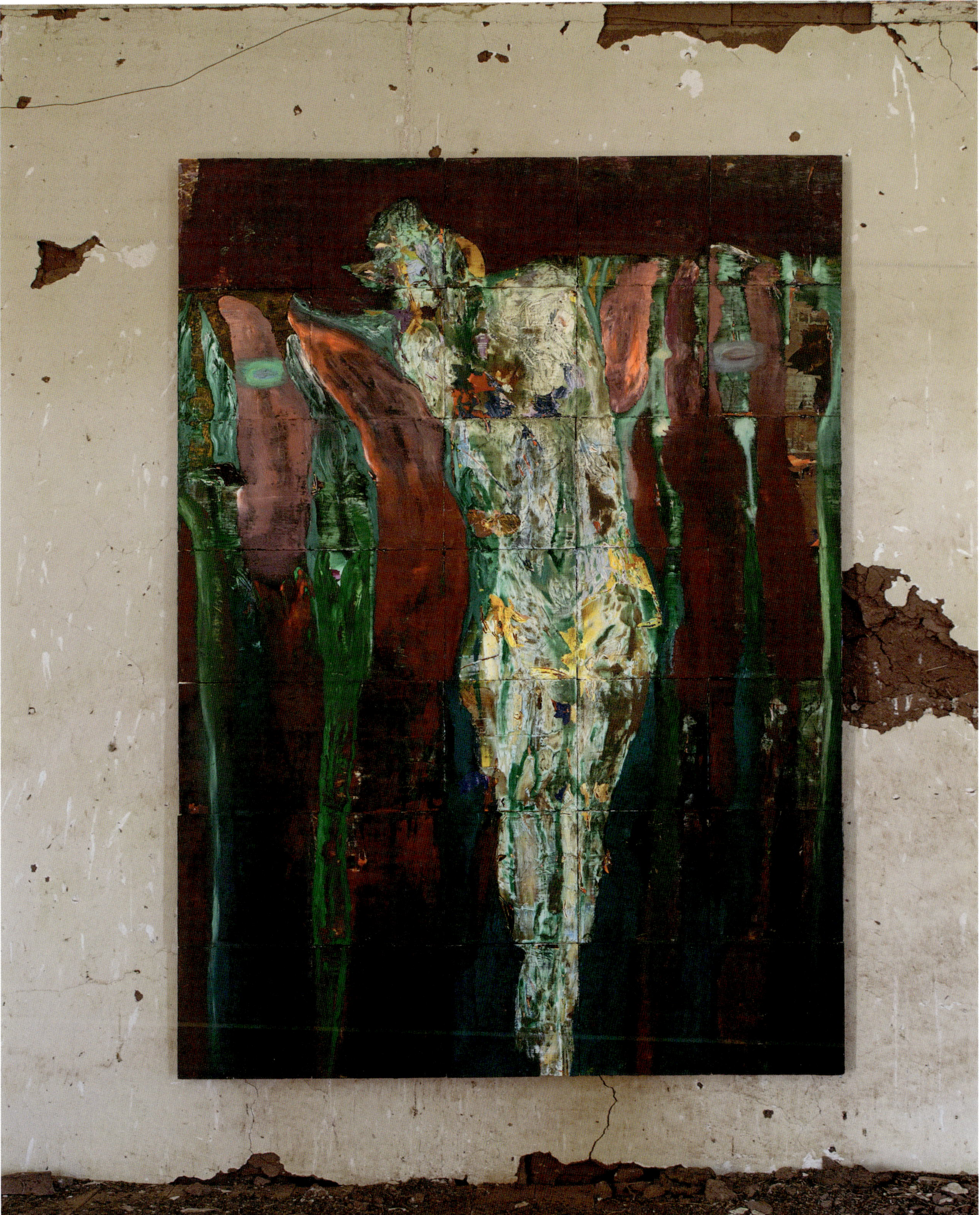

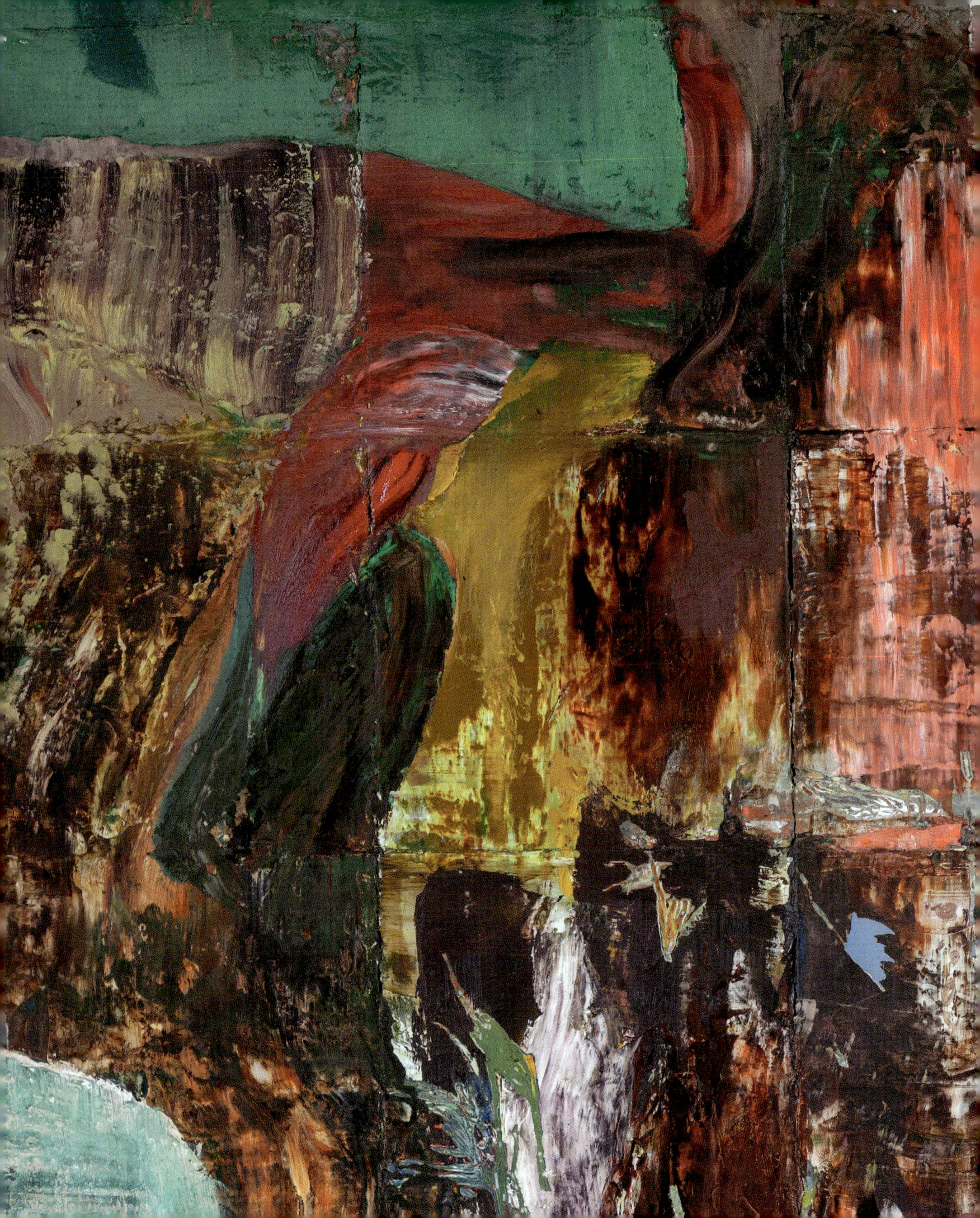

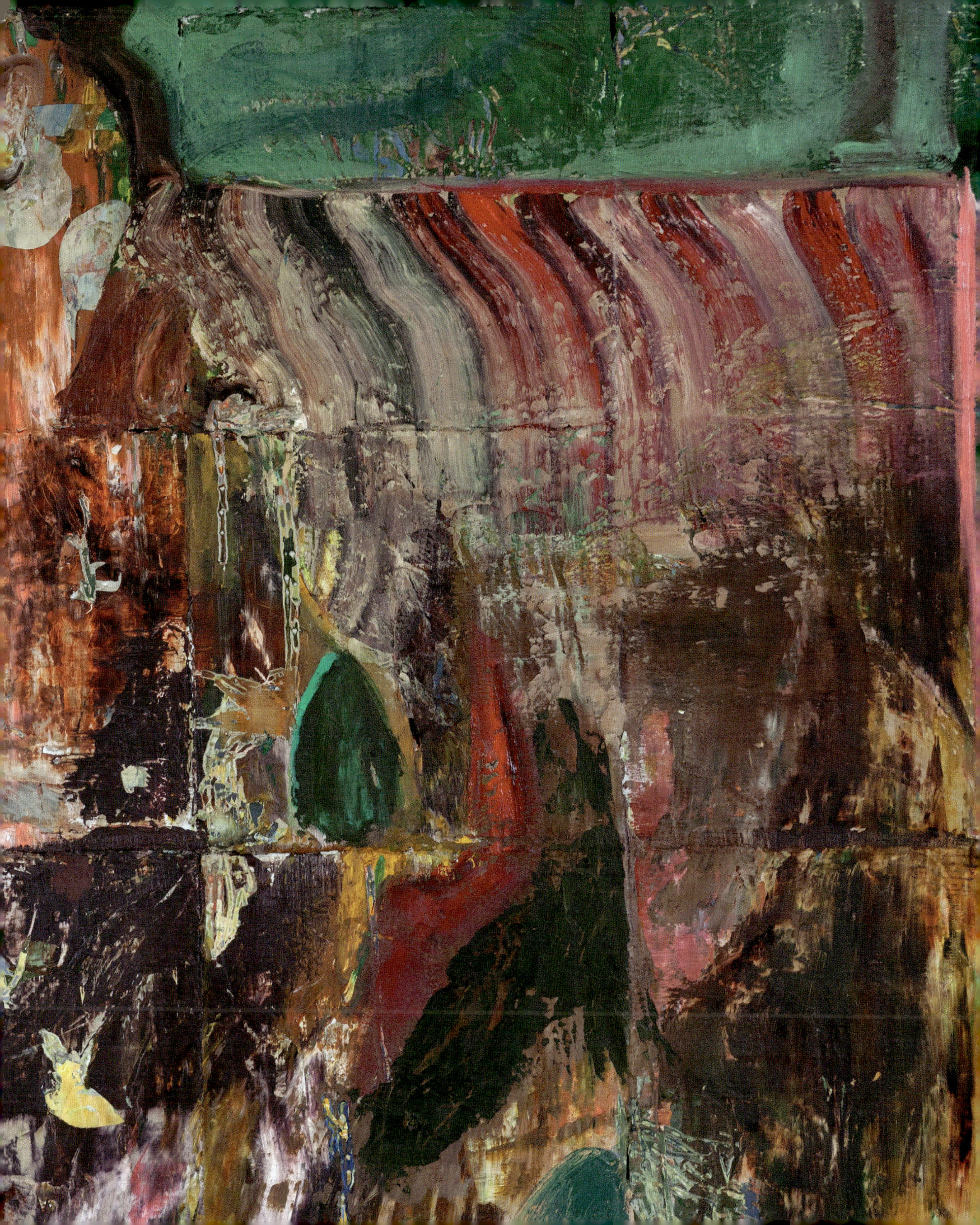

Non-Meaning (*Toward the Possibility of Genuine Discovery*)

The root word "nihil" is everywhere in culture. Perhaps the word "nihilism" comes to mind first, a pejorative in its everyday usage, commonly understood as the idea that life is meaningless and therefore not worth preserving. It is the great cultural anathema, a kind of soul-eating bedevilment that explains civilization's every spiritual malaise. We used to believe in something and now we do not.

I have asked myself, am I a nihilist? Perhaps the reason that nihilism is so vilified is precisely because we sometimes fear that life is meaningless. This is nihilism then, not out there, but right here, in each of us. So I wonder, is contempt for life related to whether or not we believe it to be meaningful? I do not know whether meaning exists independently of me in the universe, but neither do I regret if it does not. If the universe is meaningless, then I have compassion for all of us who feel lost and alone in the world. We have only each other in the vastness of space. In the absence of meaning, I am reliant only on the quality of my experience in the world to lead me to the freedom necessary to discover it naively each day. I should not limit my experience only to what matches the meaning I make of it. *Nihil* does not insist that life is meaningless, but neither does it insist the opposite.

In painting, if I insist meaning is real and that it should operate in a particular way, I am in the business of messaging through art. In fact, this is what I have done most of my life. But in *Nihil*, messaging works against the process, because the process is enfolded in the values of not-knowing and of genuine discovery. It implicitly disbelieves the meaning maker; I mistrust my own desperation to make the world appear the way I would like it.

If my touch of the surface is just as likely to be peeled off or scraped away, then no one touch insists on its own superiority; the touch is for the sake of touch, not for a picture. The image it might have contained is half missing. The color gone. Unexpected colors from earlier layers pop through the new holes made, and not necessarily in an immediately useful way. Absence is present because it overtakes earlier intentions in a kind of figure–ground reversal. Yet the intentions themselves had only ever been provisional, their futility anticipated.

In the accumulation of actions that forms the object, a trace of consciousness seems available. This feels meaningful to me, though I do not know what it means. There are times, when an image survives the process, that it would seem to the viewer that I am imparting a meaning, but that is not true in *Nihil*. To be sure, part of what constitutes my humanity is that I make meaning out of patterns in the world—either discovered or invented—which I receive as a detective receives clues in a murder case. *Nihil* is not an insistence that meaning does not exist, nor a denial of my own ordinariness; it is merely a philosophical preference to resist a flat intellectual meaning, making for the possibility of a genuinely revelatory discovery, the sort that can only come about through the process itself.

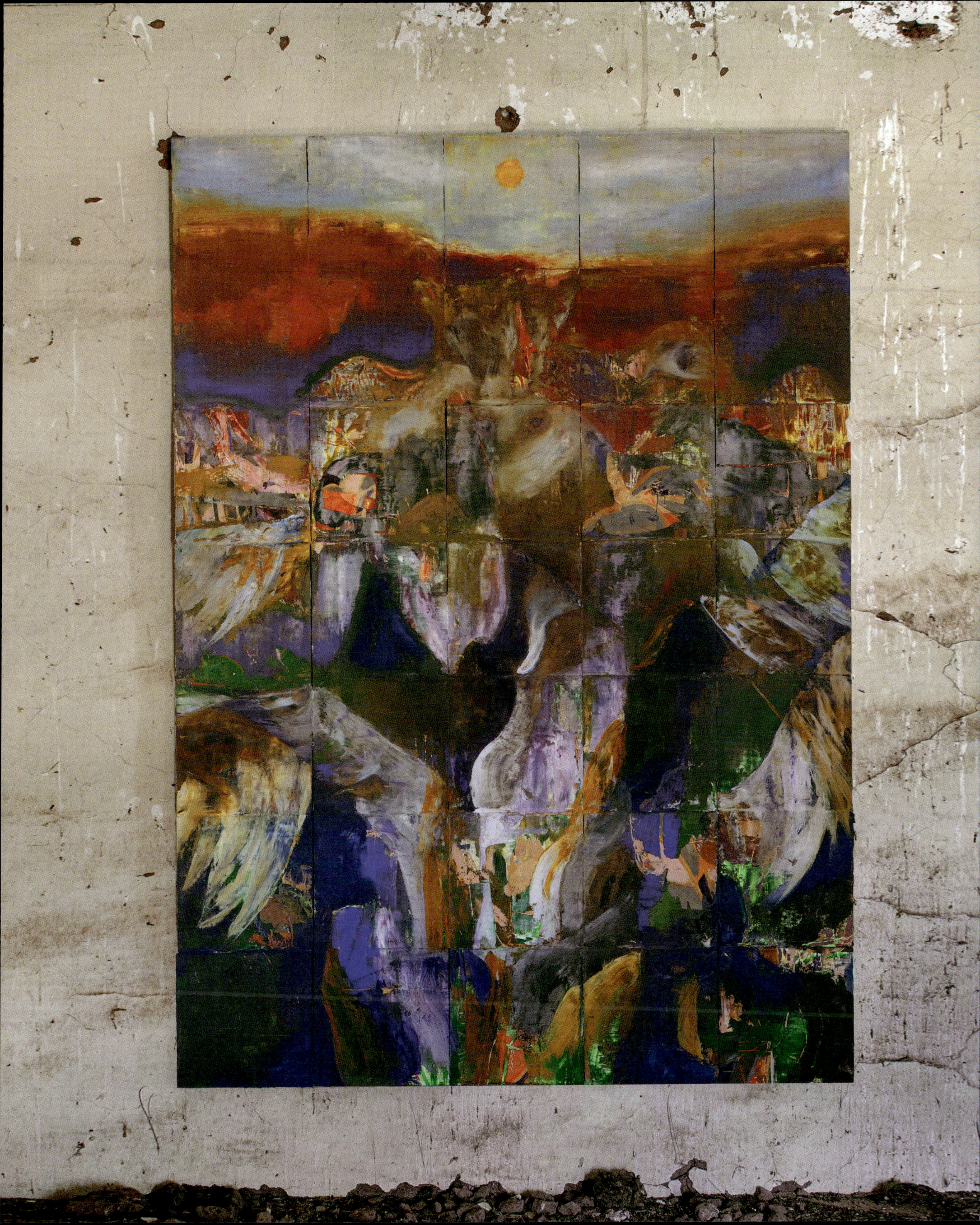

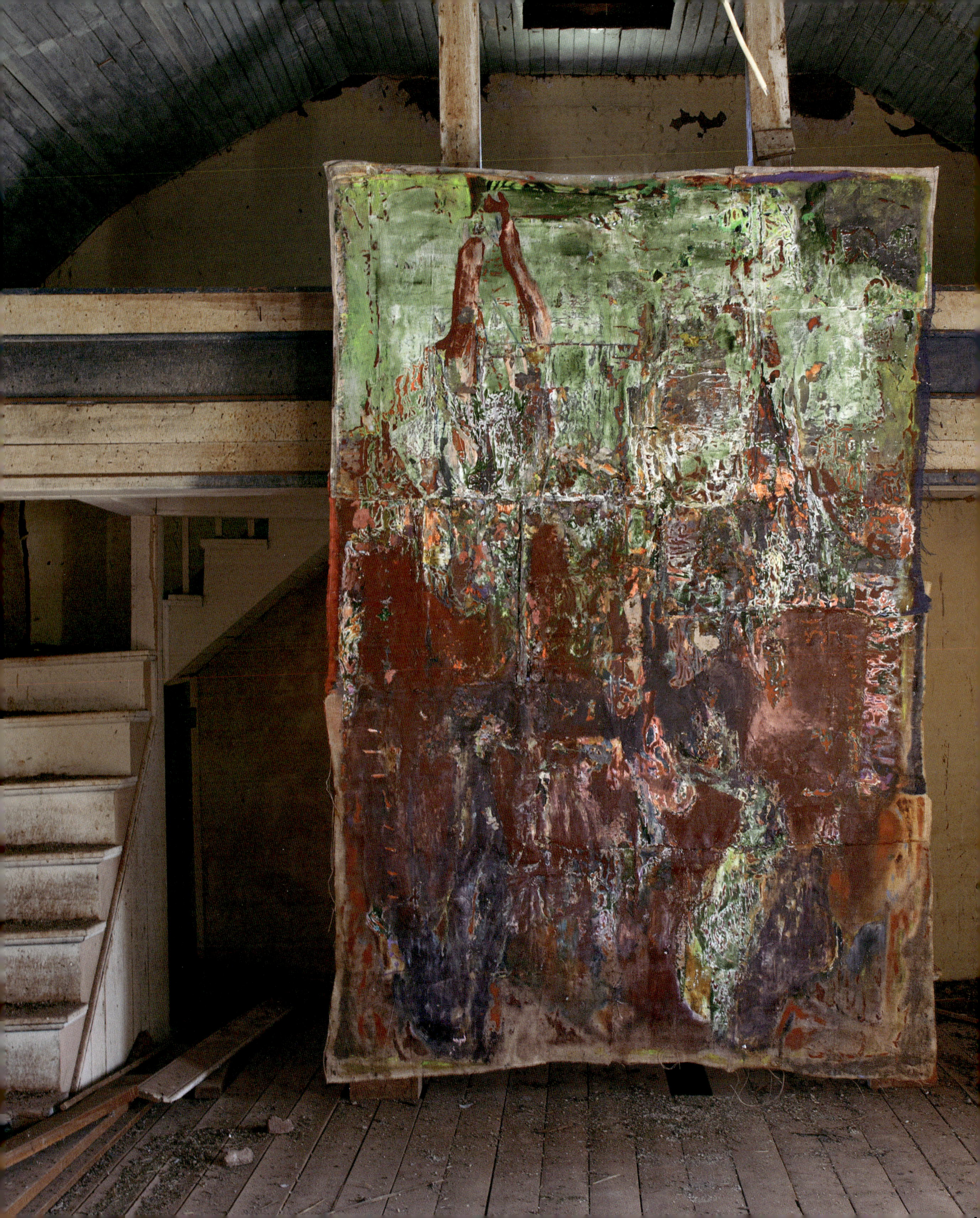

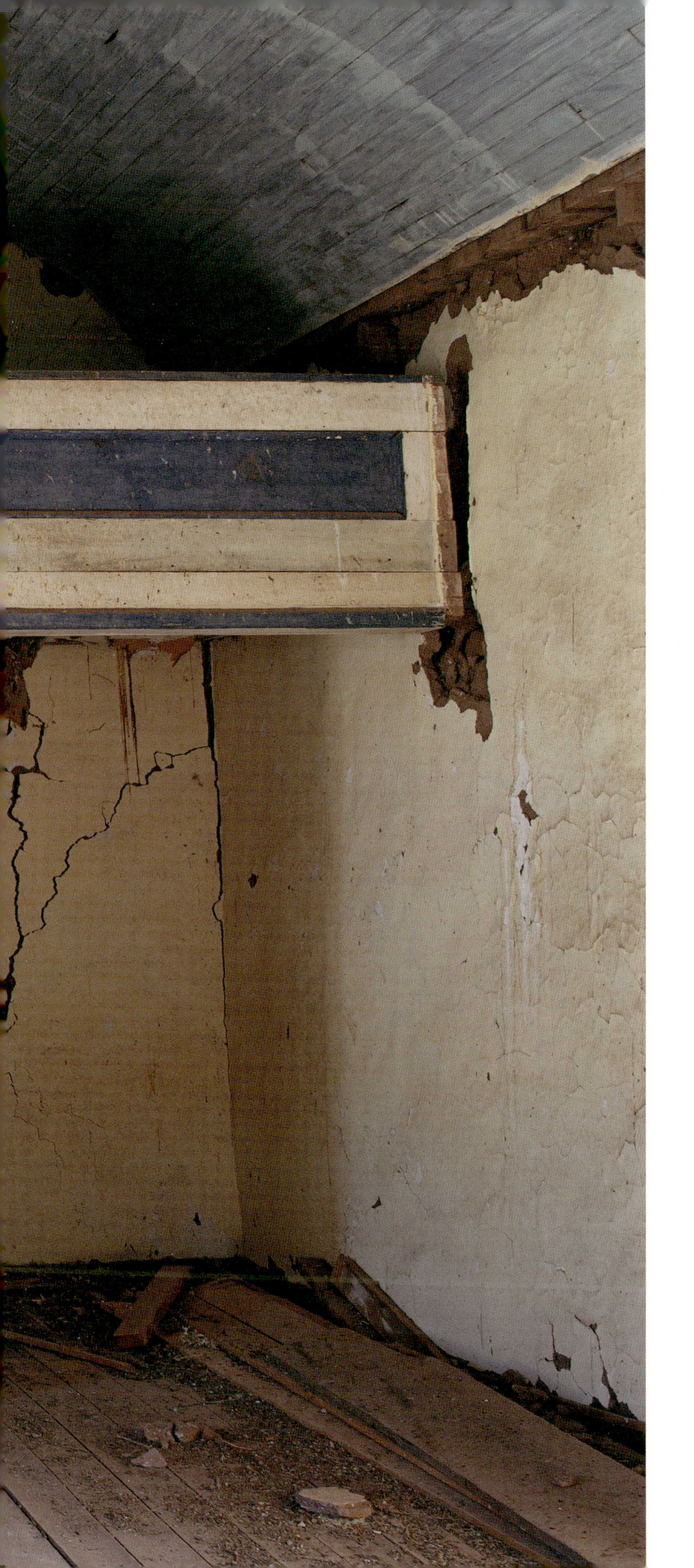

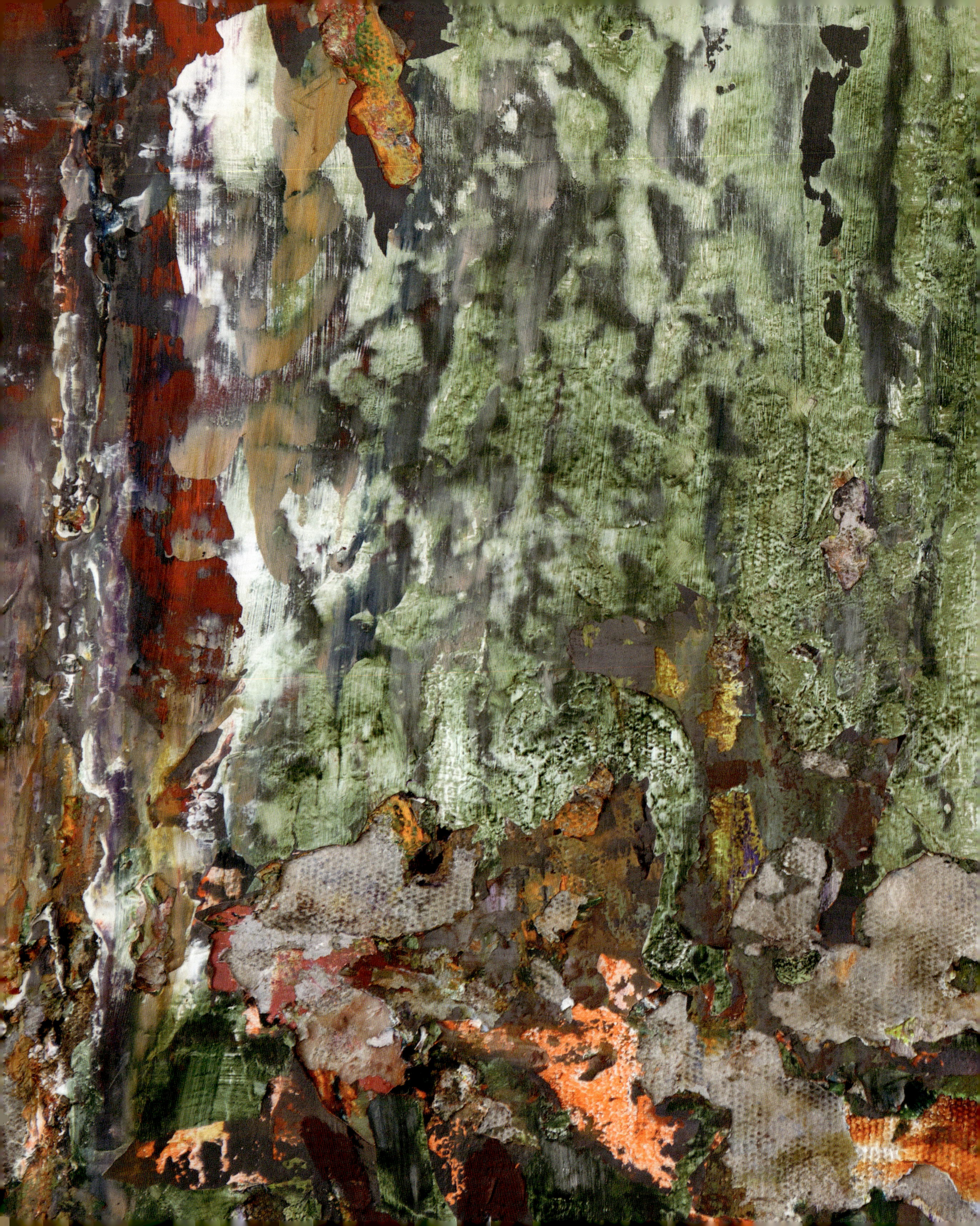

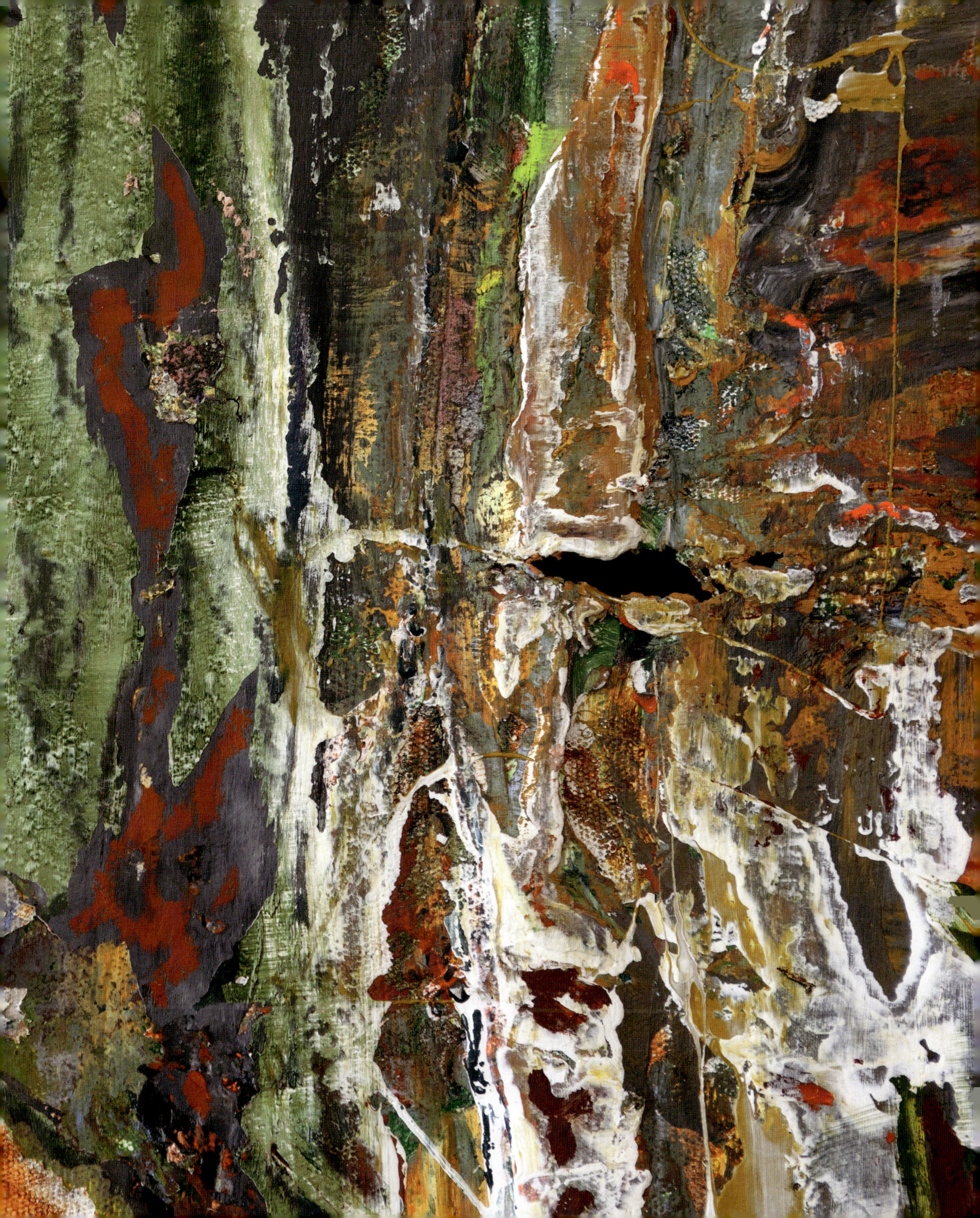

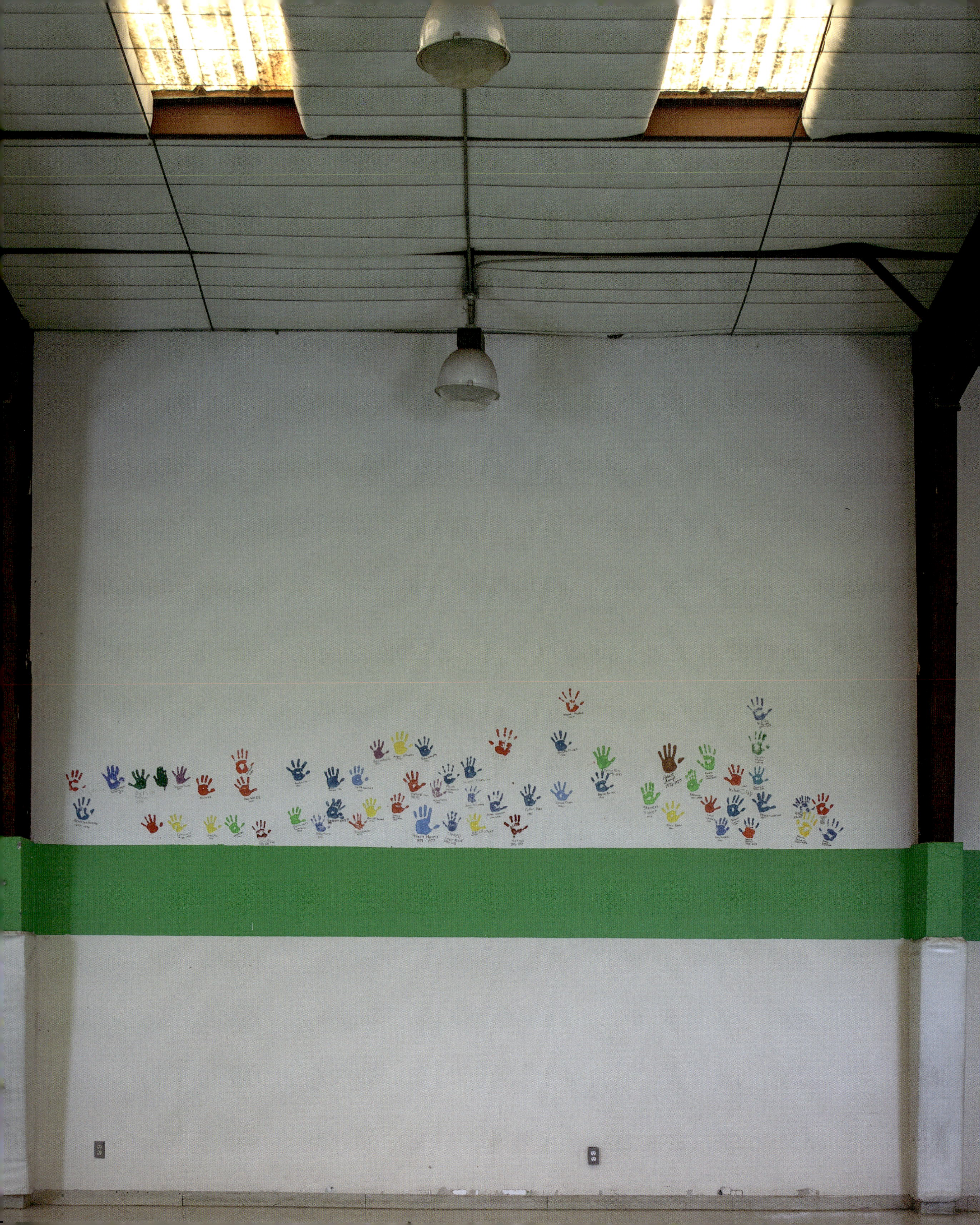

SAN ANTONIO SCHOOL

Sarah Was Ninety Years Old

One morning, when the snow was still in the mountains, I sat for meditation in a familiar area in the Sandia Mountain Wilderness, on the *Nihil* route. Before long, I heard a man's distant voice calling out for someone named Sarah. It became unthinkable to continue sitting, so I gathered my things and started down the hillside toward the voice. A little way down, I realized I had forgotten my phone and keys and turned back up the hill for them, retracing my footprints. By the time I reached them, his voice had stopped calling. I did not know what to do except sit down and wait to hear it again.

Only then did I realize I had forgotten my grandma's funeral, which was to be streamed for family members who could not be present. It would have been streaming for a while by now and if not already over, it would be soon. How strange that it was not the calling of her name that reminded me, but the silence after. Though everyone called her Sally, her birth name was Sarah. For days afterward, I searched online for missing persons in the area named Sarah, but nothing came up.

Soon after, I wanted to make something from that experience and decided to return to where I had been sitting to draw the scenery I was facing that day. I had, while in Idaho a few days earlier, made a drawing of my grandma while she slept. She died a couple days after that, shortly before her ninety-first birthday.

The absurd problem I faced was that she was not on the *Nihil* route. I decided that if I used the paper from the found Baptist instruction books that I had recovered from an abandoned bible school in Fort Sumner, I would allow myself to make a similar drawing from memory, without consulting the original. It was hard to do on that resistant surface, and her bed and pillows looked more like mountain peaks, which I decided was somehow appropriate.

From this and the mountain drawings, I layered and subtracted one image after another on the larger canvas. It was a difficult painting, and it sat unfinished for perhaps six months. When I finally went back to it, the sense of being in that place emerged on the canvas in front of me. This kind of presence is a rare occurrence. I can find my grandmother's image in it, and could point her out to a viewer, even as it probably appears to most as something akin, perhaps, to an abstract landscape. But her image remains in the painting.

I titled it *Sarah Was Ninety Years Old*, and it was the last completed of the four works that I installed in the gymnasium of the recently abandoned San Antonio Elementary School. The title, like many of my others, states a literal fact. But it is also the title of an Arvo Pärt composition, whose music was the catalyst for the entire *Nihil* schema. His title, in turn, references the Book of Genesis. In it, Sarah, at ninety, gives birth to Isaac. If the idea has meaning for me, it is simply in the way that decay and growth are part of one process, and perhaps also this: that the more we trust in that mystery, the more it offers of itself. This is something I witness on a daily basis walking through the mountains as well as in the work that I do.

Four Paintings in a Gym

Often I have commented on the reliability of the synchronous spaces for which I make *Nihil* paintings, and on how, often, it feels as if the work returns to where it began. Nowhere is this more evident than the recently abandoned San Antonio School's gymnasium in which four highly spectral anthropomorphic paintings—a rabbit figure astride a headless horse, a dog lying before a portal, a cross-legged figure with two left arms and two left legs, and a wilderness image in the outline of an old woman—are displayed on walls proliferated by handprints, those of multiple generations of the school's students and teachers.

I think it impossible as an art history lover not to see the ancient hand stencils found in caves and on rocks around the world at the very same time one stands on this basketball court. The hands on the gym walls mark time and murmur in unison from the past, just as the handprints in the caves do. One has the sense of standing in the midst of some primordial space superimposed on this one, standing somehow in all times and in all spaces. I am filled with a deep optimism that as much as things change, as much as we gain and lose along the way, the human instinct has not changed so much that we have lost our deepest capacity for connectedness within ourselves. What I see now is an echo of what we were then. I feel so alone and yet in profound relatedness to the long and short history of human life.

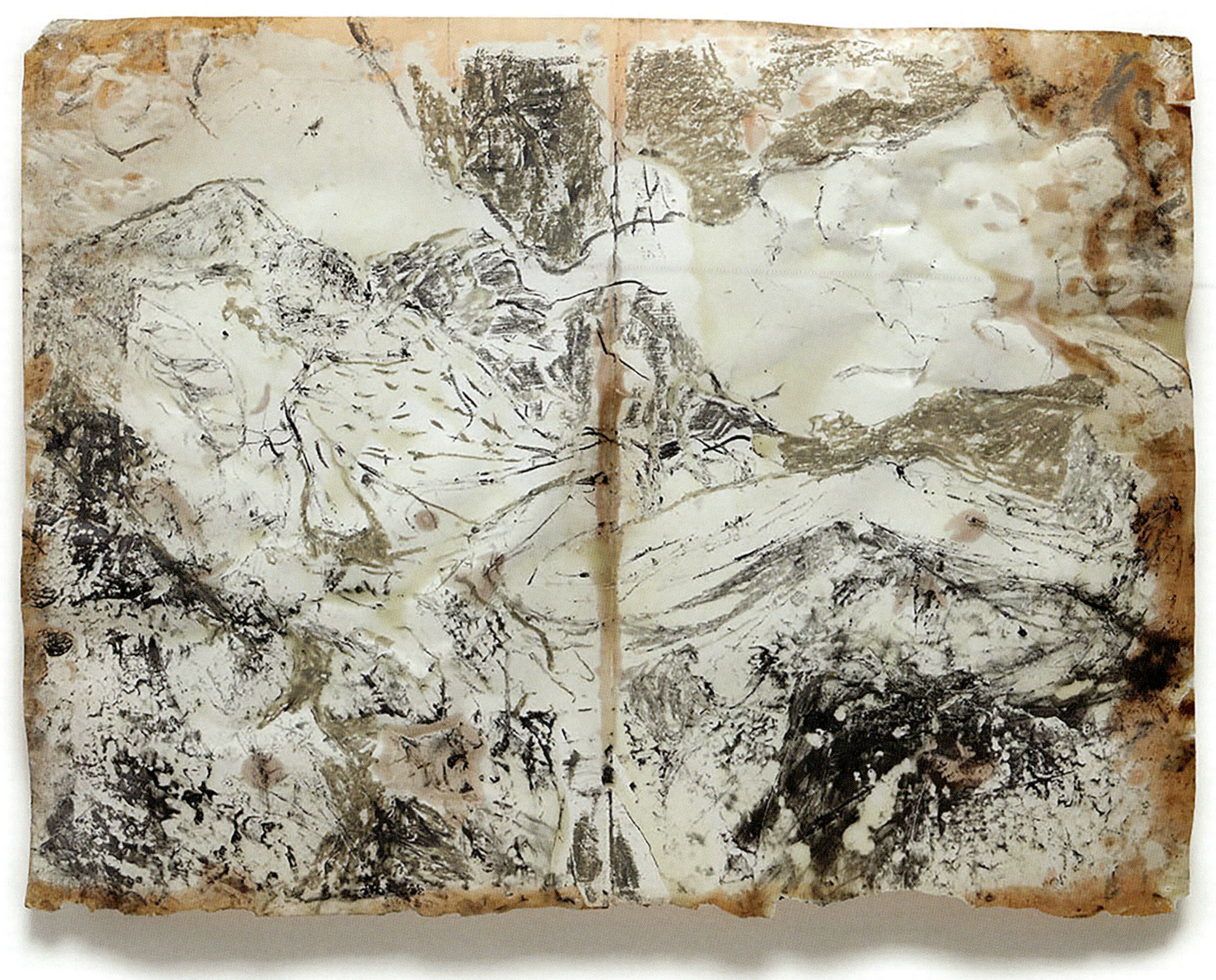

SARAH WAS NINETY YEARS OLD, GRAPHITE, CHARCOAL, OIL PASTEL, AND WAX ON FOUND BIBLE STUDY WORKBOOK PAGE, ABOUT 14 × 18 IN., ABOUT 1980–2023

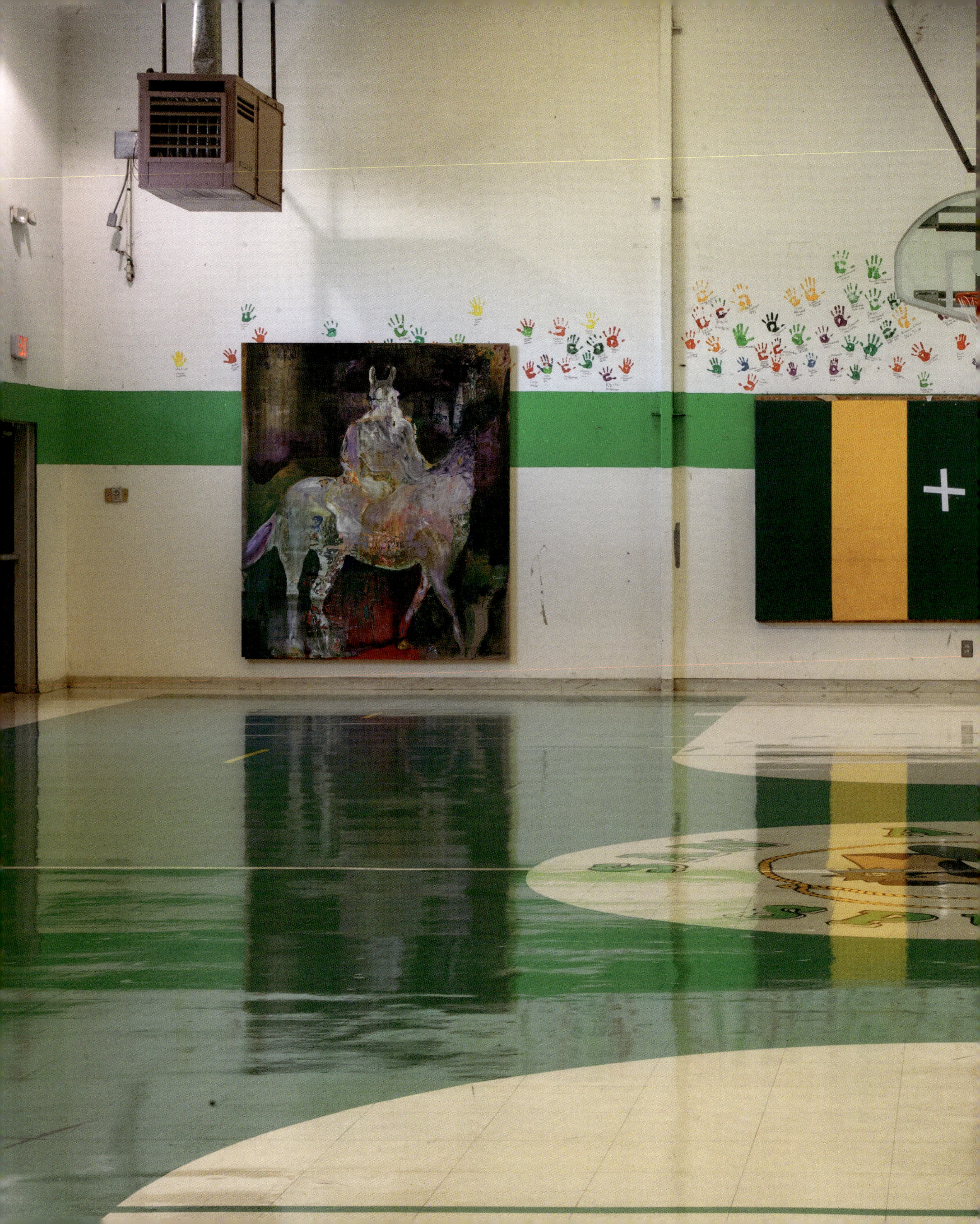

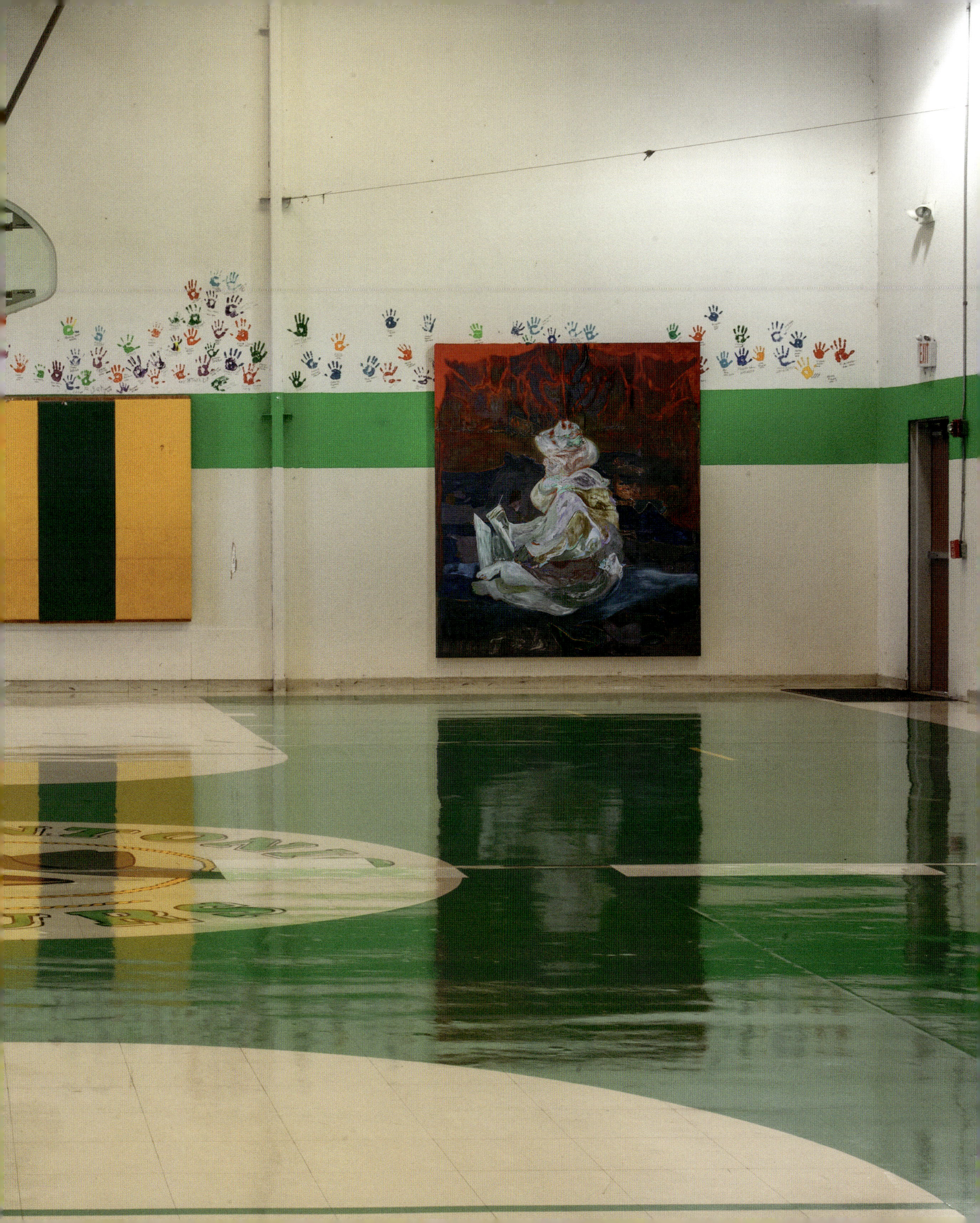

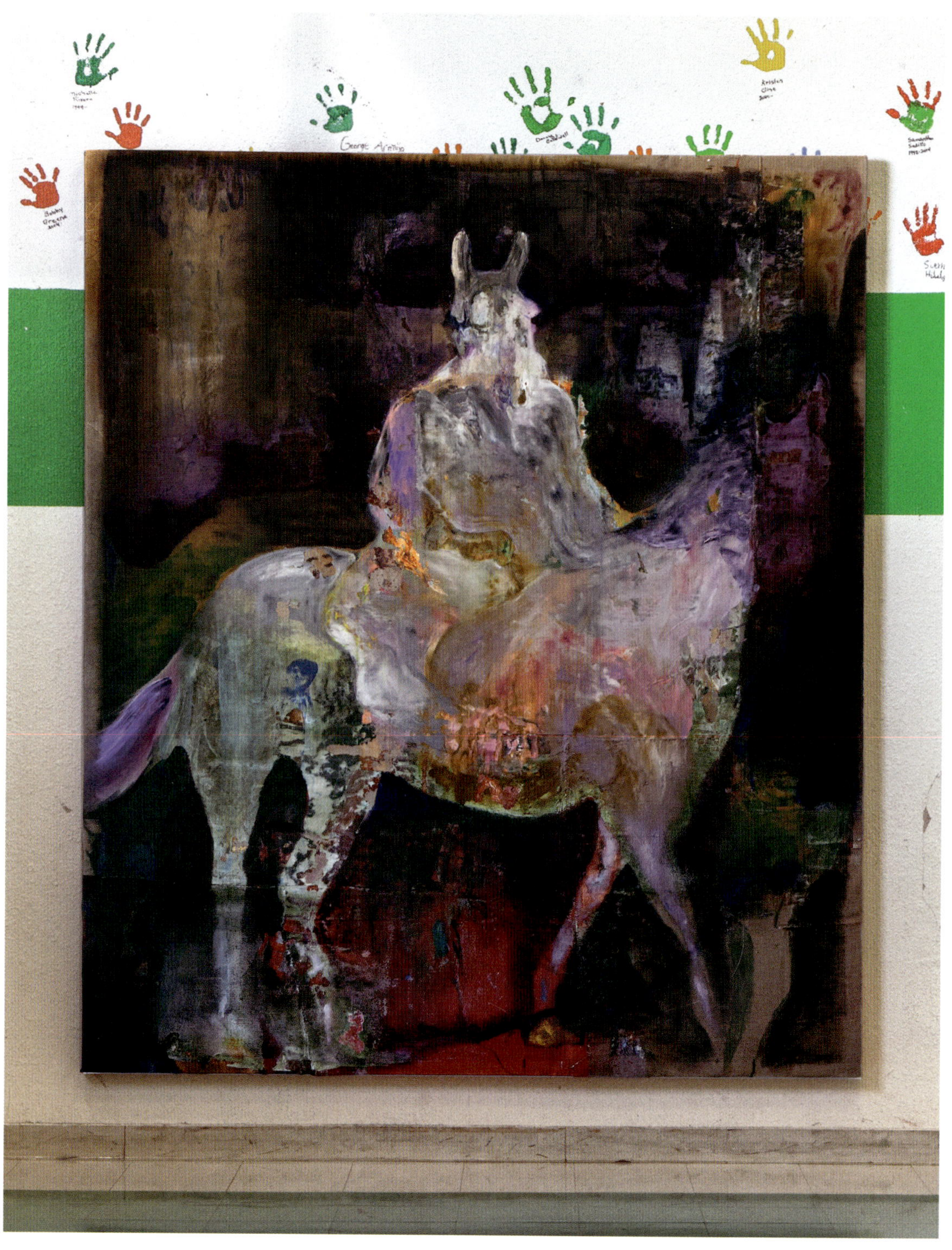

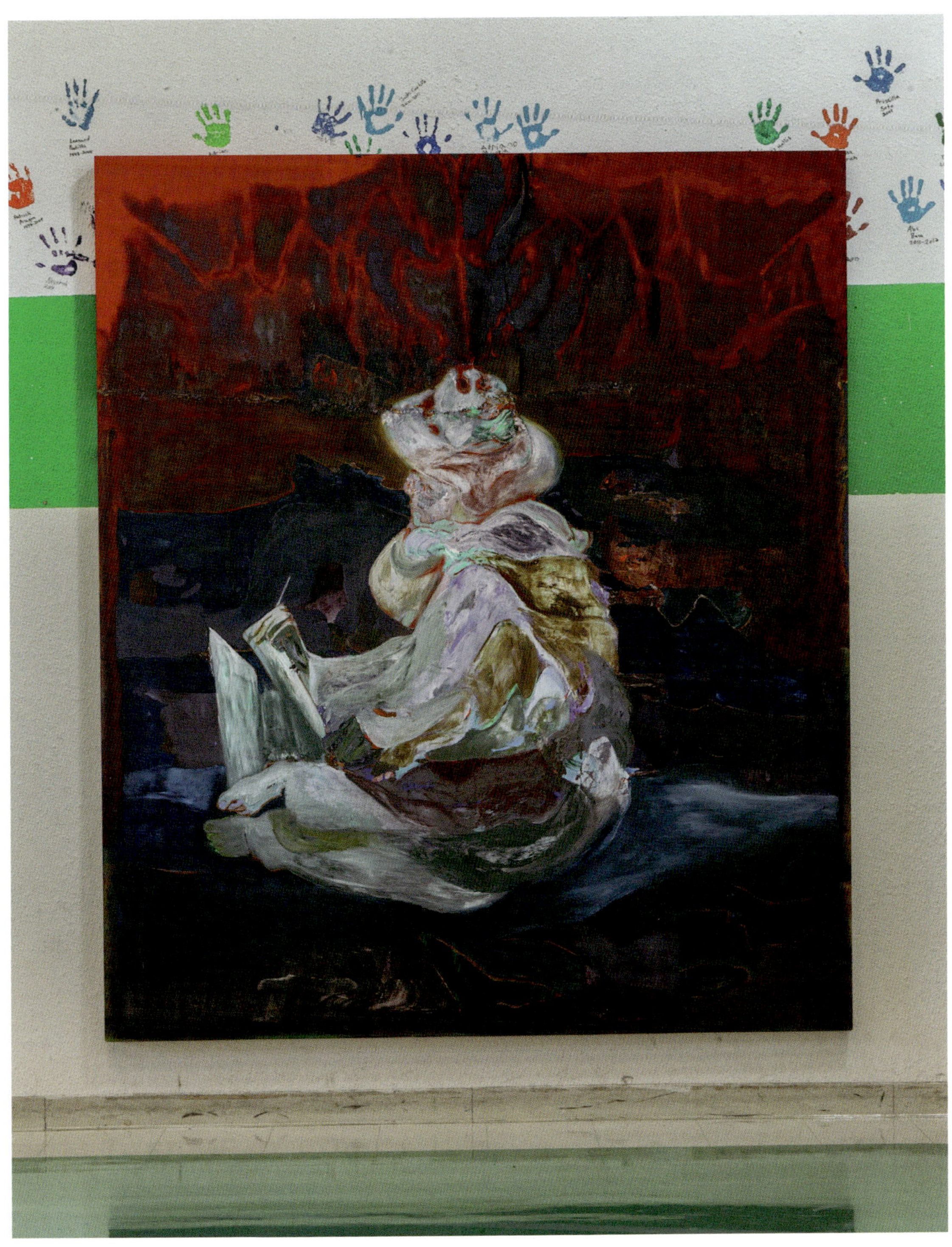

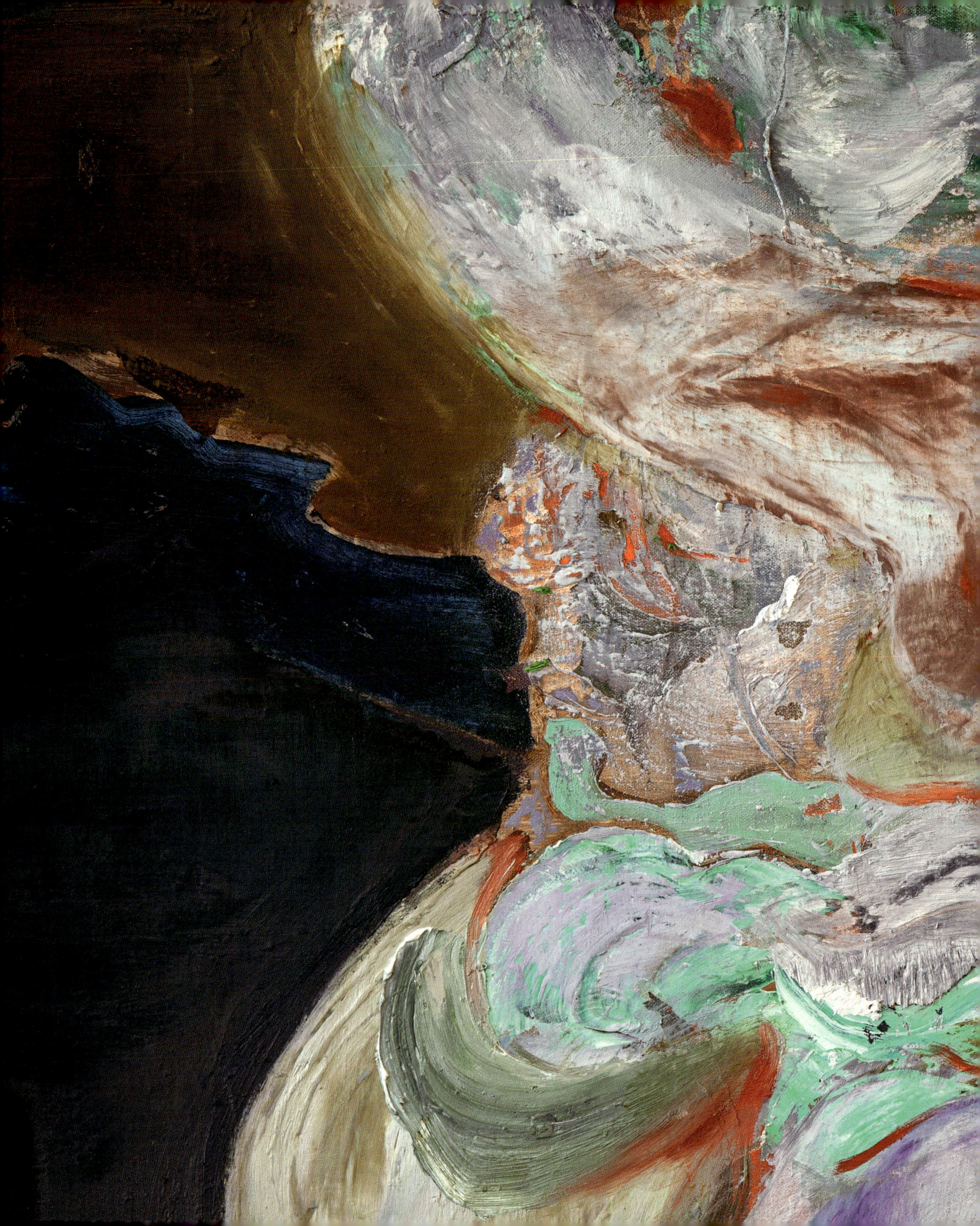

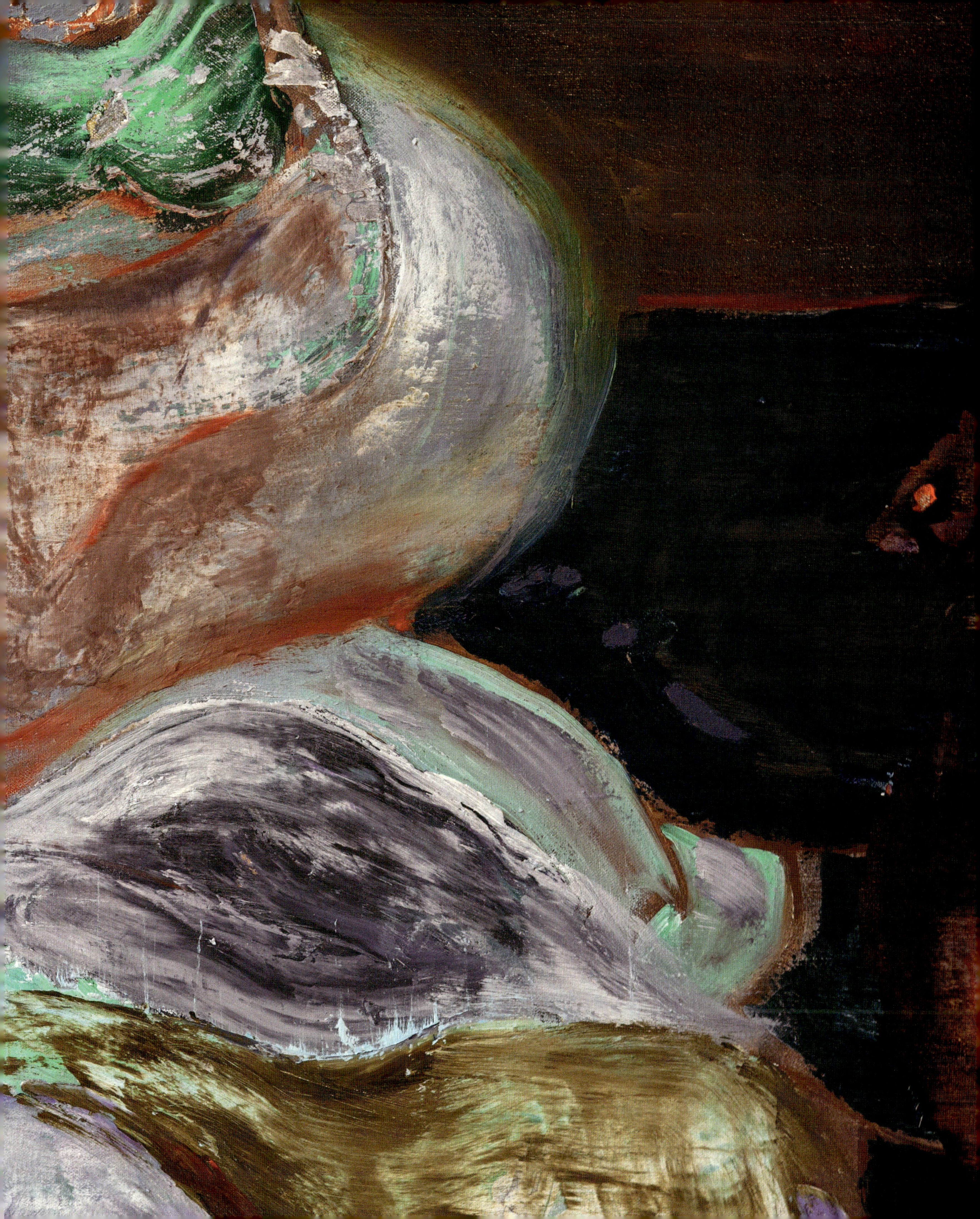

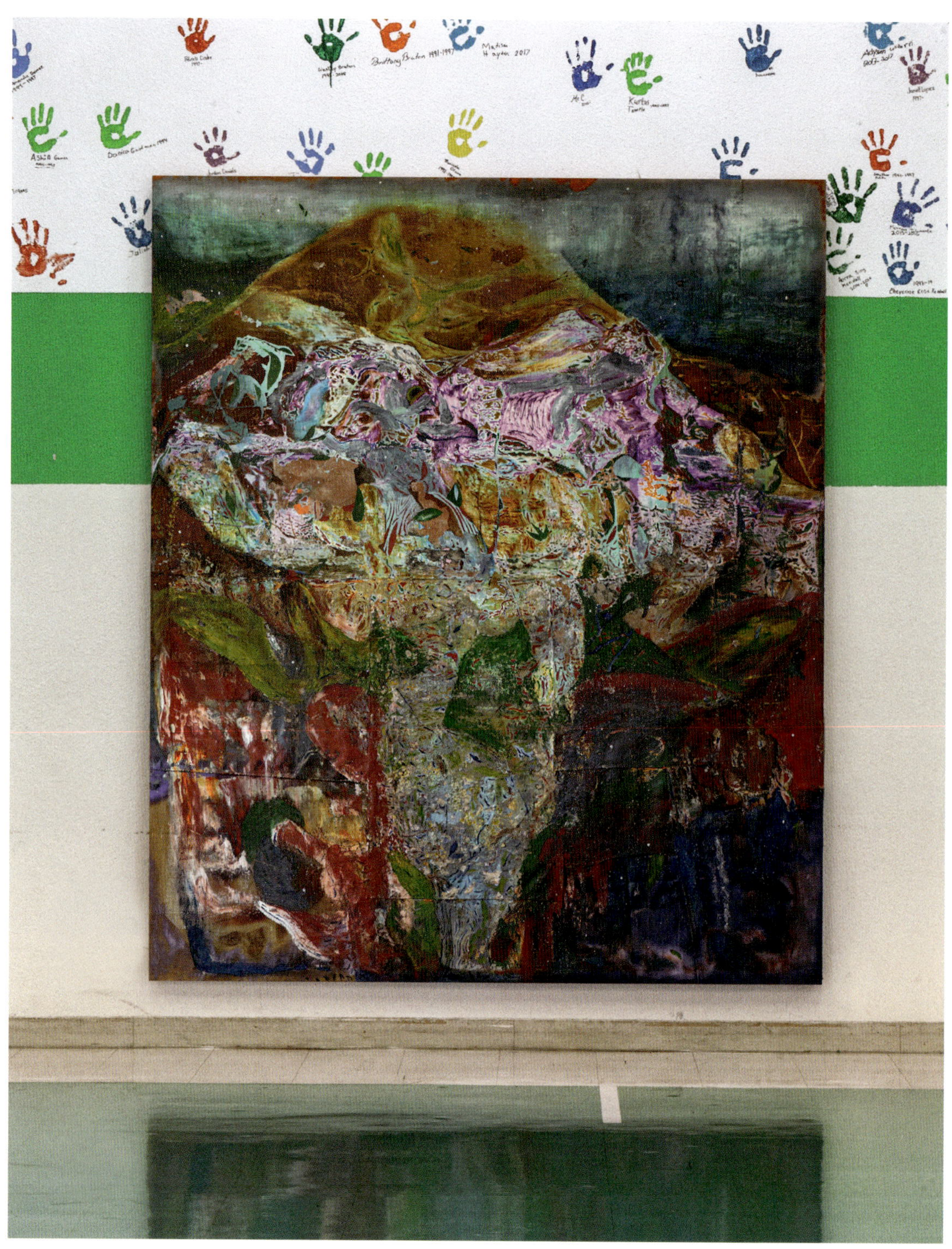

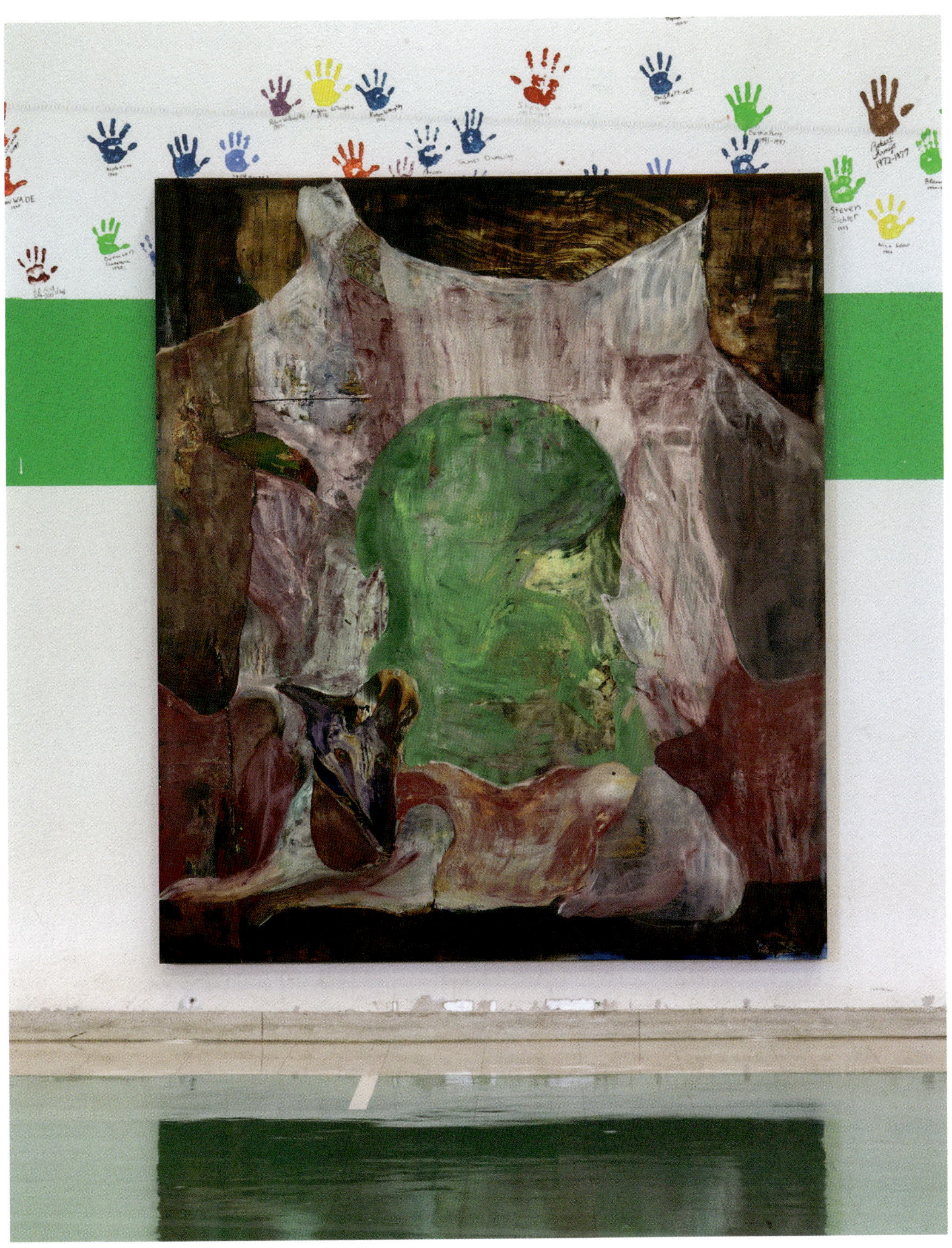

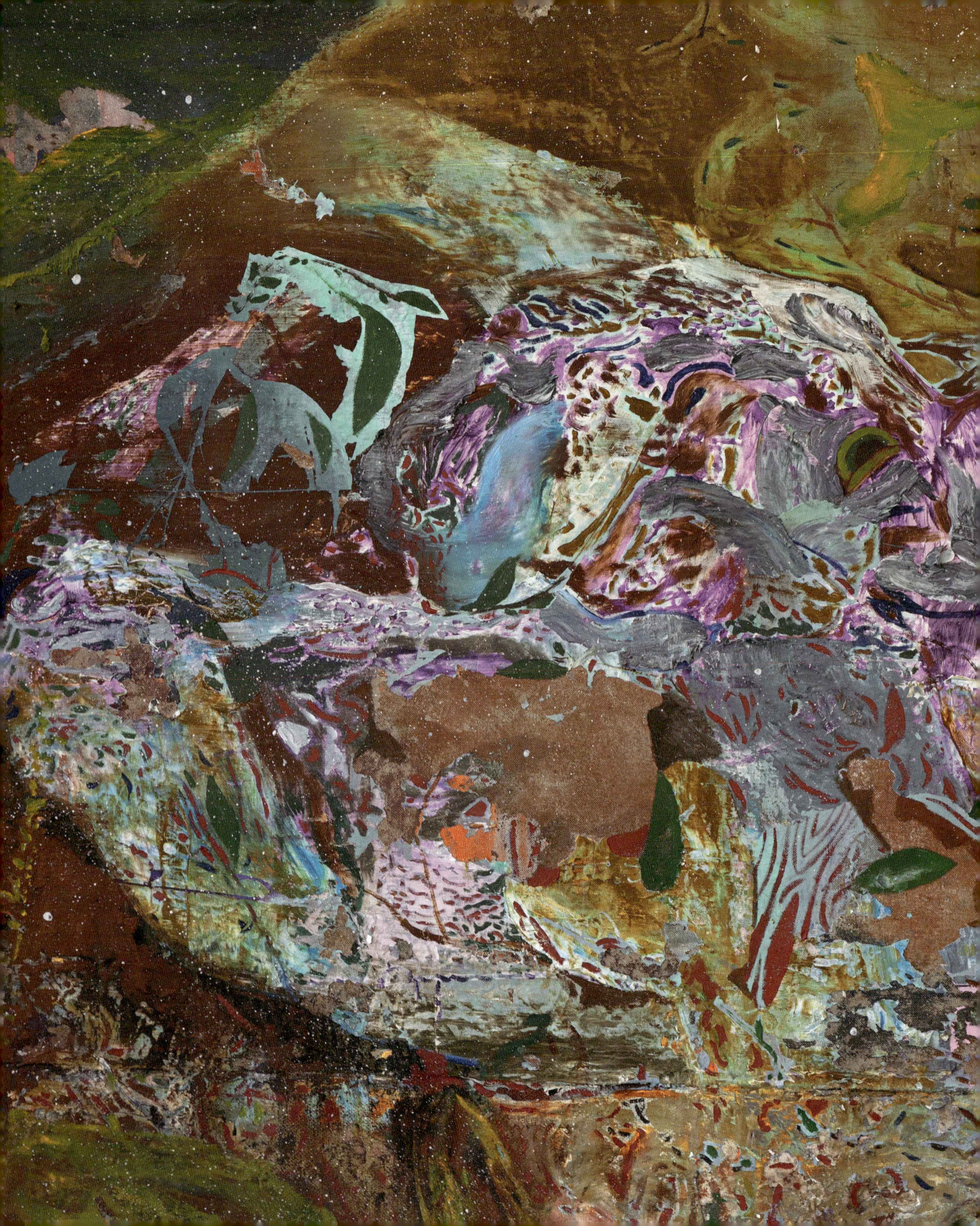

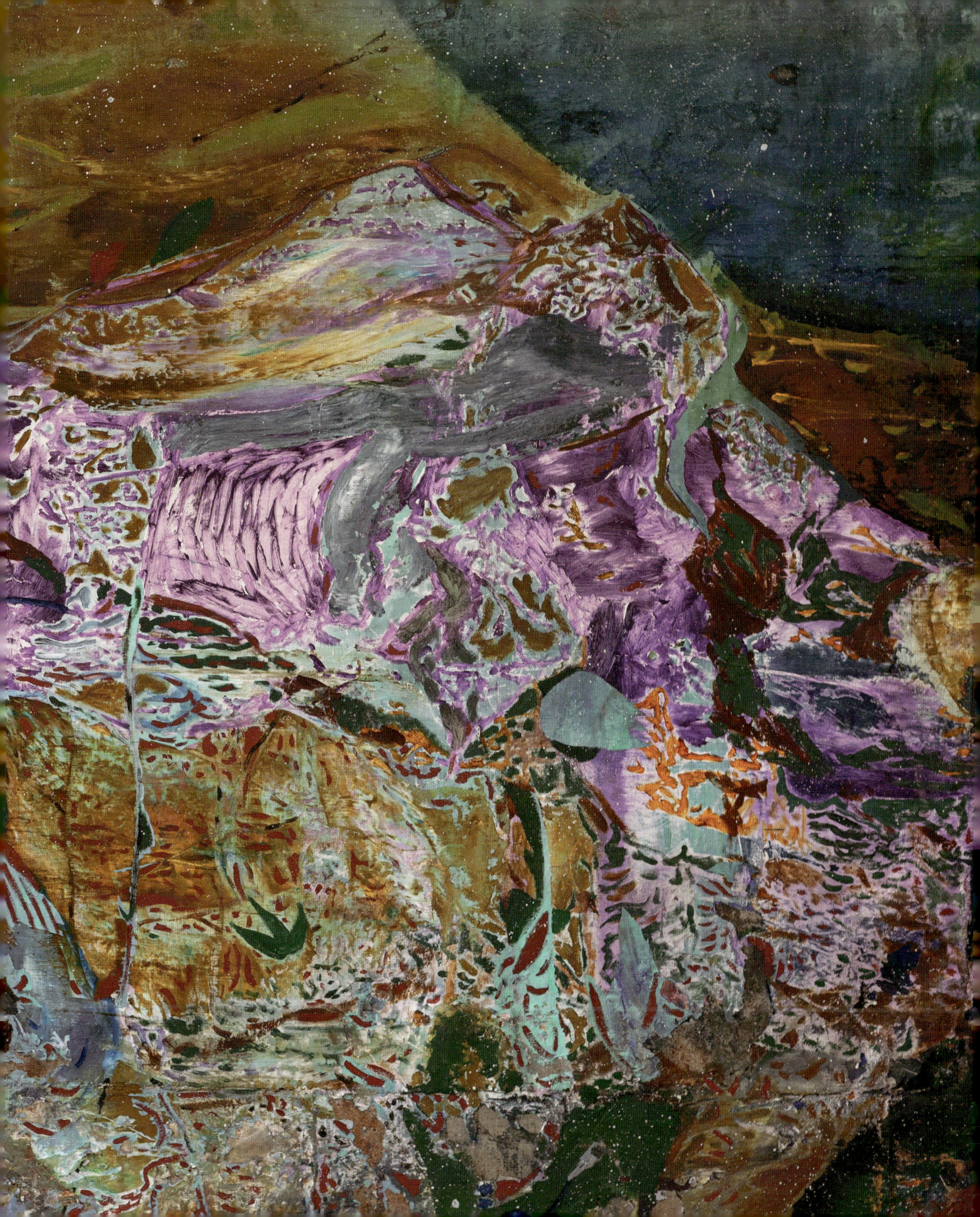

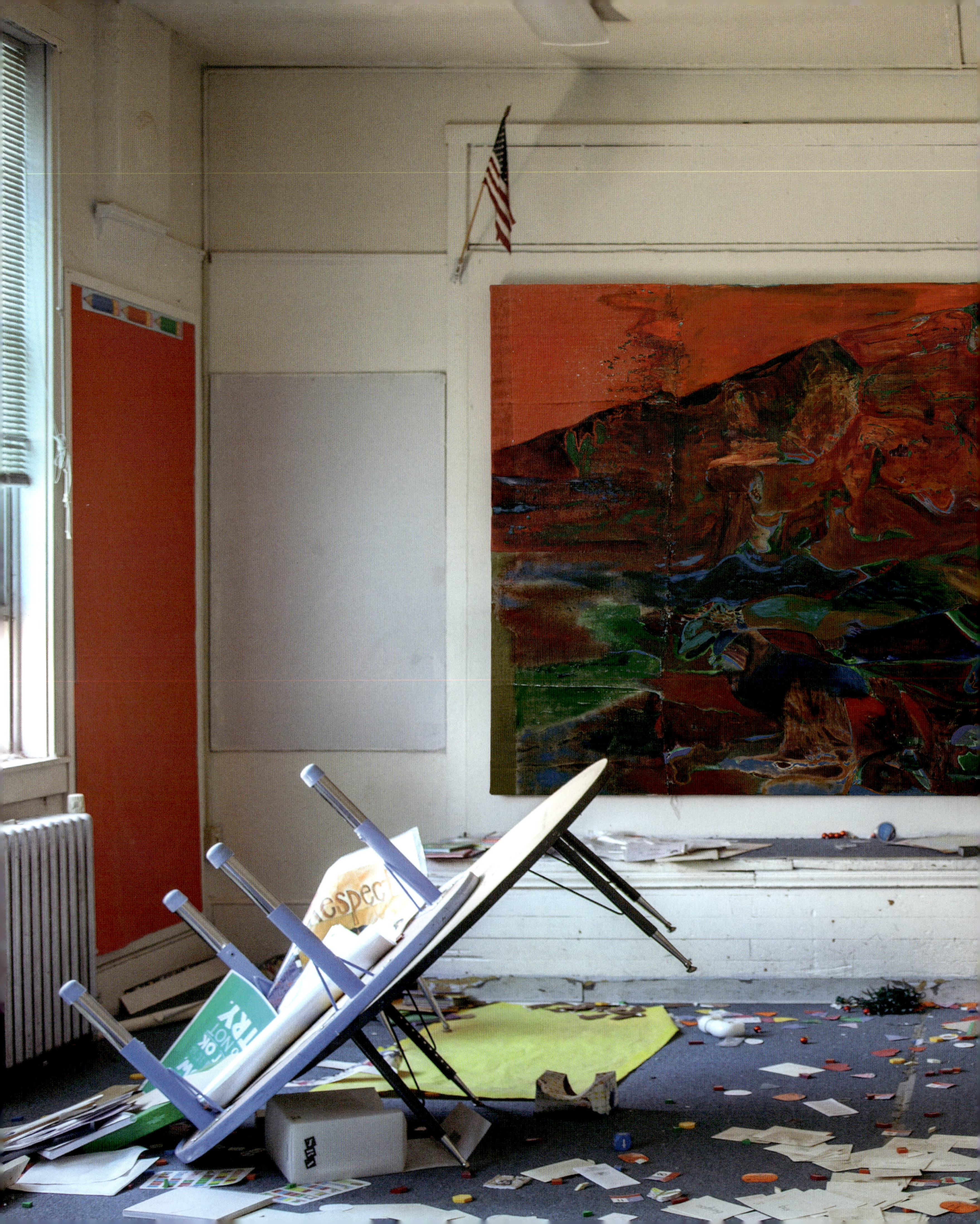

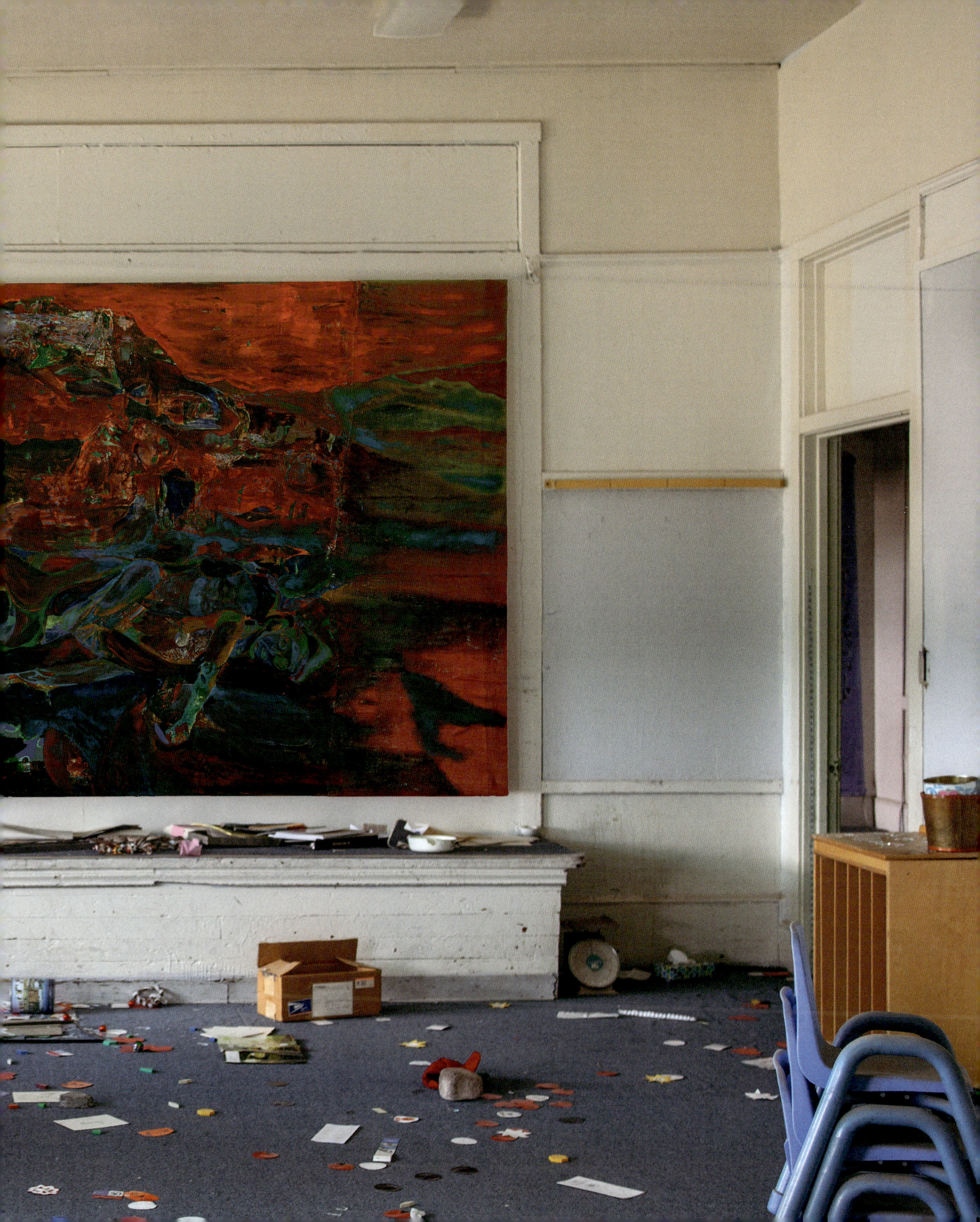

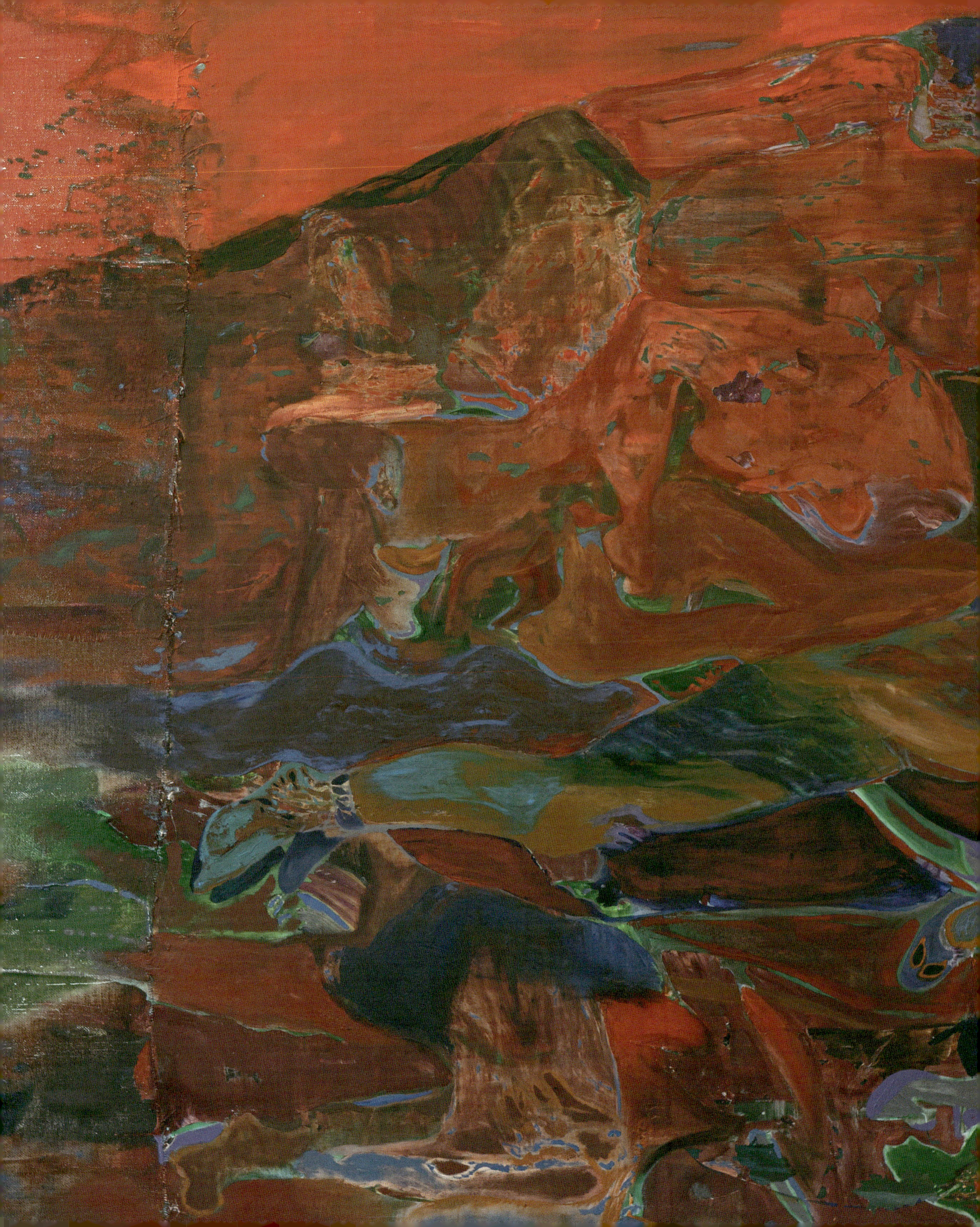

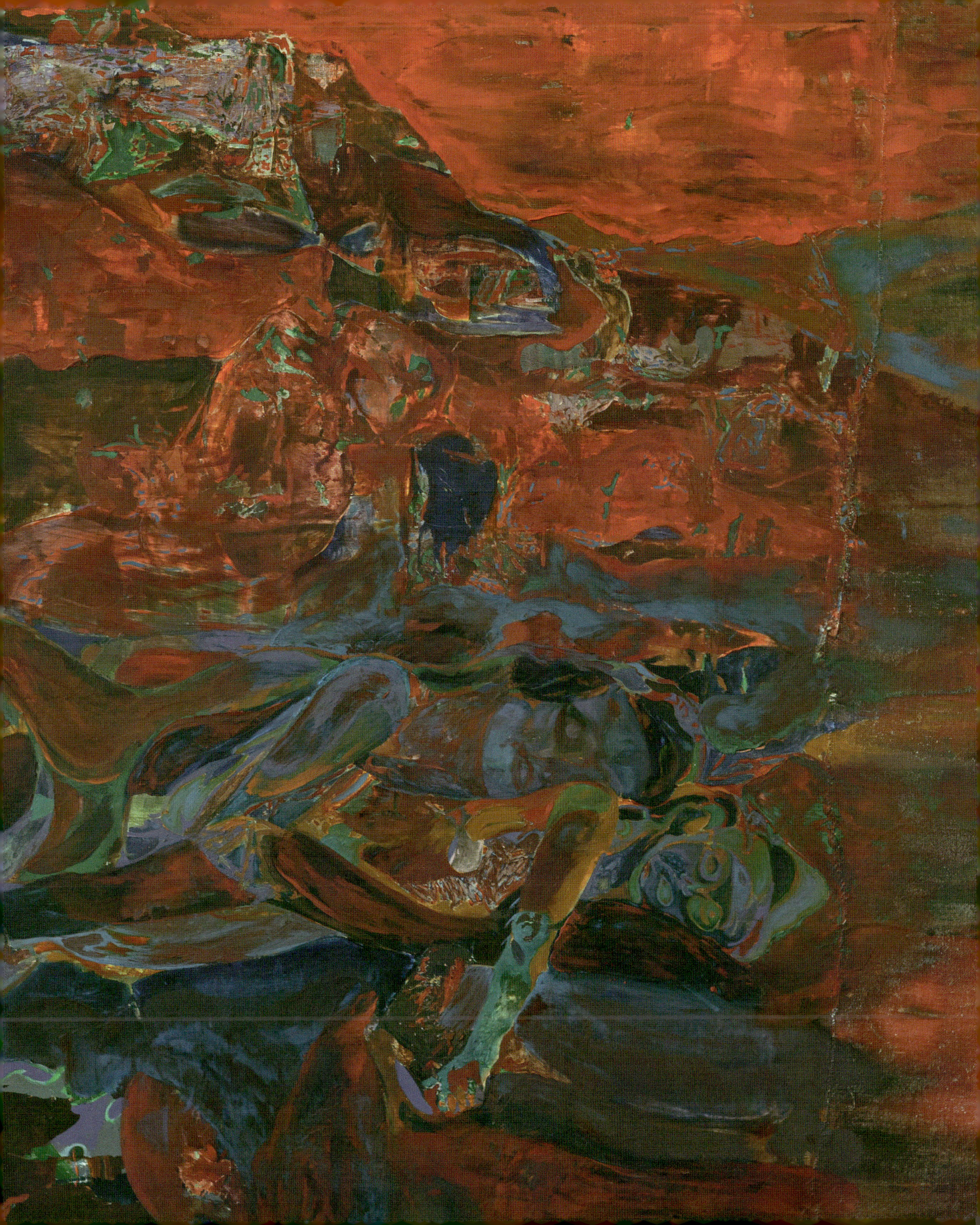

Image (*Faithful Iconoclasm*)

In *Nihil*, the image matters, but not to the painting. Whether or not the finished painting seems to hold a recognizable image is not among the considerations for deciding whether it is finished. The image marks a place to begin a process, and whether the accumulation and deterioration of the many images that come and go over the course of a painting manages to retain easy legibility is, in the end, a matter more of chance than design. The image is meant neither to convey any particular narrative nor to be categorically different from a so-called abstract painting. The painting acquires its subject through the accumulation of touches that occurs in working through images.

The value of the image, in *Nihil*, is that it dictates, to a large degree, the psychological quality of my intentions. If, for example, I make a drawing or portrait of someone I know, I think of this person in a certain way. I should always choose to draw someone I am curious about and for whom I experience genuine compassion. To draw this person is to say I choose her. The same is true about anything else I might draw: a place or animal, let's say.

Sometimes the image I draw might come from something I find printed on paper, a photograph or illustration, left behind in an abandoned building or even in a shop I find on the *Nihil* route. Perhaps it is not the picture itself I focus my intention on when I draw it, but the who, when, or what it puts me in mind of.

All that is important in my treatment of the image is that my intention is directed toward the life of the consciousness it stands for. *Nihil* works on the assumption that intention directed in this way leaves its traces on the object itself. The image is a useful field for the accumulation of intentionality and its trace. The painting is no more a narrative about the surviving imagery than it is about the buried or eviscerated image the viewer never sees.

I hear the poet Frank X. Gaspar:

"I wanted to stand in the presence of the real thing and feel it—it's never the aboutness of anything but the wailing underneath it…"[1]

1 "Late Rapturous" in the collection *Late Rapturous*, Autumn House Press, 2012.

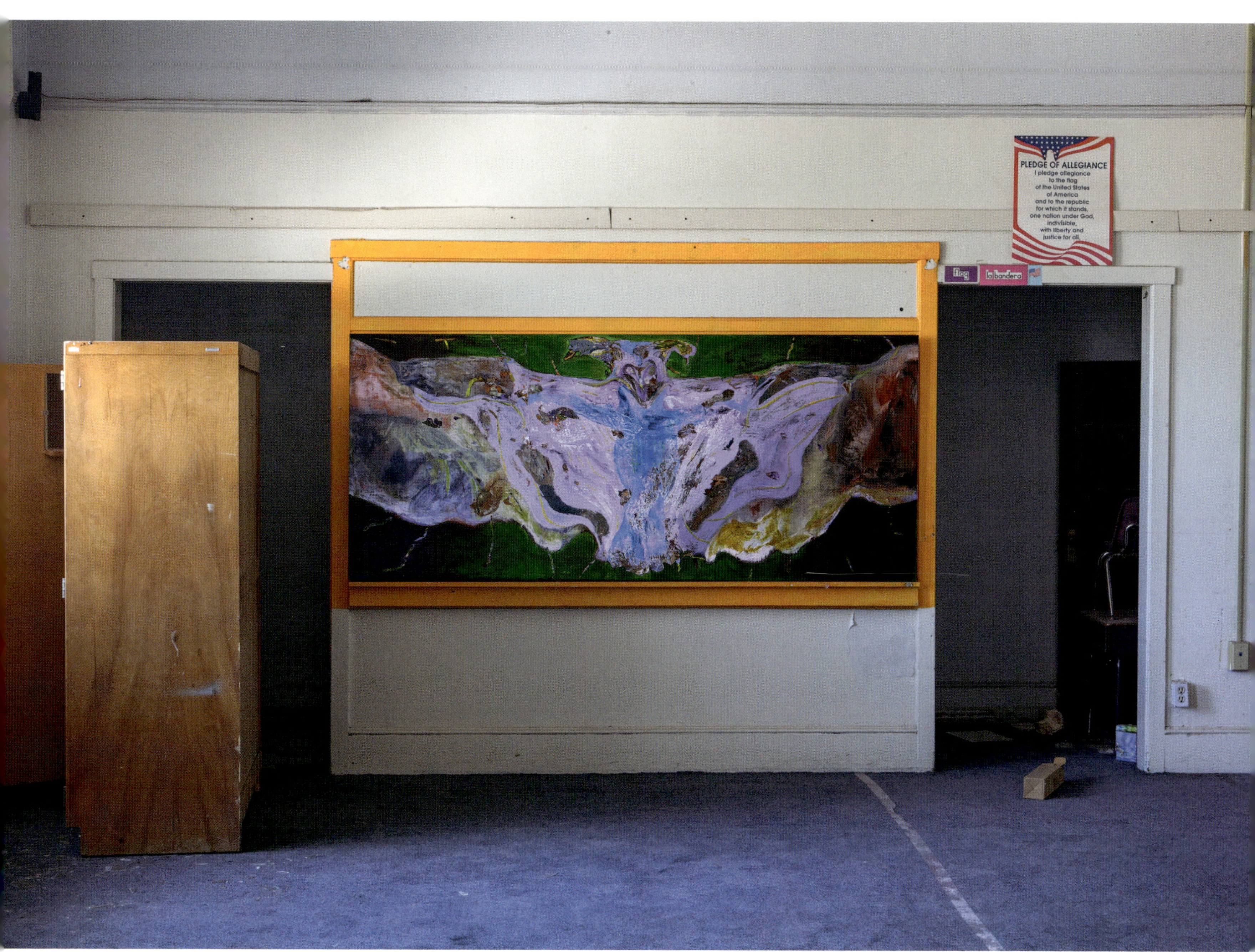
PLEDGE OF ALLEGIANCE
I pledge allegiance
to the flag
of the United States
of America
and to the republic
for which it stands,
one nation under God,
indivisible,
with liberty and
justice for all.
flag
la bandera

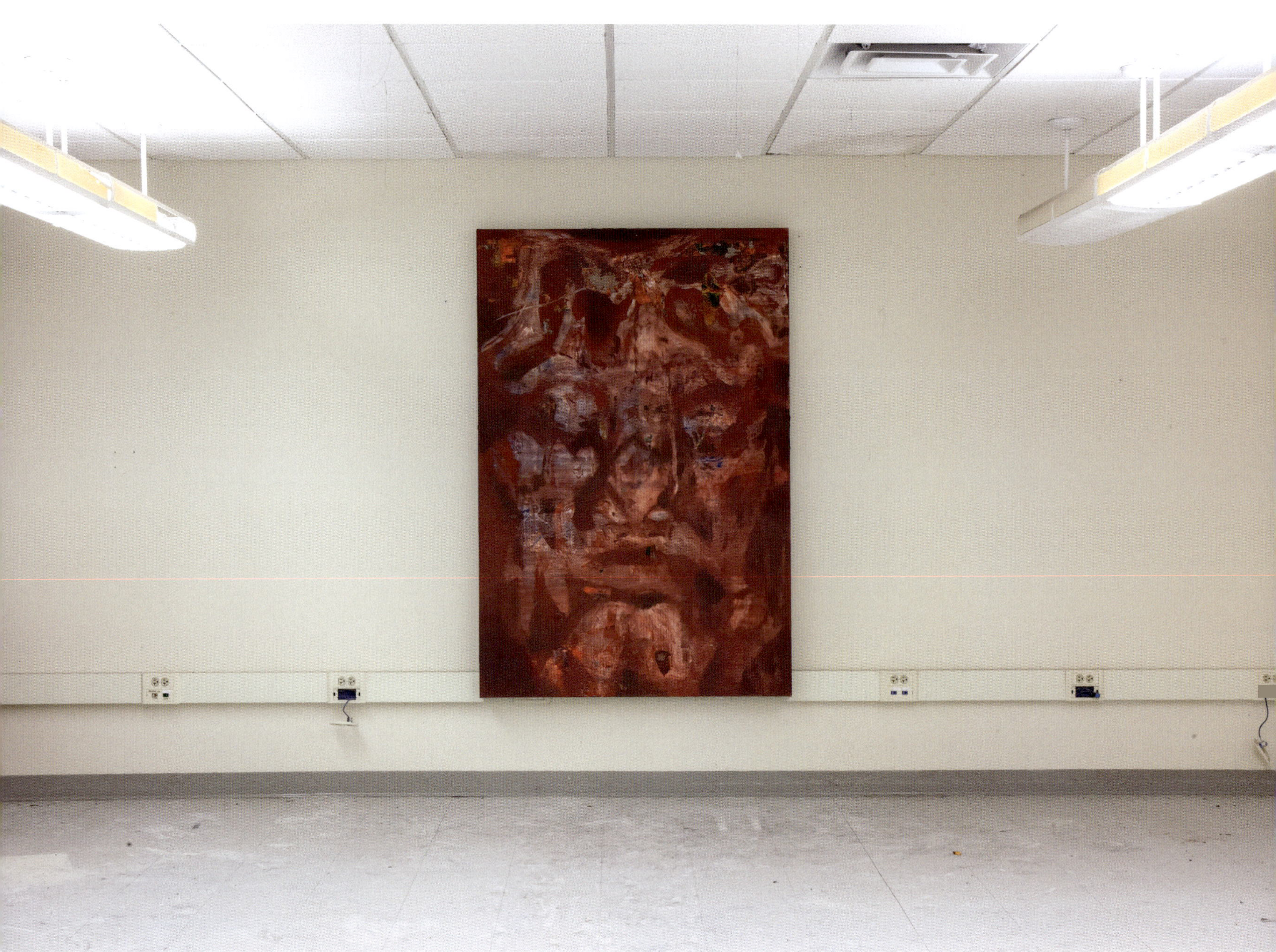

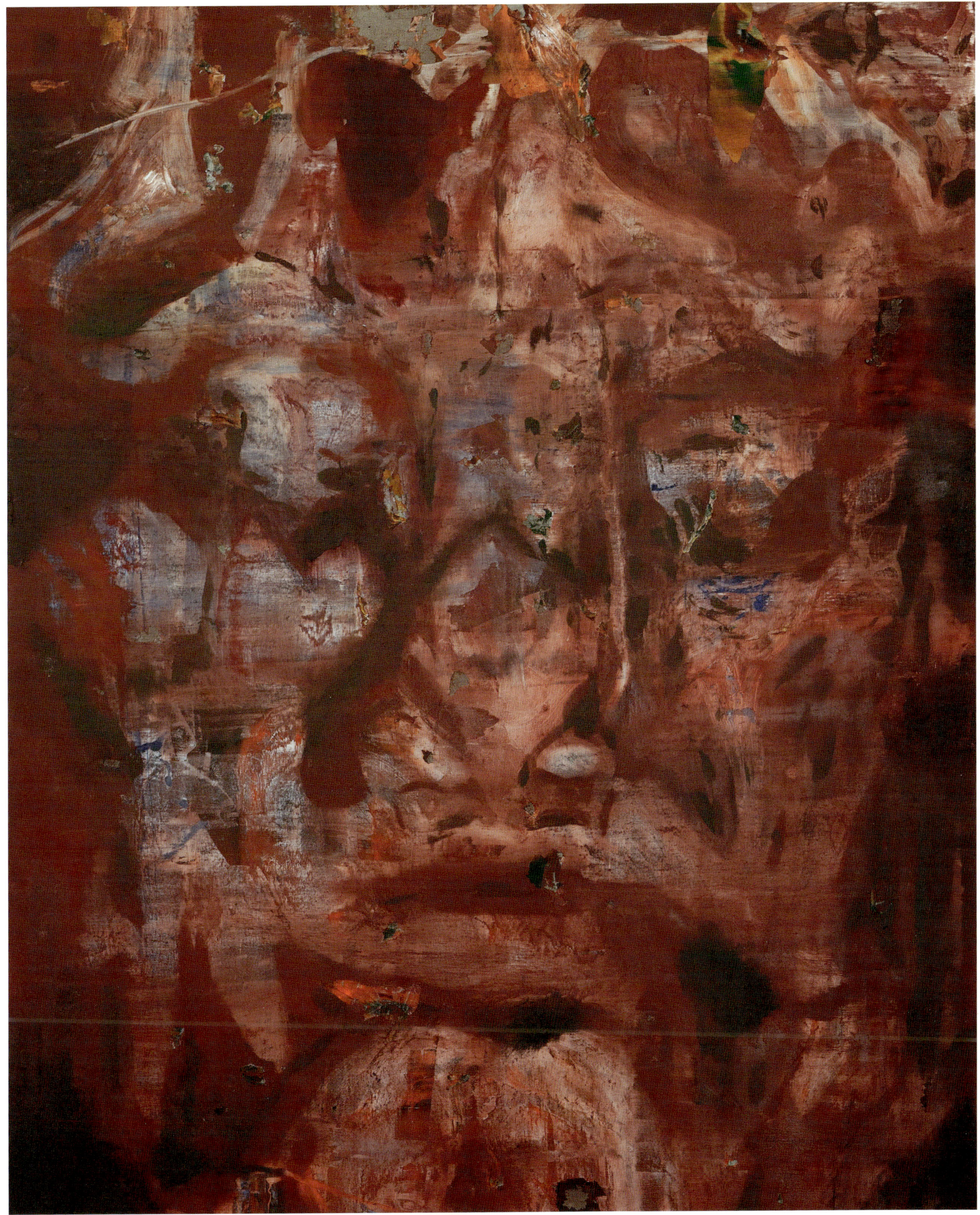

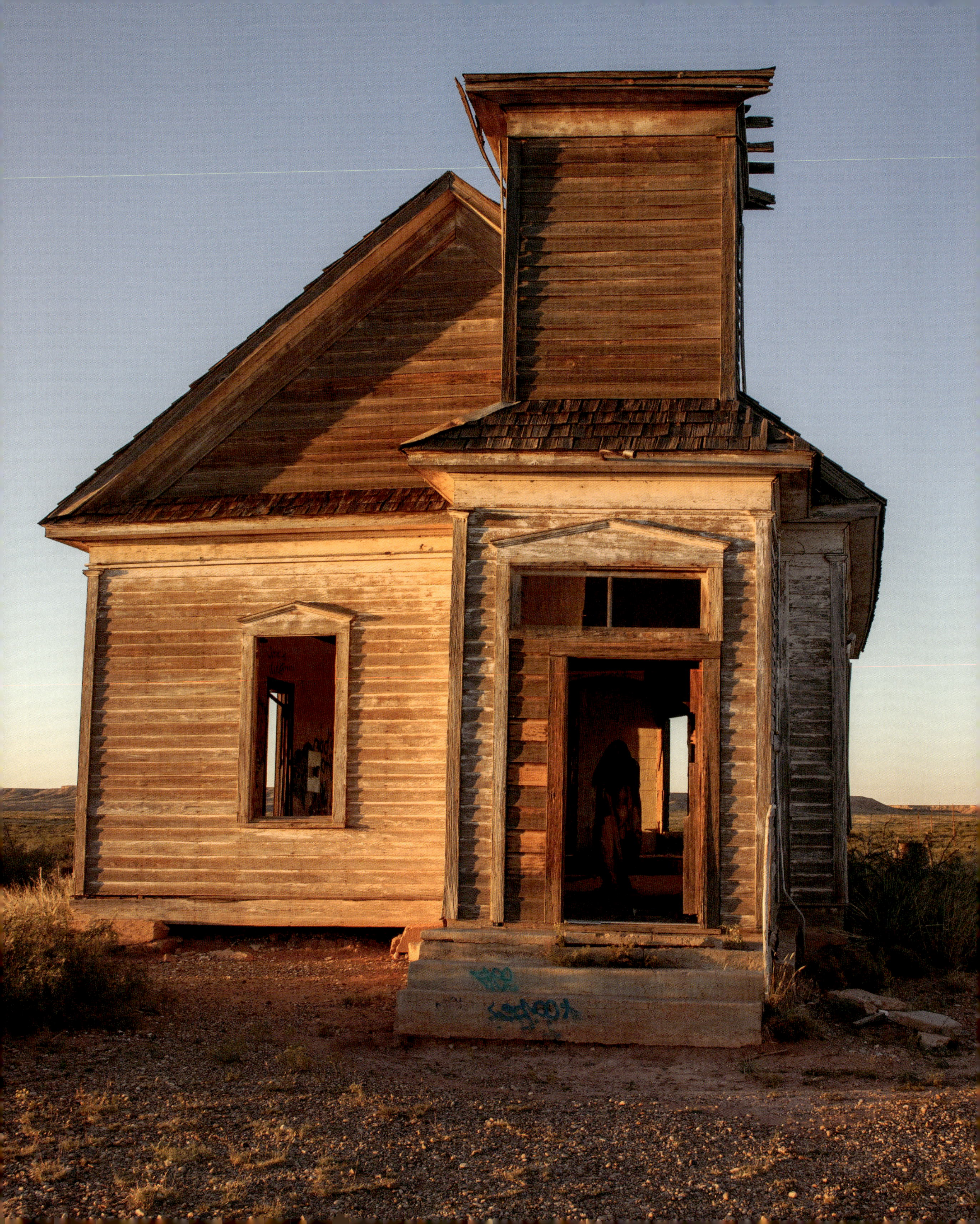

TAIBAN CHURCH

Autumn Pilgrimage

Just off Highway 60, in the desolate eastern plains of New Mexico, is the ghost town of Taiban, which happens to lie on the lower-right branch of the tree-shaped *Nihil* route. I have visited the church about once a year since first discovering it, and in that time have witnessed a total revolution of its interior graffiti. The church is not alone but, rather, bustling with unseen visitors.

To be in almost any abandoned church is to be inside something that feels very much like an individual mind. It contains a residue of the sacred but is largely neglected and unnoticed. The tagging one finds in the interior is alternately hopeful, desperate, loving, hateful, fearful, urgent, crass, horny, juvenile, cryptic, sentimental, empathetic, and hostile. Each of these tags seems like a fleeting whisper, a passing thought, like any ordinary person experiences on a daily basis, whether or not we take care to notice. The words and images engage the architecture of the Church-as-Mind, in a kind of transubstantiation of loss into yearning. Just as the tagging does this within architectural ruins, so do my figures and drawings within the ruins of Psyche.

A desire to create is made a desire to resurrect.

...

In *Autumn Pilgrimage* it had been my intention to make two figures: an adult male and a child. That a second adult figure should appear on the floor was simply the chance result of the process. When the first figure could not support its own weight, I thought to cast a second as a counterbalance that could be fastened to the first, and, by combining the two halves, would freely stand in the round.

The result was clunky, the poetry lost. It became clear that the figure's pathos was in its ephemerality, which is to do with the translucent, lightweight horsehide itself. I had only meant to move the second figure out of the way in my studio when I saw, as if for the first time, its form as it was seemingly meant to be seen, lying on the floor. By chance, two figures became three and now formed a straight line: the adult figure approached the child, who approached the prone figure.

If, in the original vision, I was following my brother or daughter, now they were following another version of me, asleep, or, perhaps, already long gone. The unexpected formation opened up a new field of imaginal encounter. The past and future came out to play. This, I had to acknowledge, was perhaps an elaborate form of self-portraiture. For if I can understand that my life is not only my own, but also the partial sum of others who come and go within my own life, who precede and proceed from me, then so am I to their lives. I exist because they do. They exist because I do.

...

Since childhood, I have feared my own disappearance, a fear I think slightly different from a fear of death, or at least an eccentric form of it. Sometimes, it feels as if I have never existed in the first place, like a ghost trying to remember the life it might once have led. Was I not going somewhere? Was something not supposed to have happened?

I have written plenty about the Archaic Brother as a personal archetype, encompassing the process by which exile and absence are given form. I have written about it as the first tenet of *Nihil* and as the childhood loss of my youngest brother from which the archetype derives much of its original meaning. I have written about how, though he would be 38 now, he, in my mind's eye, grows and ages in parallel with my daughter, now three-and-a-half as I write this (in 2023). And I have related stories of mysterious experiences: how I have felt his presence in my own body, electric currents that seemed to come up from the ground during or after meditation and pulled me to the forest or desert floor. These experiences have outmatched my clinging to rationality, which is often a kind of self-defense for fear of being disbelieved. My experience of his death was the experience of a disappearance. He was here one day and then never again.

What I have never written before now is that his death was a theft, a negligence and an injustice, which could have been avoided, and for which neither I nor anyone in my family has received closure. I have never written that the responsible party was my own father, and that his conversion to Evangelical Christianity was largely because

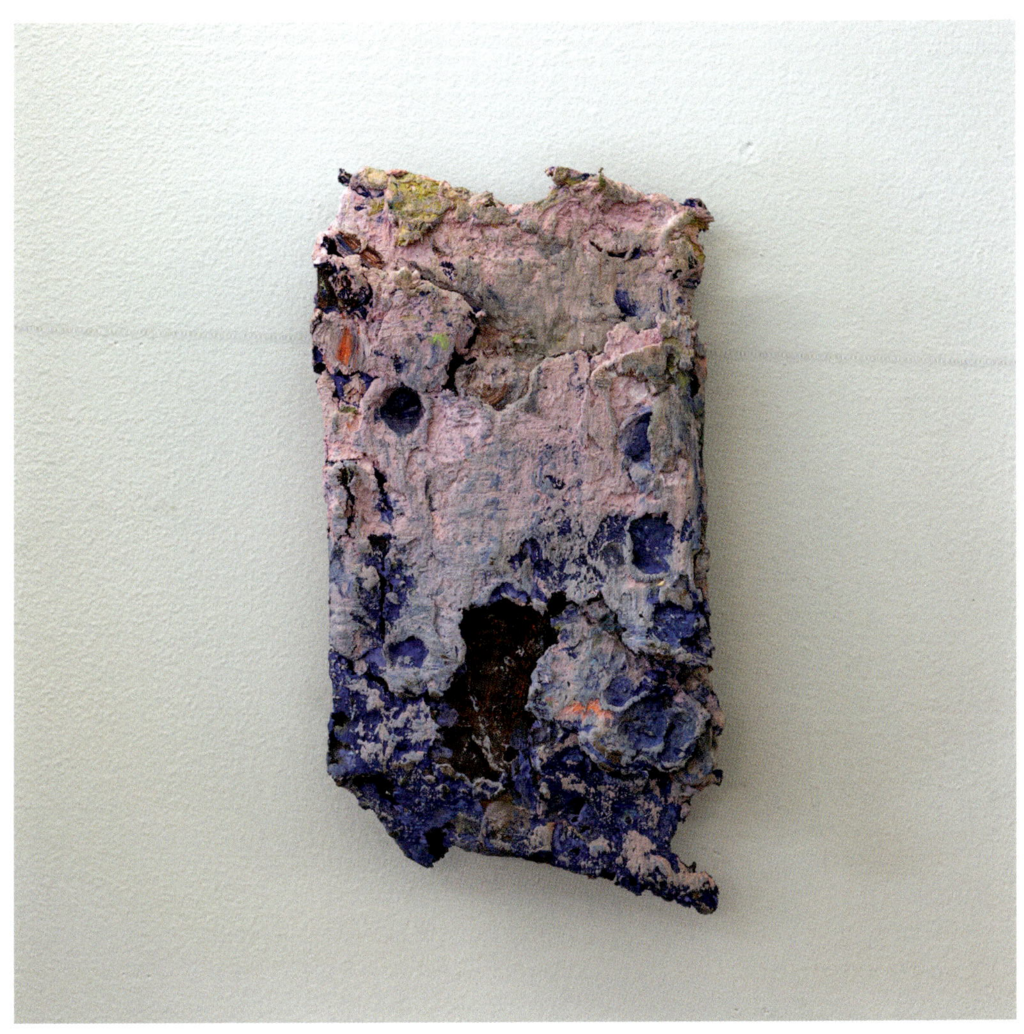

OUT OF EXISTENCE XX, OIL AND WAX ON FOUND CRUSHED TIN PAIL, ABOUT 9 × 5 IN., 2021

of my encouragement that he be baptized at the church I attended in my teens and early twenties. That I would soon thereafter leave organized religion behind as I witnessed his new fanaticism, and that he would eventually become a pastor, is a story I have simply never told any but a few friends.

In the period following Danny's death I began speaking everything twice, first in my ordinary voice, and then in a whisper. It was compulsive and deeply embarrassing. Though I cannot prove anything, I suspect that my retreat into relative solitude (as compared to average kids) to draw and tell stories in pictures was my way of capturing the repression that came from this experience, and to compensate for what I could not allow of my own voice. I suspect that is what I did, and what I do.

When I think of that child, myself, in his bedroom alone, trying to make sense of the world through his escape from it, I am filled with amazement and compassion. How did this instinct arise in him? The beauty of this unconscious strategy, to me, is in how it seemed to come from nowhere. No one else in my family made art. I have no memory of a nearby parent or adult expressing any great curiosity or showing a sense of awe about the world. And so, it is to this "nowhere" that I have grown most devoted with time. This transpersonal emptiness, this nighttime garden of inquiry, the nothing that produces everything.

In a way, the sculptural installations *Autumn Pilgrimage* and *Moon in Water* are two variations of the same imaginal encounter. They are a way of turning to my late brother and asking, "Are you here?" This is a strange question to ask, not least because I do not think I believe in ghosts. Yet I sometimes wonder if I am not hiding a part of myself in the ghost I am not ready to believe in. And not just a ghost, but a twin, a double of some kind. Though I cannot quite believe a long-lost child can hear my question, I still somehow might believe in the possibility of an answer.

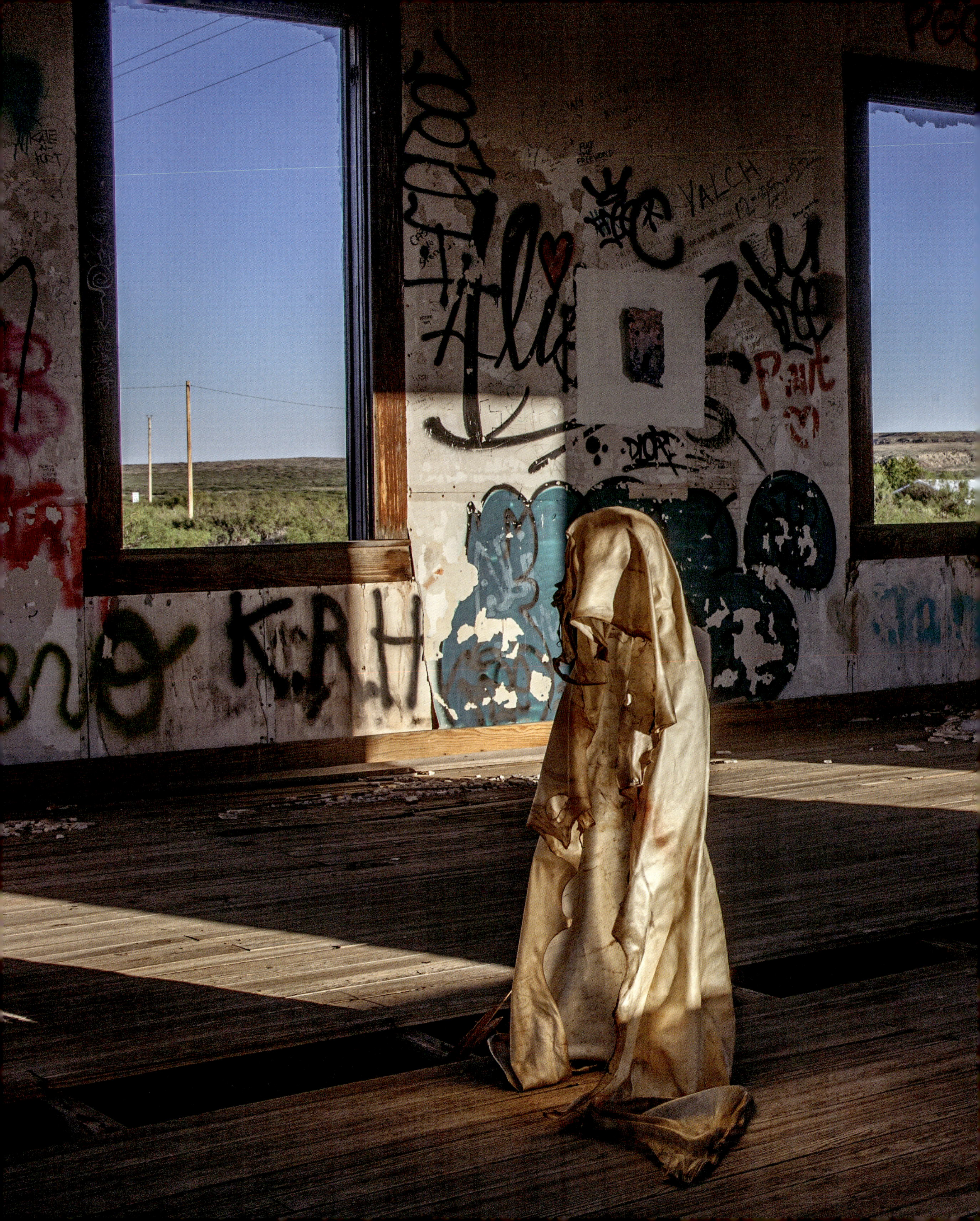
K.R.H
DIOR
YALCH

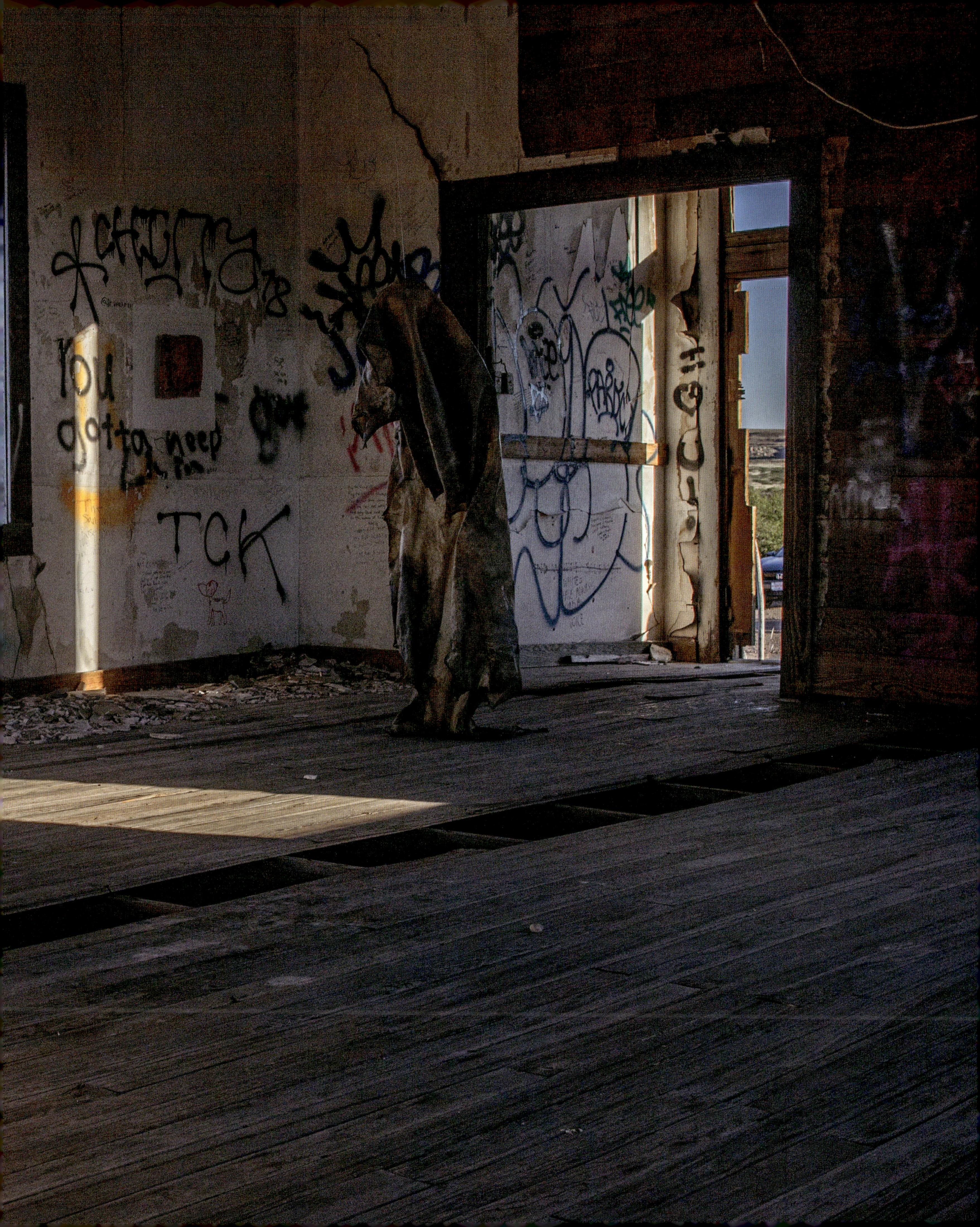
gotta keep
TCK

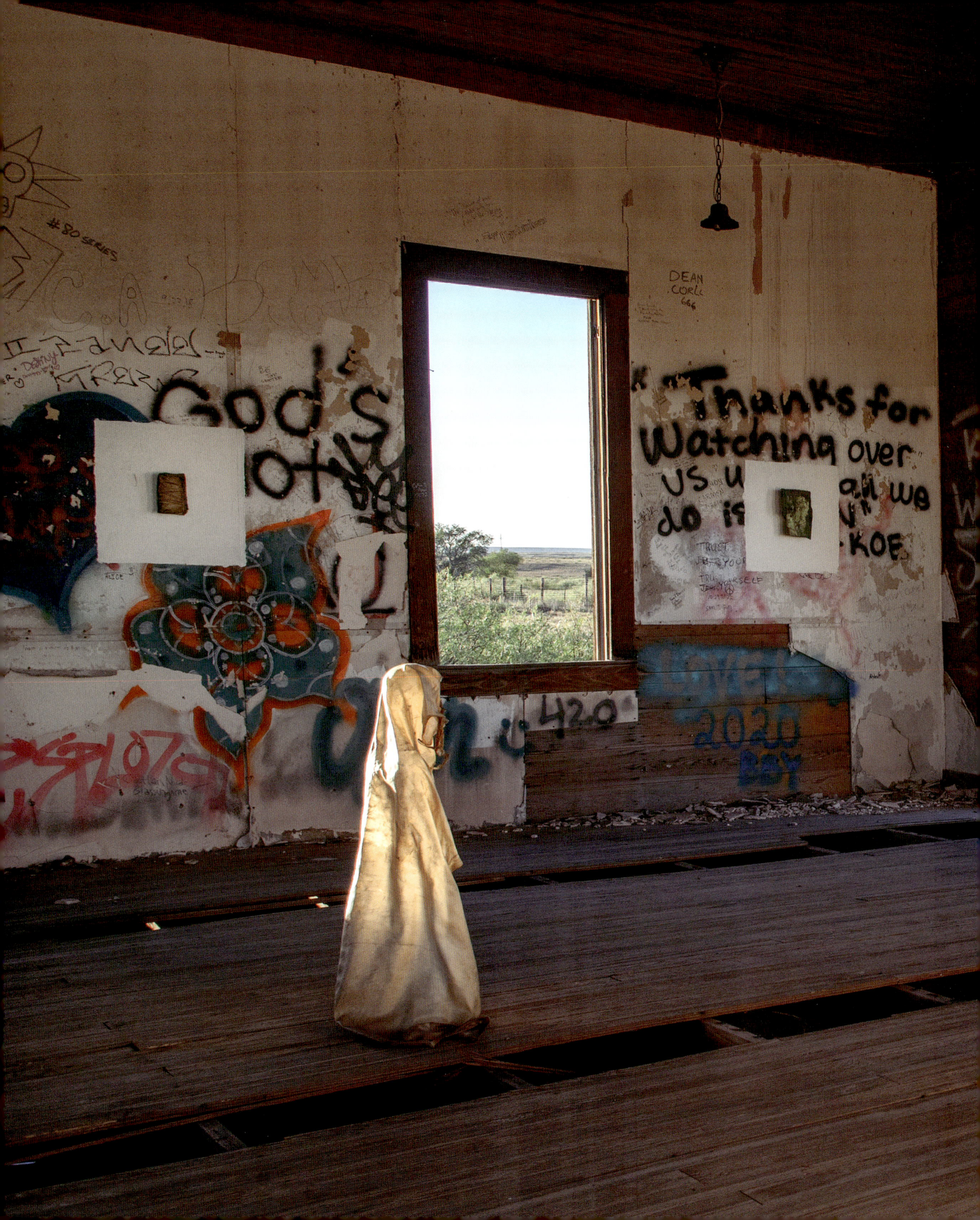
God's
"Thanks for
Watching over
DEAN
CORLL
666
#80 SERIES
420
2020

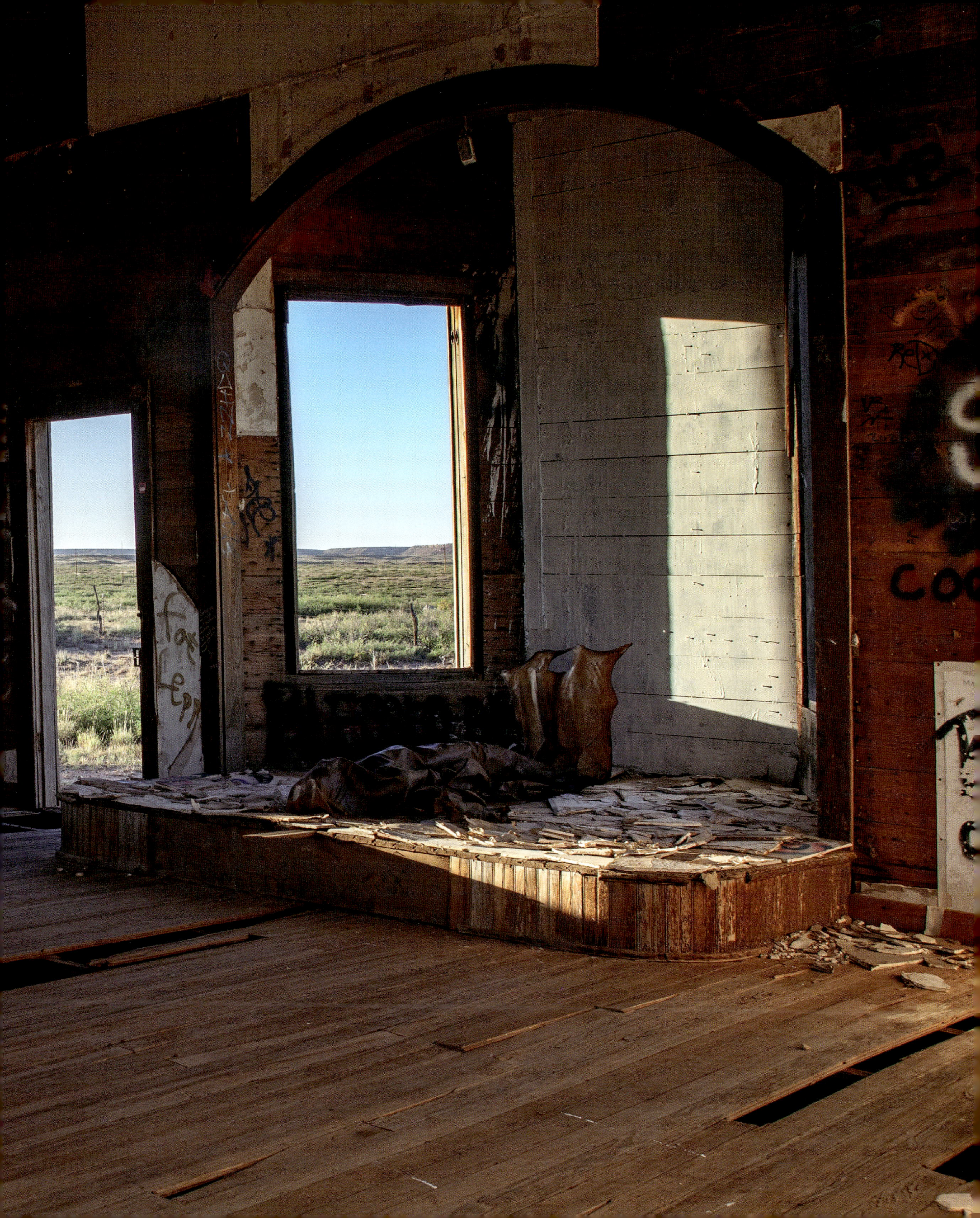

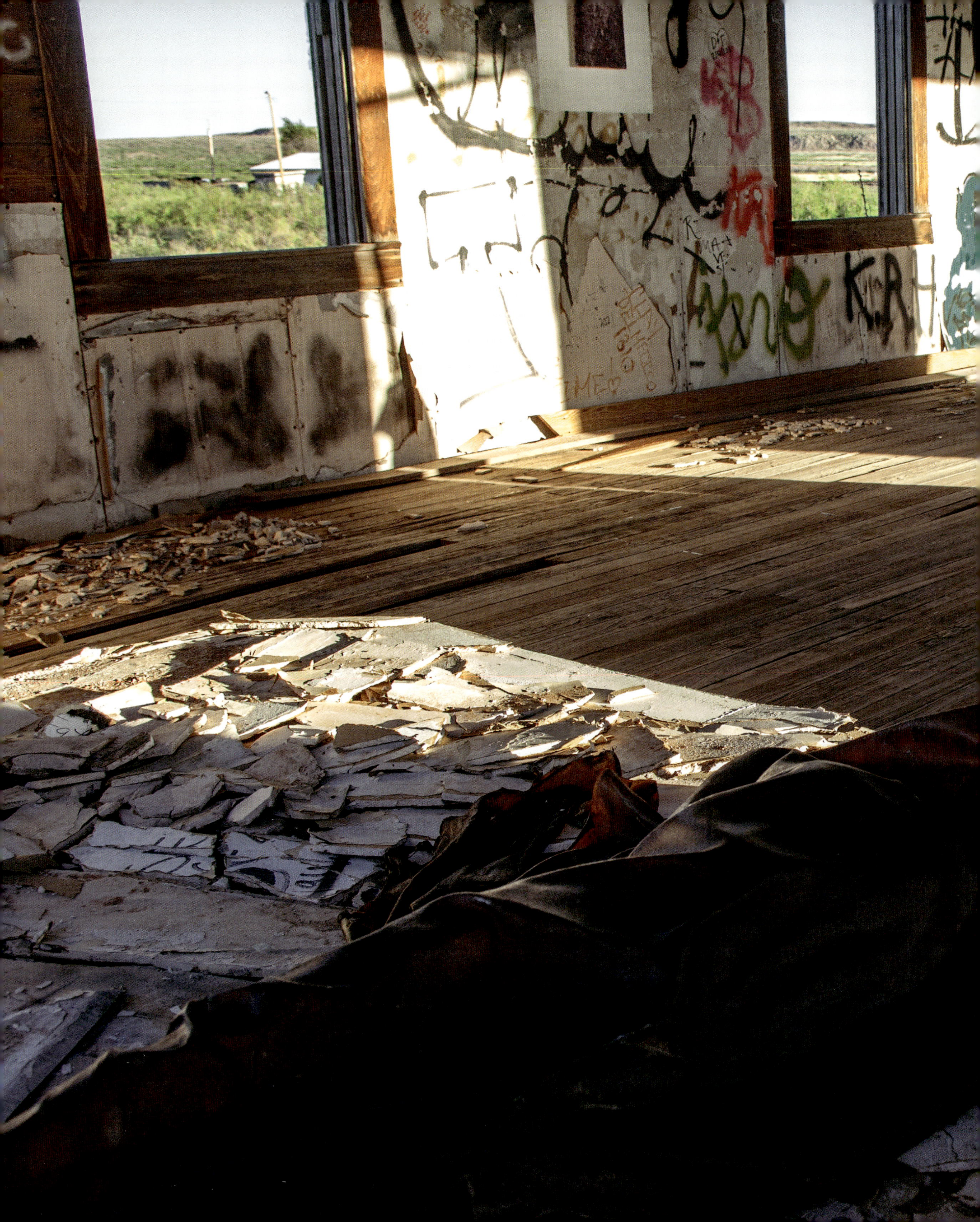

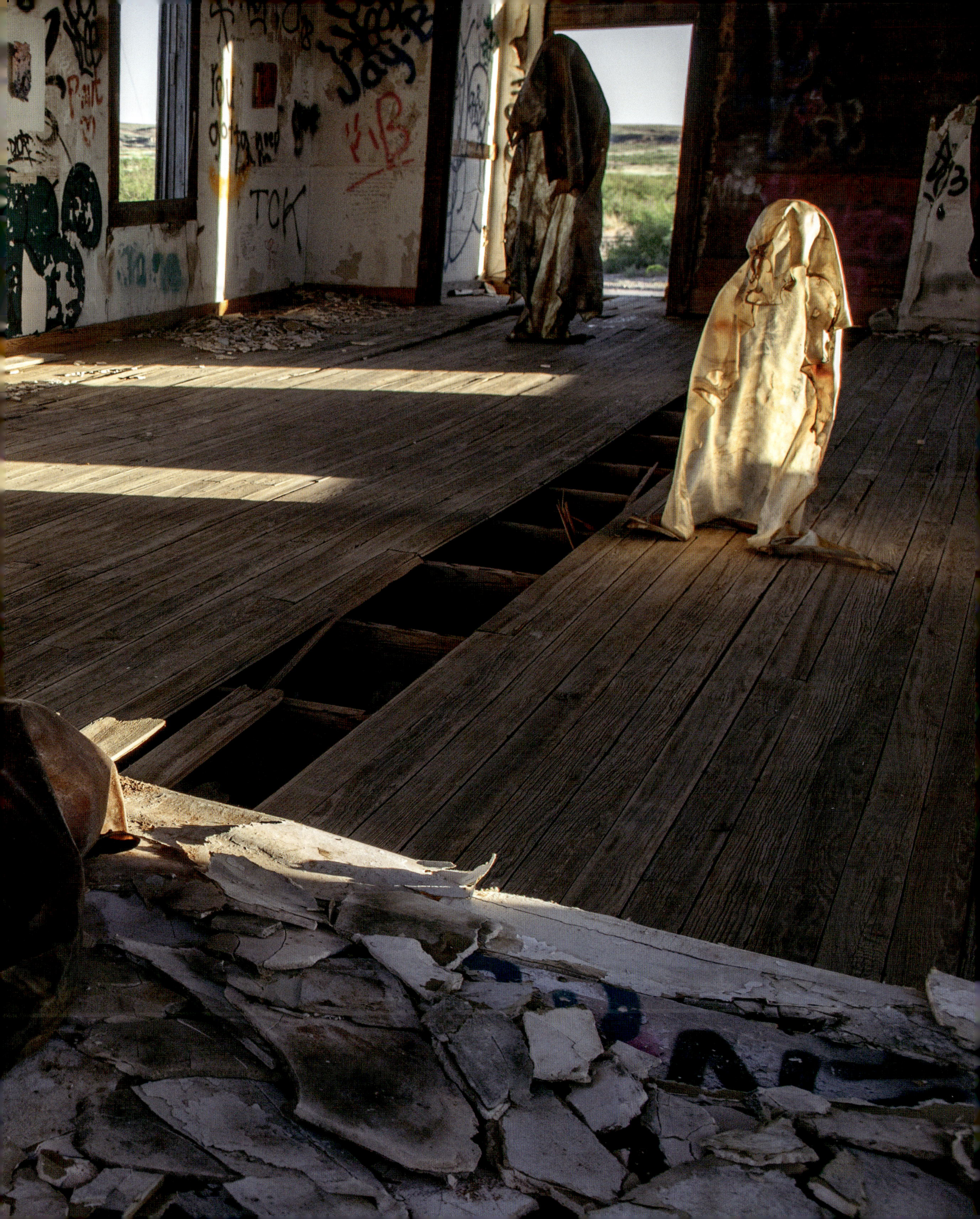
TCK

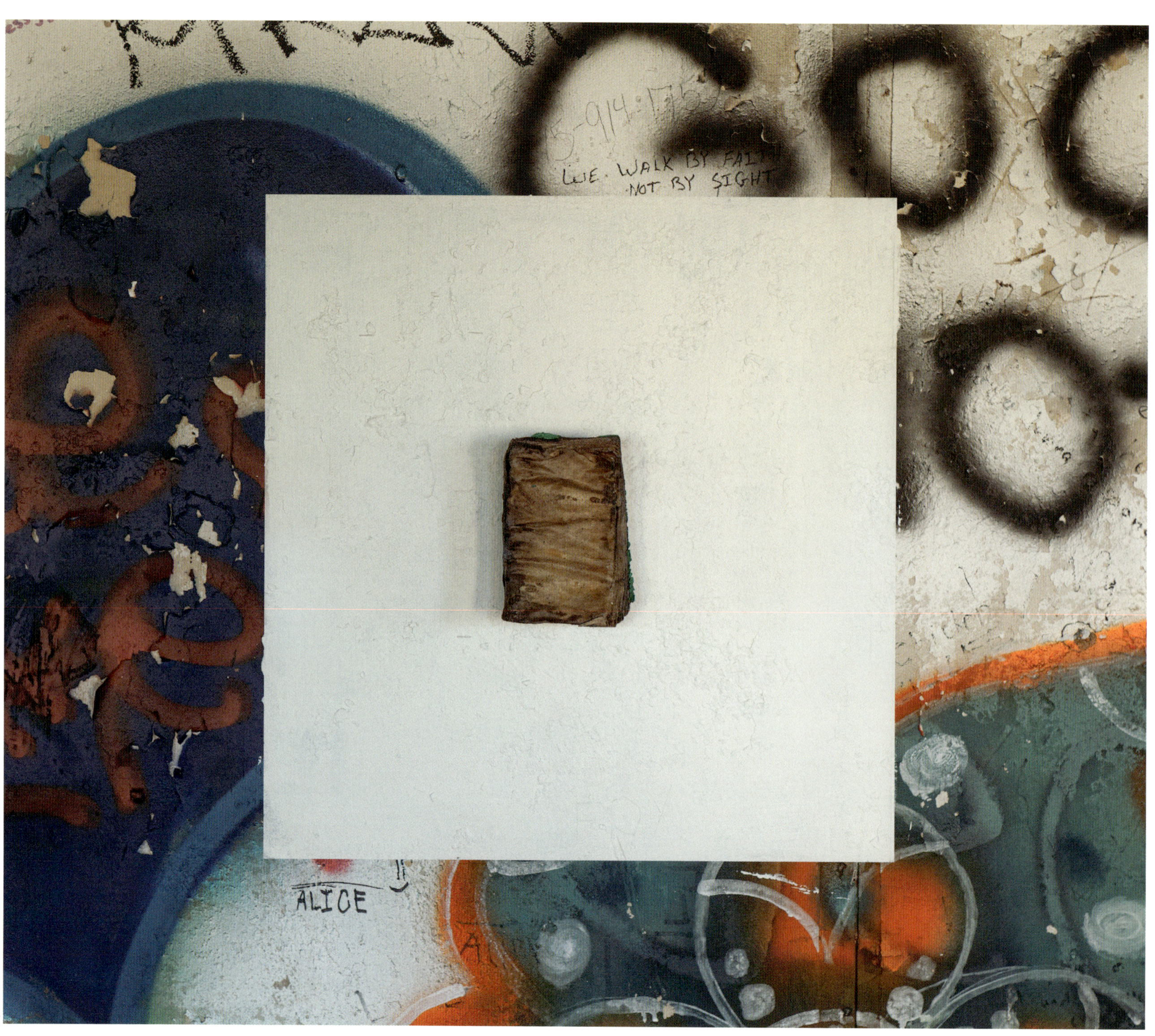
WALK BY
NOT BY SIGHT
ALICE

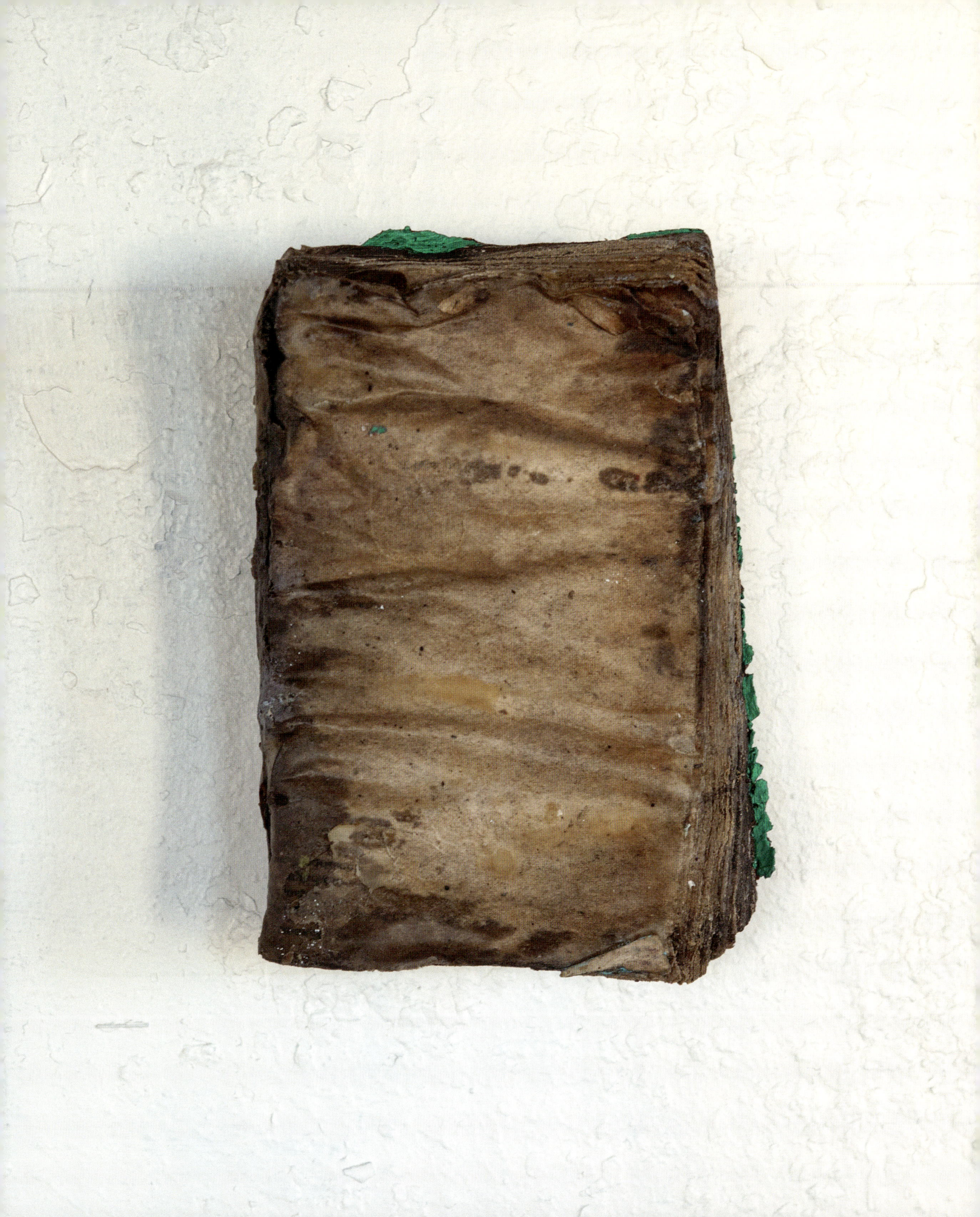

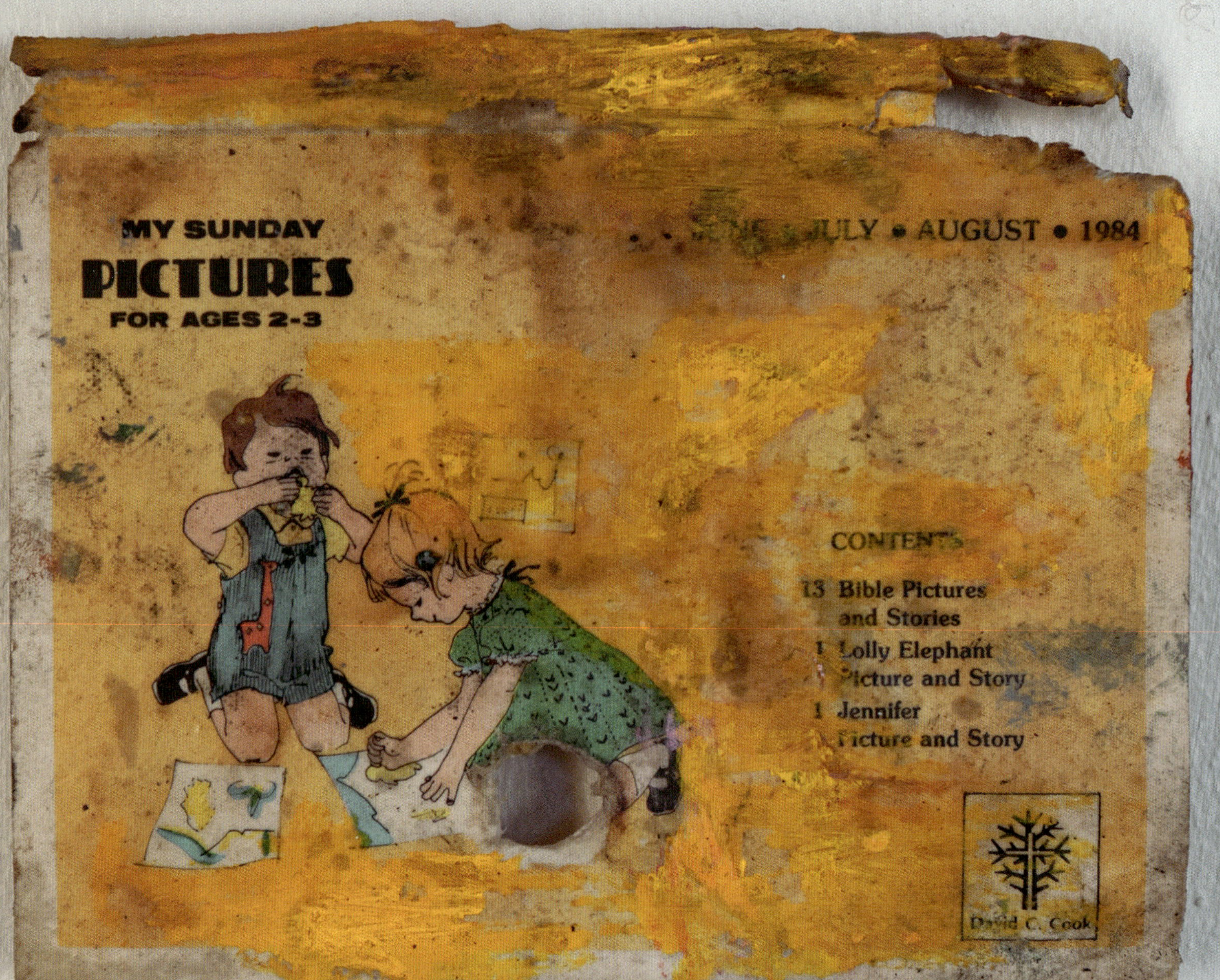

MY SUNDAY
PICTURES
FOR AGES 2-3
JULY • AUGUST • 1984
CONTENTS
13 Bible Pictures and Stories
1 Lolly Elephant Picture and Story
1 Jennifer Picture and Story
David C. Cook

Object *(Accumulated Action)*

The word "object," in *Nihil*, refers both to what I begin with (for example, the found object in the landscape, or the canvas or other fabric that has been on the studio floor collecting runoff) and to what results, the so-called "finished piece." It is the object in itself, and the experience of it, that is at the heart of my concern, rather than what the image or painting might momentarily "mean" or represent. It is the object that carries the traces of consciousness that make it what it is. Meaning is a game of ideas that cannot actually exist in the object, but depends on external forces to project cultural desires and mandates onto it. In that context, it is the game rather than the object that validates an action.

One who benefits from the object prefers the object. One who benefits from the game prefers the game.

The object I discover is the result of accumulated action upon it, whether because of the natural effects of time or because someone else has done something to it along the way. Because I think of the object as an accumulation of actions over time, I do not think of myself as painting an object. Time is my collaborator; all I can do is contribute an action to the continued formation of the object. I must think with the object, slowly, over many months, asking each day, who is the object?

Nihil understands the object as a fluctuating continuum; it does not end once I cease acting on it. Future actions will bring about the object it has yet to become. Because no one thing about it will remain fixed, it has a long life. The noun is a slow verb.

The found objects of *Nihil* are things that have been forgotten, overlooked, cast aside. To the casual observer, I am putting garbage in my truck. I look for the perfect object. I cannot describe how I know it is perfect, just that the very act of separating it from the rest seems to sacralize it. There is a piece of the Archaic Brother present. It seems to have washed up along the shores of Lethe. Once I have done all I can do with it, I must return it to its place of origin and find a new way to understand how it has changed.

It is the object that teaches me how to make a better painting. In today's promulgation of disposable images, the work must be as physical as necessary to counteract the trance of consumerism inherent in mass cultural aesthetics. The object must confront me fully, directly. It must surprise in the same way one is surprised to find moss on a boulder in the desert.

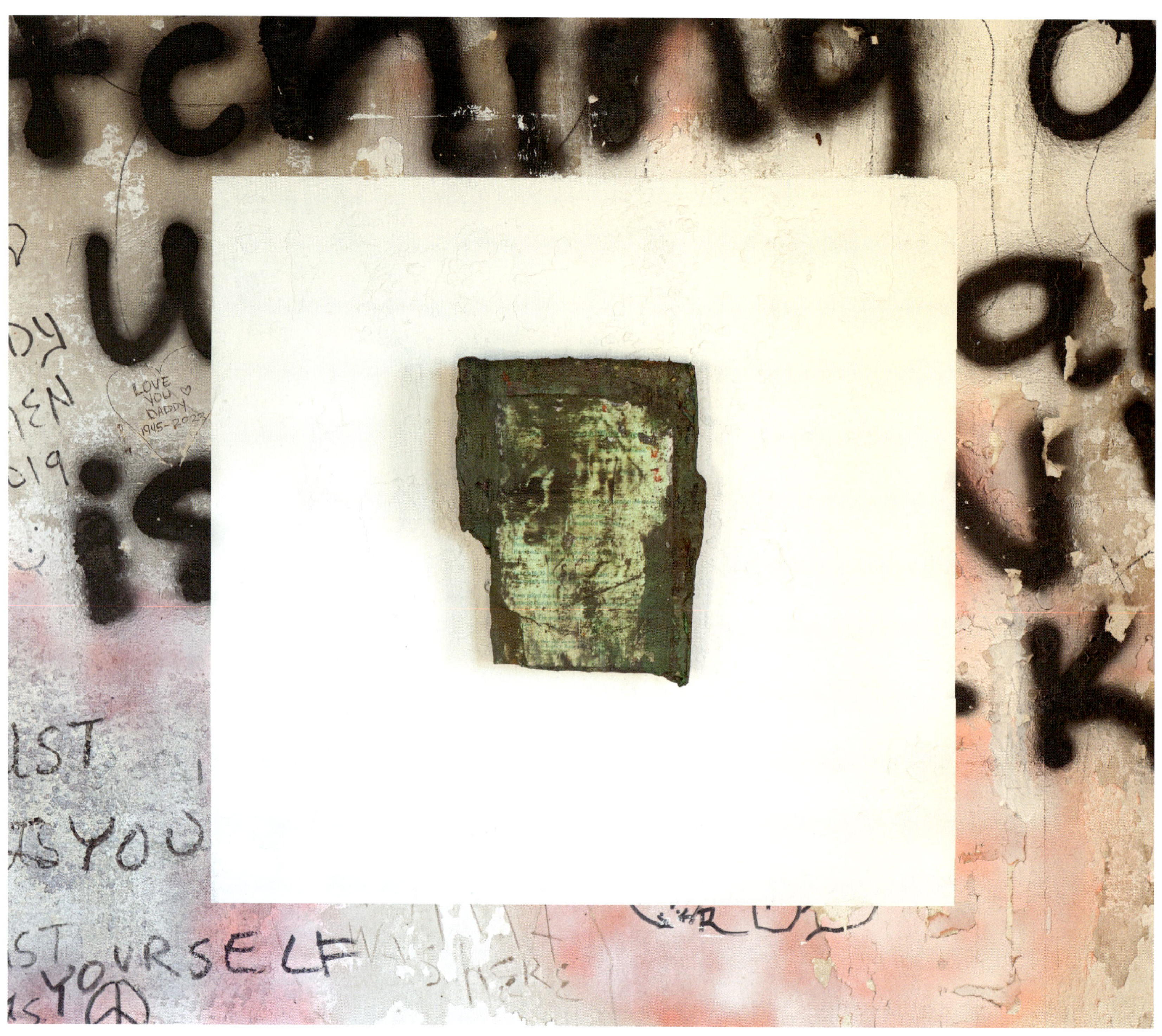
LOVE YOU DADDY
1945-2023
YOURSELF

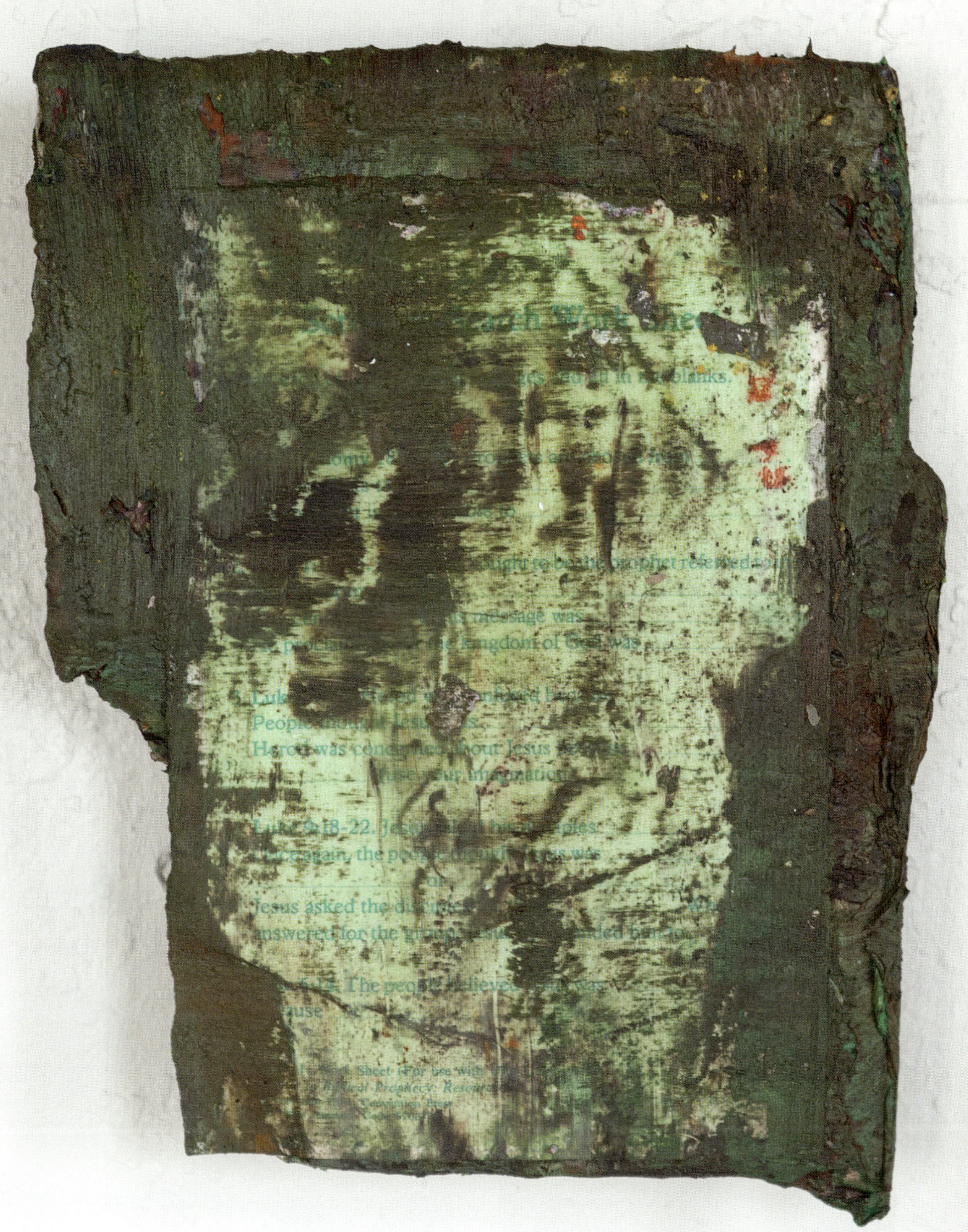

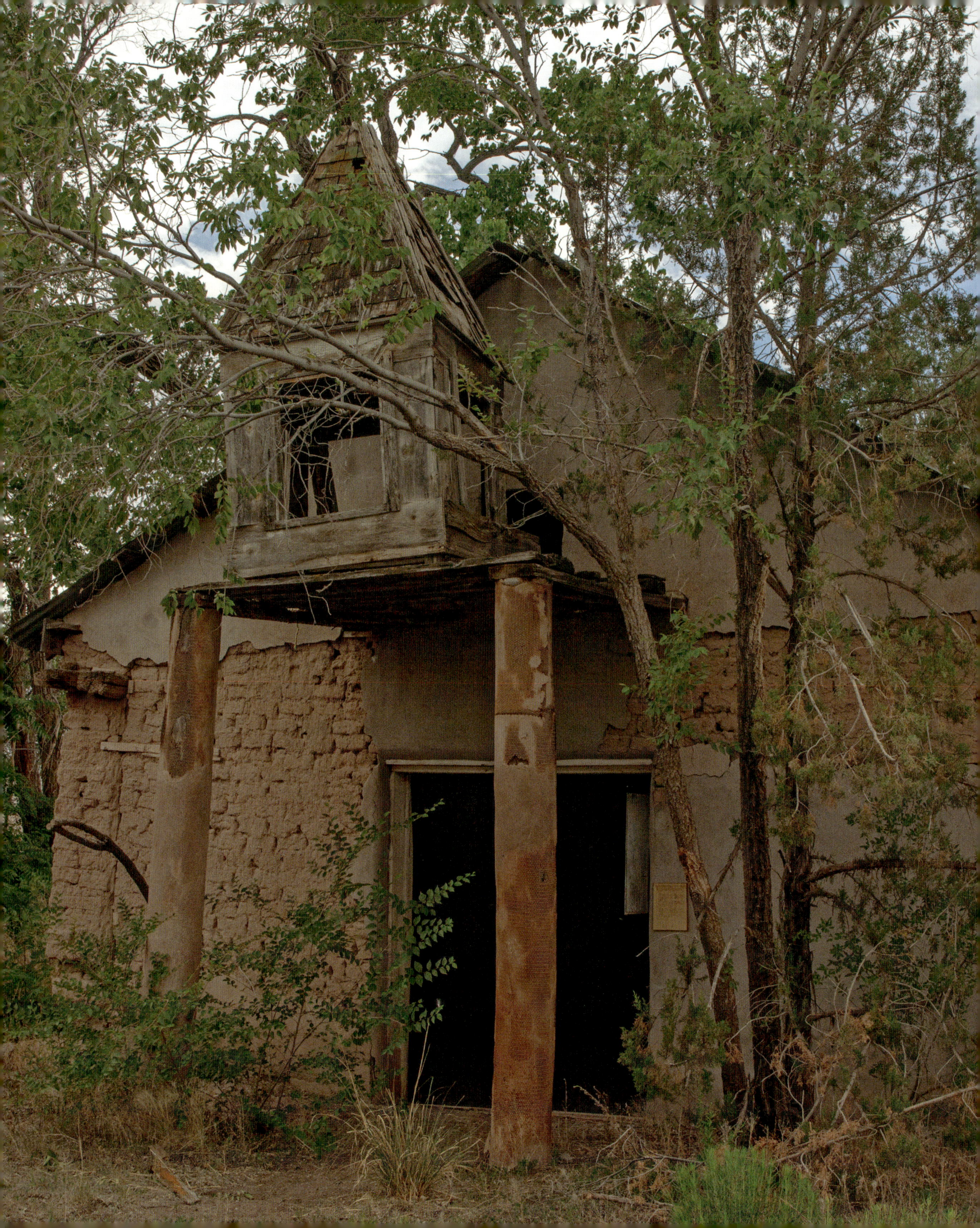

SAN ACACIA CHURCH

Moon in Water

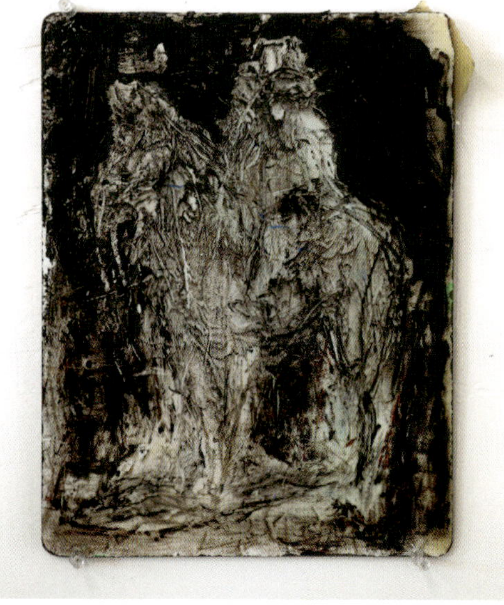

HORSE IN MOONLIGHT I, GRAPHITE, CHARCOAL, OIL PASTEL, AND WAX ON FOUND STUDENT DRY-ERASE BOARD, 11 × 8.5 IN., 2023

From the time my daughter was born until now (she is five in 2025), my brother ages with her in my mind's eye, so that they are always the same age. This began happening automatically in waking visions and dreams in her infancy.

Because of this, I imagine each of the deer-hide figures, situated on found student chairs, as my daughter and late brother, facing each other, as children of about three years, from across a small distance. I think of them as if on either side of the veil. Only later did it occur to me that the hides resemble veils, that they are translucent and formed by impressions of the head and body. The reader might know if the noun and verb versions of the word "hide" share an etymology. It seems too convenient.

Perhaps the most potent aspect of the *Nihil* experiment is that it implicitly questions the curious demarcation between interior and exterior life. In *Nihil*, the external is made internal, and vice versa. I do not think, anymore, of telling stories but of integrating experiences into the "making." What the work is about has become less important to me than what the work simply does.

A moon in water is a reflection of a moon. We assume the moon is real and its reflection false. But from an observational perspective, each is round. Each emits light. One is still, the other fluctuates. It is the fluctuation that implies the observer, the image prompting the eye, the eye prompting the image. Perhaps reality, as such, co-emerges with the self. I might think of the art I make, then, as a confirmation of that co-emergence, an artifact of the mind recognizing itself in the world.

Specific to the installation at the abandoned San Acacia church, each work is copied or doubled: the sculptural figure and each drawing. A drawing I might have made on a found student's whiteboard extracted from an abandoned school, for example, is then redrawn on a found Baptist workbook page extracted from the abandoned bible school near Fort Sumner. One substrate reacts to graphite, charcoal, oil pastel, or wax differently from the next, and that simple fact changes the drawing all by itself. The drawings on the workbook pages are less legible and seem further deteriorated from the original. You could think of the installation as existing in halves split down the middle of the church, or as one being the distorted reflection or shadow of the other. I think of the second version of each pair of works as the deteriorating memory, or dampened echo, of the other. This is true, too, of the *Moon in Water* sculpture; the second figure, if you look closely, is missing an arm.

Rawhide can be shaped only when soaking. When wet, it becomes very heavy. Positioned on the child-sized armature and left overnight, it shrinks as it dries. When I removed the hide in the first iteration, the armature's cloth and plastic arm was destroyed. This is how the idea for the entire installation came into being; I try to read every accident as a message. Rather than repair or replace the arm, I decided to position another hide on the broken armature as it was. It is a copy, which is in a more advanced stage of decay. All the drawings on found whiteboards had already been made by the time I made the sculptures. So it was that I decided to copy the drawings on the deteriorated Baptist workbook pages, and to think of one set of works as a mirror to the other.

The *Nihil* tenets make premeditated meaning-making illegal to the process. It was only due to the good luck of the hide's particular aesthetic and the simple fact of my daughter being a real child who exists on the *Nihil* route that these kinds of meanings can emerge so readily. As I have noted, the great and beautiful irony at the center of *Nihil* is that in trying to work without premeditated meaning, it seems to arise frequently and everywhere, quite without intention. The unconscious seems more readily available where other conscious choices are not.

Yet there are many shadows of doubt cast over the entire project. In fact, as the project progresses these increase. More holes in the plot. More contradictions in its principles. More performance, less of my own anonymity preserved. Some of these early blindspots are so obvious now, they cannot go unnoticed. What has so long been in the background of all of my work, long before *Nihil*, is the specter of Church. It is somewhat odd to claim that installing these works in abandoned churches is coincidence, having more to do with what sorts of abandoned buildings are available throughout the vast New Mexico landscape than with the

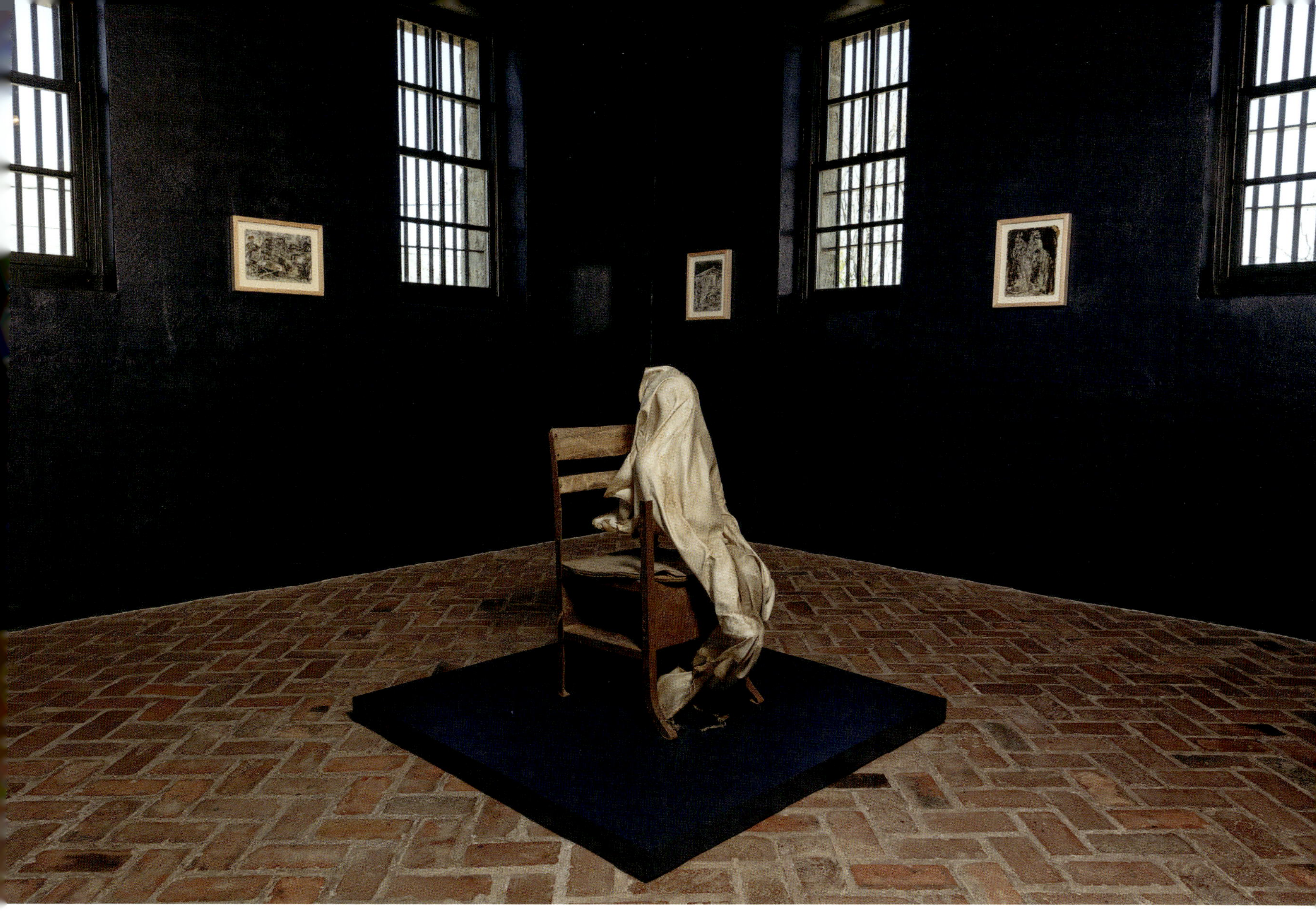

INSTALLATION VIEW FROM *NIHIL II | NOR THE MOON IN ITS WATER*, EXHIBITION AT OLD JAIL ART CENTER, ALBANY, TEXAS

meaning of Church. After all, what sort of buildings did I expect to find alongside the state's many lonely roads when I started this? How obvious it seems to me now that I sought the churches to begin with, an exteriorized projection of an interior search. *Nihil*, I now plainly see, has been an elaborate gesture made by someone coming out of a "dark night of the soul," someone lost and seeking, trying to believe, and maybe also doubting, that life is real and what we do in it matters.

I have the strangest feeling that this was an unconscious strategy all along: to bring the work into a kind of space of eternal return. It was a way of confronting what the conscious mind would not previously allow. Installing these in abandoned churches was a sideways attempt at *Aletheia,* a recovery of truth through unconcealed memory in the form of poetry and song. I did not simply stumble onto the concept at some middle stage of the *Nihil* project; it is the very word I gave to my daughter as her middle name. Coincidence and synchronicity happen often in *Nihil*, but where I go and what I make arises out of a deep need to make contact with a past for which I have no ordinary or rational access. All attempts at reclamation are also inventions of forms, of a nascent symbolism in lieu of a world I can remember as it was. This is how the collection of abandoned spaces, and my installations in them, have come to resemble a single architecture of Self, and why it seems, however irrationally, that I am returning the works to the sites from which they came.

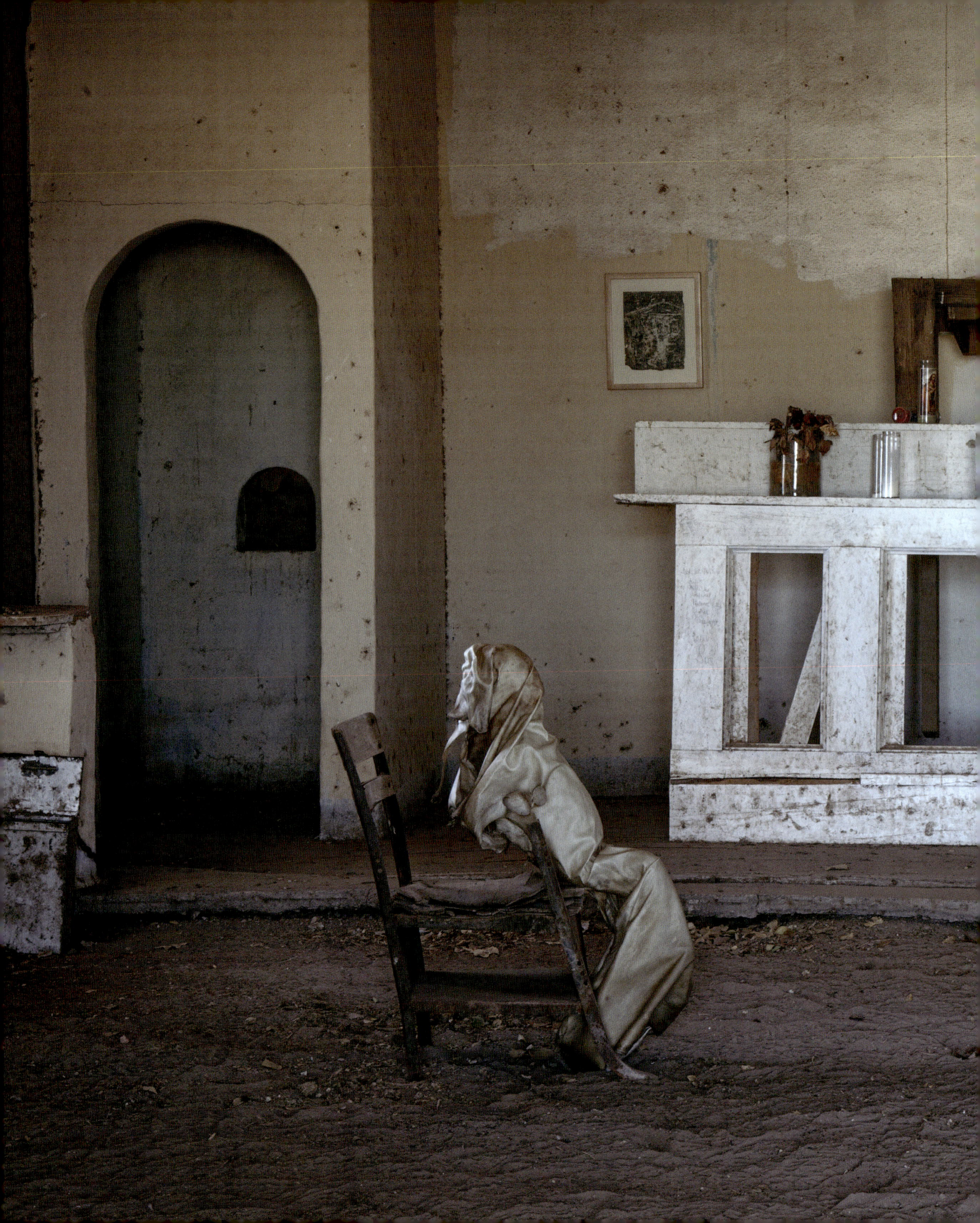

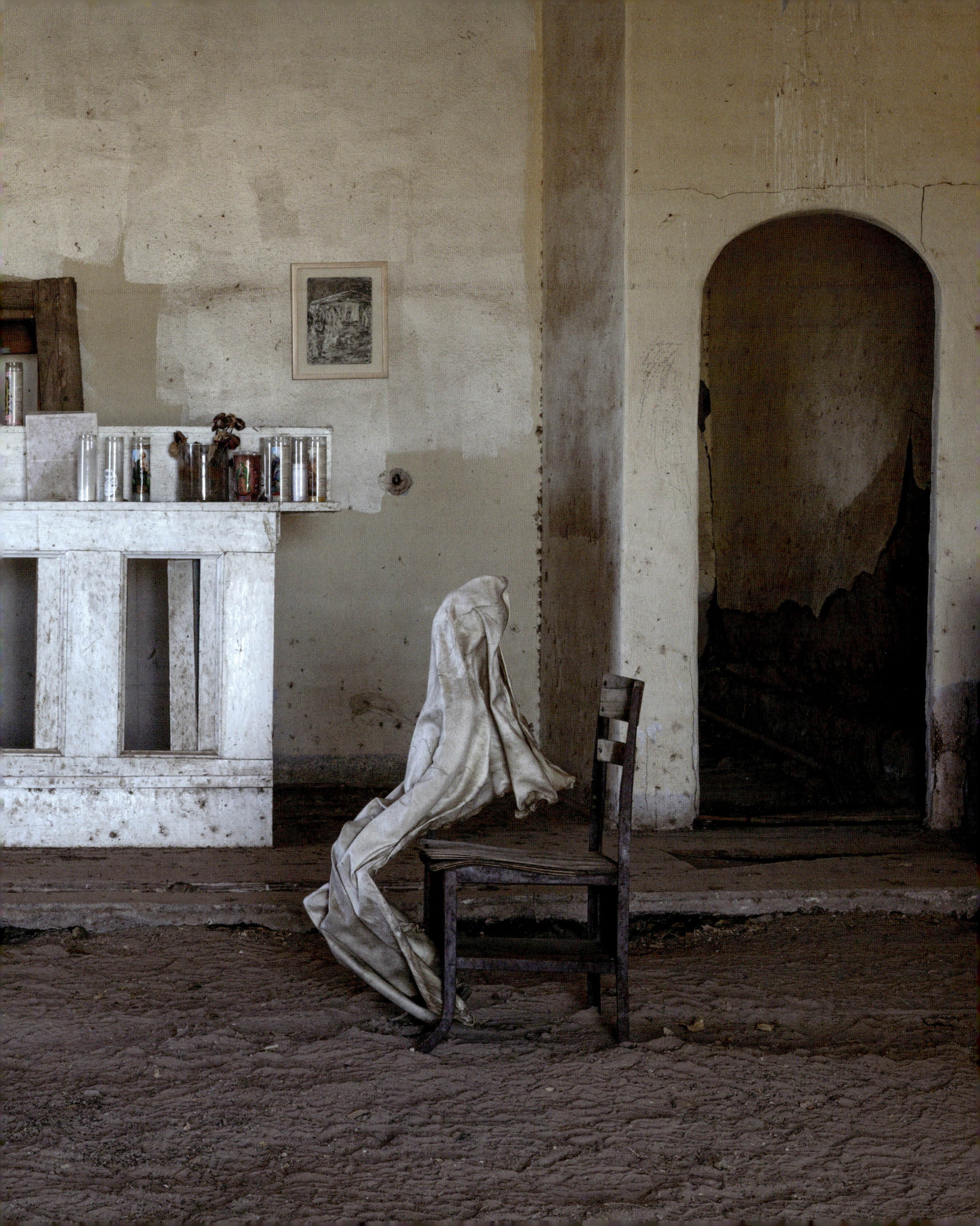

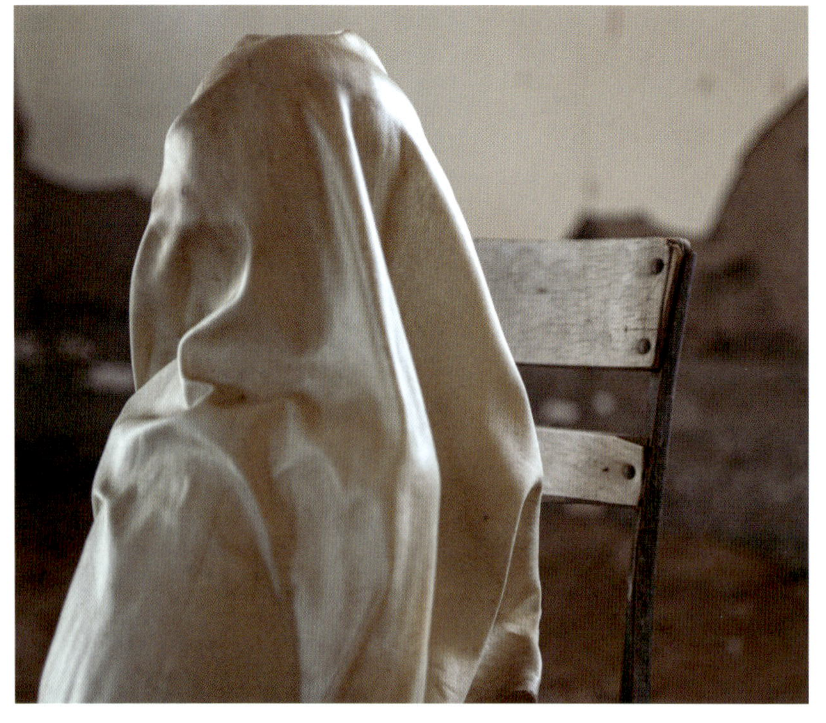
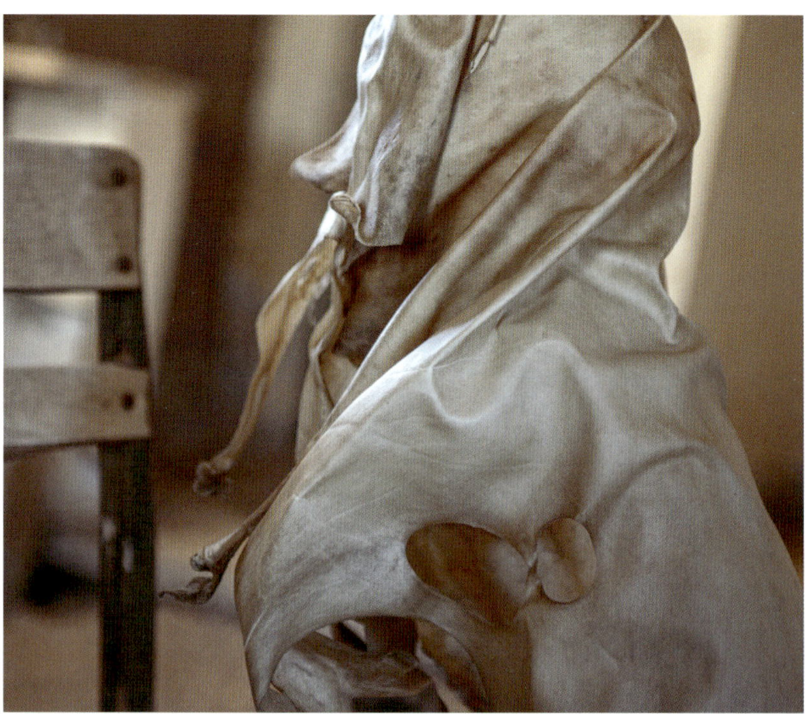
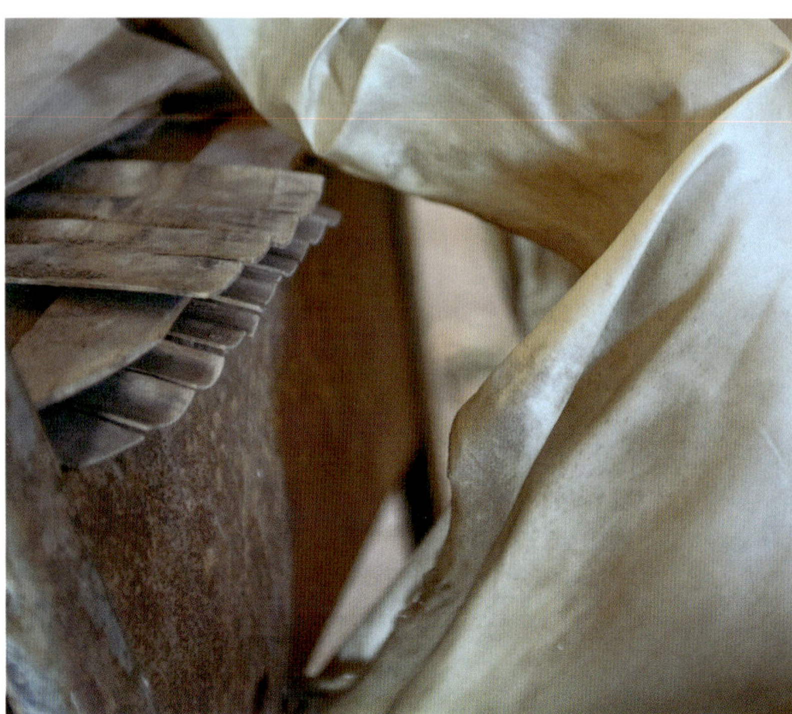
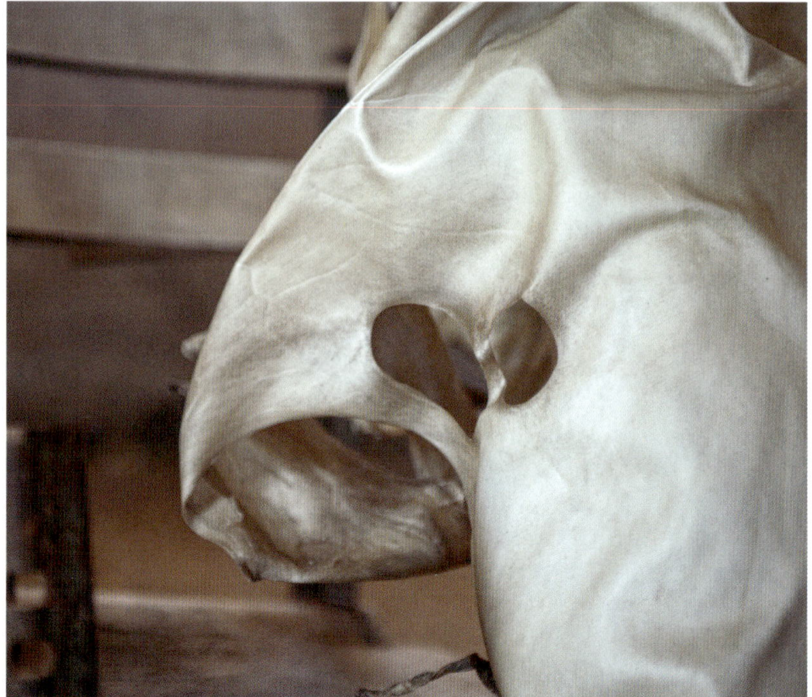

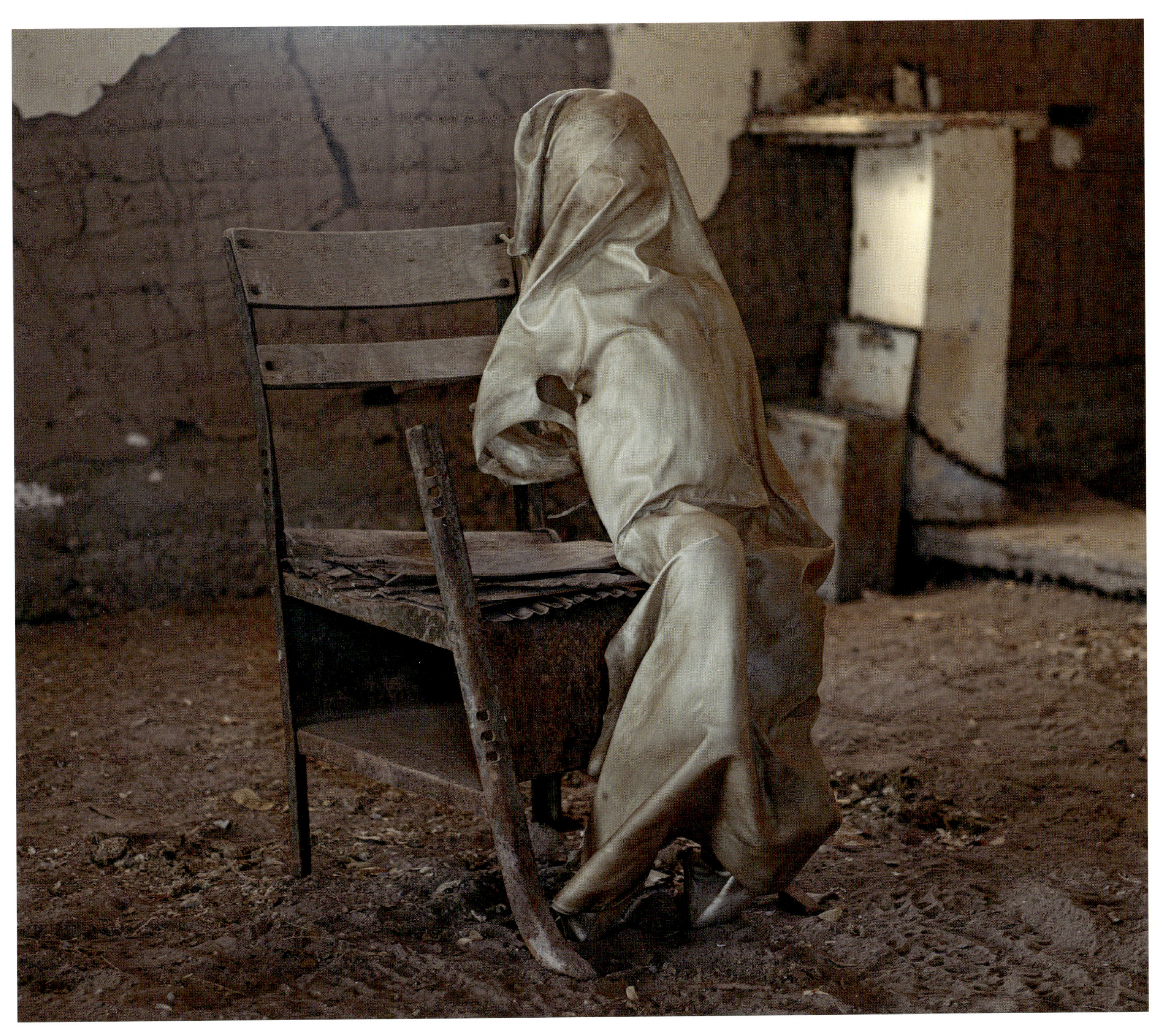

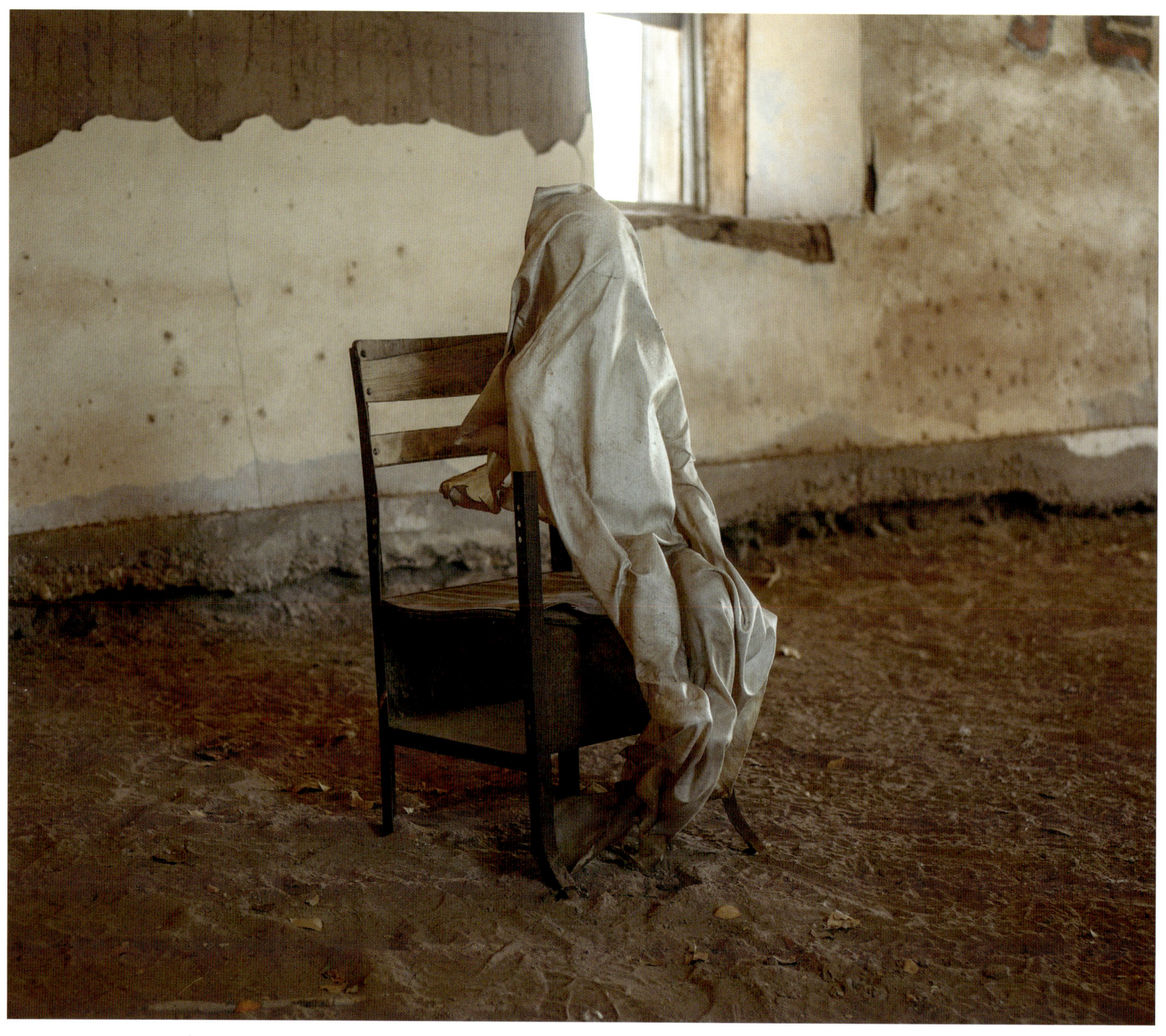

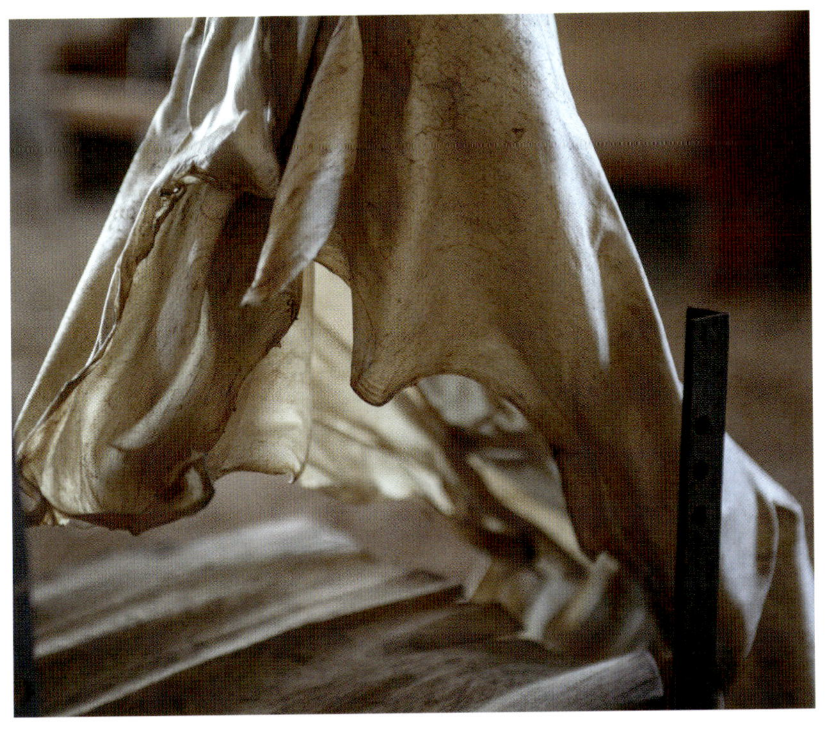
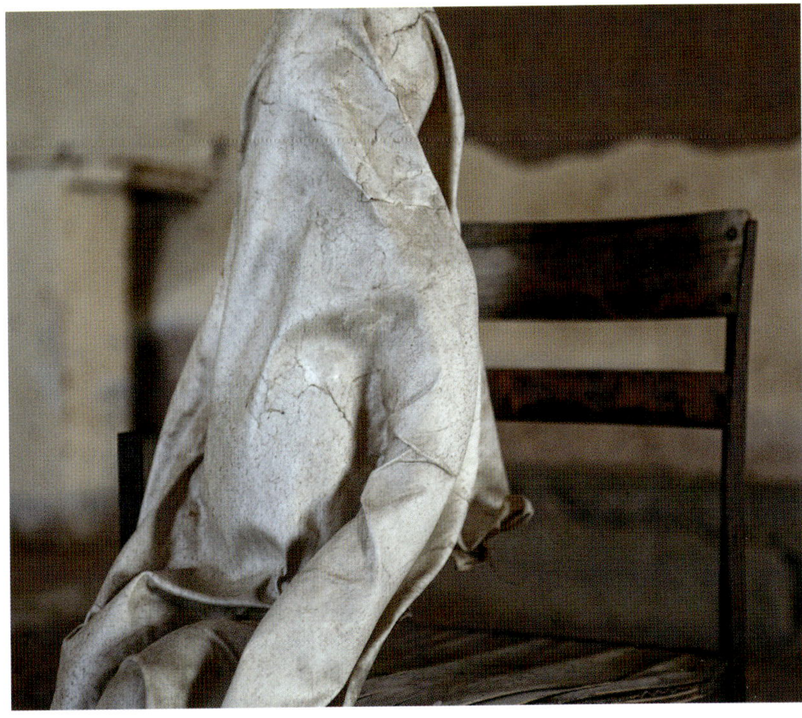
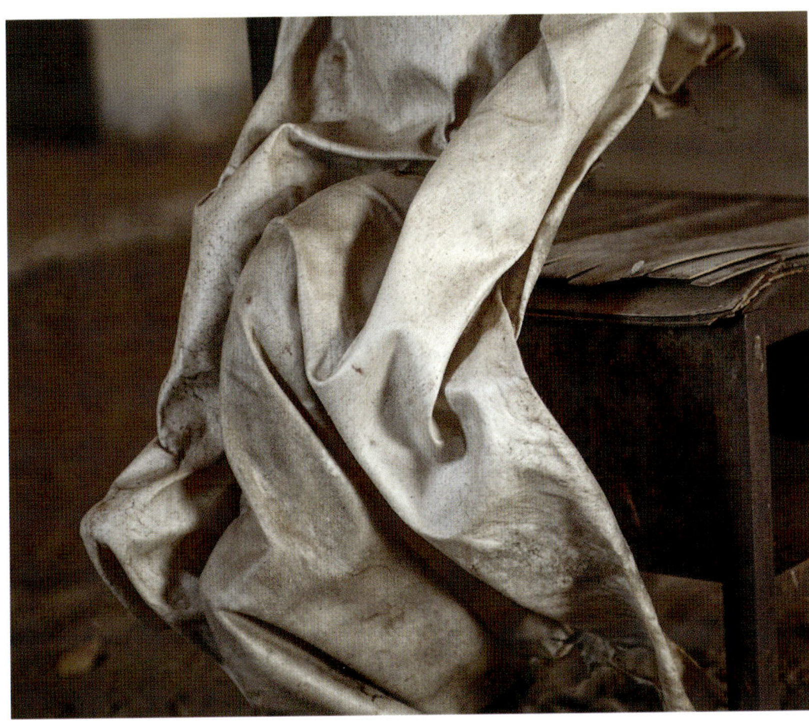
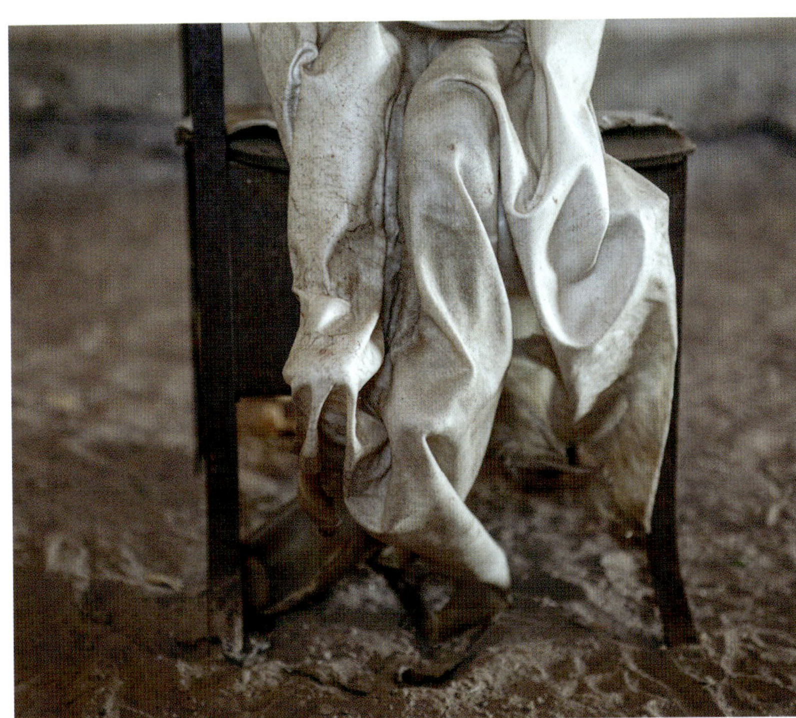

Touch (*The Unconscious Intention to Receive*)

Touch begins with the way in which one engages the physical world; one's conscious "being within" a world is the first instance of touching it. There is no rule in *Nihil* about how to look at the world. Touch should not be confused with looking, though one might well learn to touch with the eyes. The notion of touch expands out toward how one simply is in space, even in how a course might be plotted, conscious or not, through space, and in how one improvises when required.

Touch is many things. What comes into the ear, for example, touches the breath, which touches the picture that forms in the eye. I begin to understand that I both touch and am touched in the same gesture. The more points of contact I become conscious of, the more I am in contact with what is to become the painting. This is how the painting begins before painting begins.

Anything can touch the surface, hand or tool. The touch can be skilled or unskilled—actually there is no difference. None of these distinctions mean anything outside the game of meaning. Soft, patient, wild, angry, forgiving ... on and on. I am not trying to run the gamut, I am simply not that stable. The touch will unconsciously learn to settle into its individual non-importance for the sake of the accumulation, which is yet another kind of touch.

This attitude demonstrates itself at every stage:

Sitting: I am not trying to transcend the world; I hardly know it. What I want is to let go of the abstraction that had previously stood for the world.

Drawing: I am not worried about what it looks like, I am just making way through space. This is what making way looks like.

Collected objects: They are neither the garbage of the past, nor future paintings, but artifacts of an anonymous present. It is very likely the hand is unneeded, but only the hand can say. Perhaps the hand is needed to rid the object of what the hand has done.

Painting: It is not enough to make a schematic and apply the auto filter as seems enough to satisfy markets, schools, and museums today; the touch must be human and something other, inimitable by current and future AI. Someone must be there, in the work, not persona, but mind behind mind, ear behind ear.

Touch, at every stage of the process, is neither the act of giving nor forcing, but of receiving what the body believes lost. The accumulation of touches is the reformulation of its memory.

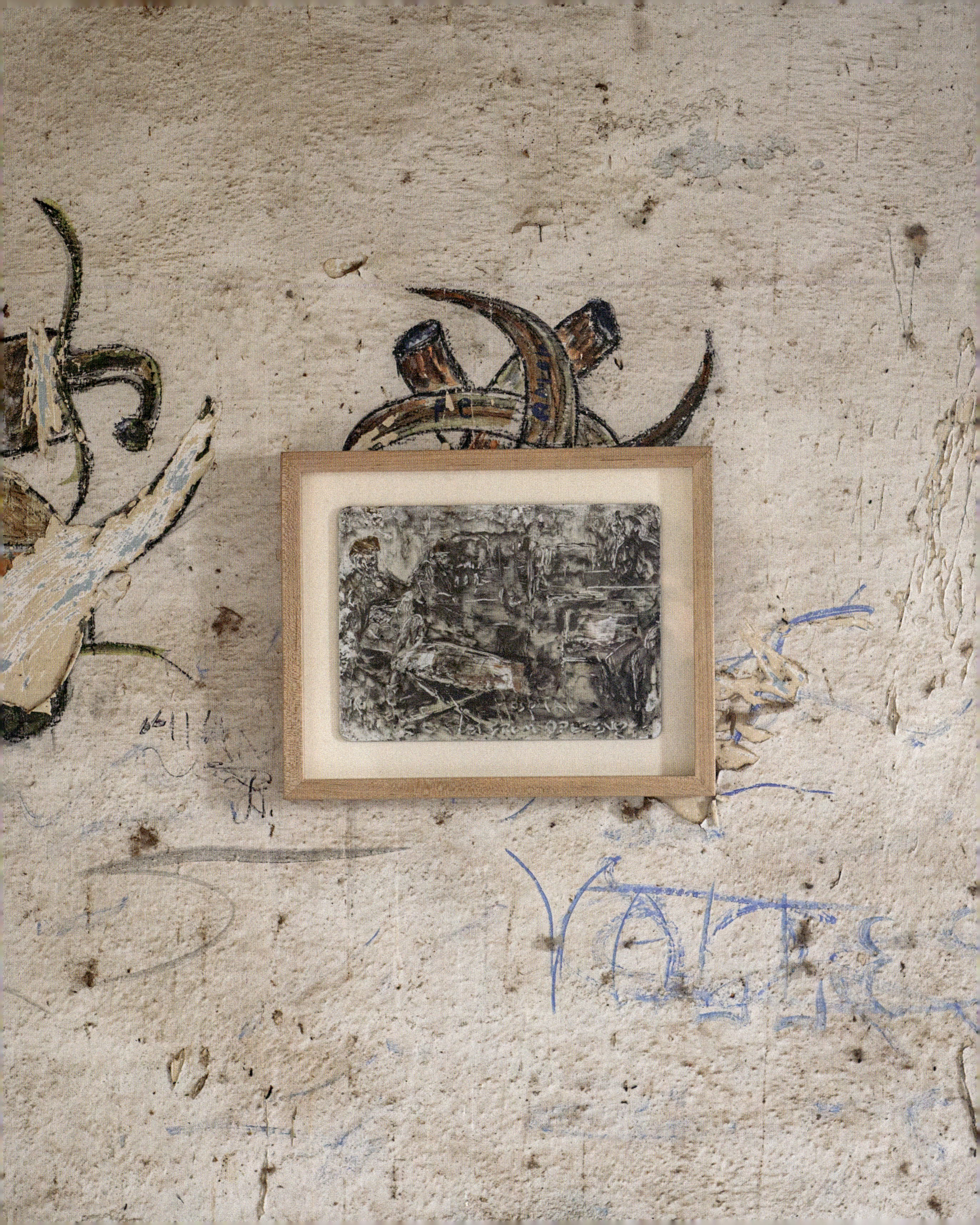

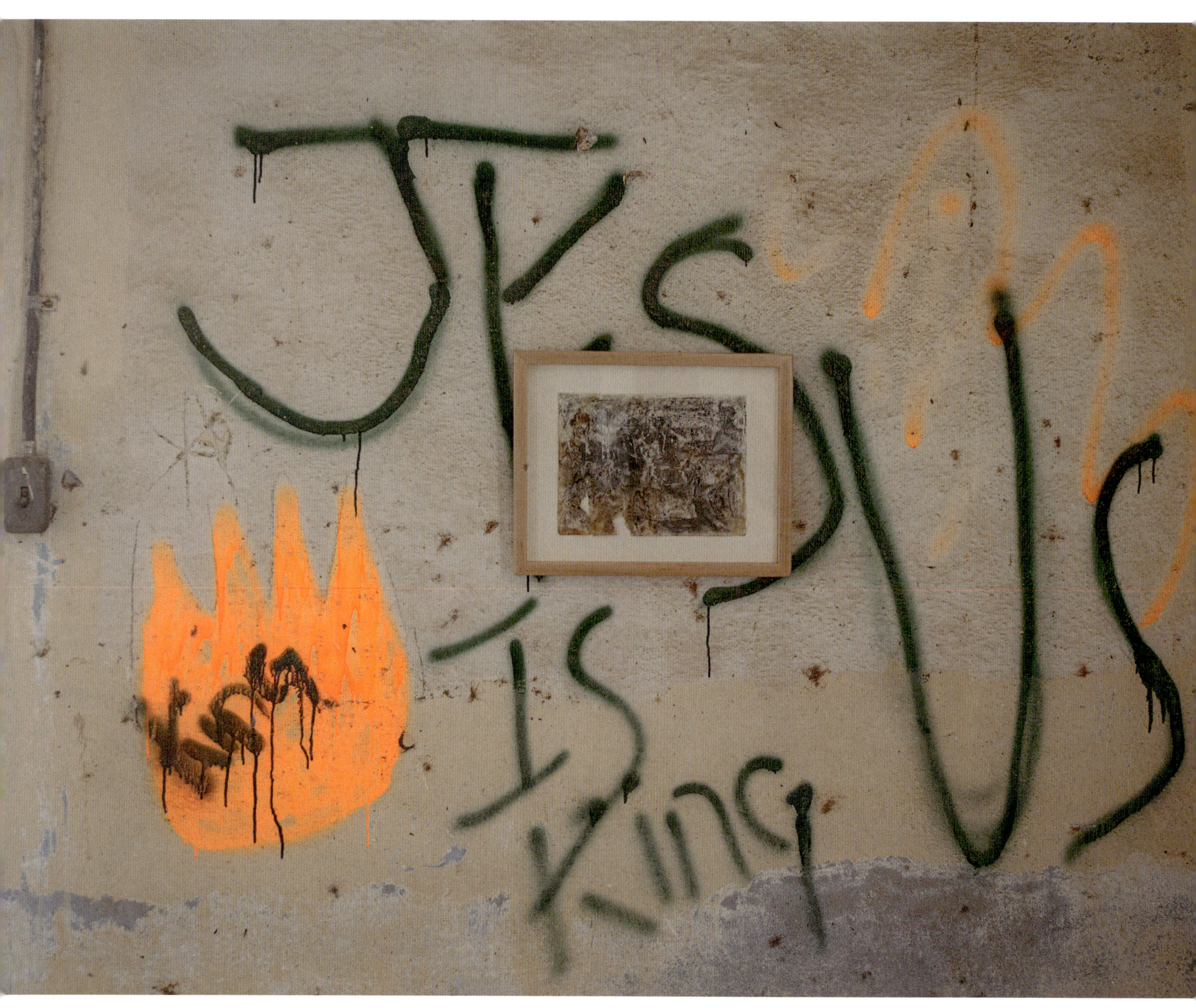
IS King

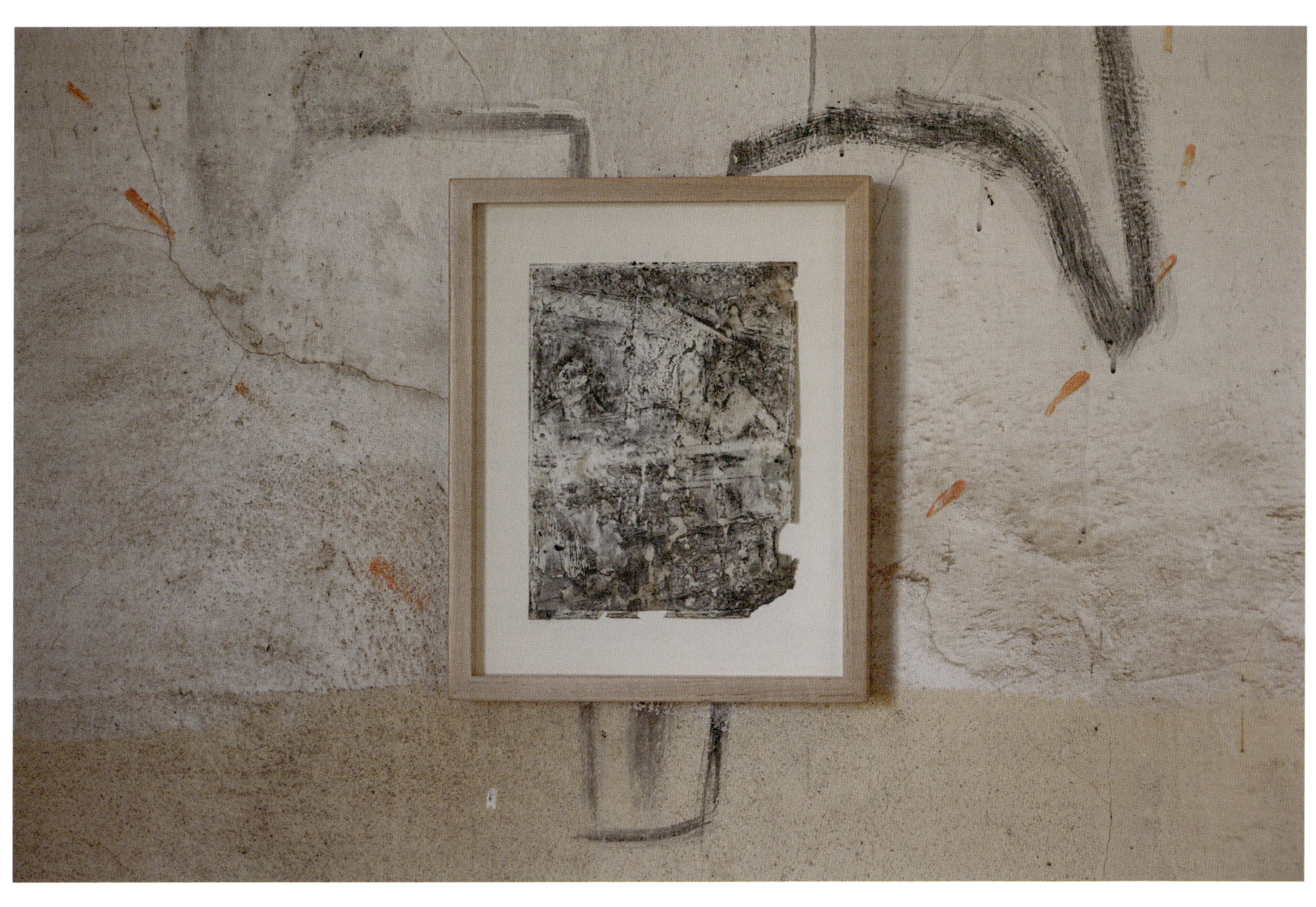

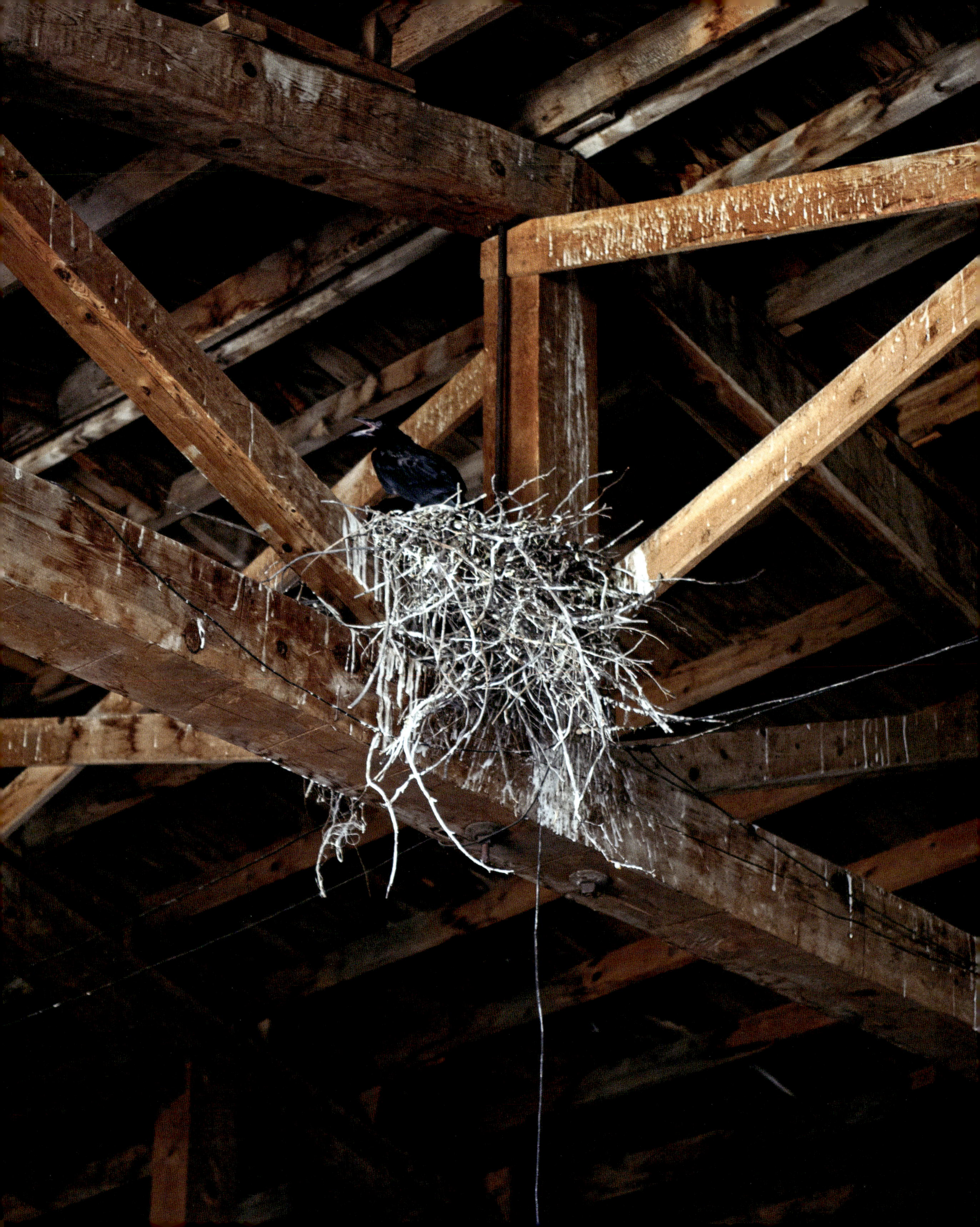

RETURN TO CEDARVALE SCHOOL

Already Paradise

At nearly 45, I am standing at the top of a ladder, which is situated on a soft, drooping, rotten wooden floor, which could collapse any second, and which definitely has some ratio of rats to rattlesnakes living beneath it. I am not the spry 40-year-old youngster I was when I came here more than four years ago. My studio manager Sam Staffan is holding the ladder. I have one arm extended as far upward as I can reach, holding a very heavy unrolled 130 × 120-inch canvas (*The Tracker or the Tracked*), which I am attempting to staple to the wooden cleat above, while bending ignorantly over the top rung of the ladder where my staple gun rests. It must appear be happening in slow motion to Sam, who might be deciding whether he will dodge or catch me when I fall. My arm-span is at full reach, and proves to be just enough. I say aloud, "This is the last time. I'm not made for this shit anymore."

Four years ago, while still living in Roswell, I packed a U-Haul with paintings, drove three hours to this selfsame New Mexico ghost town, and installed them alone in this school. I did this in the midst of the Covid pandemic, and in great anticipation of the imminent birth of our daughter, just two months away. The experience had nearly killed me then as well, but happily, cathartically.

I have often called that first abandoned school installation an "exhibition for ghosts," or, truly, an "exhibition for resident barn owl." In fact, a piece I made for the space was an overlarge barn-owl portrait, for just such an audience. I could not have anticipated how enlivening the school installation would be, how strangely better I felt to have the space to myself rather than to have a social event, however well attended. The seeming indifference of its emptiness was something akin to a religious experience. My estrangement from the culture began shifting from a kind of debilitating psychological complex to a sense of freedom and opportunity.

What I did not yet know was that putting work in an abandoned school in the middle of nowhere was the first step in forming a contemplative practice that would facilitate a personal transformation of a most important kind. I experienced a deeper sense of trust in mystery and in time, allowed that I might never find meaningful connection in the art world, and that, actually, my sense of relatedness to the broader world deepened and mattered much more to me. The install had happened spontaneously, sincerely, and irrationally without any expectation of outside response or validation. Without being aware of it, I was looking for the possibility of long-term continuance as an artist, and apparently assumed *Nihil* could go on forever. If *Nihil* is really *about* anything at all, it is to do with forming a practice in the emptiness of life in lieu of answers that never come, answers for terribly fundamental questions. Why live? Why make anything? Why say anything? Who or what is art for? Is anyone there?

All of these questions are to do with meaning and identity. Poet Christian Wiman, writing his book *My Bright Abyss* while in cancer treatment, mused, "there is a sense in which our most pressing existential question has to be outgrown before it can be answered."[1] Yet out of the inquiry came a collection of experiences, objects, and images that have given over to a surprising sort of symbolic order I could never have planned. Though it never offered answers, *Nihil* gave me something better: quiet meaningfulness.

Now life has changed again. I am an exhausted middle-aged husband and dad, and I like it that way. But over the past year or so, I have grown aware that what had begun spontaneously and in earnest was turning into a performance, a kind of window dressing, or, God forbid, a brand. The insight was gradual, but the intensity of this inner demand felt sudden, decisive: *Nihil* had reached its end. And it did so right where it began: on a hot New Mexico summer day in the abandoned Cedarvale School.

Four years ago, I installed paintings no one cared about in a part of the world few are aware of. Now I was installing a massive triptych in a gymnasium, while, unknown to me, one of my galleries was negotiating its sale to a museum I had never heard of in a country I have never visited. It is as if, like some kind of desert hermit, I have invisibly occupied an unknown land, wrestling with obscure gods and phantoms, until, finally, knowing nothing at all anymore, and desiring none of my old grief or grievances, I am obliged to stand up, dust myself off, notice that the world has changed, and that I have changed too. I recall that the first tenet of *Nihil* is "Exile and Absence." But what began as exile has welcomed me home; what was absence is now a quiet daily abundance.

1 Christian Wiman, *My Bright Abyss*, Farrar, Straus, and Giroux, 2013, p. 81.

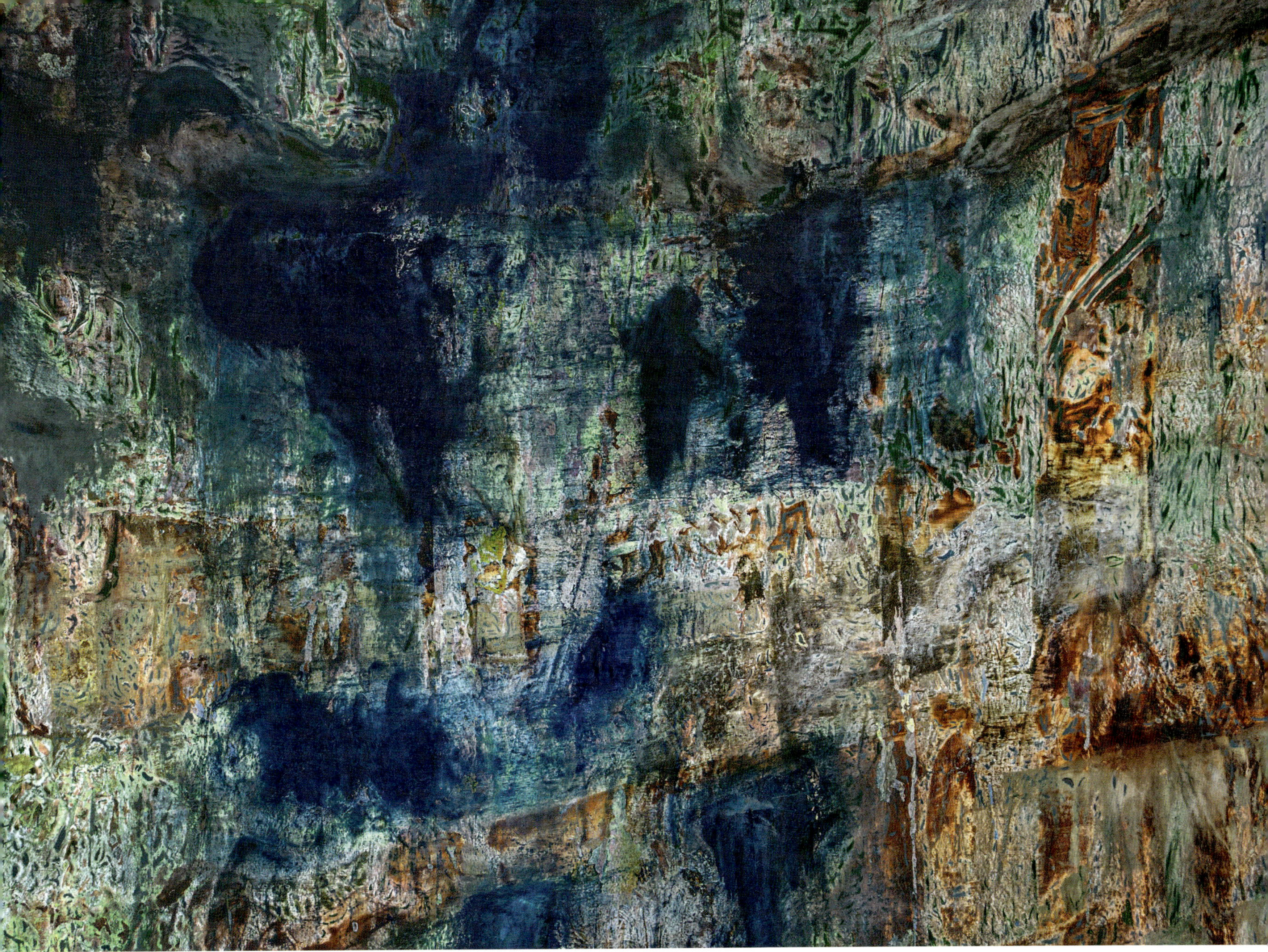

THE TRACKER OR THE TRACKED, DETAIL, MIXED MEDIA ON UNSTRETCHED CANVAS AND BURLAP, 130 × 120 IN., 2023

In the worn-out dichotomy of whether meaning is something that humans project on to a meaningless world, or whether the universe really is inherently meaningful because of God, gods, or some kind of sacred design, it seems to me that, either way, each layer of explanation begs another question, and an infinite regress begins. As usual, we are stuck in language. Belief, it seems to me, will never matter half as much as direct experience.

Nihil was never going to last forever. Yet it survives its extinction. It was the game that makes all future games possible. For it might just be that the only way forward for me is to play in that zone between meaning and meaninglessness, the sacred and absurd, and to devise a method by which to roam.

From playing a game I invented by accident, I learned how games can work, and because I understand that, I can design new ones. I can make the pieces and the board. I can set the rules and extrapolate endless sequences and combinations. The world outside has been keeping busy.

It is time to come out of the desert. There are new games to play.

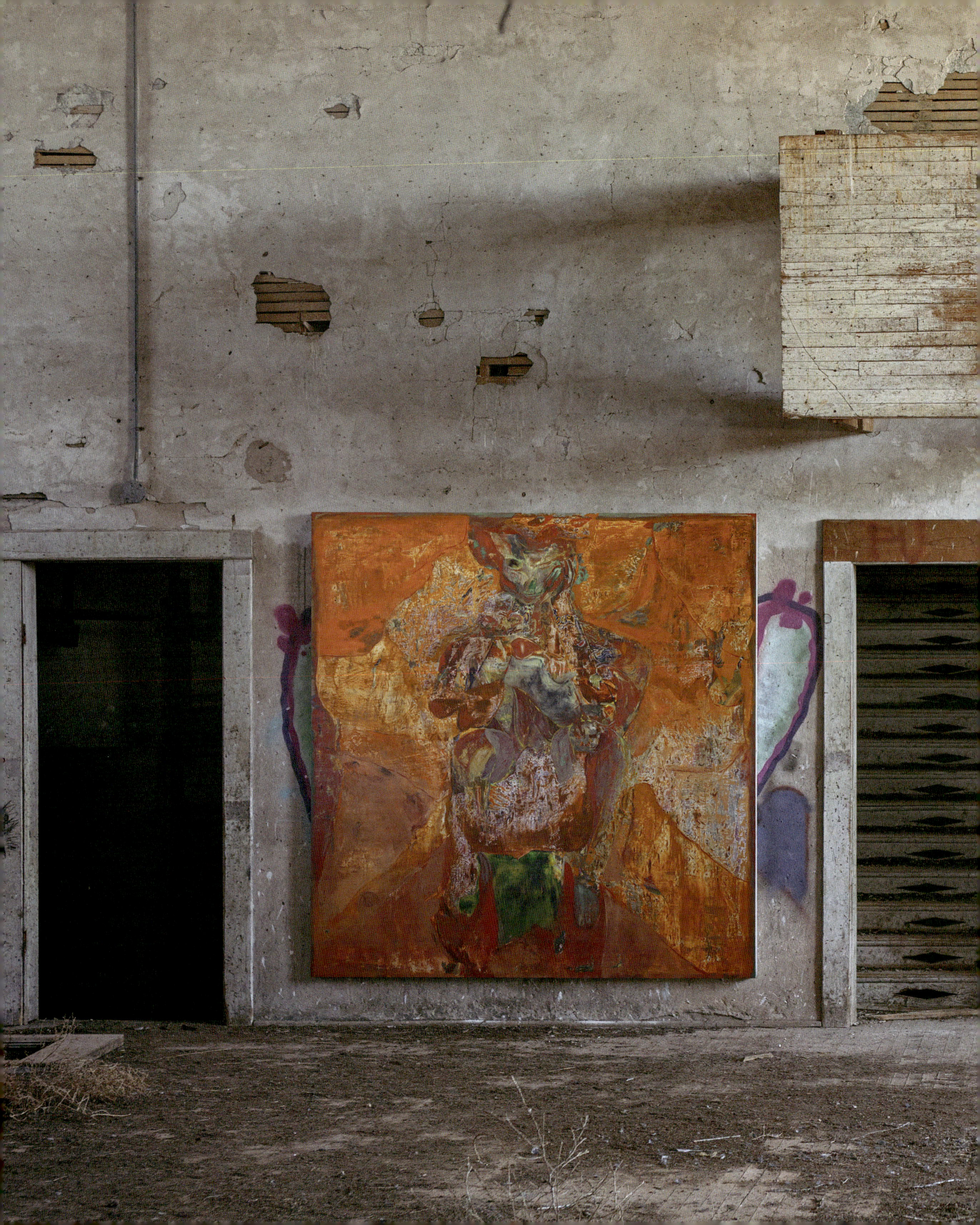

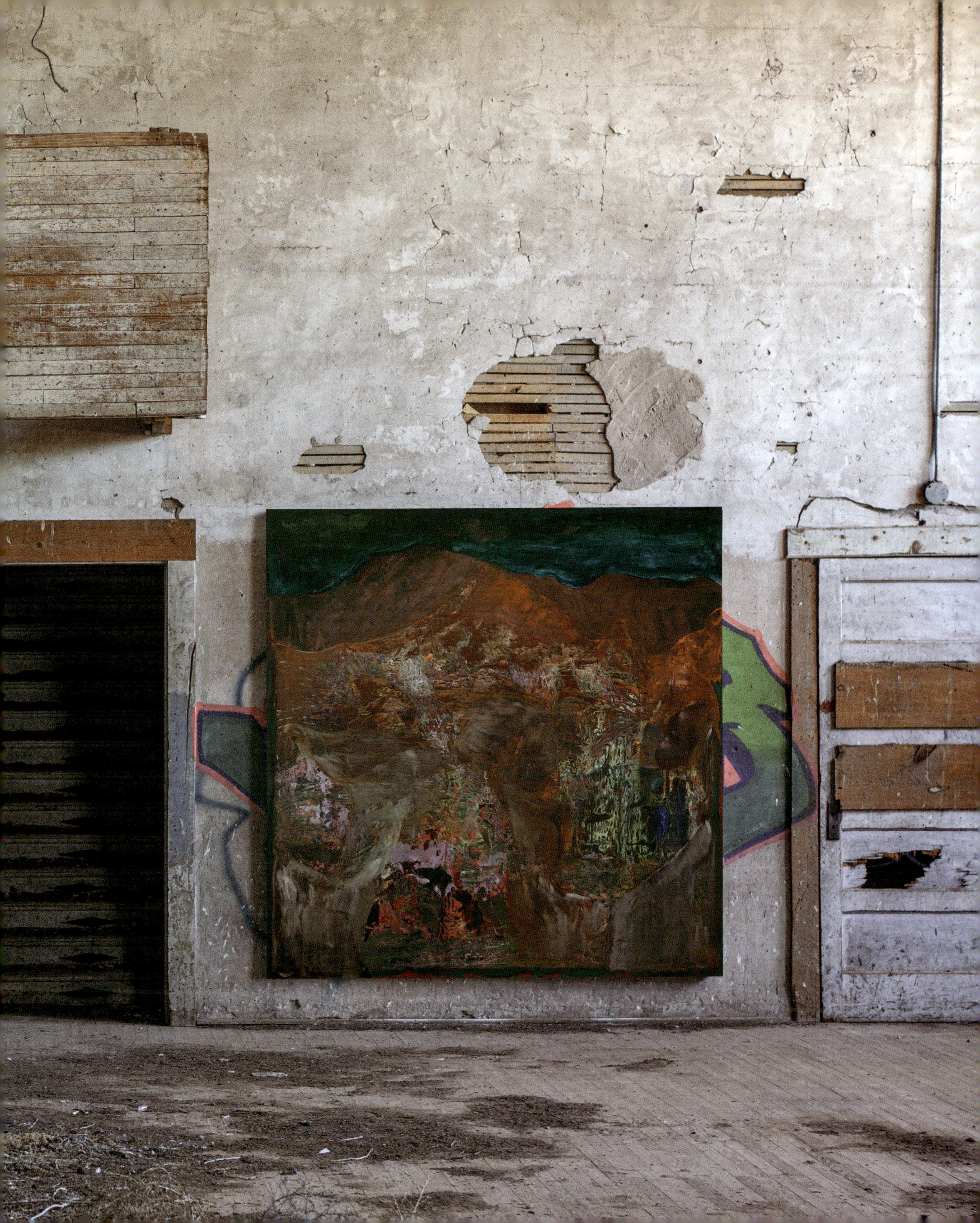

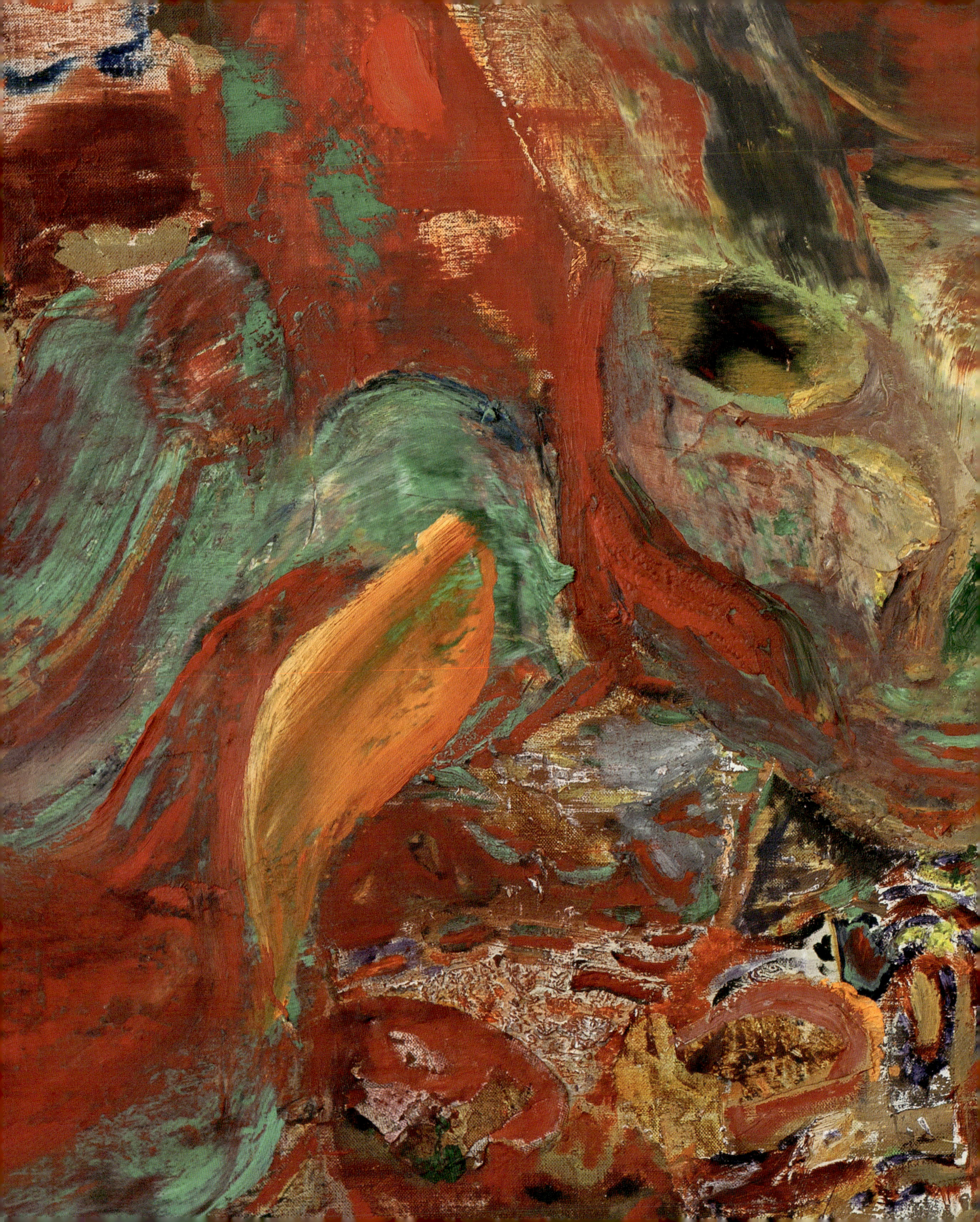

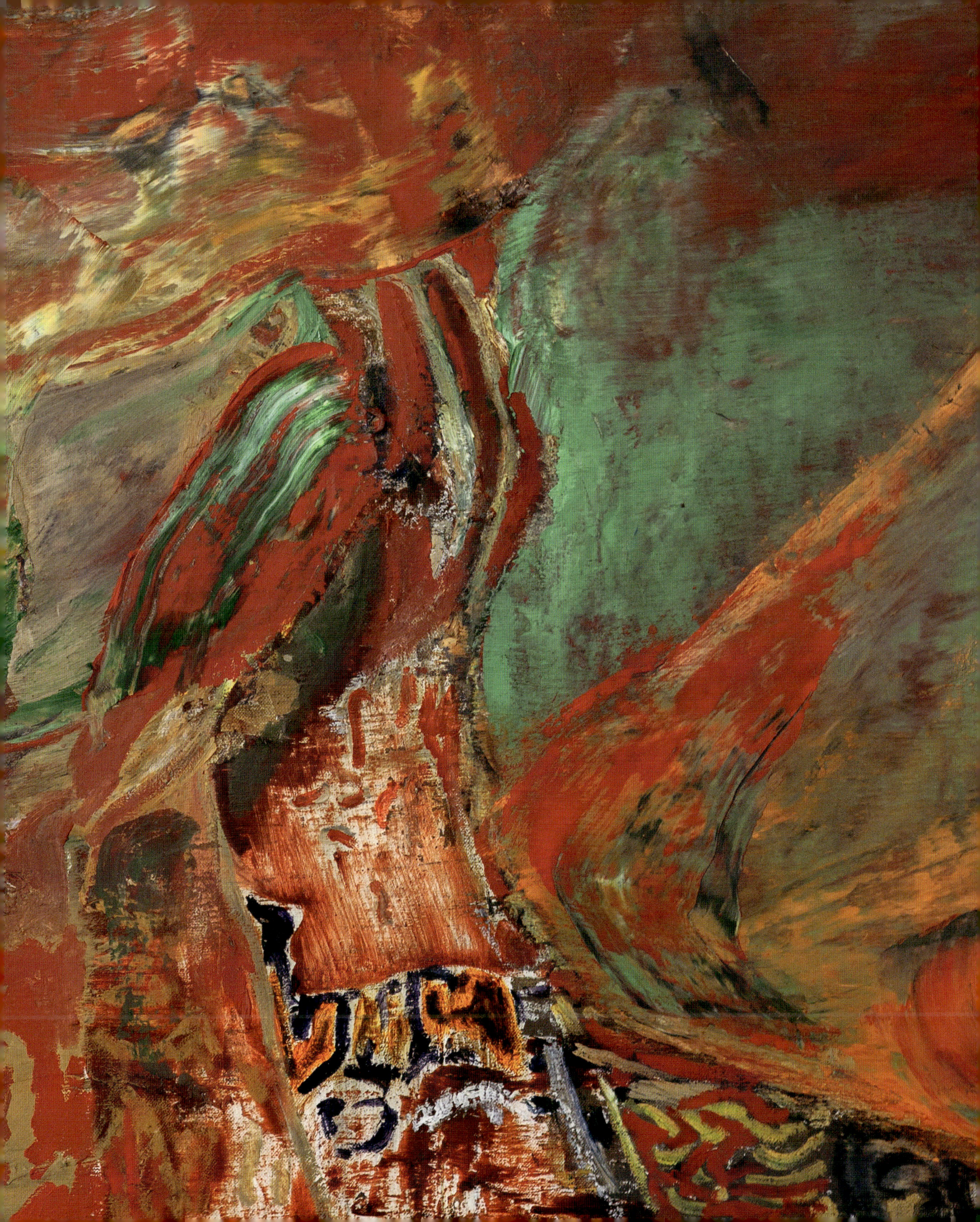

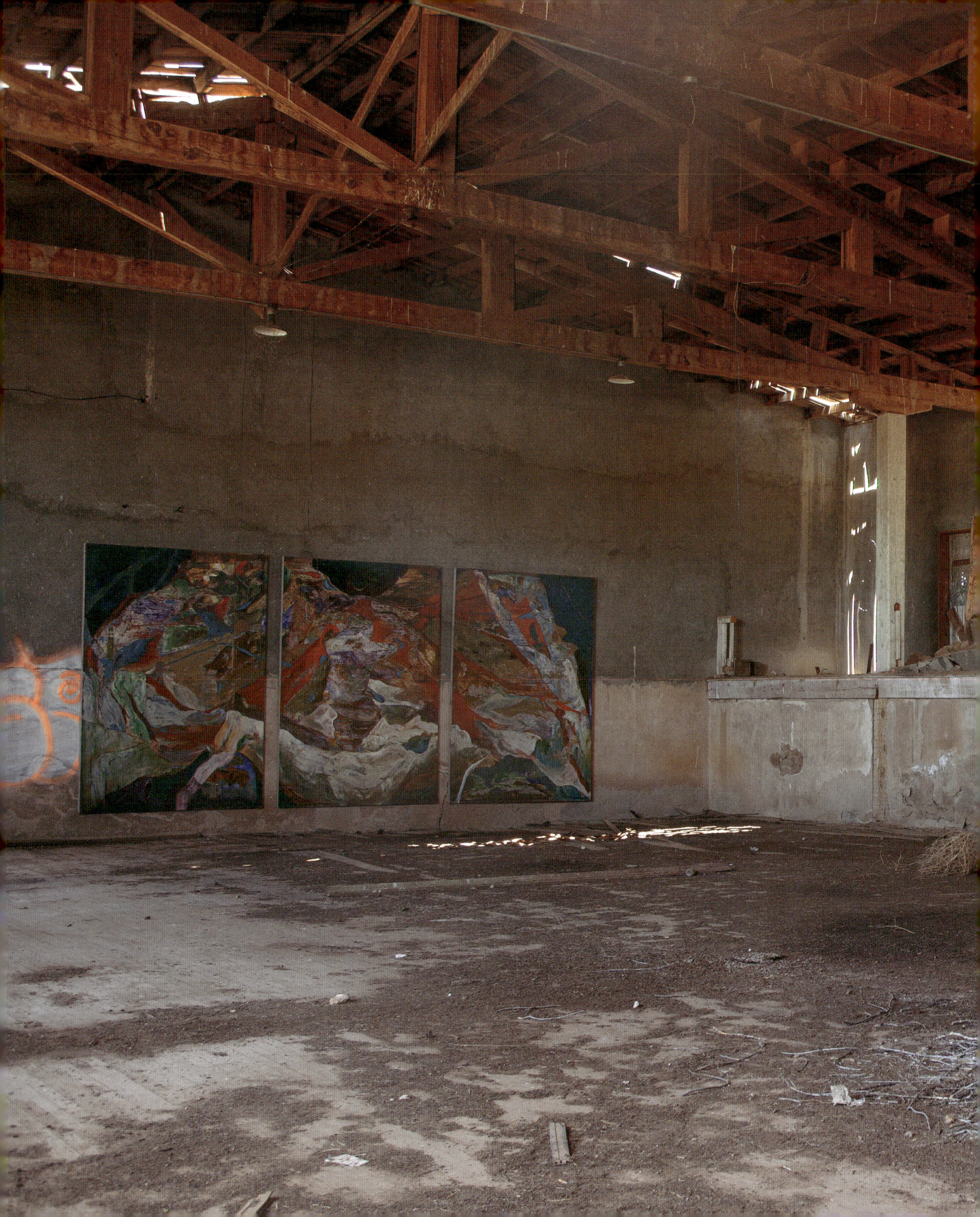

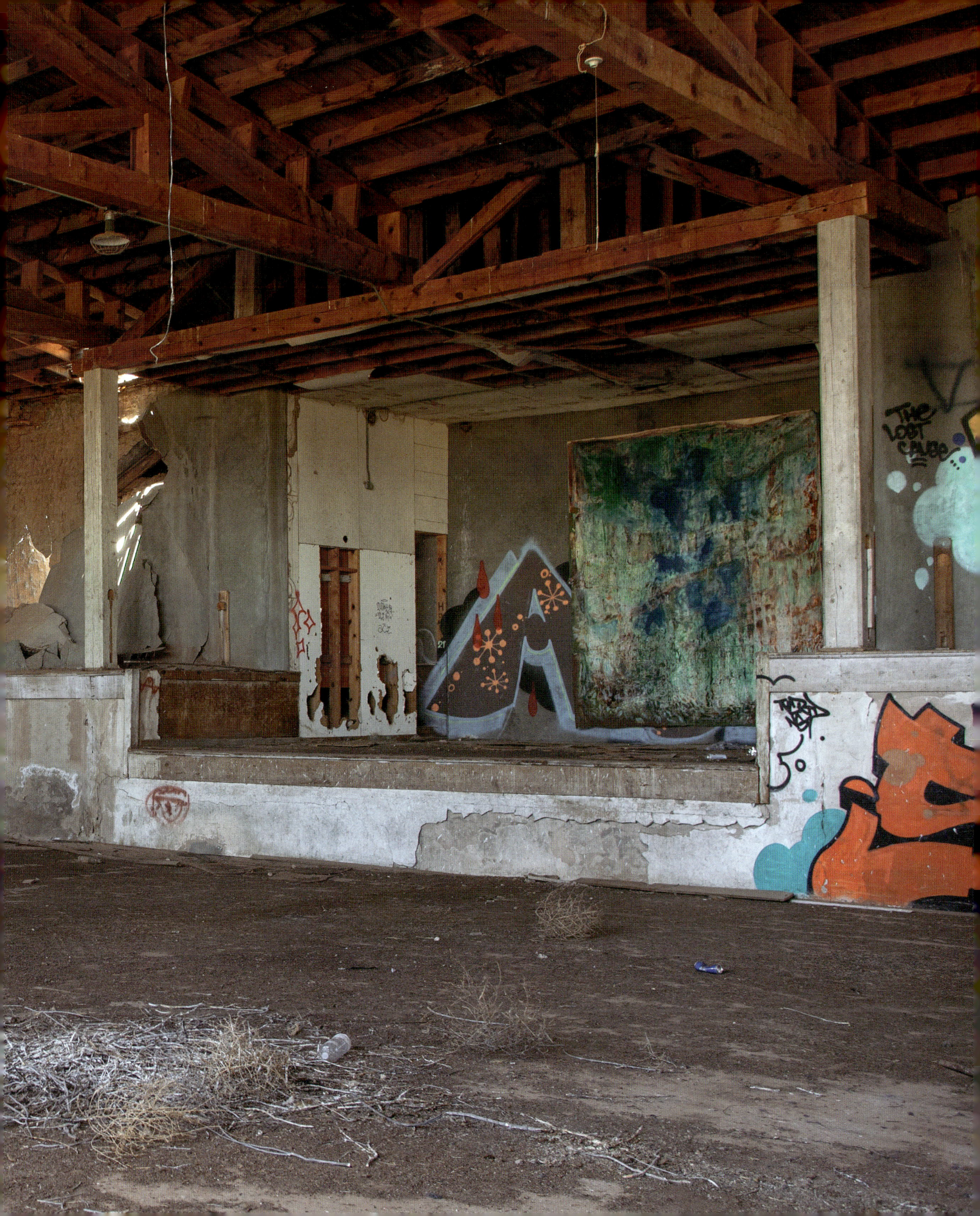
THE LOST CAUSE

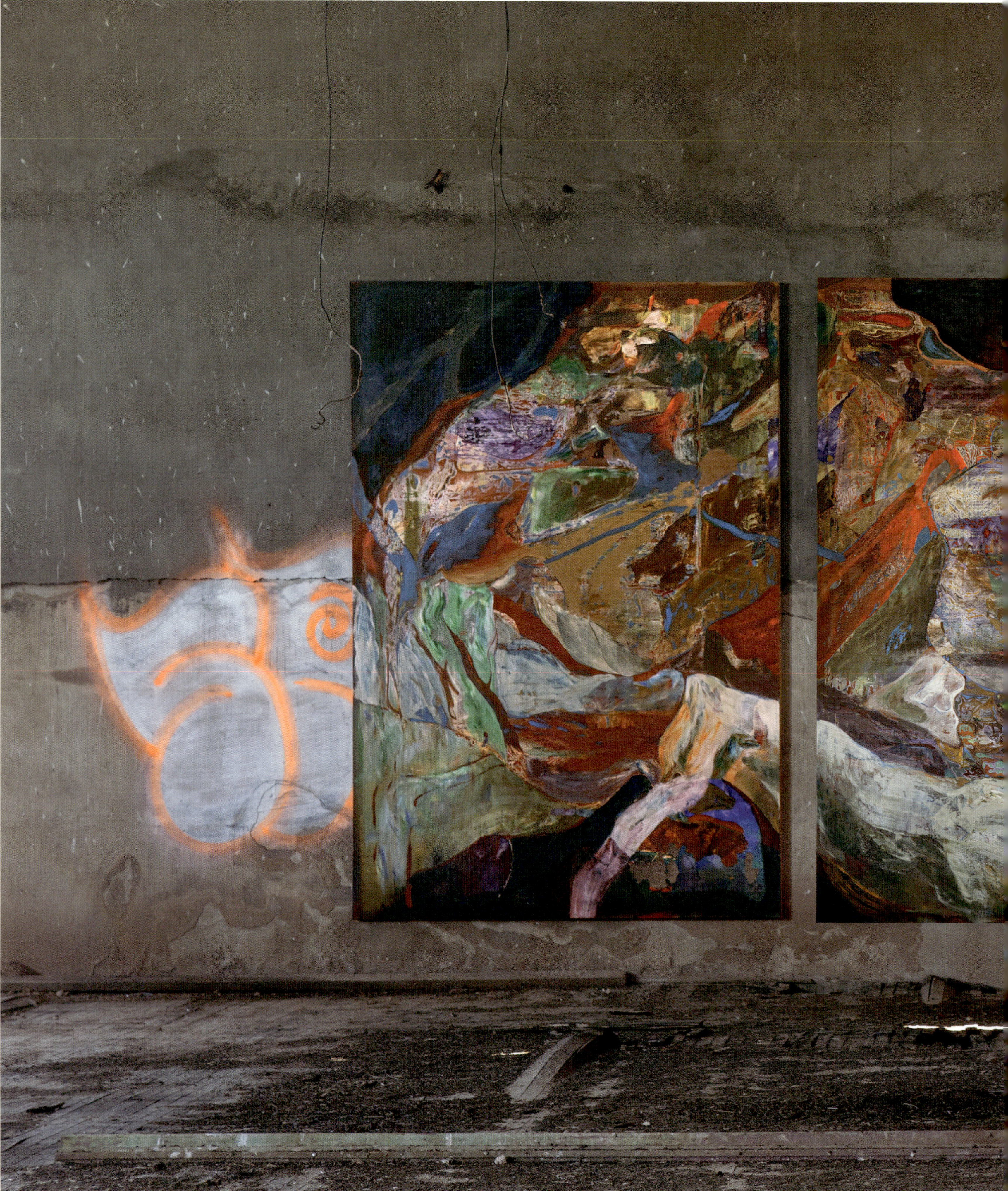

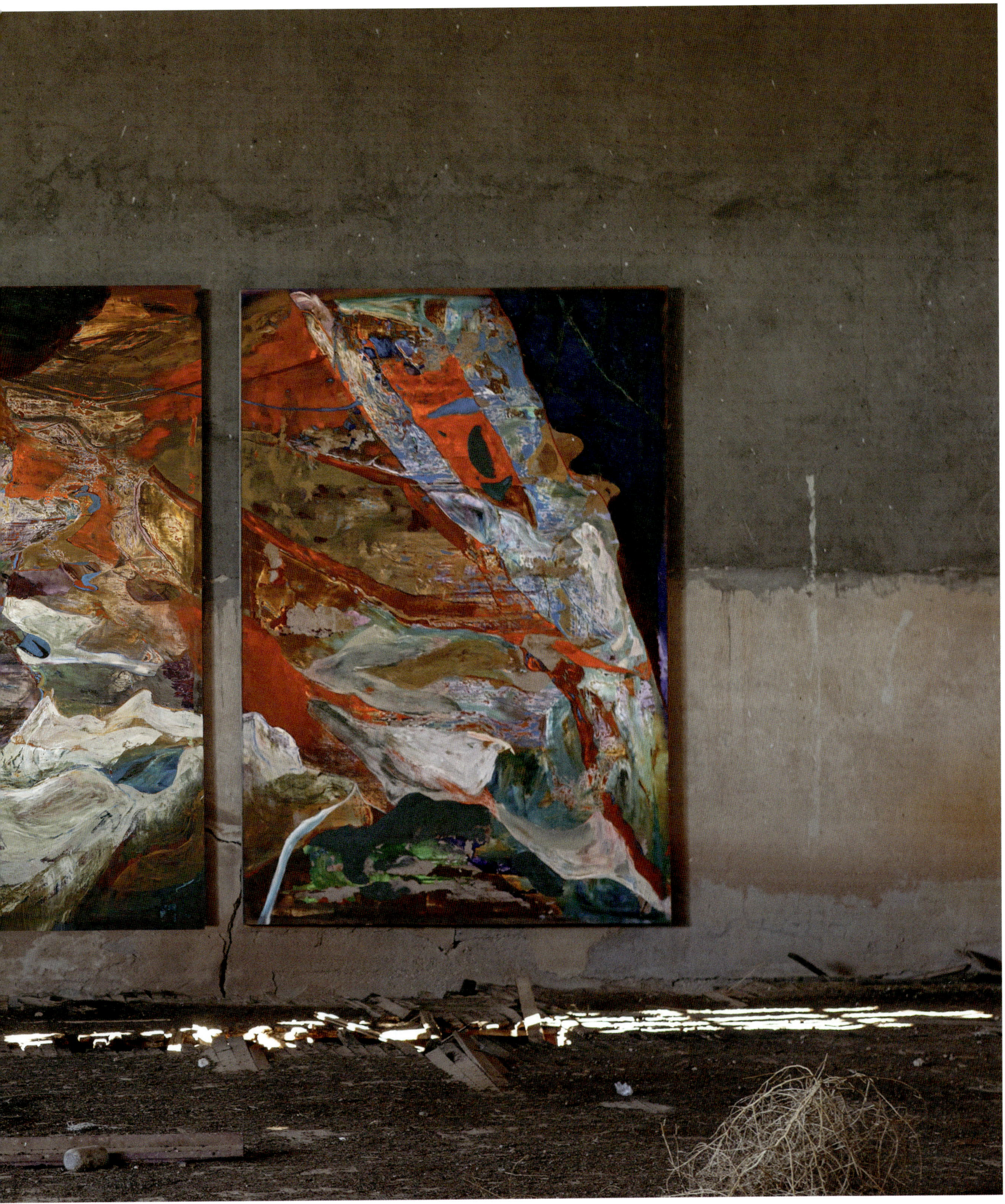

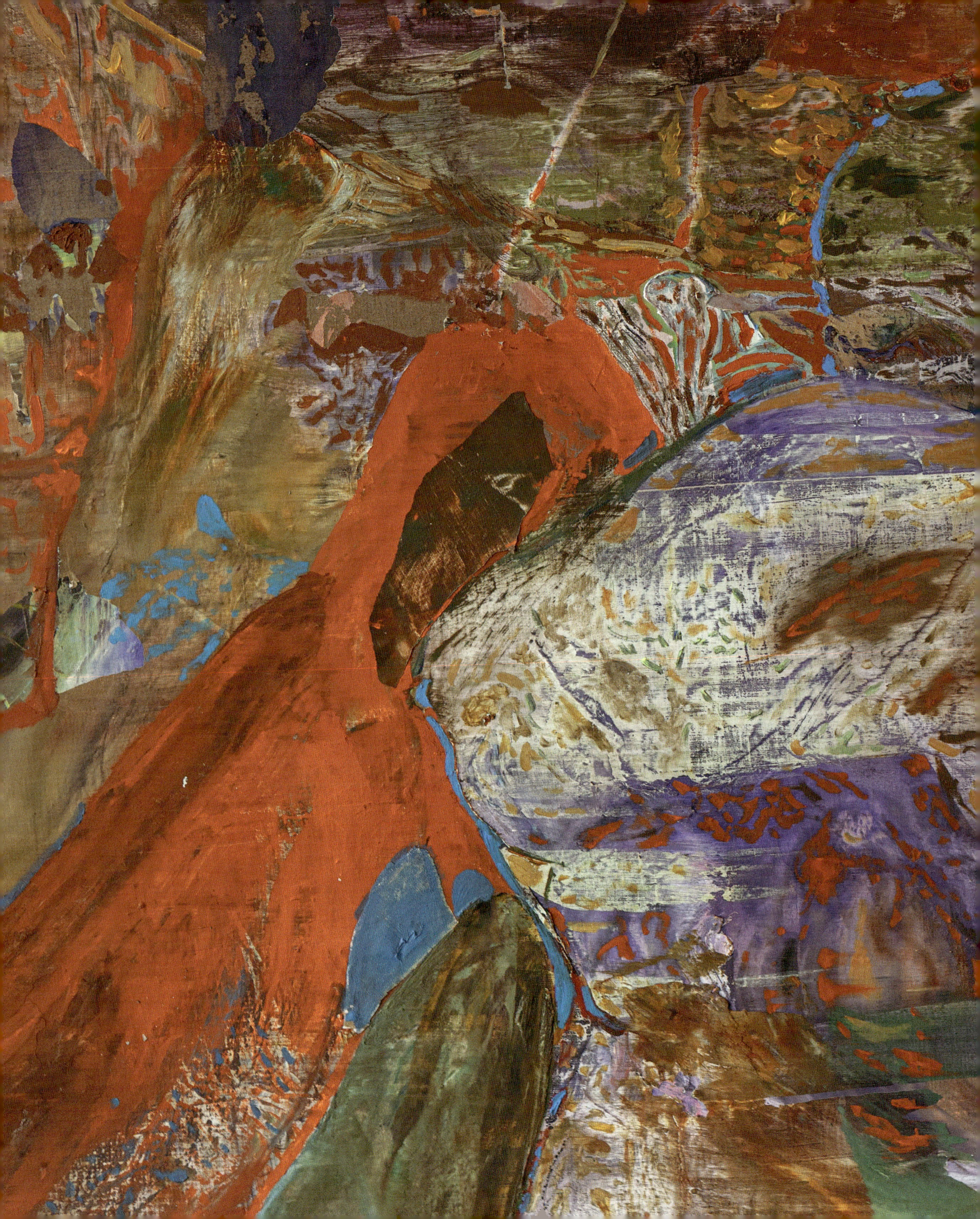

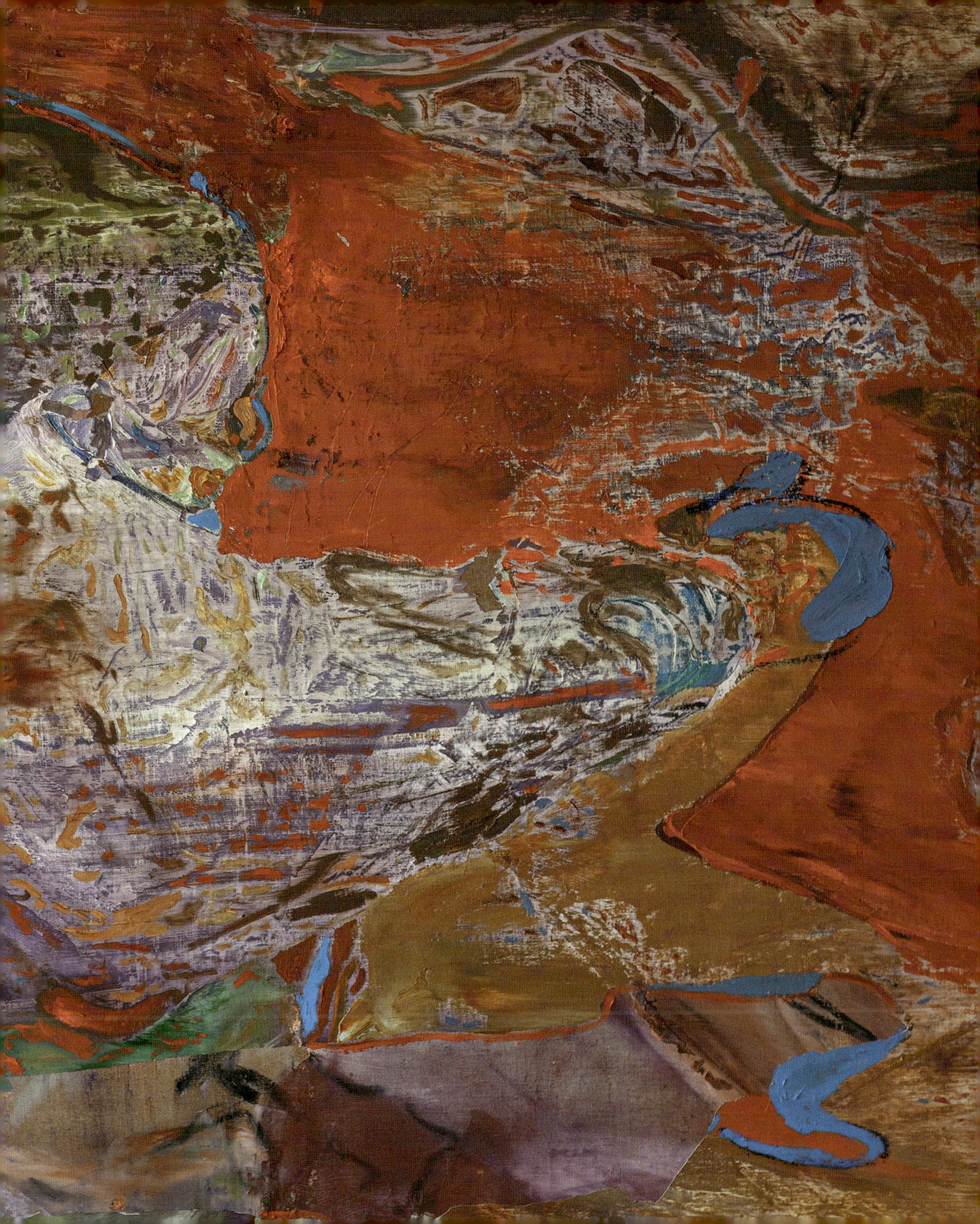

Color *(Delayed Prejudice)*

In *Nihil*, color is not planned or used strategically. There should be no conscious color preferences to make a painting in one color instead of another. Color must be incidental, contingent on a larger process, in which the palette coming forward is revealed more than designed. The assumption is that color, like anything else, will reveal itself as necessary to the overall feeling of the work.

The artwork's palette can only come about idiosyncratically. Here are some possibilities:

First, it is possible to use a preset pattern, though not one designed by me. Let us say red equals A, orange B, yellow C, and so on. If a certain piece responds to a tintinnabuli composition by Arvo Pärt, I can reference specific notes via color and layer them in the same way he layers aurally. In that way, I am forced to respond to whatever this palette gives me over several layers. The bigger the mess, the bigger the opportunity to improvise. I can never know in advance what color the final piece will be.

All drawings used as reference for paintings must be black and white or monochromatic. This is to make it impossible to preplan a palette. I cannot mix color to match an already existing color.

The tubes of paint in my painting drawers should be rearranged each time, randomly, or according to a musical pattern. When it is required to use a certain color, there is no option to deny it. Sometimes the color is an utter inconvenience to the progress made in a work. The color will sometimes be so inconvenient as to seem to "ruin" the pattern that I had been working toward. In trusting the process, however, I find again and again that the more inconveniences occur, the richer the surface eventually becomes. The only color mistake I can make is to lose faith in the process. Trusting the process, I relax into the inconvenience and accept that it has something to teach me.

When it comes to the small objects, all color used in them must be left over from previous palettes. Because of this constraint, it typically takes months to make the smallest works, and because I have little choice in the color I use, it is unlikely that the new color layer will work very well with the color underneath. That is how they become so thick. I just keep adding "bad colors" until, somehow, it arrives.

This is why *Nihil* does not really mean "nothing." If, historically, a specific color is thought to have a specific meaning, then, if I am not careful, I begin to believe it. I do not form or verbalize an intellectual belief; nevertheless, a kind of unconscious suspicion is expressed in the colors to which I default. The "nothing" of *Nihil* is in the imposed constraint: to remove intentional emotional manipulation or meaning-making from color and, by implication, to remove latent ideological underpinnings all too convenient to my sense of identity. Enforcing what are ultimately arbitrary methods for creating a palette requires the question of belief to be asked freshly each time and to make visible the unconscious tendencies that quietly rumble beneath every action.

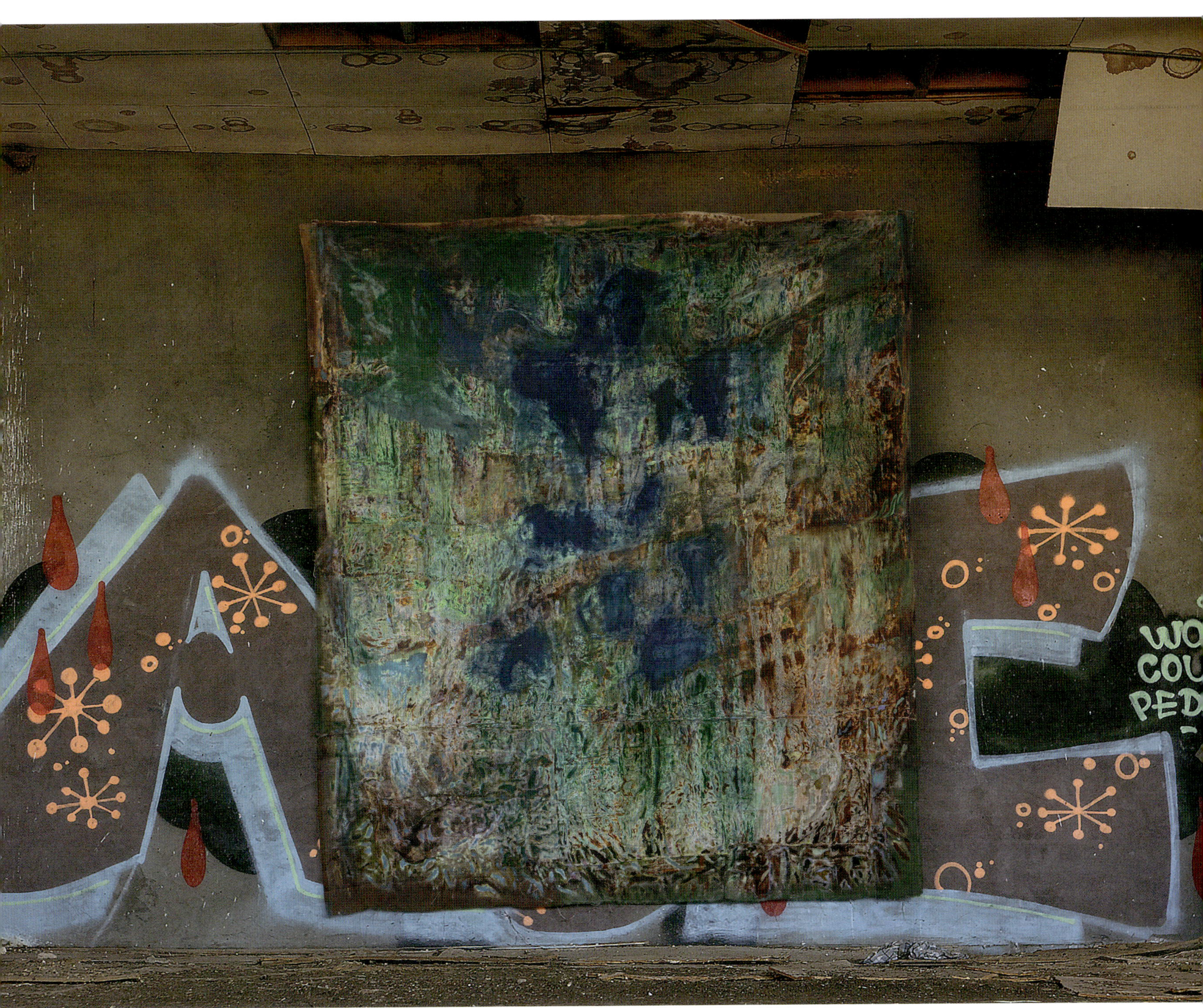

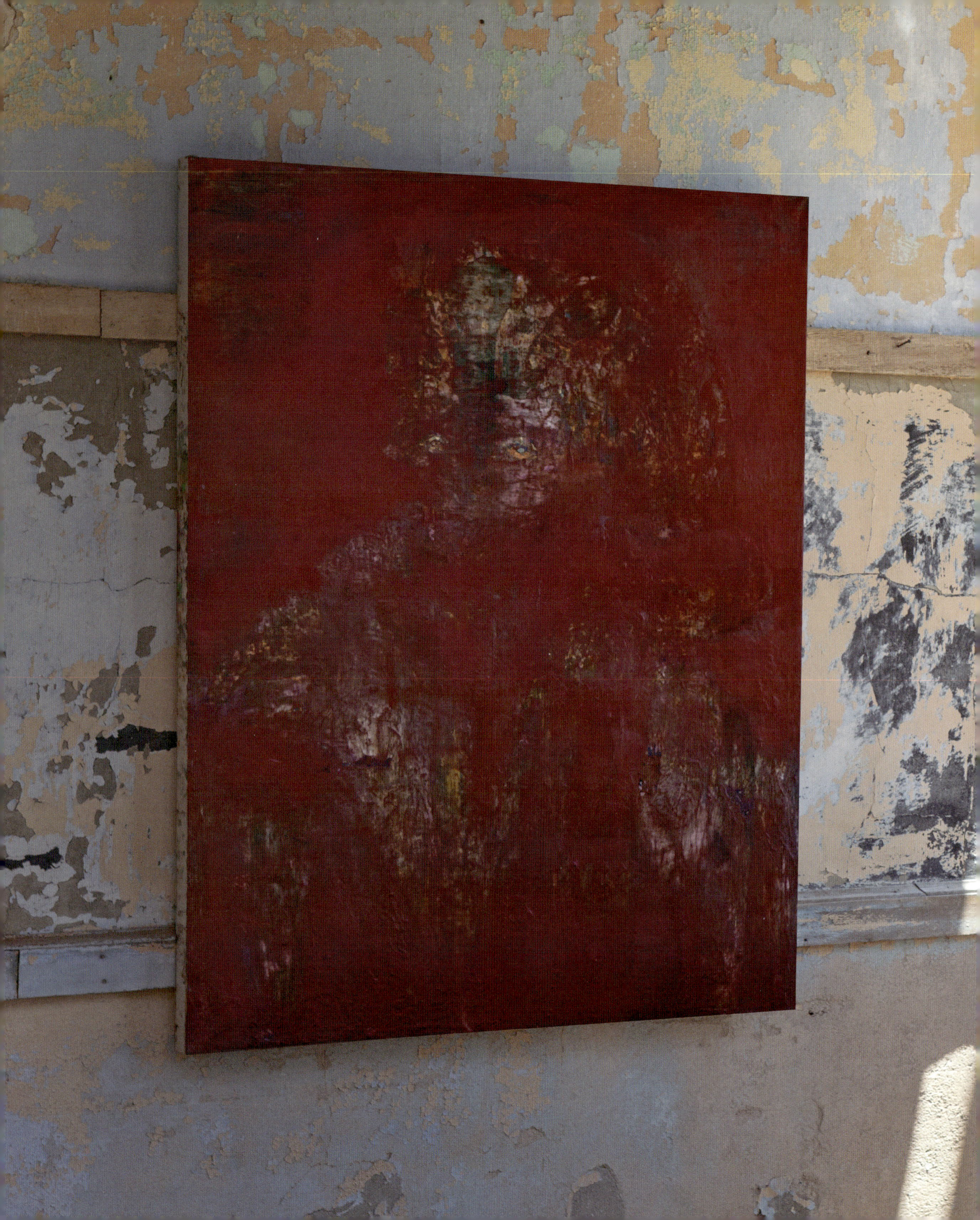

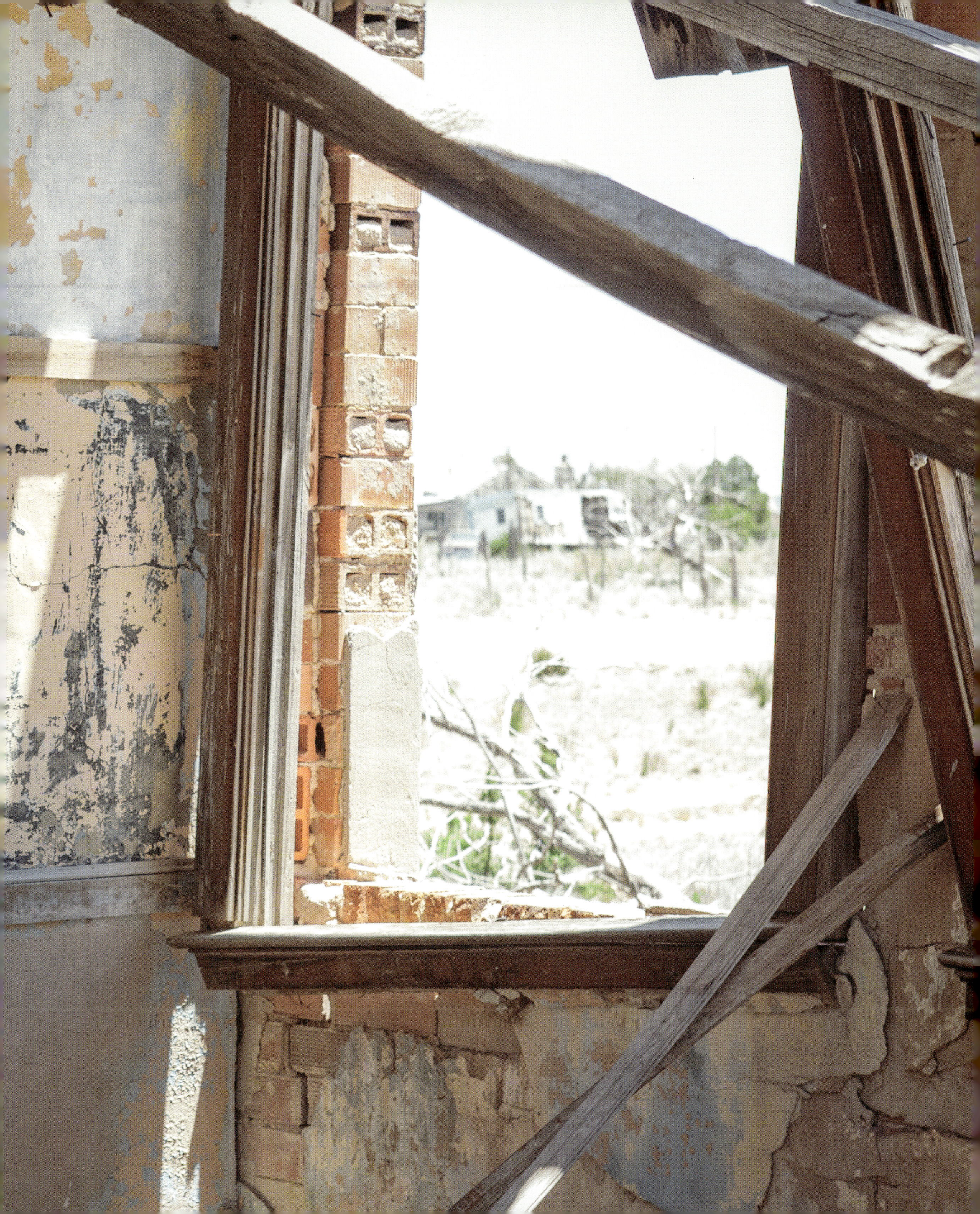

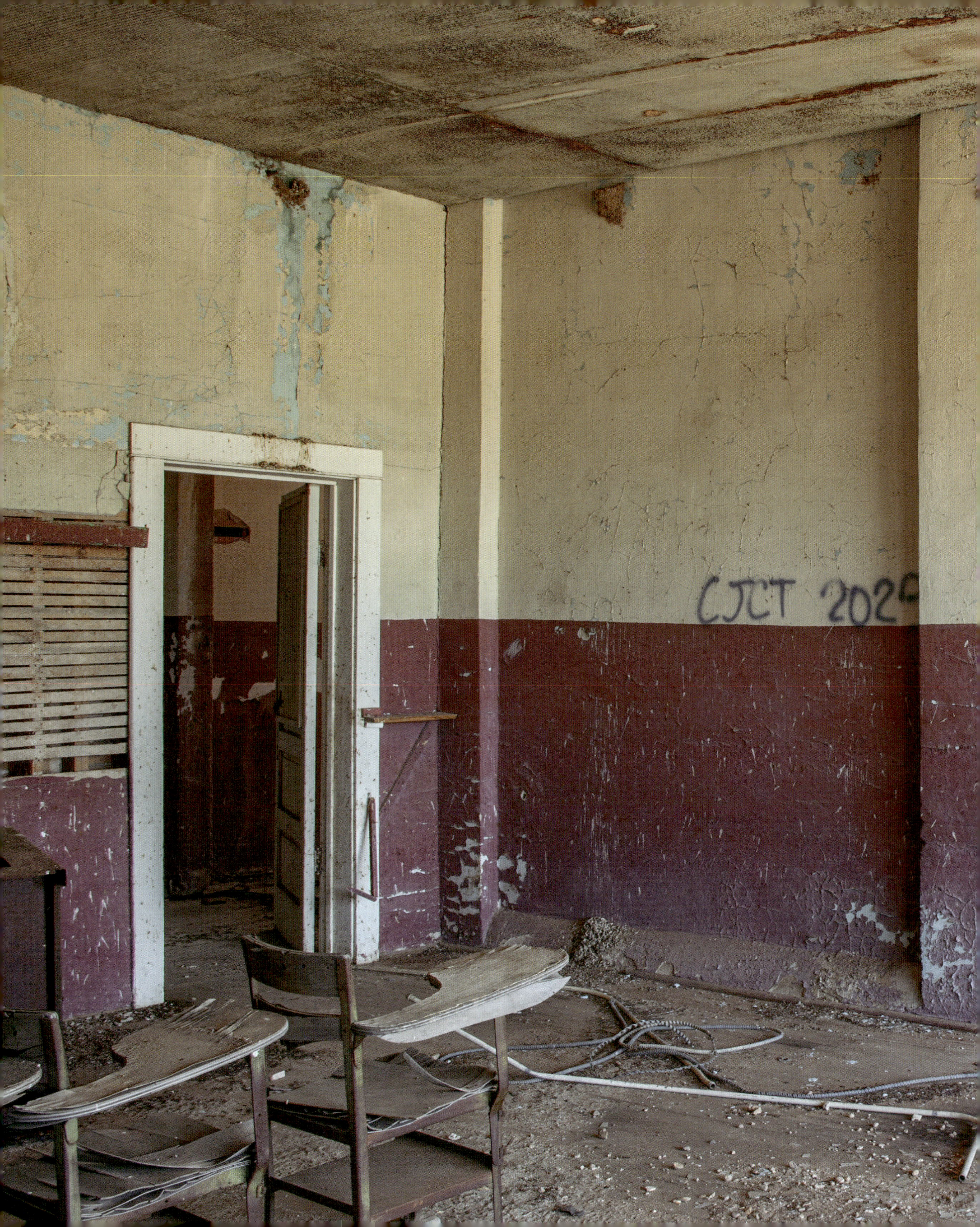
CJCT 202

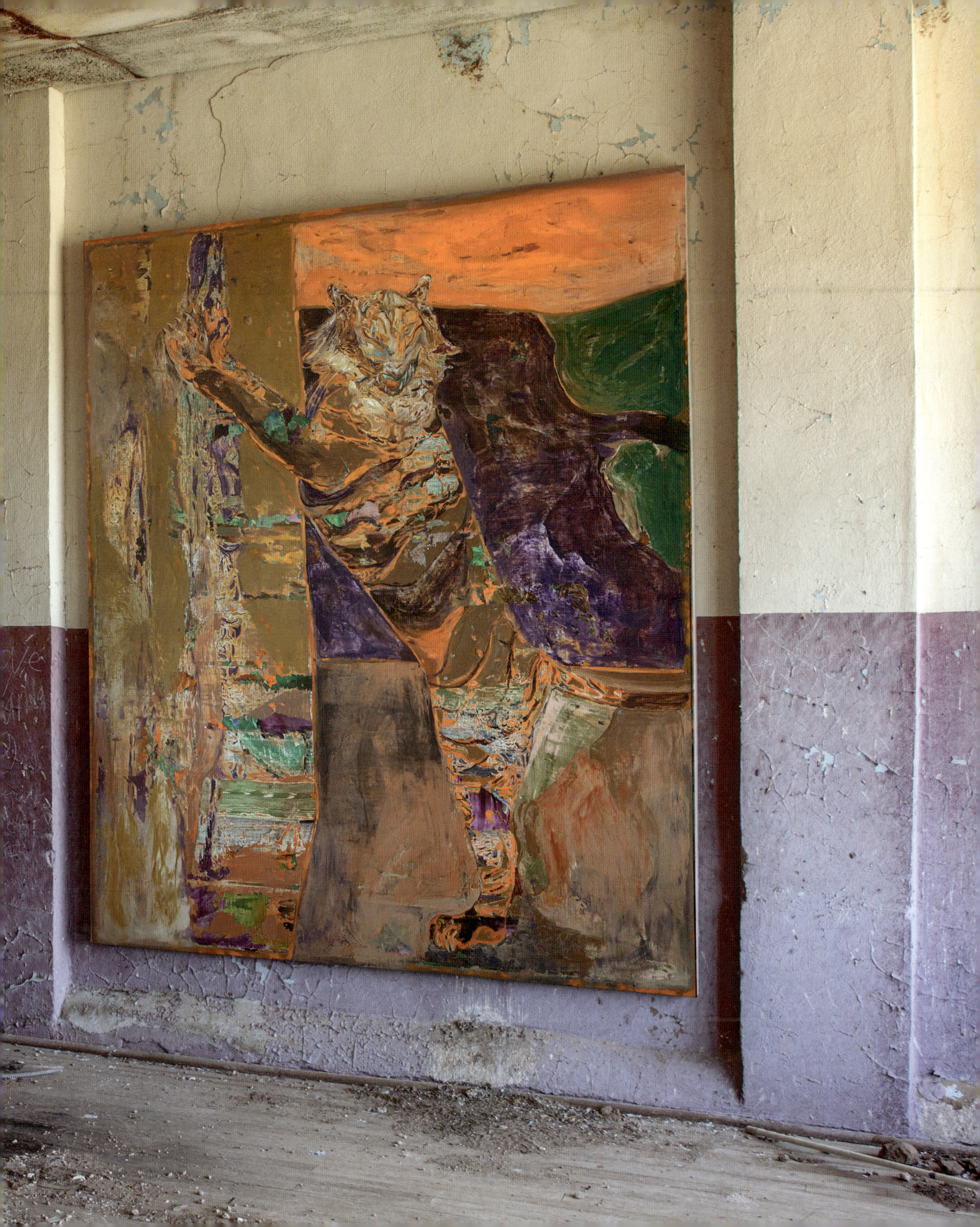

Time (*The Great Collaborator*)

The evidence of time's passage—in the landscape, an abandoned school, ancient ruin, forgotten object—is a visual clue that points toward the paradox of absence and presence so important in *Nihil*. Time is a friend making all processes possible.

The only violation of this tenet is to regard time as enemy. It is to be worked with, never against. In this way, the process cannot go wrong. For example, a layer in a painting might prove uninspiring. This is not a problem. There is no wasted time; the uninspired layer will simply take part in the overall consciousness of the work. It will contribute to the whole, however discreetly, whether it provides useful coloration peeking from underneath in later stages, or whether it simply adds to its overall sense of weariness, the necessary weight of experience grounding the work in contrast to other moments of deftness.

Time is the ubiquitous collaborator. Listening to Arvo Pärt's music is a good way to understand this. Music, in general, depends upon and must exist in time. Yet within a fixed time signature, it can either seem to expand or compress an experience of time. Pärt allows time to do a lot of the work, benefitting from the relative silence between notes, for example. This silence, in tintinnabuli, is also the expression of a gap between two voices: T-Voice (which is restricted to notes from the tonic triad) and M-Voice (which uses any tone within the chosen scale). This is, to the *Nihil* way of understanding, suggestive of the paradox in the presence of absence, where being becomes possible in the distance between myself and other. It is also the gap in the brokenness between two things; and only in brokenness can beauty be extricated. I want to know, how can my collaboration with time benefit from finding a visual approximation of this aural space that time makes possible in Pärt?

Both the opportunity and limitation in painting is that it is not confined to a linear experience of time. All considerations must fit in space, and in painting, that space is relatively flat. It is the secret of *Nihil* that a broad scale of time is present in the work as if harnessed and made expansive even if confined to what, in the scheme of things, is a small space. I must trust the process no matter what. I do not understand its alchemy; I am required only to trust it. I understand the passage of time in the object itself, with its evidence apparent, as having a deep past or a deep memory. In the addition and subtraction of layer after layer, this memory seems to regard the eternal as opposed to the momentary.

When the scale of time grows broader in the imagination, I do not fear the eventual catastrophe but accept its role in the drama. Just as there is a painting before painting, in *Nihil*, there is a painting after. Its eventual transformation will not have been an accident; I have accounted for another horizon.

In exile, I hear philosopher Emmanuel Levinas: "To renounce being the contemporary of the triumph of one's work is to envisage this triumph in *a time without me*, to aim at this world without me, to aim at a time beyond the horizon of my time, in an eschatology without hope for oneself, or in a liberation from my own time."[1]

1 Emmanuel Levinas, *Collected Philosophical Papers*, Martinus Nijhoff Publishers, 1987.

To be liberated from one's own time is what the very collaboration with time makes possible. This is true in life, in the work, and in a single work. Whatever object I might collect tells me something about the limits of my involvement with it. The touch anticipates the consciousness of time; there is what I show to you and what I do not. I am saying: the eternal is evidenced in the ephemeral, which is what every painting eventually is. The tenet of Time is a method I employ now to create a work, but more importantly, it is a method of liberating the work from my own time.

Whether memory is external to the mind or entirely dependent on it, I cannot know. Neither can I know how to differentiate between internal and external phenomena. What I do know is that my individual experience of time has little to do with its reality, whatever it is: fundamental, emergent, chimerical. I must fall in love with not knowing. Someone not yet born will find what preceded me in the painting, that piece of time I sought. The one who comes later is the one for whom it had waited.

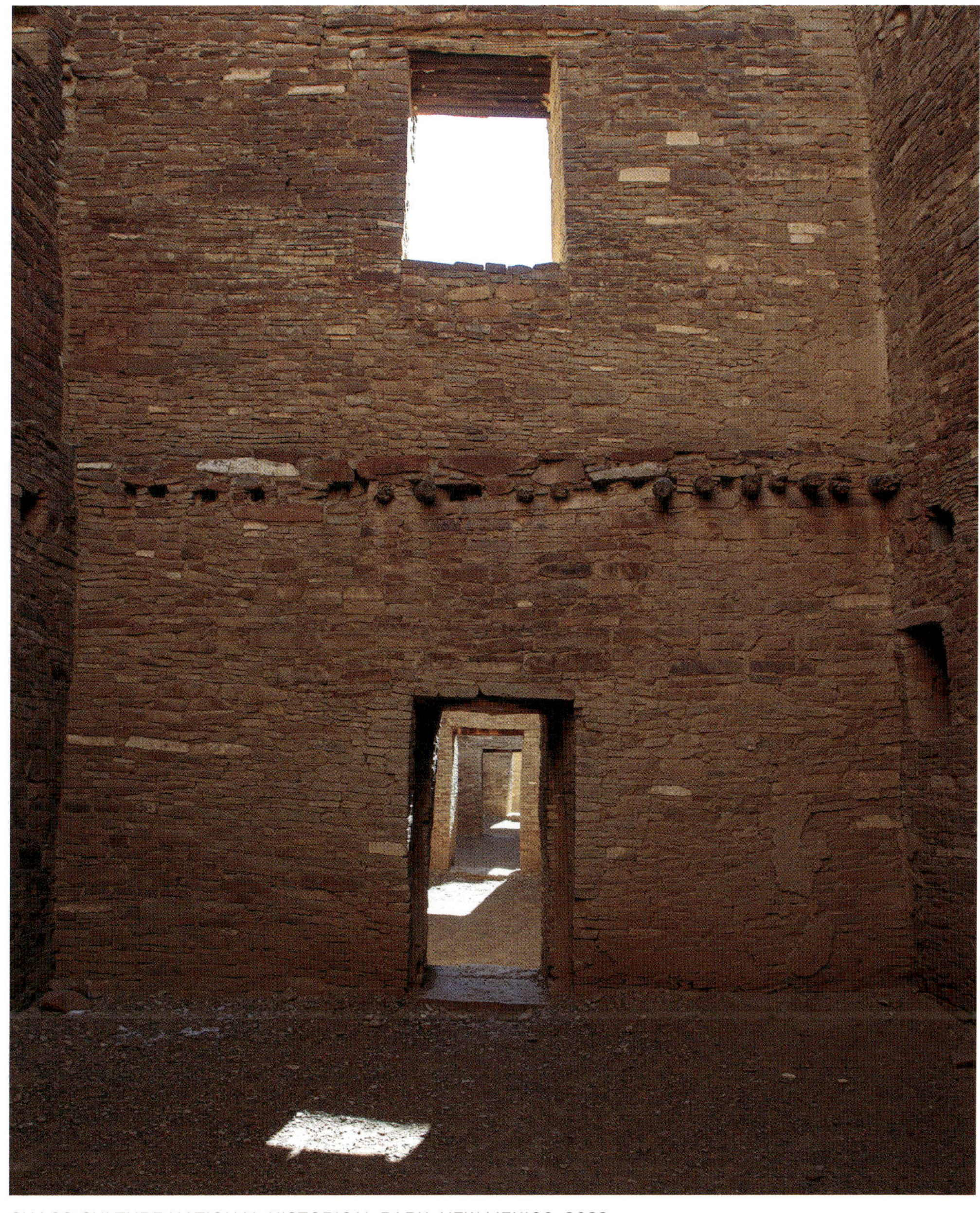

CHACO CULTURE NATIONAL HISTORICAL PARK, NEW MEXICO, 2022

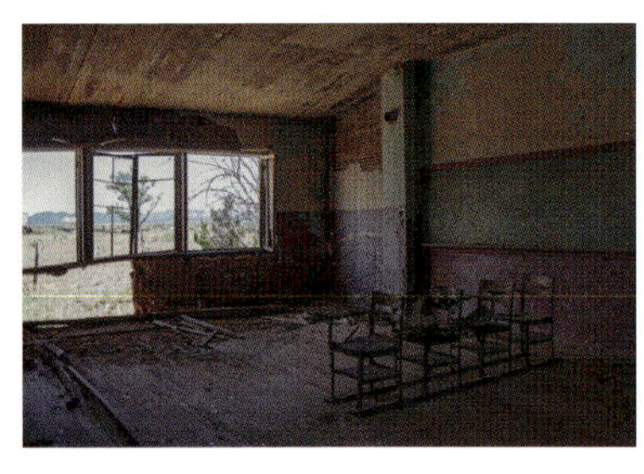

CEDARVALE SCHOOL

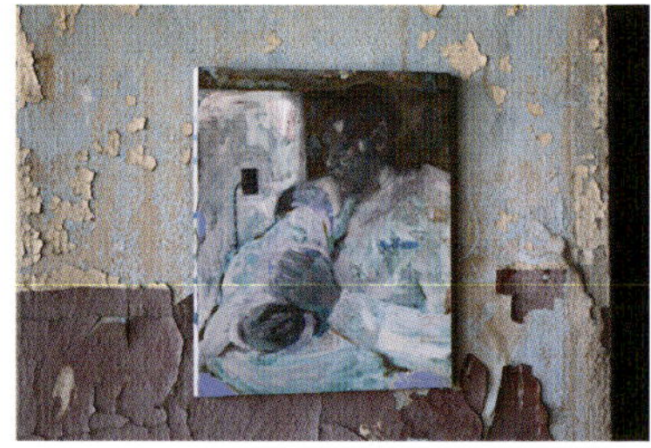

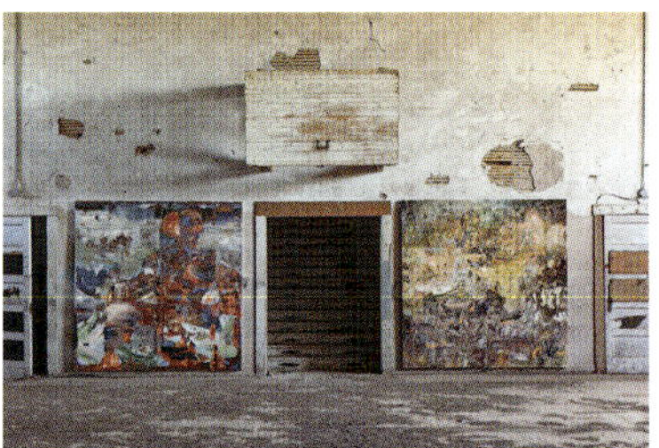

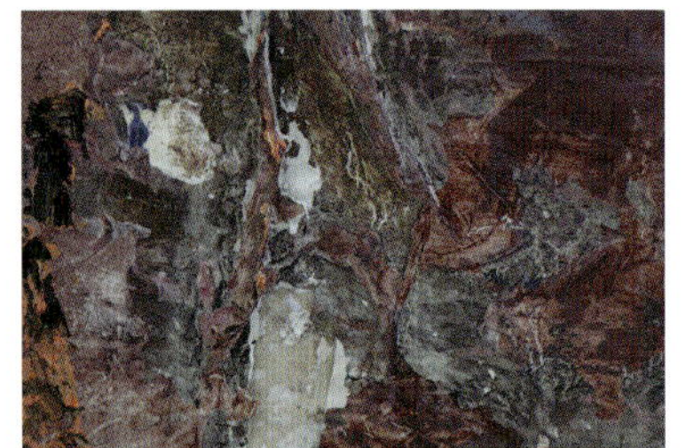

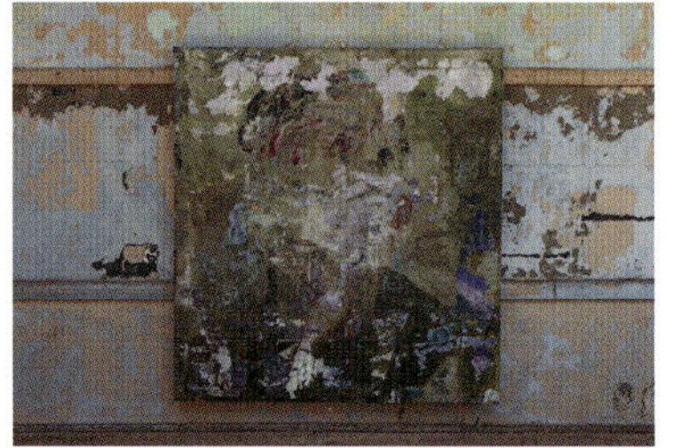

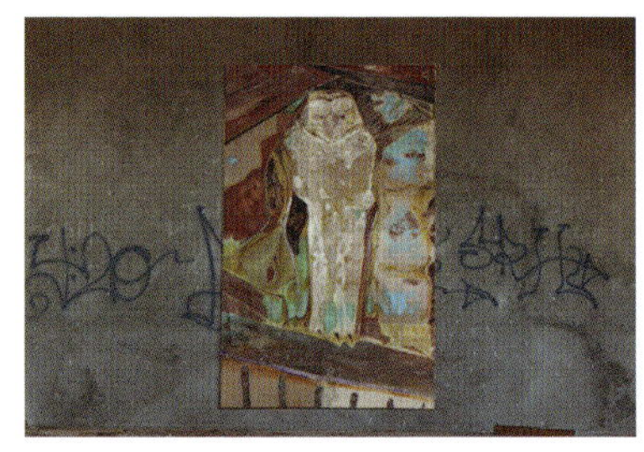

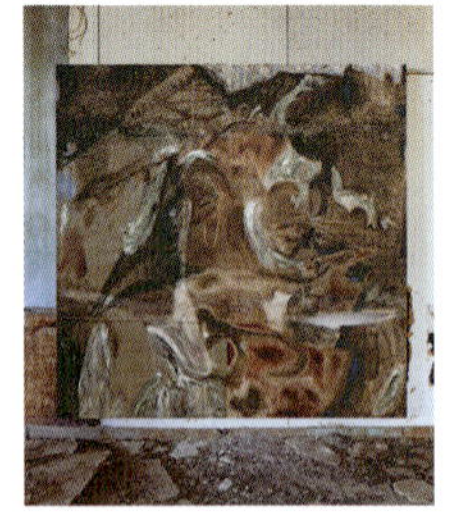

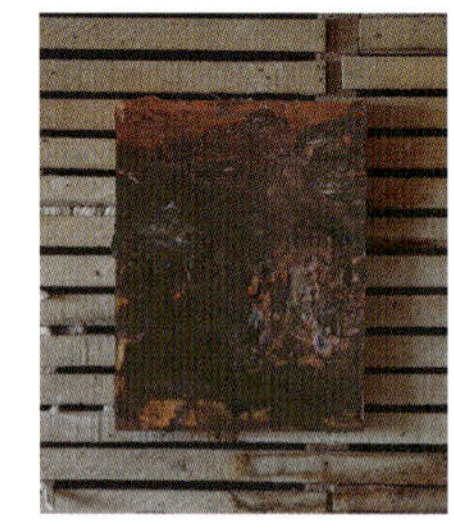

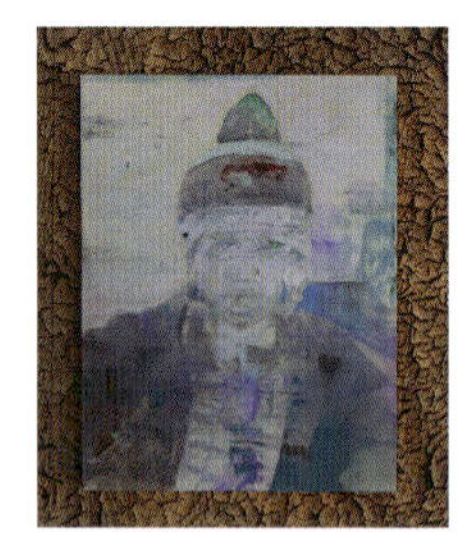

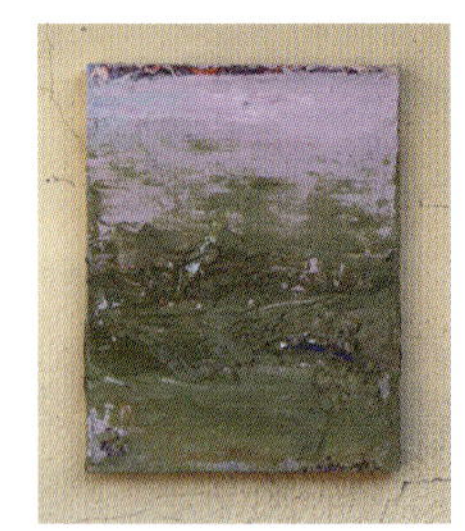

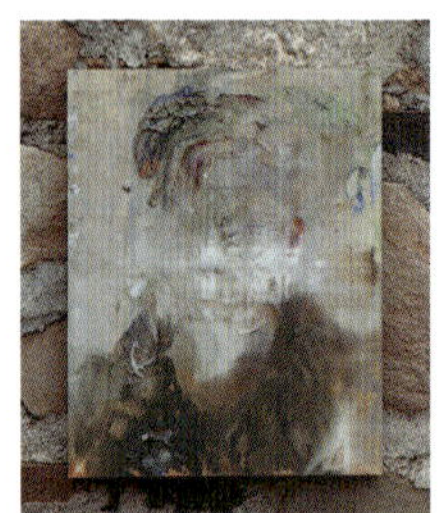

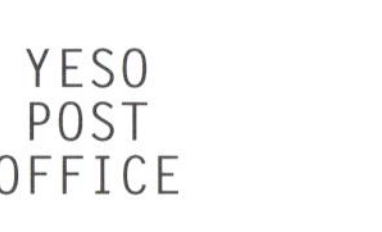

YESO POST OFFICE

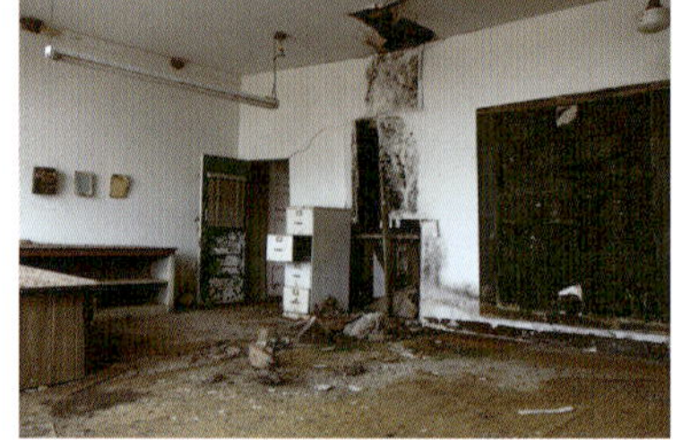

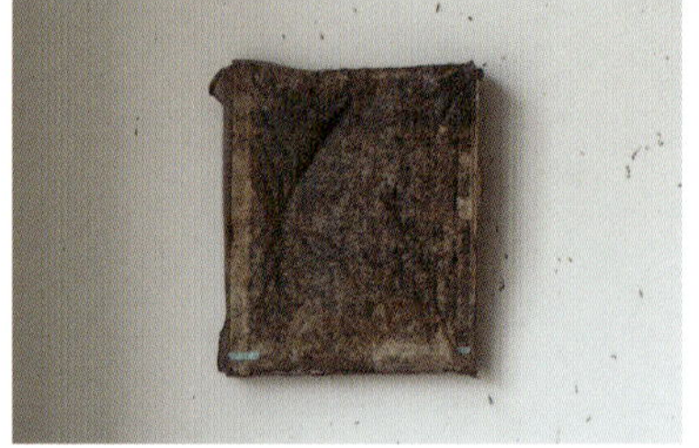

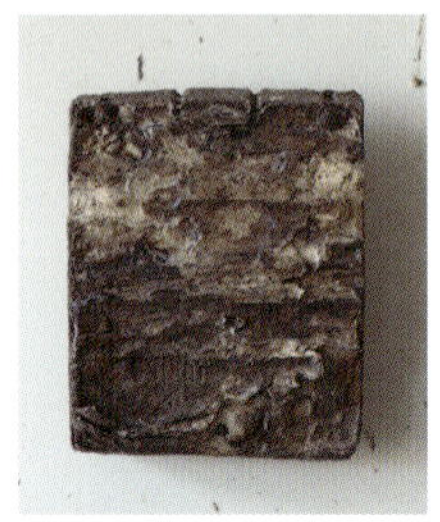

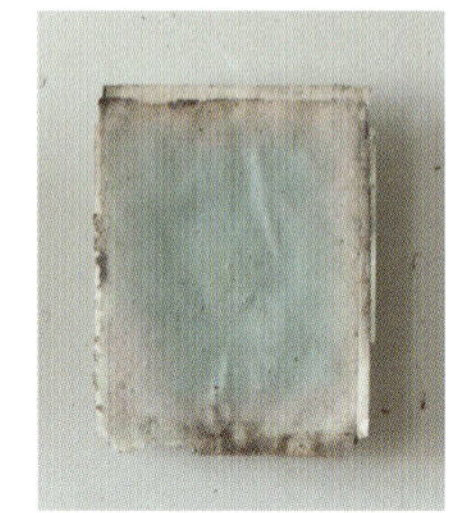

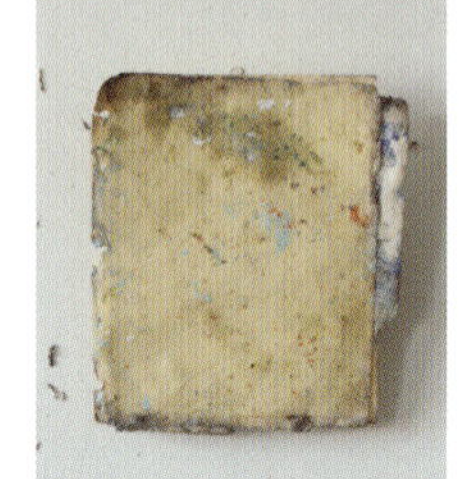

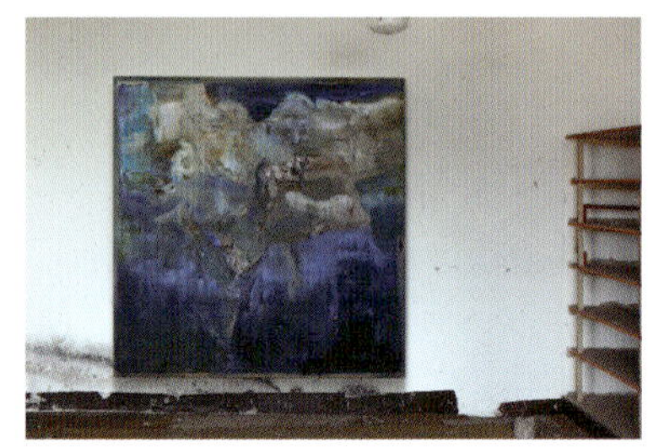

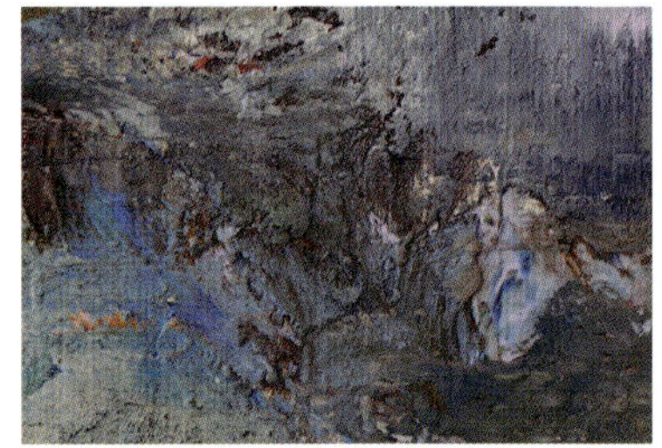

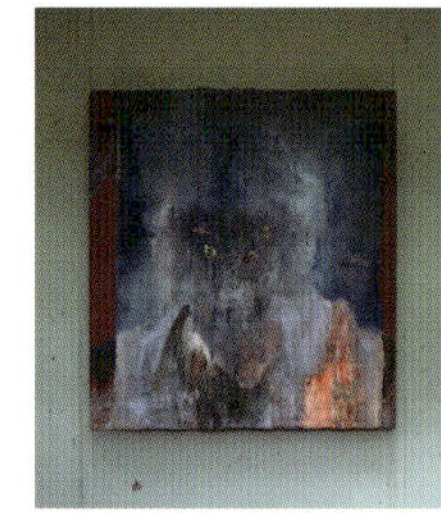

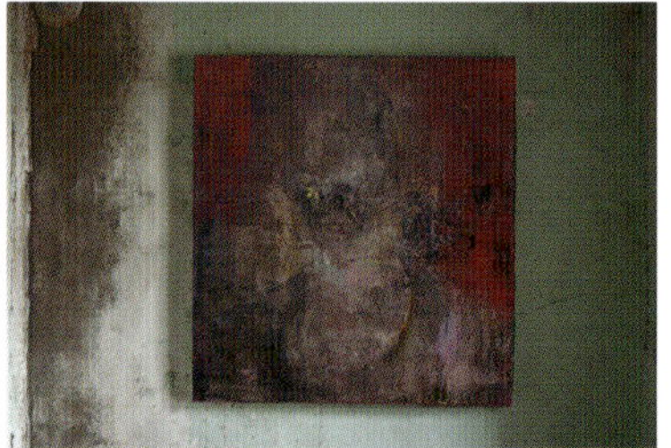

FORT SUMNER BIBLE SCHOOL

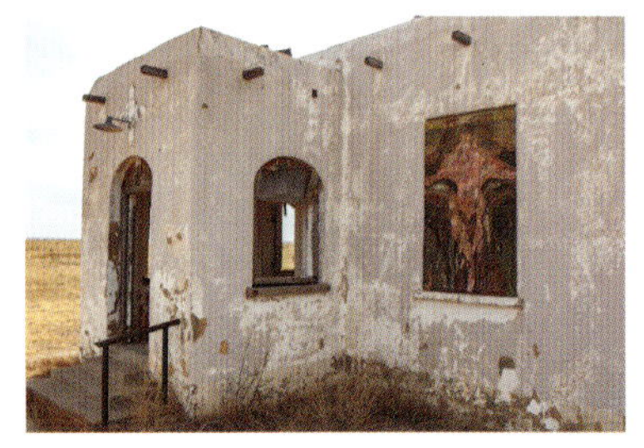

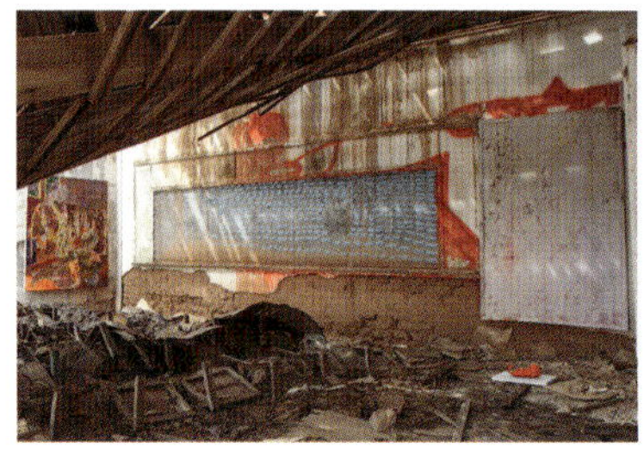

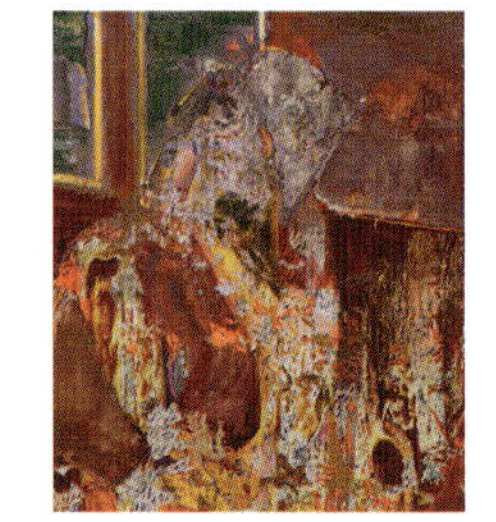

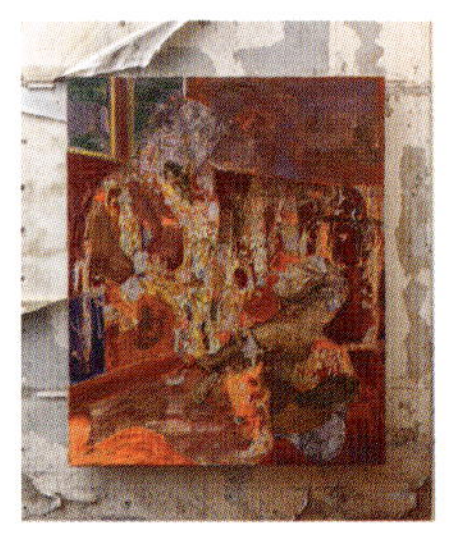

PAGES 2-3
Abandoned school in
Cedarvale, New Mexico

CEDARVALE
SCHOOL

PAGE 29
The Time Given v.I.
Ink, oil on polyester film
mounted on wood panel
9.8 × 7.9 in.
2019

PAGES 30-31
LEFT *The Time Given* | Mixed media on canvas | 89 × 87 in. | 2020 | **RIGHT** *The Smell of Fire in Winter* | Mixed media on canvas and other fabrics | 89 × 87 in. | 2012-19

PAGES 32-33
The Time Given
Detail

PAGE 34
Self-Portrait as Someone Unseen
Mixed media on canvas
72 × 66 in.
2012-19

PAGE 35
Self-Portrait as Someone Unseen
Detail

PAGES 36 and 37
A Door in the Darkness
Mixed media on burlap
120 × 72 in.
2020

PAGE 39
The Epistle of One Arriving from Among the Many Departed
Mixed media on burlap
89 × 97 in.
2020

PAGE 40
After (Us)
Mixed media on wood panel
16 × 12 in.
2019

PAGE 40
Nathaniel
Ink, oil on polyester film
mounted on wood panel
16 × 12 in.
2019

PAGE 41
Shore (Underfoot)
Mixed media on wood panel
16 × 12 in.
2020

PAGE 41
Roswell Boy
Ink, oil on polyester film
mounted on wood panel
16 × 12 in.
2019

YESO
POST
OFFICE

PAGES 46-47
Installation in an abandoned post office in Yeso, New Mexico | **RIGHT** *Book of Hours (Yeso, New Mexico, 1957)* | Mixed media and collage | 84 × 76 in. | 2021

PAGE 49
Out of Existence XIV
Mixed media on unidentified found object
18 × 22 in.
2021

PAGE 50
Out of Existence XVII
Mixed media on unidentified found object
9 × 11 × 3 in.
2021

PAGE 50
Out of Existence XVI
Mixed media on paper
12 × 9 in.
2021

PAGE 51
Out of Existence XIX
Mixed media on paper
11 × 9.5 in.
2021

PAGES 52-53
Night Swim (For Eileen)
Mixed media
82 × 78 in.
2021

PAGES 54-55
Night Swim (For Eileen)
Detail

PAGE 56
Solfeggio III
Mixed media on canvas, linen, and other fabric
50 × 45 in.
2021

PAGE 57
Solfeggio I
Mixed media on canvas, linen, and other fabric
50 × 45 in.
2021

FORT
SUMNER
BIBLE
SCHOOL

PAGES 62-63
Archaic Brother
Mixed media on canvas, linen, and burlap
82.5 × 47 in.
2022

PAGES 64-65
Installation in an abandoned bible school in Fort Sumner, New Mexico

PAGE 66
Stabat Mater
Detail

PAGE 67
Stabat Mater
Mixed media on canvas
60 × 48 in.
2022

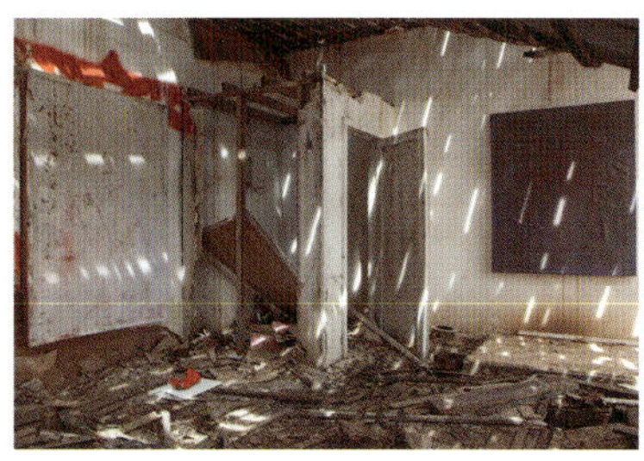
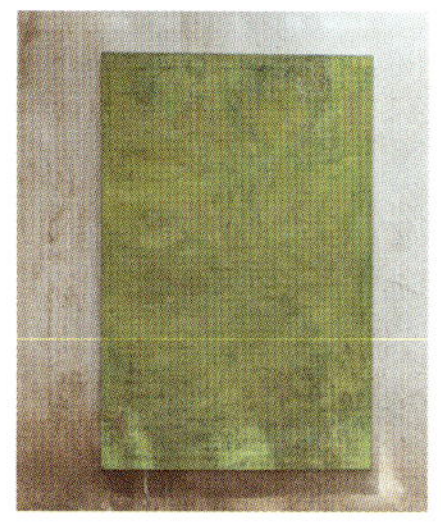
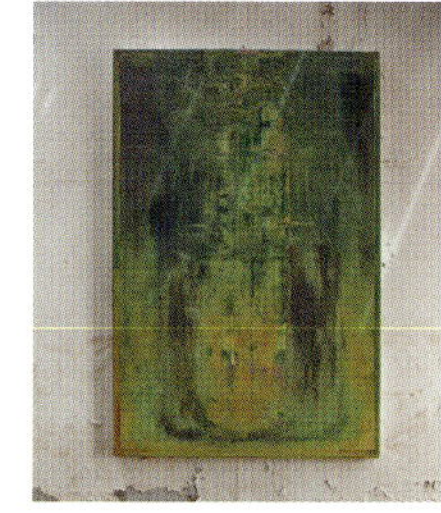

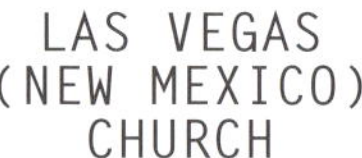

LAS VEGAS
(NEW MEXICO)
CHURCH

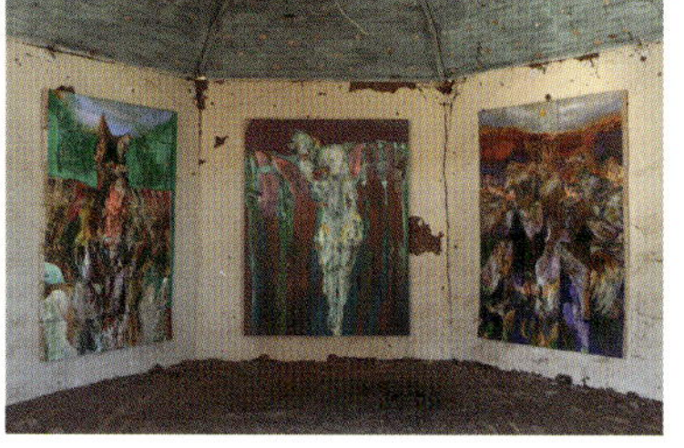
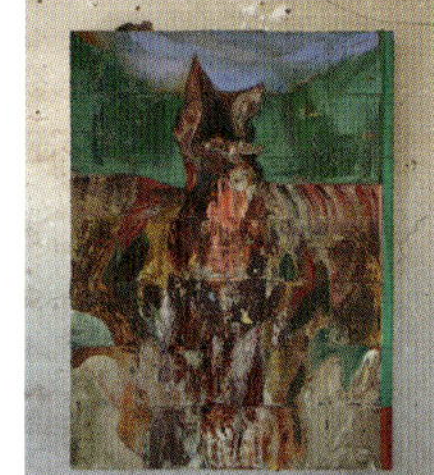
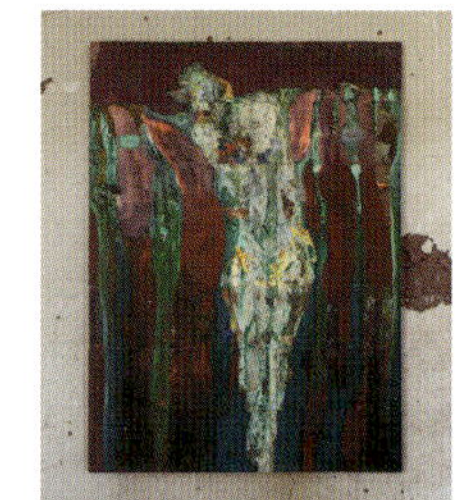
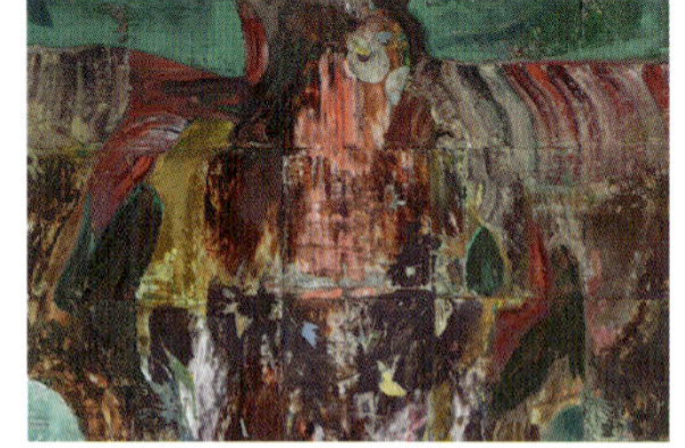
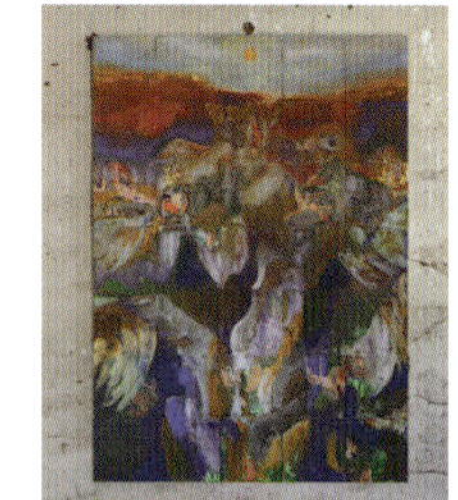
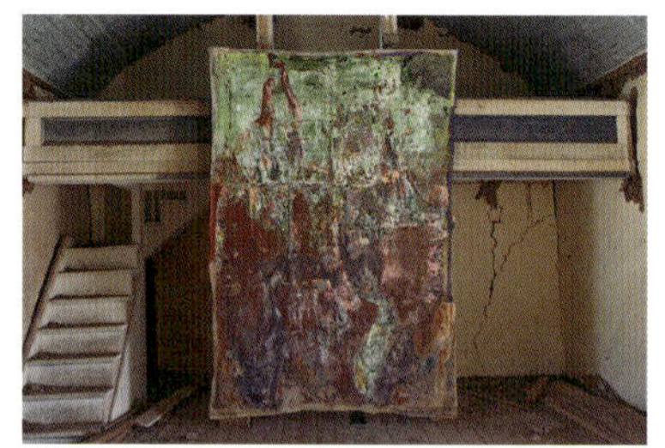
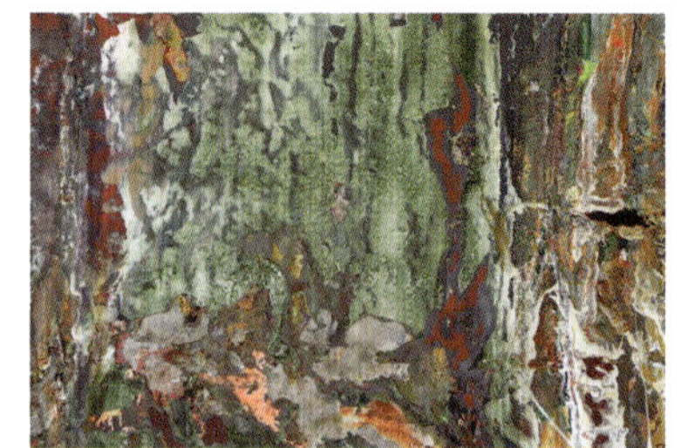

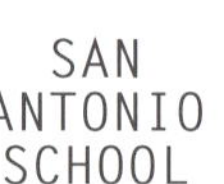

SAN
ANTONIO
SCHOOL

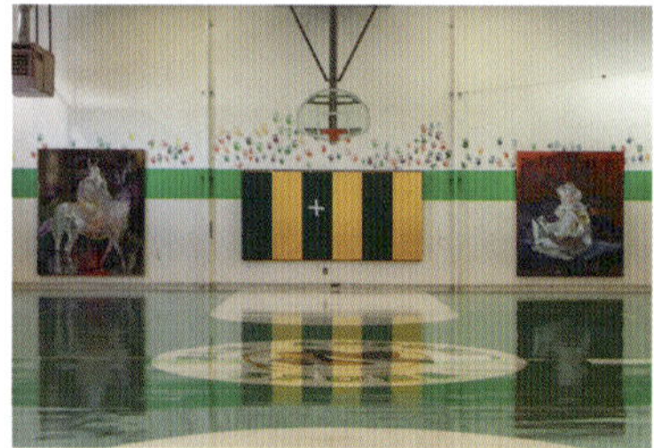
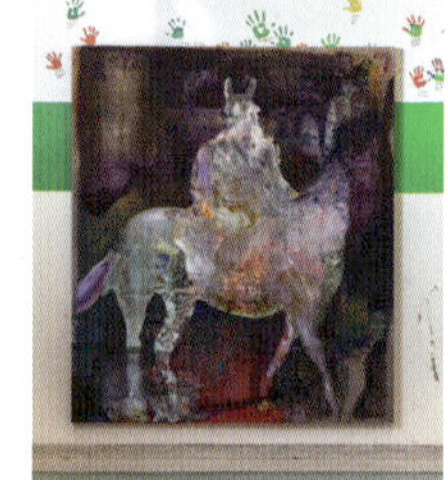
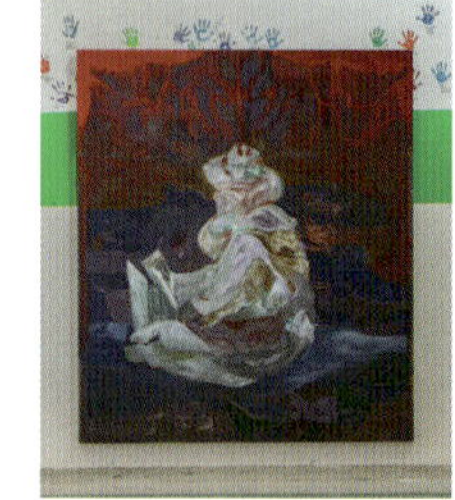
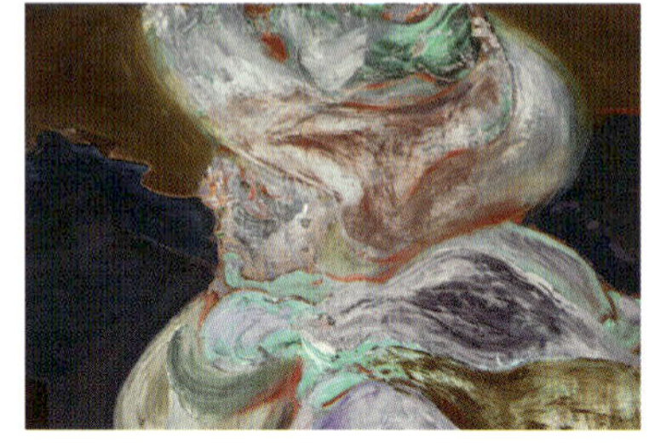
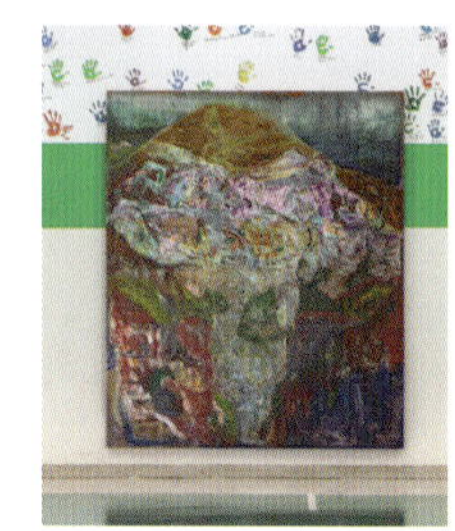
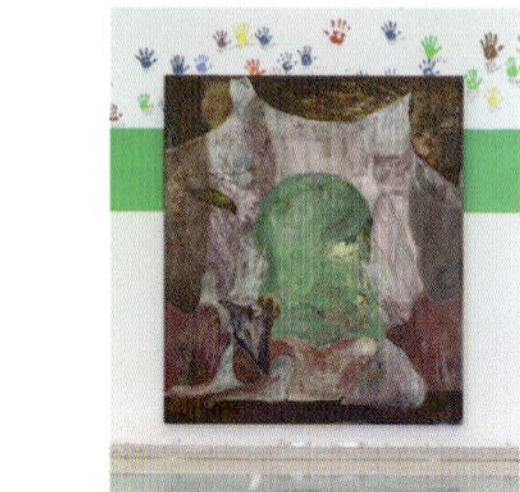
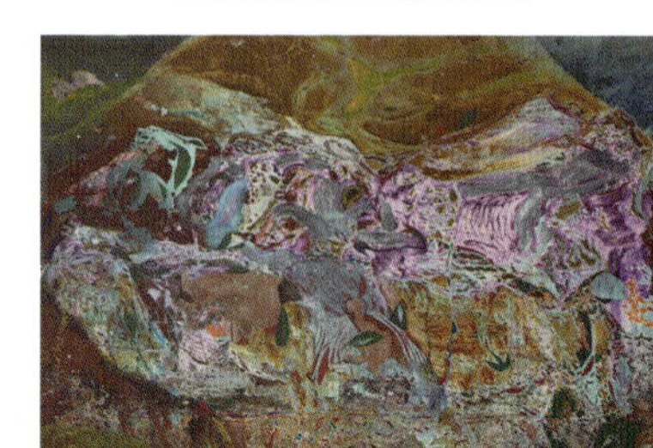
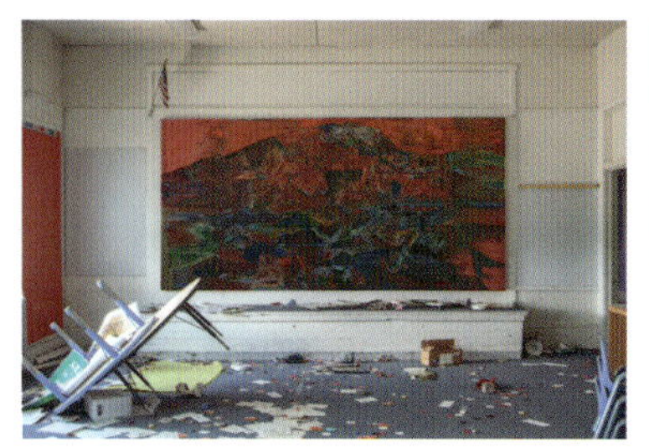
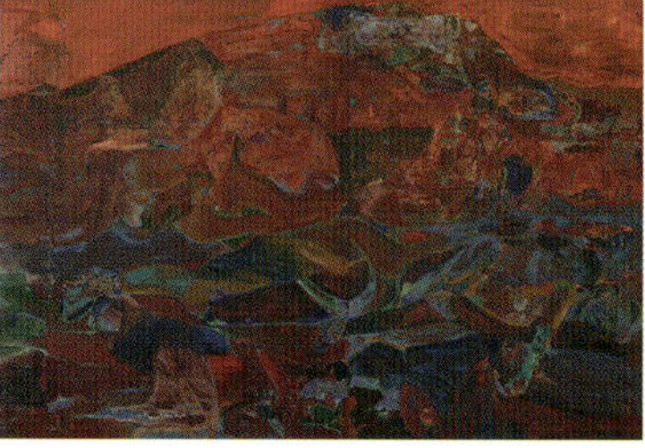
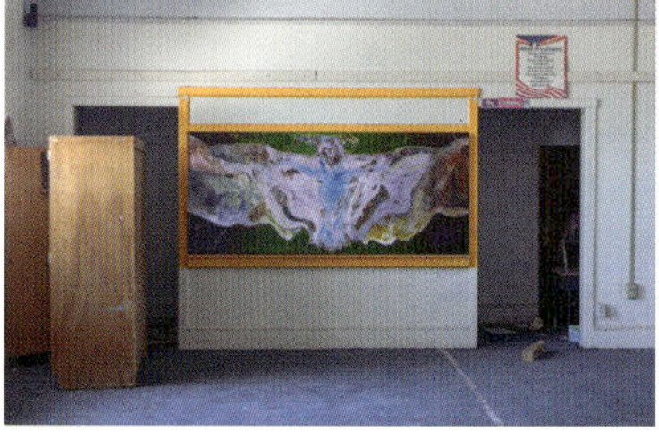
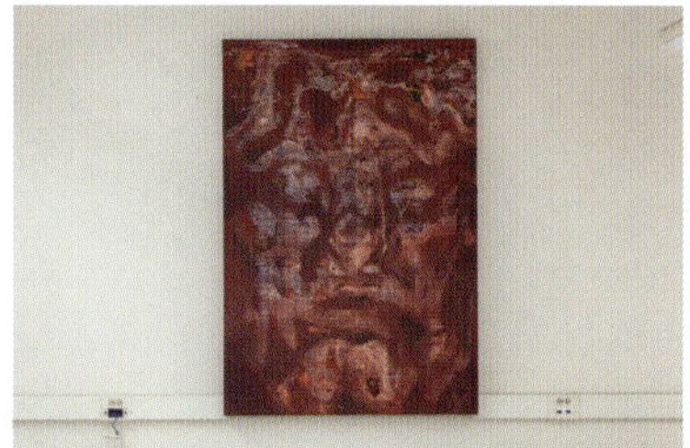

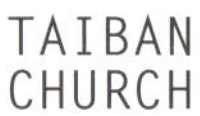

TAIBAN
CHURCH

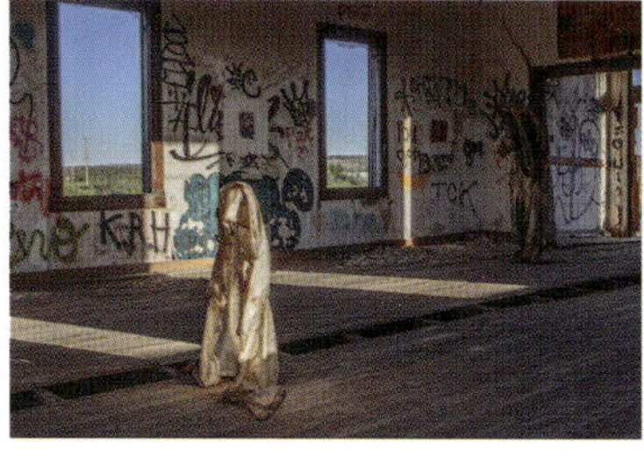
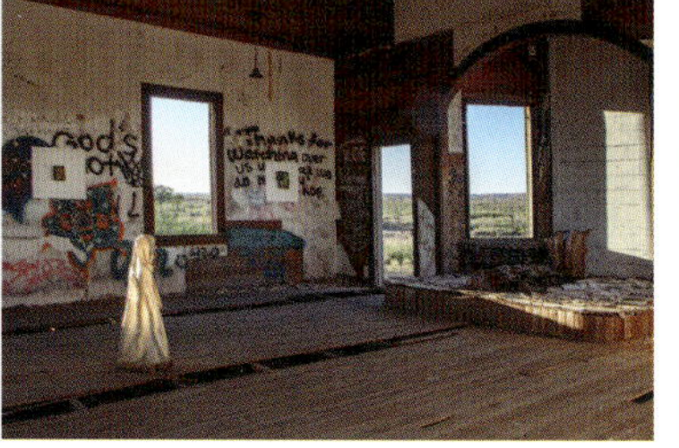
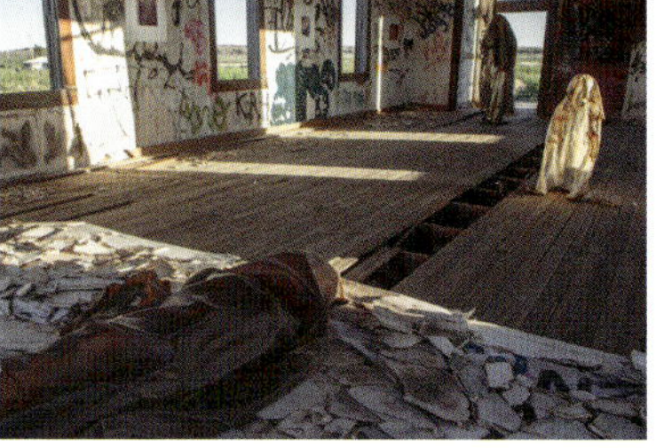

PAGES 68-69
Installation in an abandoned bible school in Fort Sumner, New Mexico | **RIGHT** *My Heart's in the Highlands (My Heart is Not Here)* | Mixed media and collage on canvas | 60 × 48 in. | 2022

PAGES 70 and 71
Out of Existence XXIV (for Lucas) | Mixed media on found bulletin board, petrified shoe in collaboration with anonymous artist | about 2000-22

PAGE 74
The Mark upon the Canyon
Mixed media on canvas
56 × 36 in.
2023

PAGE 75
Chaco I
Mixed media on canvas
56 × 36 in.
2022

LAS VEGAS (NEW MEXICO) CHURCH

PAGES 80-81
Installation in an abandoned church in Las Vegas, New Mexico

PAGE 82
A Friend Who Waits before the Bridge Leading into Fire (Vega, I Dreamt I Saw You)
Mixed media on 35 wood panels
84 × 60 in.
2022

PAGE 83
A Friend Who Waits beneath a Bridge Setting it on Fire (Deneb, I Dreamt I Saw You)
Mixed media on 35 wood panels
84 × 60 in.
2022

PAGES 84-85
A Friend Who Waits before the Bridge Leading into Fire (Vega, I Dreamt I Saw You)
Detail

PAGE 87
A Friend Who Waits beyond the Bridge Swallowed by the Fire (Altair, I Dreamt I Saw You)
Mixed media on 35 wood panels
84 × 60 in.
2022

PAGES 88-89
After the Fire (After the Flood Afterlife After Mud After Veil After Shroud After the World After the Crowd) | Mixed media on cotton drop cloth and burlap | about 120 × 80 in. | 2022

PAGES 90-91
After the Fire (After the Flood Afterlife After Mud After Veil After Shroud After the World After the Crowd)
Detail

SAN ANTONIO SCHOOL

PAGES 96-97
Installation in an abandoned school in San Antonio, New Mexico

PAGE 98
Horse in Moonlight
Mixed media on linen and burlap
100 × 84 in.
2023

PAGE 99
Painter in the Canyon (Who Paints the Moonlit Horse)
Mixed media on canvas and burlap
100 × 84 in.
2023

PAGES 100-101
Painter in the Canyon (Who Paints the Moonlit Horse)
Detail

PAGE 102
Sarah Was Ninety Years Old
Mixed media on canvas and burlap
100 × 84 in.
2023

PAGE 103
A Dog at the Tent
Mixed media on canvas and linen
100 × 84 in.
2023

PAGES 104-05
Sarah Was Ninety Years Old
Detail

PAGES 106-07
I Would Not Speak of the Mountain (Vesuvius)
Mixed media on canvas and burlap
80 × 160 in.
2023

PAGES 108-09
I Would Not Speak of the Mountain (Vesuvius)
Detail

PAGE 111
Great Mother
Mixed media on canvas
41.5 × 95 in.
2024

PAGES 112 and 113
The Unknown Collaborator (Pari Intervallo)
Mixed media on linen
73.5 × 49 in.
2023

TAIBAN CHURCH

PAGES 118-19
Autumn Pilgrimage
Rawhide forms
Dimensions variable
2023

PAGES 120-21
Autumn Pilgrimage
Rawhide forms
Dimensions variable
2023

PAGES 122-23
Autumn Pilgrimage
Rawhide forms
Dimensions variable
2023

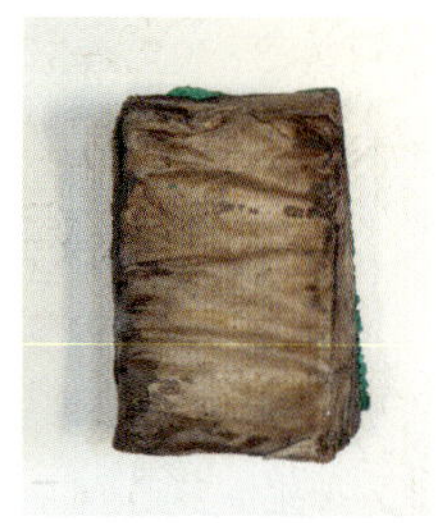
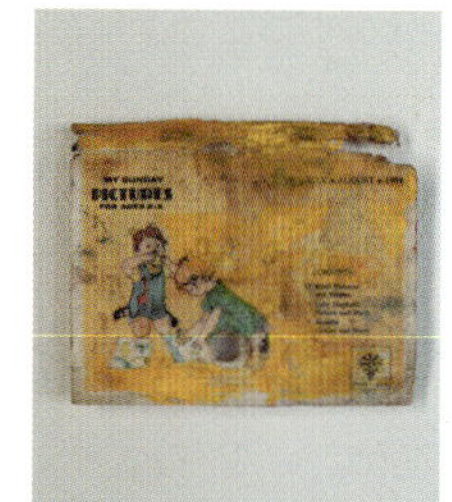
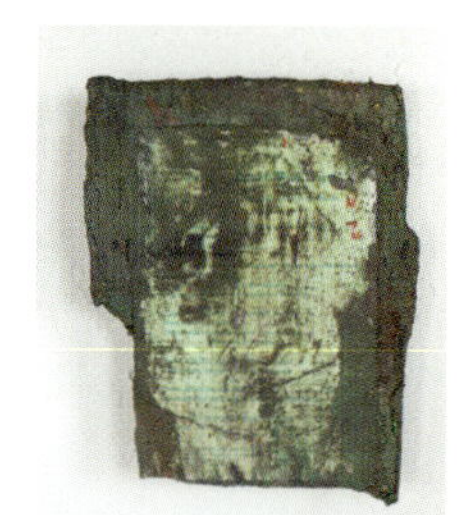

SAN
ACACIA
CHURCH

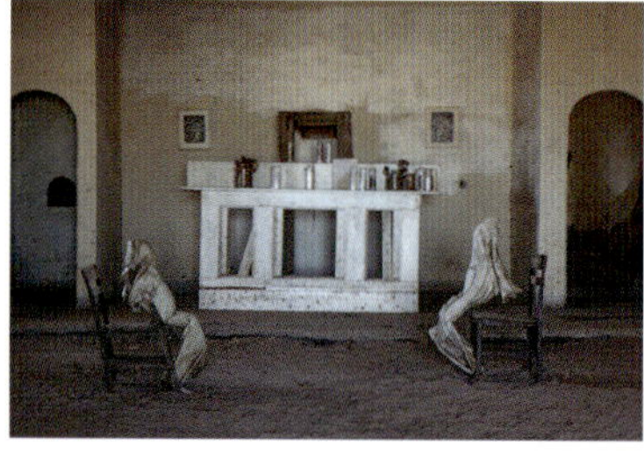
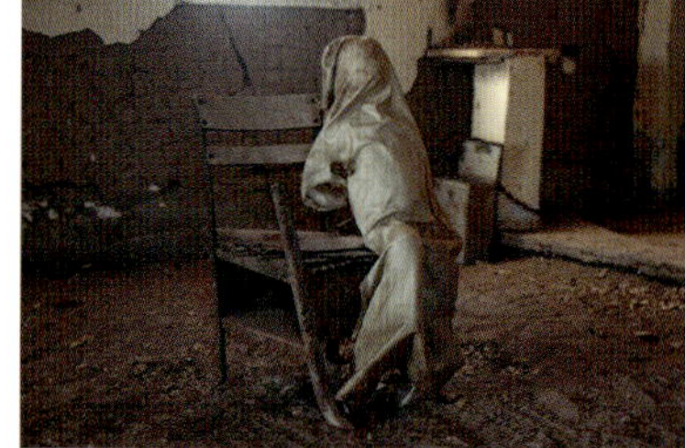
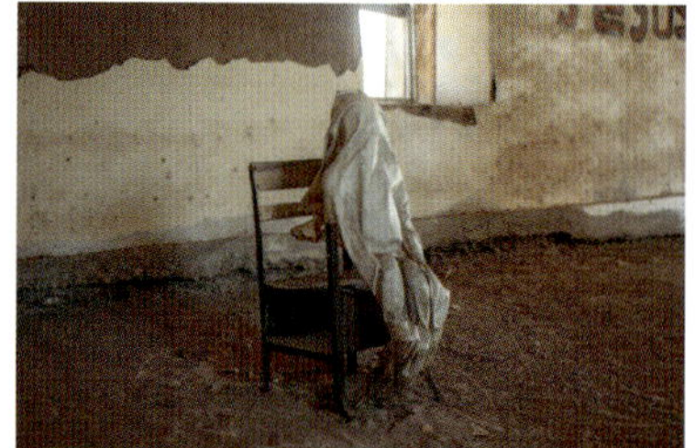
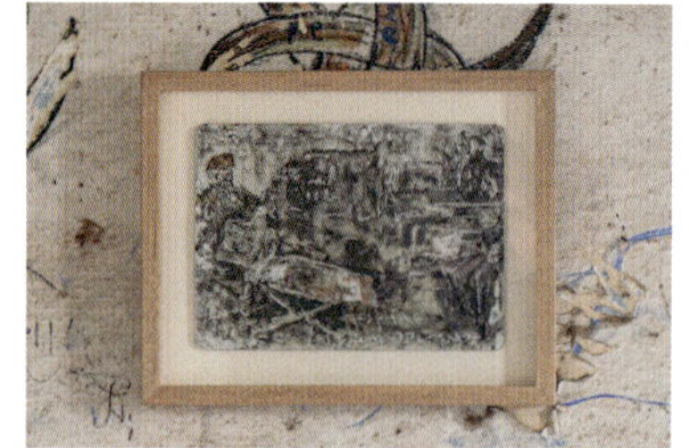
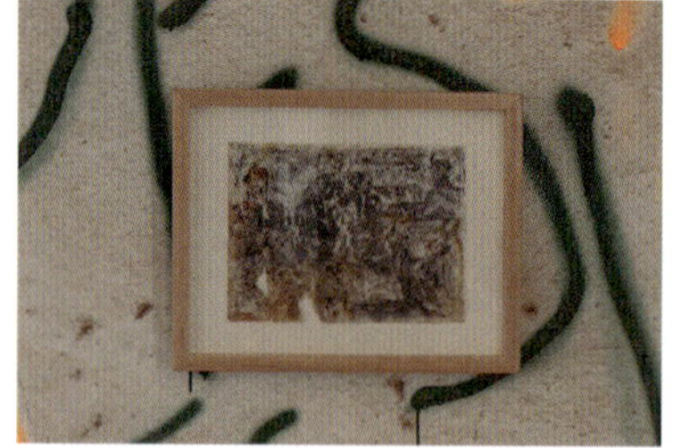
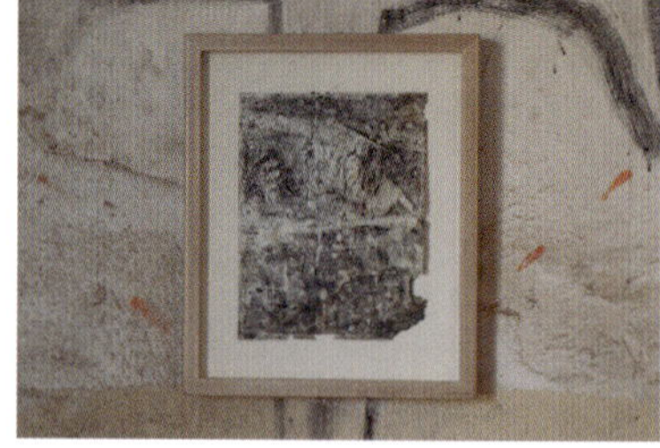

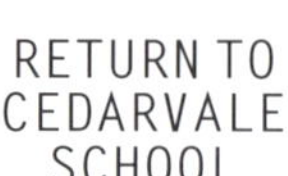

RETURN TO
CEDARVALE
SCHOOL

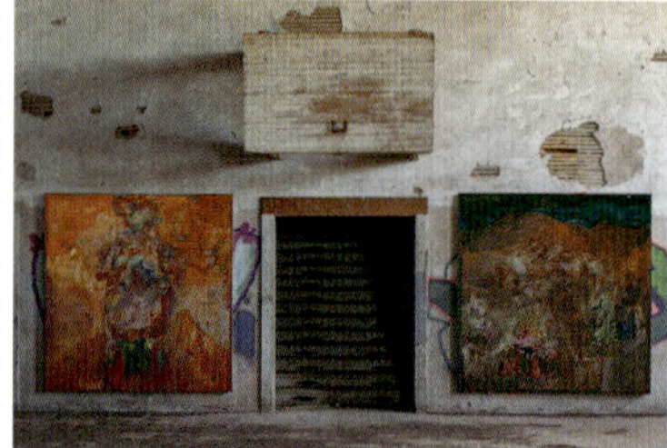
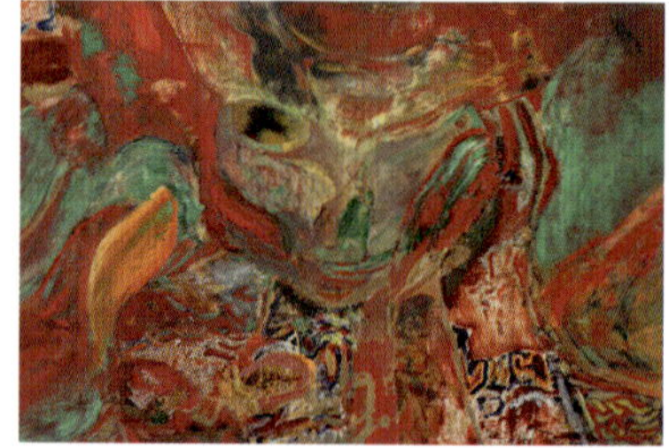
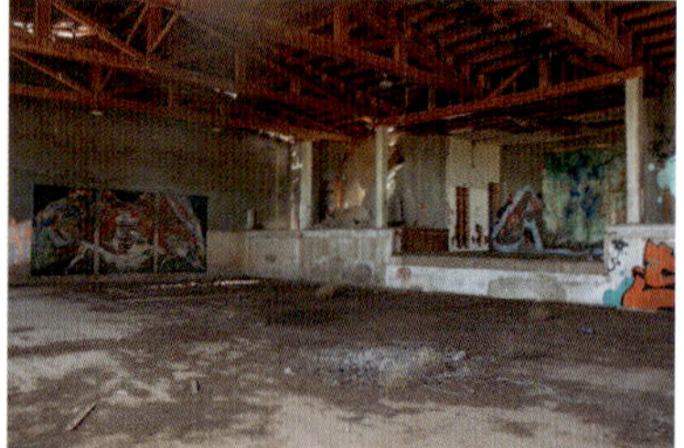
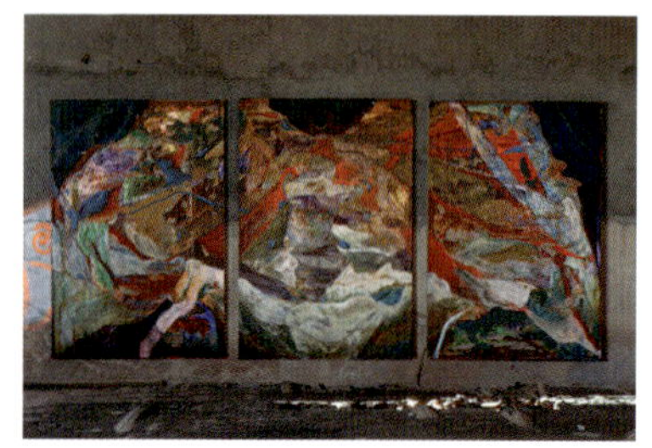
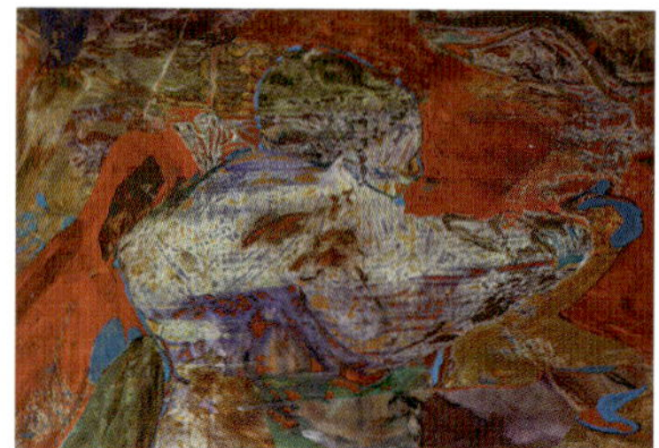
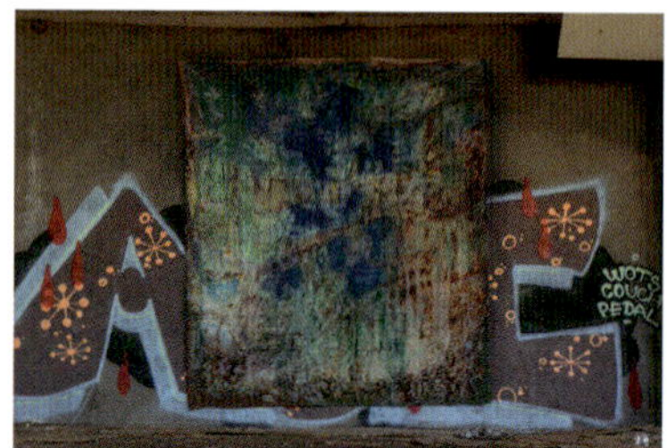
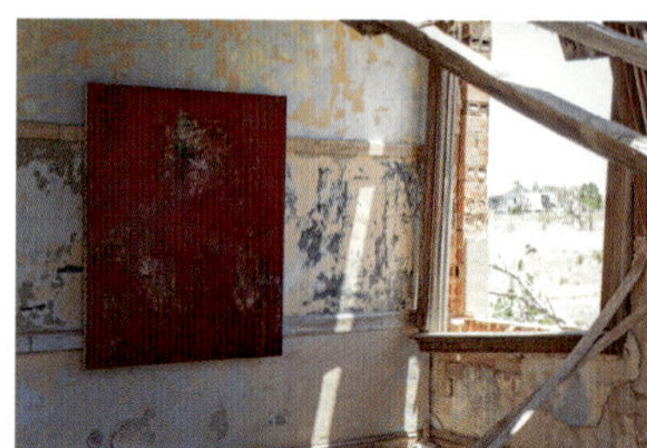
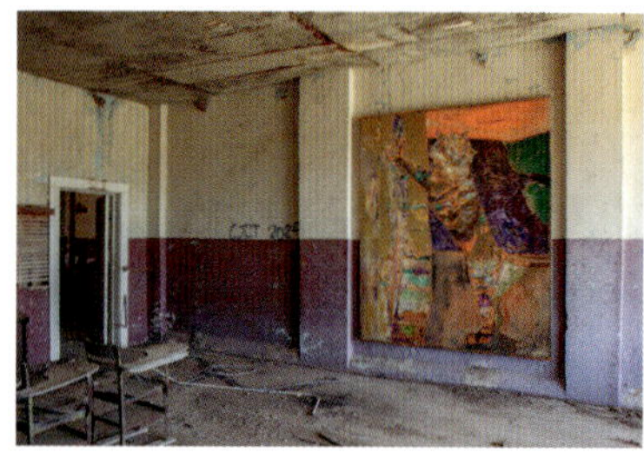

PAGES 124 and 125
Out of Existence 32
Oil and wax on found book interior
About 6.5 × 4.5 in.
About 1985-2022

PAGE 126
Out of Existence XXVII
Mixed media on found book pages
8.5 × 6 in.
About 1985-2022

PAGES 128 and 129
Out of Existence 36
Mixed media on found Baptist workbook page and unidentified found object
About 9.5 × 7.5 in.
About 1977-2023

SAN ACACIA CHURCH

PAGES 134-35
Moon in Water
Deer hide, found wood, and steel chairs
Dimensions variable
2023

PAGES 136 and 137
Moon in Water
Deer hide, found wood, and steel chairs
Dimensions variable
2023
Detail

PAGES 138 and 139
Moon in Water
Deer hide, found wood, and steel chairs
Dimensions variable
2023
Detail

PAGE 141
Mine Hospital
Charcoal, graphite, oil pastel, and wax on found whiteboard
11.5 × 8 in.
2018-23

PAGE 142
Mine Hospital II
Graphite, charcoal, oil pastel, and wax on found Baptist instruction book page
8 × 10.25 in.
1981-2023

PAGE 143
Dance Hall II
Graphite, charcoal, and wax on found Baptist instruction book page
10.5 × 8.25 in.
1981-2023

RETURN TO CEDARVALE SCHOOL

PAGES 148-49
LEFT *The Listening* | Mixed media on linen | 84 × 80 in. | 2024 | **RIGHT** *Nightfall* | Mixed media on linen | 84 × 80 in. | 2024

PAGES 150-51
The Listening
Detail

PAGES 152-53
Installation in an abandoned school in Cedarvale, New Mexico

PAGES 154-55
The Hermit
Mixed media on linen
120 × 240 in.
2024

PAGES 156-57
The Hermit
Detail

PAGE 159
The Tracker or the Tracked
Mixed media on unstretched canvas and burlap
about 130 × 120 in.
2023

PAGES 160-61
Erat Lux Vera
Mixed media on linen
60 × 48 in.
2023-24

PAGES 162-63
The Hunger Artist
Mixed media on linen
100 × 80 in.
2024

JOSHUA HAGLER worked as a visual artist for about twenty years, exhibiting in galleries and institutions around the world. In late 2017, seeking to change his life, he left Los Angeles and landed in rural New Mexico, beginning a period of artistic reinvention. This would lead, at the outset of the Covid-19 pandemic in 2020, to the *Nihil* project. In late 2024, after *Nihil*'s completion, he permanently changed his name to Æmen Ededéen, a mark, for him, of personal revolution.

Æmen lives with his wife and daughter in a high desert village at the northern foot of New Mexico's Sandia Mountains.

SELECTED EXHIBITIONS

2024
Focus: Joshua Hagler, Cris Worley Fine Arts, Dallas, Texas

Nihil II: Nor The Moon in its Water, Old Jail Art Center, Albany, Texas

Nihil III: Already Paradise, Nicodim, New York City, New York

2023
Nihil I: I Would Not Speak of the Mountain, Nicodim, Los Angeles, California

2021
Drawing in the Dark, Cris Worley Fine Arts, Dallas, Texas

The Living Circle Us, Unit London, UK

2020
Platform Series, Unit London, UK (online)

2019
Chimera, Unit London, UK

From a Corner the Sound of a Small Bird, (two person) with Maja Ruznic, Big Pictures, Los Angeles, California

2018
Love Letters to the Poorly Regarded, Roswell Museum and Art Center, Roswell, New Mexico

The River Lethe, Brand Library & Art Center, Los Angeles, California

2017
In the House is a Room into which Every River Empties, Nicole Longnecker Gallery, Houston, Texas

Missouri Parallels, Galleri Oxholm, Copenhagen, Denmark

2016
The Adopted, JAUS Gallery (traveling), Los Angeles, California

2015
The Adopted, Brandstater Gallery at La Sierra University (traveling), Riverside, California

2014
Among The Missing, (two person) with Maja Ruznic, Jack Fischer Gallery, San Francisco, California

My Name is Nobody, Avis Frank Gallery, Houston, Texas

Romancing the West, Galleri Oxholm, Copenhagen, Denmark

2013
The Unsurrendered, Figure One Gallery at University of Illinois, Champaign/Urbana, Illinois

2012
The Imagined Chase, Gallery Wendi Norris, San Francisco, California

2011
Perceptions of Religious Imagery in Natural Phenomena, 101/Exhibit (traveling), Miami, Florida

Perceptions of Religious Imagery in Natural Phenomena, Carlo V Castle (traveling), Lecce, Italy

Vessel Traces, (two person) with Joseph Cohen, San Giovanni di Dio Church, Lecce, Italy

2010
Joshua Hagler and Mayumi Ishino (two person) Babel Visningsrom for Kunst, Trondheim, Norway

Nearly Approaching Never to Pass (two person), with George Pfau, Reaves Gallery, New York City, New York

2009
72 Virgins to Die For, Frey Norris Contemporary and Modern, San Francisco, California

2007
Bring Us Rapture, Mina Dresden Gallery, San Francisco, California

SELECTED GROUP EXHIBITIONS

2024
Arcadia and Elsewhere, James Cohan, New York City, New York

Memory, Maruani Mercier, Brussels, Belgium

Observed, curated by Raffi Kalenderian and Alberto Cuadros, Miles McEnery, New York City, New York

The Ballad of the Children of the Czar, Galeria Nicodim, Bucharest, Romania

2023
DISEMBODIED, Nicodim, New York City, New York

Joshua Hagler, Devin B. Johnson, Hugo Wilson, Nicola Samori, Nicodim, Los Angeles, California

Maternity Leave: None of Women Born, Nicodim in collaboration with Green Family Foundation, Dallas, Texas

The Descendants, K11 Musea, Hong Kong

Togetherness: For Better or Worse, Green Family Art Foundation, Dallas, Texas

2022
Nassima Landau Foundation: Unit London Takeover, Nassima Landau Foundation, Tel Aviv, Israel

Unmatter, Secci, Milan, Italy

2021
Witness or Pretend, Bode Projects, Berlin, Germany

2020
Drawn Together, online group exhibition, Unit London, UK

Figure as Form, Hollis Taggart Gallery, New York City, New York

The Red Wood, online group exhibition, curated by Julia Westerbeke, San Francisco, California

TWENTYFOUR, Bricks Gallery, Copenhagen, Denmark

2019
Gardens, Last Projects, Los Angeles, California

Nuit Noire, Kashagan Galerie, curated by Hotel Triki for La Biennale de Lyon Resonance, Lyon, France

2018
Dreams and Fevers, Torrance Art Museum, Los Angeles, California

Looking for U, Unit London, UK

Paradise Lost, Patrick Painter, Inc., Los Angeles, California

With Liberty and Justice for Some, Children's Museum of the Arts, New York City, New York

2017
Figurative Futures, 101/Exhibit, Los Angeles, California

Soul Case, Durden & Ray Gallery, Los Angeles, California

The Encrypted Form, Stoerpunkt, Munich, Germany

Trust Fall, Gallery ALSO, Los Angeles, California

Two Sides of the Coin, Gallerie Gruelich, Frankfurt, Germany

Unknown Soldier, San Francisco Arts Commission Gallery, San Francisco, California

With Liberty and Justice for Some, Walter Maciel Gallery, Los Angeles; San Francisco Arts Commission Gallery, San Francisco; Berkeley Art Center (traveling), Berkeley, California

2016
Hysterical Fiction, La Estación Arte Contemporáneo, Chihuahua, Mexico

Over the Hills, Hometown Gallery, Brooklyn, New York

Werewolf, Charlie James Gallery, Los Angeles, California

2015
52nd Annual Juried Exhibition, Masur Museum of Art, Monroe, Louisiana

Angels with Dirty Faces, Galerie Ernst Hilger, Vienna, Austria

Sincerely Yours, Torrance Art Museum, Torrance, California

Tallahassee International, Florida State University Museum of Art, Tallahassee, Florida

2014
Draftpunk 2.0, Mid-Tokyo Gallery, Tokyo, Japan

Exquisite Corpse, MASS Gallery, Austin, Texas

2013
Transreal Topologies, Royal Institute, Adelaide, Australia

What the Mouth Sees, Alter Space, San Francisco, California

2012
Optic Nerve, Museum of Contemporary Art, North Miami, Florida

2010
Black Lab, The Lab, San Francisco, California

I am Solitary I am an Army, Surface Gallery, Nottingham, UK

2009
Echo, Frey Norris Gallery, San Francisco, California

2008
Close Calls, Headlands Center for the Arts, Sausalito, California

2006
Your Gallery, in association with The Saatchi Gallery, The Guardian, London, UK

2004
Contemporary Perspectives, MoCA at the Luther Burbank Center, Santa Rosa, California

BIBLIOGRAPHY

2024
Sarah Swan, "The Last Great Art Show," Galleries West, 23 December 2024: gallerieswest.ca/magazine/stories/the-last-great-art-show/

John Yau, "An Art Inhabited by Higher Spirits," *Hyperallergic*, 29 September 2024: hyperallergic.com/953667/an-art-inhabited-by-higher-spirits-joshua-hagler-nicodim-gallery/

Yoshino, "Artist Decoded," 11 November 2024: artistdecoded.com/270-Joshua-Hagler-Amen-Ededeen

2023
Zara Kand, "Joshua Hagler: 'I Would Not Speak of the Mountain," *ArtNow LA*, 8 December 2023: artnowla.com/?s=josh+hagler

Kate Mothes, "Nothing Is Not Nothing," *Dovetail Mag*, 14 December 2023: dovetailmag.com/2023/12/joshua-hagler/

2021
Matthew Bourbon, "Joshua Hagler's Exuberantly Sullen Paintings at Cris Worley Fine Arts Speak to Creation, Death," *Dallas Morning News*, 8 May 2021: joshuahagler.com/word/dallas-morning-news

New American Paintings, featured work, issue 148, June 2021

The Gentleman's Journal, "10 Emerging Artists Artists You Should Be Investing In," thegentlemansjournal.com

2020
A.Site London Podcast, interview

ArtMaze Magazine, Summer, issue 8

Hopper Prize Journal, interview, September 23, 2020: hopperprize.org/joshua-hagler-interview/

You Wanted a List, interview, June 26, 2020

2019
"Americana Incarnate Meets Hagler's Horrors," *Fault Magazine*, July 22, 2019: fault-magazine.com/2019/07/unit-london-exhibition-americana-incarnate-meets-haglers-horrors/

Artist Decoded Podcast, episode 136, interview, November 30, 2019, Los Angeles, California

Tulika Bahadur, *On Art and Aesthetics*, interview, April 2019

Cloe Chanteloube, *ICI Londres*, website, French-language review by London, UK

Beatrice Chassepot, *be-Art Magazine*, July 22, 2019

Free Seed Films, *SOHO Radio*, live interview July 18, 2019

Chris Jenkins, "Art Focus," *Arts and Collections*

London Art World Podcast, episode 19, April 11, 2019

Poppy Malby, "20 Questions," interview, *GQ Magazine*, July 14, 2019

P.C. Robinson, "Joshua Hagler Explores Fading Dichotomies in New Unit London Exhibition," *Artlyst*, July 22, 2019: artlyst.com/previews/joshua-hagler-explores-fading-dichotomies-new-unit-london-exhibition/

Mark Westall, *Fad Magazine*, July 10, 2019: fadmagazine.com/2019/07/10/chimera-is-an-exhibition-of-new-large-scale-oil-paintings-by-american-contemporary-artist-joshua-hagler/

2018
Lorraine Heitzman, *Los Angeles Art & Cake*, August 1, 2018

Peter de Kuster, *The Hero's Journey Project*: theherojourney2016.wordpress.com

Michael Livingson, "Gallery Exhibit at Glendale Library Explores Themes of Mobility," *Glendale News-Press*, July 6, 2018

Annabel Osberg, "Pick of the Week," *Artillery Magazine*, August 1, 2018

Theo Schear, *Juxtapoz Presents*, December 14, 2018

Andy Smith, "Joshua Hagler's Layered, Deconstructionist Paintings," *Hi-Fructose Magazine*, July 2018

2017
Artist Decoded, episode 67, podcast

Future Tongue, interview and video profile

2016
AF Art Magazine, artist feature, January 2016

Art & Cake, "A Conversation with Maja Ruznic and Joshua Hagler"

Artist Decoded, episode 12, podcast, January 2016

Nazish Chunara, *Venison Magazine*, summer issue

Alina Cohen, "The Art World's Most Daring—and Fun—Season," *New York Times Style Magazine*, July 2016

Karen Kedmey, *Artsy*, February 2016

2015
Ink and Other, episode 2, November 2015: inkandother.com

Max Presneill, "Eight LA Artists You Should Know," *Fabrik Magazine*, issue 26, 2015

Vogue (Italy), artist profile, June 2015

2014
DeWitt Cheng, "Among the Missing," *Art Ltd. Magazine*, July/August 2014

Christian Frock, "Among the Missing," *New York Times*, San Francisco Edition, April 28, 2014

Mikko Lautamo, *Square Cylinder*, "Among the Missing," May 18, 2014

Pickled Matter: New Faces in Contemporary Art, vol. 1, November 2014

San Francisco Chronicle, Bay Area weekend picks, May 7, 2014

2013
Mary Eisenhart, Bay Area art picks: "In the Box Beneath the City," *San Francisco Chronicle*, January 2013

Matt Fischer, "Fair Play: Notable Locals at this Year's Big artMKT & ArtPadSF Shows," *San Francisco Bay Guardian*

Courtney Malick, "To Be Announced," *Viralnet*, September 2013: viralnet.net/essays/courtneymalick.html

Gabe Scott, *Juxtapoz Magazine*, September 2013

2012
Kenneth Baker, Bay Area art picks: "The Evangelists," *San Francisco Chronicle*, April 19, 2012

DeWitt Cheng, *Visual Art Source*, April 28, 2012: visualartsource.com/index.php?page=editorial&pcID=17&aID=1179

Critical Miami, Optic Nerve 14 at MoCA, September 20, 2012: criticalmiami.com/2012/09/20/optic-nerve-14-at-moca

2011
Chiara Miglietta, *Arskey Magazine*, August 8, 2011

Brinson Renda, "Joshua Hagler at 101/exhibit," *Artcards*, October 10, 2011

Andy Ritchie, *Beautiful/Decay Magazine*, book 5

2010
Reyhan Harmanci, "Masterminds 2010," *SF Weekly*, vol. 29, no. 4

2009
Kenneth Baker, "Echo," *ARTnews Magazine*, vol. 108, no. 11

Michael Jang, "Enrich Thyself: The Finest Art at the Finest Prices," *San Francisco Magazine*

Jolene Torr, "Ever Heard of a Ritual Killing?" *ARTslant*

AWARDS & HONORS

2020
Hopper Prize Finalist

2018
Roswell Artist in Residence Program, one year, Roswell, New Mexico

2017
Alfred and Trafford Klots International Program for Artists, MICA, two months, Léhon, France

2016
Dave Bown Projects, Award of Excellence, presented by Helga Christoffersen, Assistant Curator, New Museum, New York City, New York

2015
Juror's Circle Prize, Sandra Firmin, Chief Curator, Colorado University Art Museum

Studio System Art Residency, Torrance Art Museum, one month, Torrance, California

2013
Residency, University of Illinois at Urbana-Champaign, Champaign, Illinois

2011
Martignano International Residency for Artists, six months, Martignano, Italy

2010
Lademoen Kunstnerverksteder, artist in residence, one month, Trondheim, Norway

2009
Best of the Bay Area 2009, San Francisco Magazine, San Francisco, California

2007
Finalist, Headlands Center for the Arts Tournesol Award, Sausalito, California

Xeric Foundation Grant, Boston, Massachusetts

CURATORIAL PROJECTS

2017
Wooleyes (co-curator), Washington Reid Gallery, United Cerebral Palsy of Los Angeles, California

2014
What The Mouth Sees (curator), Alter Space, San Francisco, California

2008
Founder and Director of 5 Mined Fields Studio, exhibition space, Berkeley, California

INSTITUTIONAL COLLECTIONS

Anderson Museum of Contemporary Art, Roswell, New Mexico

Azman Museum, Kuala Lumpur

Bunker Foundation (DeWoody Collection), Los Angeles

Corridor Foundation, Hong Kong

Green Family Art Foundation, Dallas

Longlati Foundation, Shanghai

Novarese Collection, Bologna, Italy

Pond Society, Shanghai

Weissman Family Collection, New York

Xiao Museum of Contemporary Art, Rizhao, Shandong, China

EDUCATION

2002
Bachelor of Fine Arts, University of Arizona, Tucson, Arizona. First-generation graduate.

PICTURE CREDITS

All images © Joshua Hagler unless listed below.

pp. 5 and 11: © Arvo Pärt Centre, Laulasmaa, Estonia, (APC) 2-1.178

p. 133 © Kevin Todora, 2024

ACKNOWLEDGMENTS

Without the past twelve years of ongoing dialogue and creative cross-pollination with my wife Maja Ruznic, I never would have arrived at the *Nihil* project. That is my first and most important thank you.

To the brilliant youngsters in my life, thank you. From the very beginning of *Nihil* and every step of the way, the gifted Samuel Staffan has played a critical collaborative role. His mind and hand are in so many parts of this book, they cannot be enumerated. The talented Lana Scholtz came aboard some time later and has contributed directly to some of the work in this book. And, before her, Julia Jameson contributed in the studio and the Las Vegas Church installation.

My profound gratitude to Adam and Catherine Hooper for making this book beautiful.

Thank you to Ben Lee Ritchie Handler and Nicodim Gallery for their moral and financial support for this book and for the *Nihil* exhibitions we mounted. Thank you to Cris Worley for taking *Nihil* seriously from the start, and to her, Patrick Kelly, and the Old Jail Art Center for the *Nihil* exhibition in such a beautifully relevant space.

I appreciate and admire the vast and important contributions made to the worlds of art and literature by John Yau, and I am forever grateful for his poet's eye and ear turned to this project. I would never have imagined an essay of John's introducing this book.

To Arvo Pärt, the greatest living composer, thank you for changing my work and my life through your music. It arrived in my ears as a great interruption, and I still cannot seem to remember whatever it was I was doing before. And, of course, thanks for permission to use your tree.

Cedra Wood, I am grateful to you for guiding me into the fire. And also into the Las Vegas church.

Stephen Fleming, thank you for the Cedarvale School, the very first one that got the whole project going.

To one of the world's greatest living artists, Elliott Hundley, my gratitude for guiding our conversations, public and private, and helping me to gain some confidence when I most needed it. Thank you.

FOR MILA ALETHEIA, ON THE OCCASION OF HER FIFTH BIRTHDAY, AND HER FORTY-FIFTH

Published in 2025 by Unicorn, an imprint of
Unicorn Publishing Group
Charleston Studio
Meadow Business Centre
Lewes BN8 5RW
www.unicornpublishing.org

ISBN 978-1-917458-01-6
10 9 8 7 6 5 4 3 2 1

Designed by hoopdesign.co.uk
Managing editor: Catherine Hooper

Colour reproduction by Pixel Colour Imaging Limited, London, E14 9RL
Printed in Malta by Gutenberg

Publication supported by

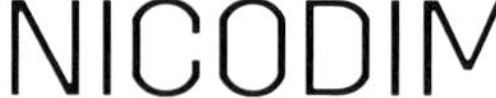